Hyundai Santa Fe Automotive Repair Manual

**by Tim Imhoff
and John H Haynes**

Member of the Guild of Motoring Writers

Models covered:

Hyundai Santa Fe - 2001 through 2006

(43050-7N3)

ABCDE
FGHIJ
KLMNO
PQ

Haynes Publishing Group
Sparkford Nr Yeovil
Somerset BA22 7JJ England

Haynes North America, Inc
861 Lawrence Drive
Newbury Park
California 91320 USA

Acknowledgements

Wiring diagrams originated exclusively for Haynes North America, Inc. by Solution Builders.

© Haynes North America, Inc. 2008

With permission from J.H. Haynes & Co. Ltd.

A book in the Haynes Automotive Repair Manual Series

Printed in the U.S.A.

ISBN-13: 978-1-56392-717-1
ISBN-10: 1-56392-717-9

Library of Congress Control Number: 2008926796

Contents

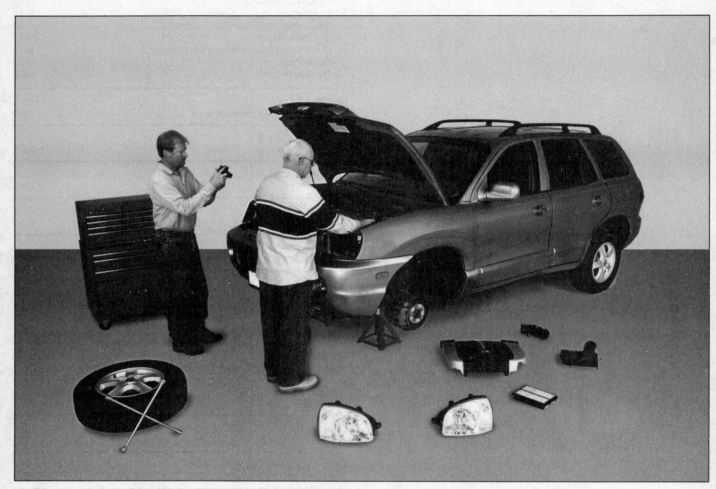

Haynes photographer and mechanic with 2004 Hyundai Santa Fe

About this manual

Its purpose

The purpose of this manual is to help you get the best value from your vehicle. It can do so in several ways. It can help you decide what work must be done, even if you choose to have it done by a dealer service department or a repair shop; it provides information and procedures for routine maintenance and servicing; and it offers diagnostic and repair procedures to follow when trouble occurs.

We hope you use the manual to tackle the work yourself. For many simpler jobs, doing it yourself may be quicker than arranging an appointment to get the vehicle into a shop and making the trips to leave it and pick it up. More importantly, a lot of money can be saved by avoiding the expense the shop must pass on to you to cover its labor and overhead costs. An added benefit is the sense of satisfaction and accomplishment that you feel after doing the job yourself.

Using the manual

The manual is divided into Chapters. Each Chapter is divided into numbered Sections, which are headed in bold type between horizontal lines. Each Section consists of consecutively numbered paragraphs.

At the beginning of each numbered Section you will be referred to any illustrations which apply to the procedures in that Section. The reference numbers used in illustration captions pinpoint the pertinent Section and the Step within that Section. That is, illustration 3.2 means the illustration refers to Section 3 and Step (or paragraph) 2 within that Section.

Procedures, once described in the text, are not normally repeated. When it's necessary to refer to another Chapter, the reference will be given as Chapter and Section number. Cross references given without use of the word "Chapter" apply to Sections and/or paragraphs in the same Chapter. For example, "see Section 8" means in the same Chapter.

References to the left or right side of the vehicle assume you are sitting in the driver's seat, facing forward.

Even though we have prepared this manual with extreme care, neither the publisher nor the author can accept responsibility for any errors in, or omissions from, the information given.

NOTE

A **Note** provides information necessary to properly complete a procedure or information which will make the procedure easier to understand.

CAUTION

A **Caution** provides a special procedure or special steps which must be taken while completing the procedure where the Caution is found. Not heeding a Caution can result in damage to the assembly being worked on.

WARNING

A **Warning** provides a special procedure or special steps which must be taken while completing the procedure where the Warning is found. Not heeding a Warning can result in personal injury.

Introduction to the Hyundai Santa Fe

This manual covers 2001 through 2006 Hyundai Santa Fe models. These vehicles are equipped with either a 2.4L four-cylinder engine, a 2.7L V6 engine or a 3.5L V6 engine.

The engine drives the front wheels through either a four or five speed automatic or a five speed manual transaxle via independent driveaxles. On all-wheel-drive models, the rear wheels are also propelled, via a driveshaft, rear differential, and rear driveaxles.

Suspension is independent at all four wheels, with MacPherson struts used at the front and coil springs with conventional shock absorbers at the rear. The rack-and-pinion steering unit is mounted on the suspension crossmember.

The brakes are disc at the front and rear on all models. Power assist is standard on all models. An Anti-lock Brake System (ABS) is standard equipment on some models and is available as an option on others.

Vehicle identification numbers

Modifications are a continuing and unpublicized process in vehicle manufacturing. Since spare parts manuals and lists are compiled on a numerical basis, the individual vehicle numbers are essential to correctly identify the component required.

Vehicle Identification Number (VIN)

This very important identification number is stamped on a plate attached to the dashboard inside the windshield on the driver's side of the vehicle (see illustration). It can also be found on the certification label located on the driver's side door post and on the right (passenger) side of the firewall. The VIN also appears on the Vehicle Certificate of Title and Registration. It contains information such as where and when the vehicle was manufactured, the model year and the body style.

VIN engine and model year codes

Two particularly important pieces of information found in the VIN are the engine code and the model year code. Counting from the left, the engine code letter designation is the 8th digit and the model year code letter designation is the 10th digit.

On the models covered by this manual the engine codes are:

B .... 2.4L four-cylinder
D .... 2.7L DOHC V6
E .... 3.5L DOHC V6

On the models covered by this manual the model year codes are:

1 2001
2 2002
3 2003
4 2004
5 2005
6 2006

Certification label

The certification label is attached to the end of the driver's door post (see illustration). The plate contains the name of the manufacturer, the month and year of production, the Gross Vehicle Weight Rating (GVWR), the Gross Axle Weight Rating (GAWR) and the certification statement.

Engine number

On four-cylinder models, the engine identification number is stamped into a machined pad on the front passenger side of the engine block, under the exhaust manifold.

On V6 models, the engine identification number is stamped into a machined pad on the front left end (driver's side) of the engine block.

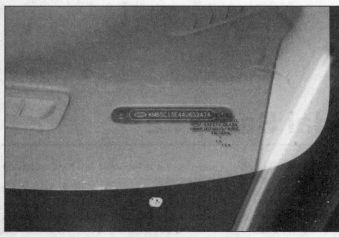

The Vehicle Identification Number (VIN) is located on a plate on top of the dash (visible through the windshield)

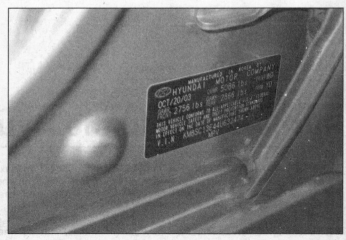

The vehicle certification label is located at the bottom of the driver's door post

Recall information

Vehicle recalls are carried out by the manufacturer in the rare event of a possible safety-related defect. The vehicle's registered owner is contacted at the address on file at the Department of Motor Vehicles and given the details of the recall. Remedial work is carried out free of charge at a dealer service department.

If you are the new owner of a used vehicle which was subject to a recall and you want to be sure that the work has been carried out, it's best to contact a dealer service department and ask about your individual vehicle - you'll need to furnish them your Vehicle Identification Number (VIN).

The table below is based on information provided by the National Highway Traffic Safety Administration (NHTSA), the body which oversees vehicle recalls in the United States. The recall database is updated constantly. For the latest information on vehicle recalls, check the NHTSA website at www.nhtsa.gov, or call the NHTSA hotline at 1-888-327-4236.

Recall date	Recall campaign number	Model(s) affected	Concern
DEC 20, 2002	03V030000	2001, 2002 Santa Fe	On certain sport utility vehicles equipped with 2.7 liter V6 engines, improperly manufactured crankshaft position sensors were installed. The sensor cases were improperly manufactured and did not meet dimensional specifications. Internal gaps within the cases allowed epoxy to contact the printed circuit board, which resulted in cracking of the printed circuit board capacitor. A damaged capacitor could result in engine stalling.
NOV 04, 2003	03V520000	2001, 2002, 2003, 2004 Santa Fe	Certain sport utility vehicles fail to comply with the requirements of federal motor vehicle safety standard no. 120, "Tire selection and rims for motor vehicles other than passenger cars." The tire pressure labels do not contain the information required by the standard.
MAR 09, 2004	04V131000	2003, 2004 Santa Fe	On certain sport utility vehicles equipped with 3.5 liter V6 engines, 4-wheel drive and antilock braking systems (ABS), if the brake pedal is depressed at speeds between 3 and 12 mph when the brake pad friction surfaces are wet, a vibration may occur between the brake discs and pads causing ABS sensor electronic signal noise to develop. At speeds below 5 mph, the ABS sensor signal noise may cause the ABS electronic control unit (ECU) to activate the ABS, extending the stopping distance, which could result in a crash.
SEP 30, 2005 NOV 16, 2005 (Hyundai of Puerto Rico)	05V450000 05V527000	2005 Santa Fe	On certain vehicles equipped with an occupant classification system (OCS) the right front seat of the vehicle may misclassify certain small children seated on the front edge of the seat as an adult. This may allow the right front airbag to deploy in a frontal collision crash or the side impact airbag to deploy in a side collision crash; severe injury or death could occur.

Buying parts

Replacement parts are available from many sources, which generally fall into one of two categories - authorized dealer parts departments and independent retail auto parts stores. Our advice concerning these parts is as follows:

Retail auto parts stores: Good auto parts stores will stock frequently needed components which wear out relatively fast, such as clutch components, exhaust systems, brake parts, tune-up parts, etc. These stores often supply new or reconditioned parts on an exchange basis, which can save a considerable amount of money. Discount auto parts stores are often very good places to buy materials and parts needed for general vehicle maintenance such as oil, grease, filters, spark plugs, belts, touch-up paint, bulbs, etc. They also usually sell tools and general accessories, have convenient hours, charge lower prices and can often be found not far from home.

Authorized dealer parts department: This is the best source for parts which are unique to the vehicle and not generally available elsewhere (such as major engine parts, transmission parts, trim pieces, etc.).

Warranty information: If the vehicle is still covered under warranty, be sure that any replacement parts purchased - regardless of the source - do not invalidate the warranty!

To be sure of obtaining the correct parts, have engine and chassis numbers available and, if possible, take the old parts along for positive identification.

Maintenance techniques, tools and working facilities

Maintenance techniques

There are a number of techniques involved in maintenance and repair that will be referred to throughout this manual. Application of these techniques will enable the home mechanic to be more efficient, better organized and capable of performing the various tasks properly, which will ensure that the repair job is thorough and complete.

Fasteners

Fasteners are nuts, bolts, studs and screws used to hold two or more parts together. There are a few things to keep in mind when working with fasteners. Almost all of them use a locking device of some type, either a lockwasher, locknut, locking tab or thread adhesive. All threaded fasteners should be clean and straight, with undamaged threads and undamaged corners on the hex head where the wrench fits. Develop the habit of replacing all damaged nuts and bolts with new ones. Special locknuts with nylon or fiber inserts can only be used once. If they are removed, they lose their locking ability and must be replaced with new ones.

Rusted nuts and bolts should be treated with a penetrating fluid to ease removal and prevent breakage. Some mechanics use turpentine in a spout-type oil can, which works quite well. After applying the rust penetrant, let it work for a few minutes before trying to loosen the nut or bolt. Badly rusted fasteners may have to be chiseled or sawed off or removed with a special nut breaker, available at tool stores.

If a bolt or stud breaks off in an assembly, it can be drilled and removed with a special tool commonly available for this purpose. Most automotive machine shops can perform this task, as well as other repair procedures, such as the repair of threaded holes that have been stripped out.

Flat washers and lockwashers, when removed from an assembly, should always be replaced exactly as removed. Replace any damaged washers with new ones. Never use a lockwasher on any soft metal surface (such as aluminum), thin sheet metal or plastic.

Fastener sizes

For a number of reasons, automobile manufacturers are making wider and wider use of metric fasteners. Therefore, it is important to be able to tell the difference between standard (sometimes called U.S. or SAE) and metric hardware, since they cannot be interchanged.

All bolts, whether standard or metric, are sized according to diameter, thread pitch and length. For example, a standard 1/2 - 13 x 1 bolt is 1/2 inch in diameter, has 13 threads per inch and is 1 inch long. An M12 - 1.75 x 25 metric bolt is 12 mm in diameter, has a thread pitch of 1.75 mm (the distance between threads) and is 25 mm long. The two bolts are nearly identical, and easily confused, but they are not interchangeable.

In addition to the differences in diameter, thread pitch and length, metric and standard bolts can also be distinguished by examining the bolt heads. To begin with, the distance across the flats on a standard bolt head is measured in inches, while the same dimension on a metric bolt is sized in millimeters (the same is true for nuts). As a result, a standard wrench should not be used on a metric bolt and a metric wrench should not be used on a standard bolt. Also, most standard bolts have slashes radiating out from the center of the head to denote the grade or strength of the bolt, which is an indication of the amount of torque that can be applied to it. The greater the number of slashes, the greater the strength of the bolt. Grades 0 through 5 are commonly used on automobiles. Metric bolts have a property class (grade) number, rather than a slash, molded into their heads to indicate bolt strength. In this case, the higher the number, the stronger the bolt. Property class numbers 8.8, 9.8 and 10.9 are commonly used on automobiles.

Strength markings can also be used to distinguish standard hex nuts from metric hex nuts. Many standard nuts have dots stamped into one side, while metric nuts are marked with a number. The greater the number of dots, or the higher the number, the greater the strength of the nut.

Metric studs are also marked on their ends according to property class (grade). Larger studs are numbered (the same as metric bolts), while smaller studs carry a geometric code to denote grade.

It should be noted that many fasteners, especially Grades 0 through 2, have no distinguishing marks on them. When such is the case, the only way to determine whether it is standard or metric is to measure the thread pitch or compare it to a known fastener of the same size.

Standard fasteners are often referred to as SAE, as opposed to metric. However, it should be noted that SAE technically refers to a non-metric fine thread fastener only. Coarse thread non-metric fasteners are referred to as USS sizes.

Since fasteners of the same size (both standard and metric) may have different strength ratings, be sure to reinstall any bolts, studs or nuts removed from your vehicle in their original locations. Also, when replacing a fastener with a new one, make sure that the new one has a strength rating equal to or greater than the original.

Tightening sequences and procedures

Most threaded fasteners should be tightened to a specific torque value (torque is the twisting force applied to a threaded component such as a nut or bolt). Overtightening the fastener can weaken it and cause it to break, while undertightening can cause it to eventually come loose. Bolts, screws and studs, depending on the material they are made of and their thread diameters, have specific torque values, many of which are noted in the Specifications at the beginning of each Chapter. Be sure to follow the torque recommendations closely. For fasteners not assigned a

Grade 1 or 2   Grade 5   Grade 8

Bolt strength marking (standard/SAE/USS; bottom - metric)

Grade	Identification
Hex Nut Grade 5	3 Dots
Hex Nut Grade 8	6 Dots

Standard hex nut strength markings

Grade	Identification
Hex Nut Property Class 9	Arabic 9
Hex Nut Property Class 10	Arabic 10

Metric hex nut strength markings

Class 10.9   Class 9.8   Class 8.8

Metric stud strength markings

specific torque, a general torque value chart is presented here as a guide. These torque values are for dry (unlubricated) fasteners threaded into steel or cast iron (not aluminum). As was previously mentioned, the size and grade of a fastener determine the amount of torque that can safely be applied to it. The figures listed here are approximate for Grade 2 and Grade 3 fasteners. Higher grades can tolerate higher torque values.

Fasteners laid out in a pattern, such as cylinder head bolts, oil pan bolts, differential cover bolts, etc., must be loosened or tightened in sequence to avoid warping the component. This sequence will normally be shown in the appropriate Chapter. If a specific pattern is not given, the following procedures can be used to prevent warping.

Initially, the bolts or nuts should be assembled finger-tight only. Next, they should be tightened one full turn each, in a criss-cross or diagonal pattern. After each one has been tightened one full turn, return to the first one and tighten them all one-half turn, following the same pattern. Finally, tighten each of them one-quarter turn at a time until each fastener has been tightened to the proper torque. To loosen and remove the fasteners, the procedure would be reversed.

Component disassembly

Component disassembly should be done with care and purpose to help ensure that

Metric thread sizes	Ft-lbs	Nm
M-6	6 to 9	9 to 12
M-8	14 to 21	19 to 28
M-10	28 to 40	38 to 54
M-12	50 to 71	68 to 96
M-14	80 to 140	109 to 154
Pipe thread sizes		
1/8	5 to 8	7 to 10
1/4	12 to 18	17 to 24
3/8	22 to 33	30 to 44
1/2	25 to 35	34 to 47
U.S. thread sizes		
1/4 - 20	6 to 9	9 to 12
5/16 - 18	12 to 18	17 to 24
5/16 - 24	14 to 20	19 to 27
3/8 - 16	22 to 32	30 to 43
3/8 - 24	27 to 38	37 to 51
7/16 - 14	40 to 55	55 to 74
7/16 - 20	40 to 60	55 to 81
1/2 - 13	55 to 80	75 to 108

Standard (SAE and USS) bolt dimensions/grade marks

G   Grade marks (bolt strength)
L   Length (in inches)
T   Thread pitch (number of threads per inch)
D   Nominal diameter (in inches)

Metric bolt dimensions/grade marks

P   Property class (bolt strength)
L   Length (in millimeters)
T   Thread pitch (distance between threads in millimeters)
D   Diameter

Micrometer set

Dial indicator set

the parts go back together properly. Always keep track of the sequence in which parts are removed. Make note of special characteristics or marks on parts that can be installed more than one way, such as a grooved thrust washer on a shaft. It is a good idea to lay the disassembled parts out on a clean surface in the order that they were removed. It may also be helpful to make sketches or take instant photos of components before removal.

When removing fasteners from a component, keep track of their locations. Sometimes threading a bolt back in a part, or putting the washers and nut back on a stud, can prevent mix-ups later. If nuts and bolts cannot be returned to their original locations, they should be kept in a compartmented box or a series of small boxes. A cupcake or muffin tin is ideal for this purpose, since each cavity can hold the bolts and nuts from a particular area (i.e. oil pan bolts, valve cover bolts, engine mount bolts, etc.). A pan of this type is especially helpful when working on assemblies with very small parts, such as the carburetor, alternator, valve train or interior dash and trim pieces. The cavities can be marked with paint or tape to identify the contents.

Whenever wiring looms, harnesses or connectors are separated, it is a good idea to identify the two halves with numbered pieces of masking tape so they can be easily reconnected.

Gasket sealing surfaces

Throughout any vehicle, gaskets are used to seal the mating surfaces between two parts and keep lubricants, fluids, vacuum or pressure contained in an assembly.

Many times these gaskets are coated with a liquid or paste-type gasket sealing compound before assembly. Age, heat and pressure can sometimes cause the two parts to stick together so tightly that they are very difficult to separate. Often, the assembly can be loosened by striking it with a soft-face hammer near the mating surfaces. A regular hammer can be used if a block of wood is placed between the hammer and the part. Do

not hammer on cast parts or parts that could be easily damaged. With any particularly stubborn part, always recheck to make sure that every fastener has been removed.

Avoid using a screwdriver or bar to pry apart an assembly, as they can easily mar the gasket sealing surfaces of the parts, which must remain smooth. If prying is absolutely necessary, use an old broom handle, but keep in mind that extra clean up will be necessary if the wood splinters.

After the parts are separated, the old gasket must be carefully scraped off and the gasket surfaces cleaned. Stubborn gasket material can be soaked with rust penetrant or treated with a special chemical to soften it so it can be easily scraped off. **Caution:** *Never use gasket removal solutions or caustic chemicals on plastic or other composite components.* A scraper can be fashioned from a piece of copper tubing by flattening and sharpening one end. Copper is recommended because it is usually softer than the surfaces to be scraped, which reduces the chance of gouging the part. Some gaskets can be removed with a wire brush, but regardless of the method used, the mating surfaces must be left clean and smooth. If for some reason the gasket surface is gouged, then a gasket sealer thick enough to fill scratches will have to be used during reassembly of the components. For most applications, a non-drying (or semi-drying) gasket sealer should be used.

Hose removal tips

Warning: *If the vehicle is equipped with air conditioning, do not disconnect any of the A/C hoses without first having the system depressurized by a dealer service department or a service station.*

Hose removal precautions closely parallel gasket removal precautions. Avoid scratching or gouging the surface that the hose mates against or the connection may leak. This is especially true for radiator hoses. Because of various chemical reactions, the rubber in hoses can bond itself to the metal spigot that the hose fits over. To remove

a hose, first loosen the hose clamps that secure it to the spigot. Then, with slip-joint pliers, grab the hose at the clamp and rotate it around the spigot. Work it back and forth until it is completely free, then pull it off. Silicone or other lubricants will ease removal if they can be applied between the hose and the outside of the spigot. Apply the same lubricant to the inside of the hose and the outside of the spigot to simplify installation.

As a last resort (and if the hose is to be replaced with a new one anyway), the rubber can be slit with a knife and the hose peeled from the spigot. If this must be done, be careful that the metal connection is not damaged.

If a hose clamp is broken or damaged, do not reuse it. Wire-type clamps usually weaken with age, so it is a good idea to replace them with screw-type clamps whenever a hose is removed.

Tools

A selection of good tools is a basic requirement for anyone who plans to maintain and repair his or her own vehicle. For the owner who has few tools, the initial investment might seem high, but when compared to the spiraling costs of professional auto maintenance and repair, it is a wise one.

To help the owner decide which tools are needed to perform the tasks detailed in this manual, the following tool lists are offered: *Maintenance and minor repair, Repair/overhaul* and *Special.*

The newcomer to practical mechanics should start off with the *maintenance and minor repair* tool kit, which is adequate for the simpler jobs performed on a vehicle. Then, as confidence and experience grow, the owner can tackle more difficult tasks, buying additional tools as they are needed. Eventually the basic kit will be expanded into the *repair and overhaul* tool set. Over a period of time, the experienced do-it-yourselfer will assemble a tool set complete enough for most repair and overhaul procedures and will add tools from the special category when it is felt that the expense is justified by the frequency of use.

Dial caliper

Hand-operated vacuum pump

Fuel pressure gauge set

Compression gauge with spark plug
hole adapter

Damper/steering wheel puller

General purpose puller

Hydraulic lifter removal tool

Valve spring compressor

Valve spring compressor

Ridge reamer

Piston ring groove cleaning tool

Ring removal/installation tool

Ring compressor

Cylinder hone

Brake hold-down spring tool

Torque angle gauge

Clutch plate alignment tool

Tap and die set

Maintenance and minor repair tool kit

The tools in this list should be considered the minimum required for performance of routine maintenance, servicing and minor repair work. We recommend the purchase of combination wrenches (box-end and open-end combined in one wrench). While more expensive than open end wrenches, they offer the advantages of both types of wrench.

Combination wrench set (1/4-inch to
    1 inch or 6 mm to 19 mm)
Adjustable wrench, 8 inch
Spark plug wrench with rubber insert
Spark plug gap adjusting tool
Feeler gauge set
Brake bleeder wrench
Standard screwdriver (5/16-inch x
    6 inch)
Phillips screwdriver (No. 2 x 6 inch)
Combination pliers - 6 inch
Hacksaw and assortment of blades
Tire pressure gauge
Grease gun
Oil can
Fine emery cloth
Wire brush
Battery post and cable cleaning tool
Oil filter wrench
Funnel (medium size)
Safety goggles
Jackstands (2)
Drain pan

Note: *If basic tune-ups are going to be part of routine maintenance, it will be necessary to purchase a good quality stroboscopic timing light and combination tachometer/dwell meter. Although they are included in the list of special tools, it is mentioned here because they are absolutely necessary for tuning most vehicles properly.*

Repair and overhaul tool set

These tools are essential for anyone who plans to perform major repairs and are in addition to those in the maintenance and minor repair tool kit. Included is a comprehensive set of sockets which, though expensive, are invaluable because of their versatility, especially when various extensions and drives are available. We recommend the 1/2-inch drive over the 3/8-inch drive. Although the larger drive is bulky and more expensive, it has the capacity of accepting a very wide range of large sockets. Ideally, however, the mechanic should have a 3/8-inch drive set and a 1/2-inch drive set.

Socket set(s)
Reversible ratchet
Extension - 10 inch
Universal joint
Torque wrench (same size drive as
    sockets)
Ball peen hammer - 8 ounce
Soft-face hammer (plastic/rubber)
Standard screwdriver (1/4-inch x 6 inch)

Standard screwdriver (stubby -
    5/16-inch)
Phillips screwdriver (No. 3 x 8 inch)
Phillips screwdriver (stubby - No. 2)
Pliers - vise grip
Pliers - lineman's
Pliers - needle nose
Pliers - snap-ring (internal and external)
Cold chisel - 1/2-inch
Scribe
Scraper (made from flattened copper
    tubing)
Centerpunch
Pin punches (1/16, 1/8, 3/16-inch)
Steel rule/straightedge - 12 inch
Allen wrench set (1/8 to 3/8-inch or
    4 mm to 10 mm)
A selection of files
Wire brush (large)
Jackstands (second set)
Jack (scissor or hydraulic type)

Note: *Another tool which is often useful is an electric drill with a chuck capacity of 3/8-inch and a set of good quality drill bits.*

Special tools

The tools in this list include those which are not used regularly, are expensive to buy, or which need to be used in accordance with their manufacturer's instructions. Unless these tools will be used frequently, it is not very economical to purchase many of them. A consideration would be to split the cost and use between yourself and a friend or friends. In addition, most of these tools can be obtained from a tool rental shop on a temporary basis.

This list primarily contains only those tools and instruments widely available to the public, and not those special tools produced by the vehicle manufacturer for distribution to dealer service departments. Occasionally, references to the manufacturer's special tools are included in the text of this manual. Generally, an alternative method of doing the job without the special tool is offered. However, sometimes there is no alternative to their use. Where this is the case, and the tool cannot be purchased or borrowed, the work should be turned over to the dealer service department or an automotive repair shop.

  Valve spring compressor
  Piston ring groove cleaning tool
  Piston ring compressor
  Piston ring installation tool
  Cylinder compression gauge
  Cylinder ridge reamer
  Cylinder surfacing hone
  Cylinder bore gauge
  Micrometers and/or dial calipers
  Hydraulic lifter removal tool
  Balljoint separator
  Universal-type puller
  Impact screwdriver
  Dial indicator set
  Stroboscopic timing light (inductive pick-up)
  Hand operated vacuum/pressure pump
  Tachometer/dwell meter
  Universal electrical multimeter
  Cable hoist
  Brake spring removal and installation tools
  Floor jack

Buying tools

For the do-it-yourselfer who is just starting to get involved in vehicle maintenance and repair, there are a number of options available when purchasing tools. If maintenance and minor repair is the extent of the work to be done, the purchase of individual tools is satisfactory. If, on the other hand, extensive work is planned, it would be a good idea to purchase a modest tool set from one of the large retail chain stores. A set can usually be bought at a substantial savings over the individual tool prices, and they often come with a tool box. As additional tools are needed, add-on sets, individual tools and a larger tool box can be purchased to expand the tool selection. Building a tool set gradually allows the cost of the tools to be spread over a longer period of time and gives the mechanic the freedom to choose only those tools that will actually be used.

Tool stores will often be the only source of some of the special tools that are needed, but regardless of where tools are bought, try to avoid cheap ones, especially when buying screwdrivers and sockets, because they won't last very long. The expense involved in replacing cheap tools will eventually be greater than the initial cost of quality tools.

Care and maintenance of tools

Good tools are expensive, so it makes sense to treat them with respect. Keep them clean and in usable condition and store them properly when not in use. Always wipe off any dirt, grease or metal chips before putting them away. Never leave tools lying around in the work area. Upon completion of a job, always check closely under the hood for tools that may have been left there so they won't get lost during a test drive.

Some tools, such as screwdrivers, pliers, wrenches and sockets, can be hung on a panel mounted on the garage or workshop wall, while others should be kept in a tool box or tray. Measuring instruments, gauges, meters, etc. must be carefully stored where they cannot be damaged by weather or impact from other tools.

When tools are used with care and stored properly, they will last a very long time. Even with the best of care, though, tools will wear out if used frequently. When a tool is damaged or worn out, replace it. Subsequent jobs will be safer and more enjoyable if you do.

How to repair damaged threads

Sometimes, the internal threads of a nut or bolt hole can become stripped, usually from overtightening. Stripping threads is an all-too-common occurrence, especially when working with aluminum parts, because aluminum is so soft that it easily strips out.

Usually, external or internal threads are only partially stripped. After they've been cleaned up with a tap or die, they'll still work. Sometimes, however, threads are badly damaged. When this happens, you've got three choices:

1) *Drill and tap the hole to the next suitable oversize and install a larger diameter bolt, screw or stud.*
2) *Drill and tap the hole to accept a threaded plug, then drill and tap the plug to the original screw size. You can also buy a plug already threaded to the original size. Then you simply drill a hole to the specified size, then run the threaded plug into the hole with a bolt and jam nut. Once the plug is fully seated, remove the jam nut and bolt.*
3) *The third method uses a patented thread repair kit like Heli-Coil or Slimsert. These*

easy-to-use kits are designed to repair damaged threads in straight-through holes and blind holes. Both are available as kits which can handle a variety of sizes and thread patterns. Drill the hole, then tap it with the special included tap. Install the Heli-Coil and the hole is back to its original diameter and thread pitch.

Regardless of which method you use, be sure to proceed calmly and carefully. A little impatience or carelessness during one of these relatively simple procedures can ruin your whole day's work and cost you a bundle if you wreck an expensive part.

Working facilities

Not to be overlooked when discussing tools is the workshop. If anything more than routine maintenance is to be carried out, some sort of suitable work area is essential.

It is understood, and appreciated, that many home mechanics do not have a good workshop or garage available, and end up removing an engine or doing major repairs outside. It is recommended, however, that the overhaul or repair be completed under the cover of a roof.

A clean, flat workbench or table of comfortable working height is an absolute necessity. The workbench should be equipped with a vise that has a jaw opening of at least four inches.

As mentioned previously, some clean, dry storage space is also required for tools, as well as the lubricants, fluids, cleaning solvents, etc. which soon become necessary.

Sometimes waste oil and fluids, drained from the engine or cooling system during normal maintenance or repairs, present a disposal problem. To avoid pouring them on the ground or into a sewage system, pour the used fluids into large containers, seal them with caps and take them to an authorized disposal site or recycling center. Plastic jugs, such as old antifreeze containers, are ideal for this purpose.

Always keep a supply of old newspapers and clean rags available. Old towels are excellent for mopping up spills. Many mechanics use rolls of paper towels for most work because they are readily available and disposable. To help keep the area under the vehicle clean, a large cardboard box can be cut open and flattened to protect the garage or shop floor.

Whenever working over a painted surface, such as when leaning over a fender to service something under the hood, always cover it with an old blanket or bedspread to protect the finish. Vinyl covered pads, made especially for this purpose, are available at auto parts stores.

Jacking and towing

Jacking

The jack supplied with the vehicle should only be used for raising the vehicle for changing a tire or placing jackstands under the frame. **Warning:** *Never crawl under the vehicle or start the engine when the jack is being used as the only means of support.*

When jacking the vehicle, the jack should be engaged with the rocker panel seam, between the two notches **(see illustration)**.

The vehicle should be on level ground with the wheels blocked and the transmission in Park (automatic). Pry off the hub cap (if equipped) using the tapered end of the lug wrench. Loosen the lug nuts one-half turn and leave them in place until the wheel is raised off the ground.

Place the jack under the side of the vehicle in the indicated position. Use the supplied wrench to turn the jackscrew clockwise until the wheel is raised off the ground. Remove the lug nuts, pull off the wheel and replace it with the spare.

With the beveled side in, reinstall the lug nuts and tighten them until snug. Lower the vehicle by turning the jackscrew counterclockwise. Remove the jack and tighten the nuts in a diagonal pattern to the torque listed in the Chapter 1 Specifications. If a torque wrench is not available, have the torque checked by a service station as soon as possible. Install the hubcap by placing it in position and using the heel of your hand or a rubber mallet to seat it.

Towing

Two-wheel drive models can be towed from the front with the front wheels off the ground, using a wheel lift type tow truck. If towed from the rear, the front wheels must be placed on a dolly. All-wheel-drive models must be towed with all four wheels off the ground. A sling-type tow truck cannot be used, as body damage will result. The best way to tow the vehicle is with a flat-bed car carrier.

In an emergency the vehicle can be towed a very short distance with a cable or chain attached to one of the towing eyelets located under the front or rear bumpers. The driver must remain in the vehicle to operate the steering and brakes (remember that power steering and power brakes will not work with the engine off). Make certain that the vehicle is in neutral with the parking brake off.

The jack fits between the notches in the rocker panel pinch-weld (there are two jacking points on each side of the vehicle)

Booster battery (jump) starting

Observe these precautions when using a booster battery to start a vehicle:

a) Before connecting the booster battery, make sure the ignition switch is in the Off position.
b) Turn off the lights, heater and other electrical loads.
c) Your eyes should be shielded. Safety goggles are a good idea.
d) Make sure the booster battery is the same voltage as the dead one in the vehicle.
e) The two vehicles MUST NOT TOUCH each other!
f) Make sure the transaxle is in Neutral (manual) or Park (automatic).
g) If the booster battery is not a maintenance-free type, remove the vent caps and lay a cloth over the vent holes.

Connect the red-colored jumper cable to the positive (+) terminal of the booster battery and the other end to the positive (+) terminal of the dead battery. Then connect one end of the black jumper cable to the negative (-) terminal of the booster battery, and the other end of the cable to a good ground, such as a bolt or bracket.

Start the engine using the booster battery, then run the booster vehicle at a fast idle for a few minutes to instill some charge in the dead battery. Let the engine idle, then disconnect the jumper cables in the reverse order of connection. The vehicle with the dead battery may have to be driven for 20 minutes or more to sufficiently recharge the battery for independent starting.

Make the booster battery cable connections in the numerical order shown (note that the negative cable of the booster battery is NOT attached to the negative terminal of the dead battery)

Automotive chemicals and lubricants

A number of automotive chemicals and lubricants are available for use during vehicle maintenance and repair. They include a wide variety of products ranging from cleaning solvents and degreasers to lubricants and protective sprays for rubber, plastic and vinyl.

Cleaners

Carburetor cleaner and choke cleaner is a strong solvent for gum, varnish and carbon. Most carburetor cleaners leave a dry-type lubricant film which will not harden or gum up. Because of this film it is not recommended for use on electrical components.

Brake system cleaner is used to remove brake dust, grease and brake fluid from the brake system, where clean surfaces are absolutely necessary. It leaves no residue and often eliminates brake squeal caused by contaminants.

Electrical cleaner removes oxidation, corrosion and carbon deposits from electrical contacts, restoring full current flow. It can also be used to clean spark plugs, carburetor jets, voltage regulators and other parts where an oil-free surface is desired.

Demoisturants remove water and moisture from electrical components such as alternators, voltage regulators, electrical connectors and fuse blocks. They are non-conductive and non-corrosive.

Degreasers are heavy-duty solvents used to remove grease from the outside of the engine and from chassis components. They can be sprayed or brushed on and, depending on the type, are rinsed off either with water or solvent.

Lubricants

Motor oil is the lubricant formulated for use in engines. It normally contains a wide variety of additives to prevent corrosion and reduce foaming and wear. Motor oil comes in various weights (viscosity ratings) from 0 to 50. The recommended weight of the oil depends on the season, temperature and the demands on the engine. Light oil is used in cold climates and under light load conditions. Heavy oil is used in hot climates and where high loads are encountered. Multi-viscosity oils are designed to have characteristics of both light and heavy oils and are available in a number of weights from 0W-20 to 20W-50.

Gear oil is designed to be used in differentials, manual transmissions and other areas where high-temperature lubrication is required.

Chassis and wheel bearing grease is a heavy grease used where increased loads and friction are encountered, such as for wheel bearings, balljoints, tie-rod ends and universal joints.

High-temperature wheel bearing grease is designed to withstand the extreme temperatures encountered by wheel bearings in disc brake equipped vehicles. It usually contains molybdenum disulfide (moly), which is a dry-type lubricant.

White grease is a heavy grease for metal-to-metal applications where water is a problem. White grease stays soft under both low and high temperatures (usually from -100 to +190-degrees F), and will not wash off or dilute in the presence of water.

Assembly lube is a special extreme pressure lubricant, usually containing moly, used to lubricate high-load parts (such as main and rod bearings and cam lobes) for initial start-up of a new engine. The assembly lube lubricates the parts without being squeezed out or washed away until the engine oiling system begins to function.

Silicone lubricants are used to protect rubber, plastic, vinyl and nylon parts.

Graphite lubricants are used where oils cannot be used due to contamination problems, such as in locks. The dry graphite will lubricate metal parts while remaining uncontaminated by dirt, water, oil or acids. It is electrically conductive and will not foul electrical contacts in locks such as the ignition switch.

Moly penetrants loosen and lubricate frozen, rusted and corroded fasteners and prevent future rusting or freezing.

Heat-sink grease is a special electrically non-conductive grease that is used for mounting electronic ignition modules where it is essential that heat is transferred away from the module.

Sealants

RTV sealant is one of the most widely used gasket compounds. Made from silicone, RTV is air curing, it seals, bonds, waterproofs, fills surface irregularities, remains flexible, doesn't shrink, is relatively easy to remove, and is used as a supplementary sealer with almost all low and medium temperature gaskets.

Anaerobic sealant is much like RTV in that it can be used either to seal gaskets or to form gaskets by itself. It remains flexible, is solvent resistant and fills surface imperfections. The difference between an anaerobic sealant and an RTV-type sealant is in the curing. RTV cures when exposed to air, while an anaerobic sealant cures only in the absence of air. This means that an anaerobic sealant cures only after the assembly of parts, sealing them together.

Thread and pipe sealant is used for sealing hydraulic and pneumatic fittings and vacuum lines. It is usually made from a Teflon compound, and comes in a spray, a paint-on liquid and as a wrap-around tape.

Chemicals

Anti-seize compound prevents seizing, galling, cold welding, rust and corrosion in fasteners. High-temperature ant-seize, usually made with copper and graphite lubricants, is used for exhaust system and exhaust manifold bolts.

Anaerobic locking compounds are used to keep fasteners from vibrating or working loose and cure only after installation, in the absence of air. Medium strength locking compound is used for small nuts, bolts and screws that may be removed later. High-strength locking compound is for large nuts, bolts and studs which aren't removed on a regular basis.

Oil additives range from viscosity index improvers to chemical treatments that claim to reduce internal engine friction. It should be noted that most oil manufacturers caution against using additives with their oils.

Gas additives perform several functions, depending on their chemical makeup. They usually contain solvents that help dissolve gum and varnish that build up on carburetor, fuel injection and intake parts. They also serve to break down carbon deposits that form on the inside surfaces of the combustion chambers. Some additives contain upper cylinder lubricants for valves and piston rings, and others contain chemicals to remove condensation from the gas tank.

Miscellaneous

Brake fluid is specially formulated hydraulic fluid that can withstand the heat and pressure encountered in brake systems. Care must be taken so this fluid does not come in contact with painted surfaces or plastics. An opened container should always be resealed to prevent contamination by water or dirt.

Weatherstrip adhesive is used to bond weatherstripping around doors, windows and trunk lids. It is sometimes used to attach trim pieces.

Undercoating is a petroleum-based, tar-like substance that is designed to protect metal surfaces on the underside of the vehicle from corrosion. It also acts as a sound-deadening agent by insulating the bottom of the vehicle.

Waxes and polishes are used to help protect painted and plated surfaces from the weather. Different types of paint may require the use of different types of wax and polish. Some polishes utilize a chemical or abrasive cleaner to help remove the top layer of oxidized (dull) paint on older vehicles. In recent years many non-wax polishes that contain a wide variety of chemicals such as polymers and silicones have been introduced. These non-wax polishes are usually easier to apply and last longer than conventional waxes and polishes.

Conversion factors

Length (distance)
Inches (in)	X	25.4	= Millimeters (mm)	X 0.0394	= Inches (in)
Feet (ft)	X	0.305	= Meters (m)	X 3.281	= Feet (ft)
Miles	X	1.609	= Kilometers (km)	X 0.621	= Miles

Volume (capacity)
Cubic inches (cu in; in^3)	X	16.387	= Cubic centimeters (cc; cm^3)	X 0.061	= Cubic inches (cu in; in^3)
Imperial pints (Imp pt)	X	0.568	= Liters (l)	X 1.76	= Imperial pints (Imp pt)
Imperial quarts (Imp qt)	X	1.137	= Liters (l)	X 0.88	= Imperial quarts (Imp qt)
Imperial quarts (Imp qt)	X	1.201	= US quarts (US qt)	X 0.833	= Imperial quarts (Imp qt)
US quarts (US qt)	X	0.946	= Liters (l)	X 1.057	= US quarts (US qt)
Imperial gallons (Imp gal)	X	4.546	= Liters (l)	X 0.22	= Imperial gallons (Imp gal)
Imperial gallons (Imp gal)	X	1.201	= US gallons (US gal)	X 0.833	= Imperial gallons (Imp gal)
US gallons (US gal)	X	3.785	= Liters (l)	X 0.264	= US gallons (US gal)

Mass (weight)
Ounces (oz)	X	28.35	= Grams (g)	X 0.035	= Ounces (oz)
Pounds (lb)	X	0.454	= Kilograms (kg)	X 2.205	= Pounds (lb)

Force
Ounces-force (ozf; oz)	X	0.278	= Newtons (N)	X 3.6	= Ounces-force (ozf; oz)
Pounds-force (lbf; lb)	X	4.448	= Newtons (N)	X 0.225	= Pounds-force (lbf; lb)
Newtons (N)	X	0.1	= Kilograms-force (kgf; kg)	X 9.81	= Newtons (N)

Pressure
Pounds-force per square inch (psi; lbf/in^2; lb/in^2)	X	0.070	= Kilograms-force per square centimeter (kgf/cm^2; kg/cm^2)	X 14.223	= Pounds-force per square inch (psi; lbf/in^2; lb/in^2)
Pounds-force per square inch (psi; lbf/in^2; lb/in^2)	X	0.068	= Atmospheres (atm)	X 14.696	= Pounds-force per square inch (psi; lbf/in^2; lb/in^2)
Pounds-force per square inch (psi; lbf/in^2; lb/in^2)	X	0.069	= Bars	X 14.5	= Pounds-force per square inch (psi; lbf/in^2; lb/in^2)
Pounds-force per square inch (psi; lbf/in^2; lb/in^2)	X	6.895	= Kilopascals (kPa)	X 0.145	= Pounds-force per square inch (psi; lbf/in^2; lb/in^2)
Kilopascals (kPa)	X	0.01	= Kilograms-force per square centimeter (kgf/cm^2; kg/cm^2)	X 98.1	= Kilopascals (kPa)

Torque (moment of force)
Pounds-force inches (lbf in; lb in)	X	1.152	= Kilograms-force centimeter (kgf cm; kg cm)	X 0.868	= Pounds-force inches (lbf in; lb in)
Pounds-force inches (lbf in; lb in)	X	0.113	= Newton meters (Nm)	X 8.85	= Pounds-force inches (lbf in; lb in)
Pounds-force inches (lbf in; lb in)	X	0.083	= Pounds-force feet (lbf ft; lb ft)	X 12	= Pounds-force inches (lbf in; lb in)
Pounds-force feet (lbf ft; lb ft)	X	0.138	= Kilograms-force meters (kgf m; kg m)	X 7.233	= Pounds-force feet (lbf ft; lb ft)
Pounds-force feet (lbf ft; lb ft)	X	1.356	= Newton meters (Nm)	X 0.738	= Pounds-force feet (lbf ft; lb ft)
Newton meters (Nm)	X	0.102	= Kilograms-force meters (kgf m; kg m)	X 9.804	= Newton meters (Nm)

Vacuum
Inches mercury (in. Hg)	X	3.377	= Kilopascals (kPa)	X 0.2961	= Inches mercury
Inches mercury (in. Hg)	X	25.4	= Millimeters mercury (mm Hg)	X 0.0394	= Inches mercury

Power
Horsepower (hp)	X	745.7	= Watts (W)	X 0.0013	= Horsepower (hp)

Velocity (speed)
Miles per hour (miles/hr; mph)	X	1.609	= Kilometers per hour (km/hr; kph)	X 0.621	= Miles per hour (miles/hr; mph)

Fuel consumption*
Miles per gallon, Imperial (mpg)	X	0.354	= Kilometers per liter (km/l)	X 2.825	= Miles per gallon, Imperial (mpg)
Miles per gallon, US (mpg)	X	0.425	= Kilometers per liter (km/l)	X 2.352	= Miles per gallon, US (mpg)

Temperature
Degrees Fahrenheit = (°C x 1.8) + 32

Degrees Celsius (Degrees Centigrade; °C) = (°F - 32) x 0.56

*It is common practice to convert from miles per gallon (mpg) to liters/100 kilometers (l/100km), where mpg (Imperial) x l/100 km = 282 and mpg (US) x l/100 km = 235

DECIMALS to MILLIMETERS

Decimal	mm	Decimal	mm
0.001	0.0254	0.500	12.7000
0.002	0.0508	0.510	12.9540
0.003	0.0762	0.520	13.2080
0.004	0.1016	0.530	13.4620
0.005	0.1270	0.540	13.7160
0.006	0.1524	0.550	13.9700
0.007	0.1778	0.560	14.2240
0.008	0.2032	0.570	14.4780
0.009	0.2286	0.580	14.7320
		0.590	14.9860
0.010	0.2540		
0.020	0.5080		
0.030	0.7620		
0.040	1.0160	0.600	15.2400
0.050	1.2700	0.610	15.4940
0.060	1.5240	0.620	15.7480
0.070	1.7780	0.630	16.0020
0.080	2.0320	0.640	16.2560
0.090	2.2860	0.650	16.5100
		0.660	16.7640
0.100	2.5400	0.670	17.0180
0.110	2.7940	0.680	17.2720
0.120	3.0480	0.690	17.5260
0.130	3.3020		
0.140	3.5560		
0.150	3.8100		
0.160	4.0640	0.700	17.7800
0.170	4.3180	0.710	18.0340
0.180	4.5720	0.720	18.2880
0.190	4.8260	0.730	18.5420
		0.740	18.7960
0.200	5.0800	0.750	19.0500
0.210	5.3340	0.760	19.3040
0.220	5.5880	0.770	19.5580
0.230	5.8420	0.780	19.8120
0.240	6.0960	0.790	20.0660
0.250	6.3500		
0.260	6.6040		
0.270	6.8580	0.800	20.3200
0.280	7.1120	0.810	20.5740
0.290	7.3660	0.820	21.8280
		0.830	21.0820
0.300	7.6200	0.840	21.3360
0.310	7.8740	0.850	21.5900
0.320	8.1280	0.860	21.8440
0.330	8.3820	0.870	22.0980
0.340	8.6360	0.880	22.3520
0.350	8.8900	0.890	22.6060
0.360	9.1440		
0.370	9.3980		
0.380	9.6520		
0.390	9.9060	0.900	22.8600
0.400	10.1600	0.910	23.1140
0.410	10.4140	0.920	23.3680
0.420	10.6680	0.930	23.6220
0.430	10.9220	0.940	23.8760
0.440	11.1760	0.950	24.1300
0.450	11.4300	0.960	24.3840
0.460	11.6840	0.970	24.6380
0.470	11.9380	0.980	24.8920
0.480	12.1920	0.990	25.1460
0.490	12.4460	1.000	25.4000

FRACTIONS to DECIMALS to MILLIMETERS

Fraction	Decimal	mm	Fraction	Decimal	mm
1/64	0.0156	0.3969	33/64	0.5156	13.0969
1/32	0.0312	0.7938	17/32	0.5312	13.4938
3/64	0.0469	1.1906	35/64	0.5469	13.8906
1/16	0.0625	1.5875	9/16	0.5625	14.2875
5/64	0.0781	1.9844	37/64	0.5781	14.6844
3/32	0.0938	2.3812	19/32	0.5938	15.0812
7/64	0.1094	2.7781	39/64	0.6094	15.4781
1/8	0.1250	3.1750	5/8	0.6250	15.8750
9/64	0.1406	3.5719	41/64	0.6406	16.2719
5/32	0.1562	3.9688	21/32	0.6562	16.6688
11/64	0.1719	4.3656	43/64	0.6719	17.0656
3/16	0.1875	4.7625	11/16	0.6875	17.4625
13/64	0.2031	5.1594	45/64	0.7031	17.8594
7/32	0.2188	5.5562	23/32	0.7188	18.2562
15/64	0.2344	5.9531	47/64	0.7344	18.6531
1/4	0.2500	6.3500	3/4	0.7500	19.0500
17/64	0.2656	6.7469	49/64	0.7656	19.4469
9/32	0.2812	7.1438	25/32	0.7812	19.8438
19/64	0.2969	7.5406	51/64	0.7969	20.2406
5/16	0.3125	7.9375	13/16	0.8125	20.6375
21/64	0.3281	8.3344	53/64	0.8281	21.0344
11/32	0.3438	8.7312	27/32	0.8438	21.4312
23/64	0.3594	9.1281	55/64	0.8594	21.8281
3/8	0.3750	9.5250	7/8	0.8750	22.2250
25/64	0.3906	9.9219	57/64	0.8906	22.6219
13/32	0.4062	10.3188	29/32	0.9062	23.0188
27/64	0.4219	10.7156	59/64	0.9219	23.4156
7/16	0.4375	11.1125	15/16	0.9375	23.8125
29/64	0.4531	11.5094	61/64	0.9531	24.2094
15/32	0.4688	11.9062	31/32	0.9688	24.6062
31/64	0.4844	12.3031	63/64	0.9844	25.0031
1/2	0.5000	12.7000	1	1.0000	25.4000

Safety first!

Regardless of how enthusiastic you may be about getting on with the job at hand, take the time to ensure that your safety is not jeopardized. A moment's lack of attention can result in an accident, as can failure to observe certain simple safety precautions. The possibility of an accident will always exist, and the following points should not be considered a comprehensive list of all dangers. Rather, they are intended to make you aware of the risks and to encourage a safety conscious approach to all work you carry out on your vehicle.

Essential DOs and DON'Ts

DON'T rely on a jack when working under the vehicle. Always use approved jackstands to support the weight of the vehicle and place them under the recommended lift or support points.

DON'T attempt to loosen extremely tight fasteners (i.e. wheel lug nuts) while the vehicle is on a jack - it may fall.

DON'T start the engine without first making sure that the transmission is in Neutral (or Park where applicable) and the parking brake is set.

DON'T remove the radiator cap from a hot cooling system - let it cool or cover it with a cloth and release the pressure gradually.

DON'T attempt to drain the engine oil until you are sure it has cooled to the point that it will not burn you.

DON'T touch any part of the engine or exhaust system until it has cooled sufficiently to avoid burns.

DON'T siphon toxic liquids such as gasoline, antifreeze and brake fluid by mouth, or allow them to remain on your skin.

DON'T inhale brake lining dust - it is potentially hazardous (see *Asbestos* below).

DON'T allow spilled oil or grease to remain on the floor - wipe it up before someone slips on it.

DON'T use loose fitting wrenches or other tools which may slip and cause injury.

DON'T push on wrenches when loosening or tightening nuts or bolts. Always try to pull the wrench toward you. If the situation calls for pushing the wrench away, push with an open hand to avoid scraped knuckles if the wrench should slip.

DON'T attempt to lift a heavy component alone - get someone to help you.

DON'T *rush or take unsafe shortcuts to finish a job.*

DON'T allow children or animals in or around the vehicle while you are working on it.

DO wear eye protection when using power tools such as a drill, sander, bench grinder, etc. and when working under a vehicle.

DO keep loose clothing and long hair well out of the way of moving parts.

DO make sure that any hoist used has a safe working load rating adequate for the job.

DO get someone to check on you periodically when working alone on a vehicle.

DO carry out work in a logical sequence and make sure that everything is correctly assembled and tightened.

DO keep chemicals and fluids tightly capped and out of the reach of children and pets.

DO remember that your vehicle's safety affects that of yourself and others. If in doubt on any point, get professional advice.

Steering, suspension and brakes

These systems are essential to driving safety, so make sure you have a qualified shop or individual check your work. Also, compressed suspension springs can cause injury if released suddenly - be sure to use a spring compressor.

Airbags

Airbags are explosive devices that can **CAUSE** injury if they deploy while you're working on the vehicle. Follow the manufacturer's instructions to disable the airbag whenever you're working in the vicinity of airbag components.

Asbestos

Certain friction, insulating, sealing, and other products - such as brake linings, brake bands, clutch linings, torque converters, gaskets, etc. - may contain asbestos or other hazardous friction material. Extreme care must be taken to avoid inhalation of dust from such products, since it is hazardous to health. If in doubt, assume that they do contain asbestos.

Fire

Remember at all times that gasoline is highly flammable. Never smoke or have any kind of open flame around when working on a vehicle. But the risk does not end there. A spark caused by an electrical short circuit, by two metal surfaces contacting each other, or even by static electricity built up in your body under certain conditions, can ignite gasoline vapors, which in a confined space are highly explosive. Do not, under any circumstances, use gasoline for cleaning parts. Use an approved safety solvent.

Always disconnect the battery ground (-) cable at the battery before working on any part of the fuel system or electrical system. Never risk spilling fuel on a hot engine or exhaust component. It is strongly recommended that a fire extinguisher suitable for use on fuel and electrical fires be kept handy in the garage or workshop at all times. Never try to extinguish a fuel or electrical fire with water.

Fumes

Certain fumes are highly toxic and can quickly cause unconsciousness and even death if inhaled to any extent. Gasoline vapor falls into this category, as do the vapors from some cleaning solvents. Any draining or pouring of such volatile fluids should be done in a well ventilated area.

When using cleaning fluids and solvents, read the instructions on the container carefully. Never use materials from unmarked containers.

Never run the engine in an enclosed space, such as a garage. Exhaust fumes contain carbon monoxide, which is extremely poisonous. If you need to run the engine, always do so in the open air, or at least have the rear of the vehicle outside the work area.

The battery

Never create a spark or allow a bare light bulb near a battery. They normally give off a certain amount of hydrogen gas, which is highly explosive.

Always disconnect the battery ground (-) cable at the battery before working on the fuel or electrical systems.

If possible, loosen the filler caps or cover when charging the battery from an external source (this does not apply to sealed or maintenance-free batteries). Do not charge at an excessive rate or the battery may burst.

Take care when adding water to a non maintenance-free battery and when carrying a battery. The electrolyte, even when diluted, is very corrosive and should not be allowed to contact clothing or skin.

Always wear eye protection when cleaning the battery to prevent the caustic deposits from entering your eyes.

Household current

When using an electric power tool, inspection light, etc., which operates on household current, always make sure that the tool is correctly connected to its plug and that, where necessary, it is properly grounded. Do not use such items in damp conditions and, again, do not create a spark or apply excessive heat in the vicinity of fuel or fuel vapor.

Secondary ignition system voltage

A severe electric shock can result from touching certain parts of the ignition system (such as the spark plug wires) when the engine is running or being cranked, particularly if components are damp or the insulation is defective. In the case of an electronic ignition system, the secondary system voltage is much higher and could prove fatal.

Hydrofluoric acid

This extremely corrosive acid is formed when certain types of synthetic rubber, found in some O-rings, oil seals, fuel hoses, etc. are exposed to temperatures above 750-degrees F (400-degrees C). The rubber changes into a charred or sticky substance containing the acid. *Once formed, the acid remains dangerous for years. If it gets onto the skin, it may be necessary to amputate the limb concerned.*

When dealing with a vehicle which has suffered a fire, or with components salvaged from such a vehicle, wear protective gloves and discard them after use.

Troubleshooting

Contents

This Section provides an easy reference guide to the more common problems which may occur during the operation of your vehicle. These problems and their possible causes are grouped under headings denoting various components or systems, such as Engine, Cooling system, etc. They also refer you to the Chapter and/or Section which deals with the problem.

Remember that successful troubleshooting is not a mysterious art practiced only by professional mechanics. It is simply the result of the right knowledge combined with an intelligent, systematic approach to the problem. Always work by a process of elimination, starting with the simplest solution and working through to the most complex - and never overlook the obvious. Anyone can run the gas tank dry or leave the lights on overnight, so don't assume that you are exempt from such oversights.

Finally, always establish a clear idea of why a problem has occurred and take steps to ensure that it doesn't happen again. If the electrical system fails because of a poor connection, check the other connections in the system to make sure that they don't fail as well. If a particular fuse continues to blow, find out why - don't just replace one fuse after another. Remember, failure of a small component can often be indicative of potential failure or incorrect functioning of a more important component or system.

Engine

1 Engine will not rotate when attempting to start

1   Battery terminal connections loose or corroded (Chapter 1).
2   Battery discharged or faulty (Chapter 1).
3   Automatic transaxle not completely engaged in Park (Chapter 7).
4   Broken, loose or disconnected wiring in the starting circuit (Chapters 5 and 12).
5   Starter motor pinion jammed in flywheel ring gear (Chapter 5).
6   Starter solenoid faulty (Chapter 5).
7   Starter motor faulty (Chapter 5).
8   Ignition switch faulty (Chapter 12).
9   Starter pinion or flywheel teeth worn or broken (Chapter 5).

2 Engine rotates but will not start

1   Fuel tank empty.
2   Fuel cut switch activated due to vehicle impact (Chapter 4).
3   Battery discharged (engine rotates slowly) (Chapter 5).
4   Battery terminal connections loose or corroded (Chapter 1).
5   Leaking fuel injector(s), faulty fuel pump, pressure regulator, etc. (Chapter 4).
6   Fuel not reaching fuel rail (Chapter 4).
7   Ignition components damp or damaged (Chapter 5).
8   Worn, faulty or incorrectly gapped spark plugs (Chapter 1).
9   Broken, loose or disconnected wiring in the starting circuit (Chapter 5).
10   Broken, loose or disconnected wires at the ignition coil(s) or faulty coil(s) (Chapter 5).
11   Faulty camshaft or crankshaft position sensor (Chapter 6).

3 Engine hard to start when cold

1   Battery discharged or low (Chapter 1).
2   Malfunctioning fuel system (Chapter 4).
3   Faulty cold start injector (Chapter 4).
4   Injector(s) leaking (Chapter 4).
5   Faulty coolant temperature sensor (Chapter 6).

4 Engine hard to start when hot

1   Air filter clogged (Chapter 1).
2   Fuel not reaching the fuel injection system (Chapter 4).
3   Corroded battery connections, especially ground (Chapter 1).

5 Starter motor noisy or excessively rough in engagement

1   Pinion or flywheel gear teeth worn or broken (Chapter 5).
2   Starter motor mounting bolts loose or missing (Chapter 5).

6 Engine starts but stops immediately

1   Loose or faulty electrical connections at coil(s) or alternator (Chapter 5).
2   Insufficient fuel reaching the fuel injector(s) (Chapters 1 and 4).
3   Vacuum leak at the gasket between the intake manifold/plenum and throttle body (Chapters 1 and 4).

7 Oil puddle under engine

1   Oil pan gasket and/or oil pan drain bolt washer leaking (Chapter 2).
2   Oil pressure sending unit leaking (Chapter 2).
3   Valve covers leaking (Chapter 2).
4   Engine oil seals leaking (Chapter 2).
5   Oil pump housing leaking (Chapter 2).

8 Engine lopes while idling or idles erratically

1   Vacuum leakage (Chapters 2 and 4).
2   Leaking EGR valve (Chapter 6).
3   Air filter clogged (Chapter 1).
4   Fuel pump not delivering sufficient fuel to the fuel injection system (Chapter 4).
5   Leaking head gasket (Chapter 2).
6   Timing belt and/or sprockets worn (Chapter 2).
7   Camshaft lobes worn (Chapter 2).

9 Engine misses at idle speed

1   Spark plugs worn or faulty (Chapter 1).
2   Faulty spark plug wires (Chapter 1).
3   Vacuum leaks (Chapter 1).
4   Fault in engine management system (Chapter 6).
5   Uneven or low compression (Chapter 2).

10 Engine misses throughout driving speed range

1   Fuel filter clogged and/or impurities in the fuel system (Chapter 1).
2   Low fuel output at the injector(s) (Chapter 4).
3   Faulty or worn spark plugs (Chapter 1).
4   Fault in engine management system (Chapter 6).
5   Faulty emission system components (Chapter 6).
6   Low or uneven cylinder compression pressures (Chapter 2).
7   Weak or faulty ignition coil(s) (Chapter 5).
8   Vacuum leak in fuel injection system, intake manifold/plenum, air control valve or vacuum hoses (Chapter 4).

11 Engine stumbles on acceleration

1   Spark plugs fouled (Chapter 1).
2   Fuel injection system faulty (Chapter 4).
3   Fuel filter clogged (Chapters 1 and 4).
4   Fault in engine management system (Chapter 6).
5   Intake manifold or plenum air leak (Chapters 2 and 4).

12 Engine surges while holding accelerator steady

1   Intake air leak (Chapter 4).
2   Fuel pump faulty (Chapter 4).
3   Loose fuel injector wire harness connectors (Chapter 4).
4   Defective ECM or information sensor (Chapter 6).

13 Engine stalls

1 Fuel filter clogged and/or water and impurities in the fuel system (Chapters 1 and 4).
2 Ignition components damp or damaged (Chapter 5).
3 Faulty emissions system components (Chapter 6).
4 Faulty or incorrectly gapped spark plugs (Chapter 1).
5 Vacuum leak in the fuel injection system, intake manifold or vacuum hoses (Chapters 2 and 4).
6 Valve clearances incorrectly set (Chapter 1).

14 Engine lacks power

1 Fault in engine management system (Chapter 6).
2 Faulty or worn spark plugs (Chapter 1).
3 Fuel injection system malfunction (Chapter 4).
4 Faulty coil(s) (Chapter 5).
5 Brakes binding (Chapter 9).
6 Automatic transaxle fluid level incorrect (Chapter 1).
7 Fuel filter clogged and/or impurities in the fuel system (Chapters 1 and 4).
8 Emissions control systems not functioning properly (Chapter 6).
9 Low or uneven cylinder compression pressures (Chapter 2).
10 Obstructed exhaust system (Chapter 4).

15 Engine backfires

1 Emission control system not functioning properly (Chapter 6).
2 Fault in engine management system (Chapter 6).
3 Faulty spark plug insulator (Chapter 1).
4 Fuel injection system malfunction (Chapter 4).
5 Vacuum leak at fuel injector(s), intake manifold, air control valve or vacuum hoses (Chapters 2 and 4).
6 Valve clearances incorrectly set and/or valves sticking (Chapter 1).

16 Pinging or knocking engine sounds during acceleration or uphill

1 Incorrect grade of fuel.
2 Fault in engine management system (Chapter 6).
3 Fuel injection system faulty (Chapter 4).
4 Improper or damaged spark plug(s) (Chapter 1).
5 Vacuum leak (Chapters 2 and 4).
6 Defective knock sensor (Chapter 6).

17 Engine runs with oil pressure light on

1 Low oil level (Chapter 1).
2 Short in wiring circuit (Chapter 12).
3 Faulty oil pressure sender (Chapter 2).
4 Worn engine bearings and/or oil pump (Chapter 2).

18 Engine diesels (continues to run) after switching off

1 Excessive engine operating temperature (Chapter 3).
2 Fault in engine management system (Chapter 6).

Engine electrical system

19 Battery will not hold a charge

1 Alternator drivebelt defective or not adjusted properly (Chapter 1).
2 Battery electrolyte level low (Chapter 1).
3 Battery terminals loose or corroded (Chapter 1).
4 Alternator not charging properly (Chapter 5).
5 Loose, broken or faulty wiring in the charging circuit (Chapter 5).
6 Short in vehicle wiring (Chapter 12).
7 Internally defective battery (Chapters 1 and 5).

20 Alternator light fails to go out

1 Faulty alternator or charging circuit (Chapter 5).
2 Alternator drivebelt defective or out of adjustment (Chapter 1).
3 Alternator voltage regulator inoperative (Chapter 5).

21 Alternator light fails to come on when key is turned on

1 Warning light bulb defective (Chapter 12).
2 Fault in the printed circuit, dash wiring or bulb holder (Chapter 12).

Fuel system

22 Excessive fuel consumption

1 Dirty or clogged air filter element (Chapter 1).
2 Fault in engine management system (Chapter 6).

3 Emissions systems not functioning properly (Chapter 6).
4 Fuel injection system not functioning properly (Chapter 4).
5 Low tire pressure or incorrect tire size (Chapter 1).

23 Fuel leakage and/or fuel odor

1 Leaking fuel feed or return line (Chapters 1 and 4).
2 Tank overfilled.
3 Evaporative canister filter clogged (Chapters 1 and 6).
4 Fuel injection system not functioning properly (Chapter 4).

Cooling system

24 Overheating

1 Insufficient coolant in system (Chapter 1).
2 Water pump defective (Chapter 3).
3 Radiator core blocked or grille restricted (Chapter 3).
4 Thermostat faulty (Chapter 3).
5 Electric coolant fan blades broken or cracked (Chapter 3).
6 Radiator cap not maintaining proper pressure (Chapter 3).
7 Fault in engine management system (Chapter 6).

25 Overcooling

1 Faulty thermostat (Chapter 3).
2 Inaccurate temperature gauge sending unit (Chapter 3)

26 External coolant leakage

1 Deteriorated/damaged hoses; loose clamps (Chapters 1 and 3).
2 Water pump defective (Chapter 3).
3 Leakage from radiator core or coolant reservoir bottle (Chapter 3).
4 Engine drain or water jacket core plugs leaking (Chapter 2).

27 Internal coolant leakage

1 Leaking cylinder head gasket (Chapter 2).
2 Cracked cylinder bore or cylinder head (Chapter 2).

28 Coolant loss

1 Too much coolant in system (Chapter 1).

2 Coolant boiling away because of overheating (Chapter 3).
3 Internal or external leakage (Chapter 3).
4 Faulty radiator cap (Chapter 3).

29 Poor coolant circulation

1 Inoperative water pump (Chapter 3).
2 Restriction in cooling system (Chapters 1 and 3).
3 Water pump drivebelt defective/out of adjustment (Chapter 1).
4 Thermostat sticking (Chapter 3).

Automatic transaxle

Note: *Due to the complexity of the automatic transaxle, it is difficult for the home mechanic to properly diagnose and service this component. For problems other than the following, the vehicle should be taken to a dealer or transaxle shop.*

30 Fluid leakage

1 Automatic transaxle fluid is a deep red color. Fluid leaks should not be confused with engine oil, which can easily be blown onto the transaxle by air flow.
2 To pinpoint a leak, first remove all built-up dirt and grime from the transaxle housing with degreasing agents and/or steam cleaning. Then drive the vehicle at low speeds so air flow will not blow the leak far from its source. Raise the vehicle and determine where the leak is coming from. Common areas of leakage are:
   a) *Pan (Chapters 1 and 7)*
   b) *Dipstick tube (Chapters 1 and 7)*
   c) *Transaxle oil lines (Chapter 7)*
   d) *Speed sensor (Chapter 7)*
   e) *Differential drain plug (Chapters 1 and 7)*

31 Transaxle fluid brown or has a burned smell

1 Transaxle fluid overheated (Chapter 1).
2 Clutch friction discs and/or bands burned.

32 General shift mechanism problems

1 Chapter 7 deals with checking and adjusting the shift linkage on automatic transaxles. Common problems which may be attributed to poorly adjusted linkage are:
   a) *Engine starting in gears other than Park or Neutral.*

b) *Indicator on shifter pointing to a gear other than the one actually being used.*
c) *Vehicle moves when in Park.*
2 Refer to Chapter 7 for the shift linkage adjustment procedure.

33 Transaxle will not downshift with accelerator pedal pressed to the floor

These transaxles are electronically controlled. Check for trouble codes stored in the PCM (see Chapter 6).

34 Engine will start in gears other than Park or Neutral

Transmission Range (TR) sensor malfunctioning (Chapter 7).

35 Transaxle slips, shifts roughly, is noisy or has no drive in forward or reverse gears

There are many probable causes for the above problems, but the home mechanic should be concerned with only one possibility - fluid level. Before taking the vehicle to a repair shop, check the level and condition of the fluid as described in Chapter 1. Correct the fluid level as necessary or change the fluid and filter if needed. If the problem persists, have a professional diagnose the cause.

Driveaxles

36 Clicking noise in turns

Worn or damaged outboard CV joint (Chapter 8).

37 Shudder or vibration during acceleration

1 Excessive toe-in (Chapter 10).
2 Worn or damaged inboard or outboard CV joints (Chapter 8).
3 Sticking inboard CV joint assembly (Chapter 8).

38 Vibration at highway speeds

1 Out-of-balance front wheels and/or tires (Chapters 1 and 10).
2 Out-of-round front tires (Chapters 1 and 10).
3 Worn CV joint(s) (Chapter 8).

Brakes

Note: *Before assuming that a brake problem exists, make sure that:*
   a) *The tires are in good condition and properly inflated (Chapter 1).*
   b) *The front end alignment is correct.*
   c) *The vehicle is not loaded with weight in an unequal manner.*

39 Vehicle pulls to one side during braking

1 Incorrect tire pressures (Chapter 1).
2 Front end out of alignment (have the front end aligned).
3 Front or rear tires not matched to one another.
4 Restricted brake lines or hoses (Chapter 9).
5 Malfunctioning caliper assembly (Chapter 9).
6 Loose suspension parts (Chapter 10).
7 Loose calipers (Chapter 9).
8 Excessive wear of brake pad material or disc on one side.

40 Noise (high-pitched squeal when the brakes are applied)

Front and/or rear disc brake pads worn out. Replace pads with new ones immediately (Chapter 9).

41 Brake roughness or chatter (pedal pulsates)

1 Excessive lateral runout (Chapter 9).
2 Uneven pad wear (Chapter 9).
3 Defective disc (Chapter 9).

42 Excessive brake pedal effort required to stop vehicle

1 Malfunctioning power brake booster (Chapter 9).
2 Partial system failure (Chapter 9).
3 Excessively worn pads (Chapter 9).
4 Piston in caliper stuck or sluggish (Chapter 9).
5 Brake pads contaminated with oil, grease or brake fluid (Chapter 9).
6 New pads installed and not yet seated. It will take a while for the new material to seat against the disc.

43 Excessive brake pedal travel

1 Partial brake system failure (Chapter 9).
2 Insufficient fluid in master cylinder (Chapters 1 and 9).
3 Air trapped in system (Chapters 1 and 9).

44 Dragging brakes

1 Incorrect adjustment of brake light switch (Chapter 9).
2 Master cylinder pistons not returning correctly (Chapter 9).
3 Restricted brakes lines or hoses (Chapters 1 and 9).
4 Incorrect parking brake adjustment (Chapter 9).

45 Grabbing or uneven braking action

1 Malfunction of proportioning valve (Chapter 9).
2 Malfunction of power brake booster unit (Chapter 9).
3 Binding brake pedal mechanism (Chapter 9).

46 Brake pedal feels spongy when depressed

1 Air in hydraulic lines (Chapter 9).
2 Master cylinder mounting bolts loose (Chapter 9).
3 Master cylinder defective (Chapter 9).

47 Brake pedal travels to the floor with little resistance

1 Little or no fluid in the master cylinder reservoir caused by leaking caliper piston(s) (Chapter 9).
2 Loose, damaged or disconnected brake lines (Chapter 9).
3 Defective master cylinder (Chapter 9).

48 Parking brake does not hold

Parking brake improperly adjusted (Chapters 1 and 9).

Suspension and steering systems
Note: *Before attempting to diagnose the suspension and steering systems, perform the following preliminary checks:*

a) *Tires for wrong pressure and uneven wear.*
b) *Steering universal joints from the column to the rack and pinion for loose connectors or wear.*
c) *Front and rear suspension and the steering gear assembly for loose or damaged parts.*
d) *Out-of-round or out-of-balance tires, bent rims and loose and/or rough wheel bearings.*

49 Vehicle pulls to one side

1 Mismatched or uneven tires (Chapter 10).
2 Broken or sagging springs (Chapter 10).
3 Wheel alignment (Chapter 10).
4 Front brake dragging (Chapter 9).

50 Abnormal or excessive tire wear

1 Wheel alignment (Chapter 10).
2 Sagging or broken springs (Chapter 10).
3 Tire out of balance (Chapter 10).
4 Worn strut damper (Chapter 10).
5 Overloaded vehicle.
6 Tires not rotated regularly.

51 Wheel makes a thumping noise

1 Blister or bump on tire (Chapter 10).
2 Improper strut damper action (Chapter 10).

52 Shimmy, shake or vibration

1 Tire or wheel out-of-balance or out-of-round (Chapter 10).
2 Loose or worn wheel bearings (Chapters 1, 8 and 10).
3 Worn tie-rod ends (Chapter 10).
4 Worn lower balljoints (Chapters 1 and 10).
5 Excessive wheel runout (Chapter 10).
6 Blister or bump on tire (Chapter 10).

53 Hard steering

1 Lack of lubrication at balljoints, tie-rod ends and steering gear assembly (Chapter 10).
2 Front wheel alignment (Chapter 10).
3 Low tire pressure(s) (Chapters 1 and 10).

54 Poor returnability of steering to center

1 Lack of lubrication at balljoints and tie-rod ends (Chapter 10).
2 Binding in balljoints (Chapter 10).
3 Binding in steering column (Chapter 10).
4 Lack of lubricant in steering gear assembly (Chapter 10).
5 Front wheel alignment (Chapter 10).

55 Abnormal noise at the front end

1 Lack of lubrication at balljoints and tie-rod ends (Chapters 1 and 10).
2 Damaged strut mounting (Chapter 10).
3 Worn control arm bushings or tie-rod ends (Chapter 10).
4 Loose stabilizer bar (Chapter 10).
5 Loose wheel nuts (Chapters 1 and 10).
6 Loose suspension bolts (Chapter 10)

56 Wander or poor steering stability

1 Mismatched or uneven tires (Chapter 10).
2 Lack of lubrication at balljoints and tie-rod ends (Chapters 1 and 10).
3 Worn strut assemblies (Chapter 10).
4 Loose stabilizer bar (Chapter 10).
5 Broken or sagging springs (Chapter 10).
6 Wheels out of alignment (Chapter 10).

57 Erratic steering when braking

1 Wheel bearings worn (Chapter 10).
2 Broken or sagging springs (Chapter 10).
3 Leaking wheel cylinder or caliper (Chapter 9).
4 Warped brake discs (Chapter 9).

58 Excessive pitching and/or rolling around corners or during braking

1 Loose stabilizer bar (Chapter 10).
2 Worn strut dampers or mountings (Chapter 10).
3 Broken or sagging springs (Chapter 10).
4 Overloaded vehicle.

59 Suspension bottoms

1 Overloaded vehicle.
2 Worn strut dampers (Chapter 10).
3 Incorrect, broken or sagging springs (Chapter 10).

60 Cupped tires

1 Front wheel or rear wheel alignment (Chapter 10).
2 Worn strut dampers (Chapter 10).
3 Wheel bearings worn (Chapter 10).
4 Excessive tire or wheel runout (Chapter 10).
5 Worn balljoints (Chapter 10).

61 Excessive tire wear on outside edge

1 Inflation pressures incorrect (Chapter 1).
2 Excessive speed in turns.
3 Front end alignment incorrect (excessive toe-in). Have professionally aligned.
4 Suspension arm bent or twisted (Chapter 10).

62 Excessive tire wear on inside edge

1　Inflation pressures incorrect (Chapter 1).
2　Front end alignment incorrect (toe-out). Have professionally aligned.
3　Loose or damaged steering components (Chapter 10).

63 Tire tread worn in one place

1　Tires out of balance.

2　Damaged wheel. Inspect and replace if necessary.
3　Defective tire (Chapter 1).

64 Excessive play or looseness in steering system

1　Wheel bearing(s) worn (Chapter 10).
2　Tie-rod end loose (Chapter 10).
3　Steering gear loose (Chapter 10).
4　Worn or loose steering intermediate shaft (Chapter 10).

65 Rattling or clicking noise in steering gear

1　Steering gear loose (Chapter 10).
2　Steering gear defective.

Chapter 1
Tune-up and routine maintenance

Contents

Specifications

Recommended lubricants and fluids

Note: *Listed here are manufacturer recommendations at the time this manual was written. Manufacturers occasionally upgrade their fluid and lubricant specifications, so check with your auto parts store for current recommendations.*

Engine oil type	API "certified for gasoline engines"
Viscosity	See accompanying chart
Fuel	Refer to owner's manual
Coolant	Ethylene-glycol based for use with aluminum, 50/50 mix with water
Transaxle	Diamond or SK SP-III automatic transmission fluid or equivalent
Brake fluid type	DOT 3 or DOT 4 brake fluid
Power steering system fluid	PSF 3 power steering fluid
Transfer case (AWD models)	API GL-5 SAE 80W-90 hypoid gear oil
Rear differential (AWD models)	API GL-5 SAE 80W-90 hypoid gear oil

Engine oil viscosity chart

1-a3 HAYNES

Capacities*

Engine oil (including filter)	
Four-cylinder and 3.5L V6 engines	4.5 quarts (4.3 liters)
2.7L V6 engine	4.7 quarts (4.5 liters)
Coolant	
Four-cylinder engine	7.7 quarts (7.3 liters)
2.7L V6 engine	9.1 quarts (8.6 liters)
3.5L V6 engine	8.7 quarts (8.2 liters)
Automatic transaxle	Up to 8.9 quarts (8.5 liters)**
Manual transaxle	2.4 quarts (2.3 liters)
Transfer case (AWD models)	Fill to bottom of fill hole
Rear differential (AWD models)	1.2 quarts (1.1 liters)

*Note: *All capacities approximate. Add as necessary to bring to the appropriate level.*

**Note: *This is a dry-fill capacity. The best way to determine the amount of fluid to add during a routine fluid change is to measure the amount drained. When refilling, add that amount initially, then check the fluid level and add a little at a time, as necessary. It is important not to overfill the transaxle.*

Ignition system

Spark plug	
Four-cylinder engine	NGK PGR5C-11 or equivalent
V6 engines	NGK PFR5N-11, RC10PYP4 or equivalent
Gap	0.039 to 0.043 inch (1.0 to 1.1 mm)
Engine firing order	
Four-cylinder engine	1-3-4-2
V6 engine	1-2-3-4-5-6

Brakes

Disc brake pad lining thickness (minimum)	1/16 inch (1.5 mm)

Torque specifications

Note: *One foot-pound (ft-lb) of torque is equivalent to 12 inch-pounds (in-lbs) of torque. Torque values below approximately 15 ft-lbs are expressed in inch-pounds, since most foot-pound torque wrenches are not accurate at these smaller values.*

	Ft-lbs (unless otherwise indicated)	Nm
Automatic transaxle		
Drain plug	23	32
Pan bolts	67 in-lbs	8
Filter bolts	96 in-lbs	11
Transfer case drain and fill plugs	27	36
Differential housing drain and fill plugs	27	36
Engine oil pan drain plug	22 to 33	30 to 45
Spark plugs	15 to 22	20 to 30
Fuel filter fitting nuts	22 to 29	30 to 40
Wheel lug nuts	66 to 81	90 to 110

Cylinder numbering - four-cylinder engine

Cylinder numbering - V6 engines

V6 engine compartment (3.5L V6 shown)

1 Brake fluid reservoir
2 Air filter housing
3 Fuse/relay box
4 Battery
5 Automatic transaxle dipstick

6 Engine cover (remove for access to spark plugs)
7 Engine oil dipstick
8 Radiator cap

9 Engine oil filler cap
10 Windshield washer fluid reservoir
11 Power steering fluid reservoir
12 Engine coolant reservoir

Typical 2WD front underside components

1	Engine splash shield (remove for access to engine oil drain plug and transmission drain plug)	5	Steering gear
2	Front brake caliper	6	Outer driveaxle boot
3	Brake hose	7	Balljoint
4	Inner driveaxle boot		

Typical 2WD rear underside components

1 Muffler
2 Shock absorber
3 Lower control arm
4 Trailing arm
5 Stabilizer bar
6 Coil spring
7 Upper control arm

Hyundai Santa Fe Maintenance Schedule

The maintenance intervals in this manual are provided with the assumption that you, not the dealer, will be doing the work. These are the minimum maintenance intervals recommended by the factory for vehicles that are driven daily. If you wish to keep your vehicle in peak condition at all times, you may wish to perform some of these procedures even more often. Because frequent maintenance enhances the efficiency, performance and resale value of your car, we encourage you to do so. If you drive in dusty areas, tow a trailer, idle or drive at low speeds for extended periods or drive for short distances (less than four miles) in below freezing temperatures, shorter intervals are also recommended.

When your vehicle is new, it should be serviced by a factory authorized dealer service department to protect the factory warranty. In many cases, the initial maintenance check is done at no cost to the owner.

Every 250 miles (400 km) or weekly, whichever comes first

Check the engine oil level (Section 4)
Check the engine coolant level (Section 4)
Check the windshield washer fluid level (Section 4)
Check the brake fluid level (Section 4)
Check the power steering fluid level (Section 4)
Check the automatic transaxle fluid level (Section 4)
Check the tires and tire pressures (Section 5)

Every 3000 miles (4,800 km) or 3 months, whichever comes first

All items listed above plus:
Change the engine oil and oil filter (Section 6)

Every 5000 miles (8000 km) or 6 months, whichever comes first

All items listed above plus:
Check and service the battery (Section 7)
Rotate the tires (Section 8)
Inspect and replace if necessary the windshield wiper blades (Section 9)
Inspect and replace if necessary all underhood hoses (Section 10)
Check the cooling system (Section 11)
Inspect the brake system (Section 12)

Every 15,000 miles (24,000 km) or 18 months, whichever comes first

All items listed above plus:
Inspect the suspension, steering components and driveaxle boots (Section 13)*
Inspect the exhaust system (Section 14)

Every 30,000 miles (48,000 km) or 36 months, whichever comes first

All items listed above plus:
Replace the air filter (Section 15)*
Inspect the fuel system (Section 16)
Replace interior ventilation filter (Section 17)*
Check and replace (if necessary) the PCV valve (Section 18)
Change the brake fluid (Section 19)

Every 50,000 miles (80,500 km) or 60 months, whichever comes first

Service the cooling system (drain, flush and refill) (Section 24) (after the initial 100,000-mile [160,000 km] or 120-month service)
Replace the fuel filter (Section 27)

Every 60,000 miles (96,000 km) or 72 months, whichever comes first

All items listed above plus:
Check and adjust if necessary the engine drivebelts (Section 20) (after the initial 60,000-mile [96,000 km] or 72-month check)
Change the automatic transaxle fluid (Section 21)**
Change the transfer case (AWD models and manual transaxle lubricant) (Section 22)**
Change the rear differential lubricant (AWD models) (Section 23)**

100,000 miles (160,000 km) or 120 months, whichever comes first - thereafter every 50,000 miles (80,500 km) or 60 months, whichever comes first

Service the cooling system (drain, flush and refill) (Section 24)

Every 120,000 miles (193,000 km) or 144 months, whichever comes first

Replace the spark plugs (Section 25)
Check the ignition system components (Section 26)

* *This item is affected by "severe" operating conditions as described below. If your vehicle is operated under "severe" conditions, inspect all maintenance indicated with an asterisk (*) at 3000 mile/3 month intervals and perform maintenance or replace parts as necessary. Severe conditions are indicated if you mainly operate your vehicle under one or more of the following conditions:*

Operating in dusty areas
Idling for extended periods and/or low speed operation
Operating when outside temperatures remain below freezing and when most trips are less than 4 miles

** *If used for trailer towing, change the transaxle, transfer case or rear differential fluid lubricant every 30,000 miles (Section 21, Section 22 or Section 23)*

2   Introduction

This Chapter is designed to help the home mechanic maintain his vehicle for peak performance, economy, safety and long life.

Included is a master maintenance schedule, followed by sections dealing specifically with each item on the schedule. Visual checks, adjustments, component replacement and other helpful items are included. Refer to the accompanying illustrations of the engine compartment and the underside of the vehicle for the location of various components.

Servicing your vehicle in accordance with the mileage/time maintenance schedule and the following Sections will provide it with a planned maintenance program that should result in a long and reliable service life. This is a comprehensive plan, so maintaining some items but not others at the specified service intervals won't produce the same results.

As you service your vehicle, you will discover that many of the procedures can - and should - be grouped together because of the nature of the particular procedure you're performing or because of the close proximity of two otherwise unrelated components to one another.

For example, if the vehicle is raised for any reason, you should inspect the exhaust, suspension, steering and fuel systems while you're under the vehicle. When you're rotating the tires, it makes good sense to check the brakes and wheel bearings since the wheels are already removed.

Finally, let's suppose you have to borrow or rent a torque wrench. Even if you only need to tighten the spark plugs, you might as well check the torque of as many critical fasteners as time allows.

The first step of this maintenance program is to prepare yourself before the actual work begins. Read through all Sections pertinent to the procedures you're planning to do, then make a list of and gather together all the parts and tools you will need to do the job. If it looks as if you might run into problems during a particular segment of some procedure, seek advice from your local parts man or dealer service department.

3   Tune-up general information

The term tune-up is used in this manual to represent a combination of individual operations rather than one specific procedure.

If, from the time the vehicle is new, the routine maintenance schedule is followed closely and frequent checks are made of fluid levels and high wear items, as suggested throughout this manual, the engine will be kept in relatively good running condition and the need for additional work will be minimized.

More likely than not, however, there will be times when the engine is running poorly due to lack of regular maintenance. This is even more likely if a used vehicle, which has not received regular and frequent maintenance checks, is purchased. In such cases, an engine tune-up will be needed outside of the regular routine maintenance intervals.

The first step in any tune-up or engine diagnosis to help correct a poor running engine would be a cylinder compression check. A check of the engine compression (see Chapter 2 Part C) will give valuable information regarding the overall performance of many internal components and should be used as a basis for tune-up and repair procedures. If, for instance, a compression check indicates serious internal engine wear, a conventional tune-up will not help the running condition of the engine and would be a waste of time and money. Also in Chapter 2, Part C is information on checking engine vacuum, which also gives information on the engine's state-of-tune and condition.

The following series of operations are those most often needed to bring a generally poor-running engine back into a proper state of tune.

Minor tune-up

Check all engine related fluids (Section 4)
Clean, inspect and test the battery (Section 7)
Check all underhood hoses (Section 10)
Check the cooling system (Section 11)
Check the air filter (Section 15)
Check and adjust the drivebelts (Section 20)

Major tune-up

All items listed under Minor tune-up, plus . . .
Replace the air filter (Section 15)
Check the fuel system (Section 16)
Replace the spark plugs (Section 25)
Replace the fuel filter (Section 27)
Check the charging system (Chapter 5)

4   Fluid level checks (every 250 miles [400 km] or weekly)

1   Fluids are an essential part of the lubrication, cooling, brake, clutch and other systems. Because these fluids gradually become depleted and/or contaminated during normal operation of the vehicle, they must be periodically replenished. See *Recommended lubricants and fluids* and *Capacities* at the beginning of this Chapter before adding fluid to any of the following components. **Note:** *The vehicle must be on level ground before fluid levels can be checked.*

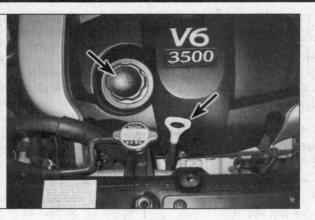

4.2 The engine oil dipstick is mounted on the front (radiator) side of the engine; the threaded oil filler cap is located on the valve cover - to prevent dirt from contaminating the engine, always make sure the area around this opening is clean before removing the cap

Engine oil

Refer to illustrations 4.2 and 4.4

2   The engine oil level is checked with a dipstick located at the front side of the engine **(see illustration).** The dipstick extends through a metal tube from which it protrudes down into the engine oil pan.

3   The oil level should be checked before the vehicle has been driven, or about 5 minutes after the engine has been shut off. If the oil is checked immediately after driving the vehicle, some of the oil will remain in the upper engine components, producing a low reading on the dipstick.

4   Pull the dipstick from the tube and wipe all the oil from the end with a clean rag or paper towel. Insert the clean dipstick all the way back into its metal tube and pull it out again. Observe the oil at the end of the dipstick. At its highest point, the level should be between the lower and upper marks **(see illustration).**

5   It takes one quart of oil to raise the level from the lower mark to the upper mark on the dipstick. Do not allow the level to drop below the lower mark or oil starvation may cause engine damage. Conversely, overfilling the engine (adding oil above the upper mark) may cause oil-fouled spark plugs, oil leaks or oil seal failures.

6   Remove the threaded cap from the valve cover to add oil **(see illustration 4.2).** Use a funnel to prevent spills. After adding the oil, install the filler cap hand tight. Start the engine and look carefully for any small leaks around the oil filter or drain plug. Stop the engine and check the oil level again after it has had sufficient time to drain from the upper block and cylinder head galleys.

7   Checking the oil level is an important preventive maintenance step. A continually dropping oil level indicates oil leakage through damaged seals, from loose connections, or past worn rings or valve guides. If the oil looks milky in color or has water droplets in it, a cylinder head gasket may be blown. The engine should be checked immediately. The condition of the oil should also be checked. Each time you check the oil level, slide your thumb and index finger up the dipstick before wiping off the oil. If you see small dirt or metal particles clinging to the dipstick, the oil should be changed (see Section 8).

Engine coolant

Refer to illustration 4.8

Warning: *Do not allow antifreeze to come in contact with your skin or painted surfaces of the vehicle. Flush contaminated areas immediately with plenty of water. Don't store new coolant or leave old coolant lying around where it's accessible to children or pets - they're attracted by its sweet smell. Ingestion of even a small amount of coolant can be fatal! Wipe up garage floor and drip pan spills immediately. Keep antifreeze containers covered and repair cooling system leaks as soon as they're noticed.*

8   All models use a coolant surge tank connected to the top of the radiator **(see illustration).** **Warning:** *Never remove the cap from the coolant surge tank unless the engine is completely cool. Serious burns can result.*

9   The coolant level should be checked regularly. It must be between the Full and Low lines on the tank. The level will vary with the temperature of the engine. When the engine is cold, the coolant level should be at or slightly above the Low mark on the tank. Once the engine has warmed up, the level should be at or near the Full mark. If it isn't, allow the fluid in the tank to cool, then remove the cap from the reservoir and add coolant to bring the level up to the Full line. Use only the type of coolant listed in this Chapter's Specifications or in your owner's manual. Do not use supplemental inhibitors or additives. If only a small amount of coolant is required to bring the system up to the proper level, water can be used. However, repeated additions of

water will dilute the recommended antifreeze and water solution. In order to maintain the proper ratio of antifreeze and water, it is advisable to top up the coolant level with the correct mixture. If the coolant level drops within a short time after replenishment, there may be a leak in the system. Inspect the radiator, hoses, engine coolant filler cap, drain plugs, air bleeder plugs and water pump. If no leak is evident, have the radiator cap pressure tested. **Warning:** *Never remove the radiator pressure cap when the engine is running or has just been shut down, because the cooling system is hot. Escaping steam and scalding liquid could cause serious injury.*

10   If it is necessary to open the radiator cap, wait until the system has cooled completely, then wrap a thick cloth around the cap and turn it to the first stop. If any steam escapes, wait until the system has cooled further, then remove the cap.

11   When checking the coolant level, always note its condition. It should be relatively clear. If it is brown or rust colored, the system should be drained, flushed and refilled. Even if the coolant appears to be normal, the corrosion inhibitors wear out with use, so it must be replaced at the specified intervals.

12   Do not allow antifreeze to come in contact with your skin or painted surfaces of the vehicle. Flush contacted areas immediately with plenty of water.

Windshield washer fluid

Refer to illustration 4.13

13   Fluid for the windshield washer system is stored in a plastic reservoir that is located at the right front corner of the engine compartment **(see illustration).** In milder climates, plain water can be used to top up the reservoir, but the reservoir should be kept no more than two-thirds full to allow for expansion should the water freeze. In colder climates, the use of a specially designed windshield washer fluid, available at your dealer and any auto parts store, will help lower the freezing point of the fluid. Mix the solution with water in accordance with the manufacturer's directions on the container. Do not use regular antifreeze. It will damage the vehicle's paint.

4.4 The oil level should be at or near the upper mark on the dipstick - if it isn't, add enough oil to bring the level to or near the upper mark (it takes one quart to raise the level from the lower mark to the upper mark)

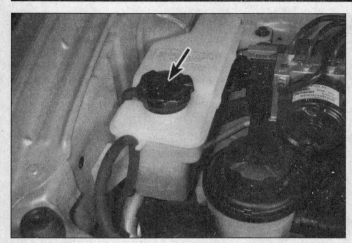

4.8 The coolant reservoir (surge tank) is located at the passenger side of the engine compartment

4.13 The windshield washer fluid reservoir is located at the right front corner of the engine compartment

Brake fluid

Refer to illustration 4.15

14 The brake master cylinder is mounted on the front of the power booster unit in the engine compartment.

15 To check the fluid level of the brake master cylinder reservoir, simply look at the MAX and MIN marks on the reservoir **(see illustration)**. The level should be within the specified distance from the maximum fill line.

16 If the level is low, wipe the top of the reservoir cover with a clean rag to prevent contamination of the brake system before lifting the cover.

17 Add only the specified brake fluid to the brake reservoir (refer to *Recommended lubricants and fluids* at the front of this Chapter or your owner's manual). Mixing different types of brake fluid can damage the system. Fill the brake master cylinder reservoir only to the dotted line - this brings the fluid to the correct level when you put the cover back on. **Warn-**

ing: *Use caution when filling the reservoir - brake fluid can harm your eyes and damage painted surfaces. Do not use brake fluid that has been opened for more than one year or has been left open. Brake fluid absorbs moisture from the air. Excess moisture can cause a dangerous loss of braking.*

18 While the reservoir cap is removed, inspect the master cylinder reservoir for contamination. If deposits, dirt particles or water droplets are present, the system should be drained and refilled (see Chapter 9).

19 After filling the reservoir to the proper level, make sure the lid is properly seated to prevent fluid leakage and/or system pressure loss.

20 The brake fluid in the master cylinder will drop slightly as the brake pads at each wheel wear down during normal operation. If the master cylinder requires repeated replenishing to keep it at the proper level, this is an indication of leakage in the brake system, which should be corrected immediately. Check all

brake lines and connections, along with the wheel cylinders and booster (see Section 12 for more information).

21 If, upon checking the master cylinder fluid level, you discover the reservoir empty or nearly empty, the brake system should be thoroughly inspected for leaks (see Chapter 9 for more information on the brake system).

Power steering fluid

Refer to illustration 4.25

22 Unlike manual steering, the power steering system relies on fluid that may, over a period of time, require replenishing.

23 The fluid reservoir for the power steering pump is located near the front of the engine.

24 For the check, the front wheels should be pointed straight ahead and the engine should be off.

25 The reservoir is translucent plastic and the fluid level can be checked visually **(see illustration)**.

4.15 The brake fluid should be kept between the Min and Max marks on the reservoir

4.25 The power steering fluid reservoir is located on the right side of the engine compartment - the reservoir is translucent, so the fluid level can be checked either hot or cold without removing the cap

4.32a The automatic transaxle dipstick is located next to the battery

26   If additional fluid is required, pour the specified type directly into the reservoir, using a funnel to prevent spills.

27   If the reservoir requires frequent fluid additions, all power steering hoses, hose connections, the power steering pump and the steering gear assembly should be carefully checked for leaks.

Automatic transaxle fluid

Refer to illustrations 4.32a, 4.32b and 4.32c

28   The level of the automatic transaxle fluid should be carefully maintained. Low fluid level can lead to slipping or loss of drive, while overfilling can cause foaming, loss of fluid and transaxle damage.

29   The transaxle fluid level should only be checked when the transaxle is hot (at its normal operating temperature). If the vehicle has just been driven over 10 miles (15 miles in a frigid climate), and the fluid temperature is 160 to 175-degrees F, the transaxle is hot. **Caution:** *If the vehicle has just been driven for a long time at high speed or in city traffic in hot weather, or if it has been pulling a trailer, an accurate fluid level reading cannot be obtained. Allow the fluid to cool down for about 30 minutes.*

30   If the vehicle has not just been driven, park the vehicle on level ground, set the parking brake and start the engine.

31   While the engine is idling, depress the brake pedal and move the selector lever through all the gear ranges, beginning and ending in Park.

32   With the engine still idling, remove the dipstick from its tube **(see illustration)**. Check the level of the fluid on the dipstick **(see illustration)** and note its condition.

33   Wipe the fluid from the dipstick with a clean rag and reinsert it back into the filler tube until the cap seats.

34   Pull the dipstick out again and note the fluid level. If the transaxle is cold, the level should be in the COLD or COOL range on the dipstick. If it is hot, the fluid level should be in the HOT range. If the level is at the low side of either range, add the specified automatic transaxle fluid through the dipstick tube with a funnel.

35   Add just enough of the recommended fluid to fill the transaxle to the proper level. It takes about one pint to raise the level from the low mark to the high mark when the fluid is hot, so add the fluid a little at a time and keep checking the level until it is correct.

36   The condition of the fluid should also be checked along with the level. If the fluid at the end of the dipstick is black or a dark reddish brown color, or if it emits a burned smell, the fluid should be changed (see Section 21). If you are in doubt about the condition of the fluid, purchase some new fluid and compare the two for color and smell.

Transfer case lubricant (AWD models)

Warning: *If the vehicle is equipped with electronically modulated air suspension, make sure that the height control switch is turned off.*

37   The transfer case does not have a dipstick. To check the fluid level, raise the vehicle and support it securely on jackstands. On the side of the transfer case housing, you will see a plug - remove it. If the lubricant level is correct, it should be up to the lower edge of the hole.

38   If the transaxle needs more lubricant (if the level is not up to the hole), use a syringe or a gear oil pump to add more. Stop filling the transaxle when the lubricant begins to run out the hole.

39   Install the plug and tighten it securely. Drive the vehicle a short distance, then check for leaks.

Rear differential lubricant level (AWD models)

40   Raise the vehicle and support it securely on jackstands.

41   Using the appropriate wrench, unscrew the plug from the rear differential.

42   Use your little finger to reach inside the housing to feel the lubricant level. The level should be at or near the bottom of the plug hole. If it isn't, add the recommended lubricant through the plug hole with a syringe or squeeze bottle.

43   Install the plug and tighten it securely. Check for leaks after the first few miles of driving.

4.32b If the automatic transaxle fluid is cold, the level should be near the Cold mark on the dipstick . . .

4.32c . . . if it's at normal operating temperature, the level should be near the Hot mark on the other side

5   Tire and tire pressure checks (every 250 miles [400 km] or weekly)

Refer to illustrations 5.2, 5.3, 5.4a, 5.4b and 5.8

1   Periodic inspection of the tires may spare you from the inconvenience of being stranded with a flat tire. It can also provide you with vital information regarding possible problems in the steering and suspension systems before major damage occurs.

2   Normal tread wear can be monitored with a simple, inexpensive device known as a tread depth indicator **(see illustration)**. When the tread depth reaches approximately 1/16-inch, replace the tire(s) (preferably long before that).

3   Note any abnormal tread wear **(see illustration)**. Tread pattern irregularities such as cupping, flat spots and more wear on one side than the other are indications of front end

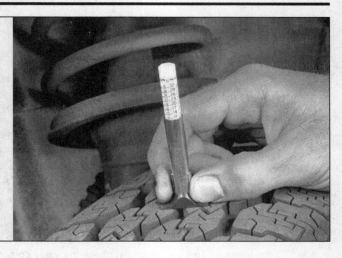

5.2 Use a tire tread depth gauge to monitor tire wear - they are available at auto parts stores and service stations and cost very little

alignment and/or balance problems. If any of these conditions are noted, take the vehicle to a tire shop or service station to correct the problem.

4   Look closely for cuts, punctures and embedded nails or tacks. Sometimes a tire will hold its air pressure for a short time or leak down very slowly even after a nail has embedded itself into the tread. If a slow leak persists, check the valve stem core to make

UNDERINFLATION

CUPPING

Cupping may be caused by:
- Underinflation and/or mechanical irregularities such as out-of-balance condition of wheel and/or tire, and bent or damaged wheel.
- Loose or worn steering tie-rod or steering idler arm.
- Loose, damaged or worn front suspension parts.

OVERINFLATION

INCORRECT TOE-IN OR EXTREME CAMBER

FEATHERING DUE TO MISALIGNMENT

5.3 This chart will help you determine the condition of your tires, the probable cause(s) of abnormal wear and the corrective action necessary

5.4a If a tire loses air on a steady basis, check the valve core first to make sure it's snug (special inexpensive wrenches are commonly available at auto parts stores)

5.4b If the valve core is tight, raise the corner of the vehicle with the low tire and spray a soapy water solution onto the tread as the tire is turned slowly - slow leaks will cause small bubbles to appear

sure it is tight **(see illustration)**. Examine the tread for an object that may have embedded itself into the tire or for a "plug" that may have begun to leak (radial tire punctures are repaired with a plug that is inserted into the hole). If a puncture is suspected, it can be easily verified by spraying a solution of soapy water onto the puncture area **(see illustration)**. The soapy solution will bubble if there is a leak. Unless the puncture is inordinately large, a tire shop or gas station can usually repair the punctured tire.

5   Carefully inspect the inner sidewall of each tire for evidence of brake fluid leakage. If you see any, inspect the brakes immediately.

6   Correct tire air pressure adds miles to the lifespan of the tires, improves mileage and enhances overall ride quality. Tire pressure cannot be accurately estimated by looking at a tire, particularly if it is a radial. A tire pressure gauge is therefore essential. Keep an accurate gauge in the glove box. The pressure gauges fitted to the nozzles of air hoses at gas stations are often inaccurate.

7   Always check tire pressure when the tires are cold. "Cold," in this case, means the vehicle has not been driven over a mile in the three hours preceding a tire pressure check. A pressure rise of four to eight pounds is not uncommon once the tires are warm.

8   Unscrew the valve cap protruding from the wheel or hubcap and push the gauge firmly onto the valve **(see illustration)**. Note the reading on the gauge and compare this figure to the recommended tire pressure shown on the tire placard in the glove box. Be sure to reinstall the valve cap to keep dirt and moisture out of the valve stem mechanism. Check all four tires and, if necessary, add enough air to bring them up to the recommended pressure levels.

9   Don't forget to keep the spare tire inflated to the specified pressure (consult your owner's manual).

---

6   Engine oil and oil filter change (every 3000 miles [4,800 km] or 3 months)

Refer to illustrations 6.2, 6.7, 6.13 and 6.15
Warning: *If the vehicle is equipped with electronically modulated air suspension, make sure that the height control switch is turned off.*

1   Frequent oil changes are the best preventive maintenance the home mechanic can give the engine, because aging oil becomes diluted and contaminated, which leads to premature engine wear.

2   Make sure that you have all the necessary tools before you begin this procedure **(see illustration).** You should also have plenty of rags or newspapers handy for mopping up any spills.

3   Access to the underside of the vehicle is greatly improved if the vehicle can be lifted on a hoist, driven onto ramps or supported by jackstands. **Warning:** *Do not work under a vehicle which is supported only by a bumper, hydraulic or scissors-type jack.*

4   If this is your first oil change, get under

the vehicle and familiarize yourself with the location of the oil drain plug. The engine and exhaust components will be warm during the actual work, so try to anticipate any potential problems before the engine and accessories are hot.

5   Park the vehicle on a level spot. Start the engine and allow it to reach its normal operating temperature (the needle on the temperature gauge should be at least above the bottom mark). Warm oil and sludge will flow out more easily. Turn off the engine when it's warmed up. Remove the filler cap.

6   Raise the vehicle and support it securely on jackstands. **Warning:** *To avoid personal injury, never get beneath a vehicle when it is supported by only by a jack. The jack provided with your vehicle is designed solely for raising the vehicle to remove and replace the wheels. Always use jackstands to support the vehicle when it becomes necessary to place your body underneath the vehicle.*

7   Being careful not to touch the hot exhaust components, place the drain pan under the drain plug in the bottom of the pan and remove the plug **(see illustration)**. You

5.8 To extend the life of your tires, check the air pressure at least once a week with an accurate gauge (don't forget the spare!)

6.2 These tools are required when changing the engine oil and filter

1   **Drain pan** - *It should be fairly shallow in depth, but wide in order to prevent spills*
2   **Rubber gloves** - *When removing the drain plug and filter, it is inevitable that you will get oil on your hands (the gloves will prevent burns)*
3   **Breaker bar** - *Sometimes the oil drain plug is pretty tight and a long breaker bar is needed to loosen it*
4   **Socket** - *To be used with the breaker bar or a ratchet (must be the correct size to fit the drain plug)*
5   **Filter wrench** - *This is a metal band-type wrench, which requires clearance around the filter to be effective*
6   **Filter wrench** - *This type fits on the bottom of the filter and can be turned with a ratchet or beaker bar (different size wrenches are available for different types of filters)*

6.7 Use the proper size box-end wrench or socket to remove the oil drain plug without rounding off the corners

may want to wear gloves while unscrewing the plug the final few turns if the engine is really hot.

8   Allow the old oil to drain into the pan. It may be necessary to move the pan farther under the engine as the oil flow slows to a trickle. Inspect the old oil for the presence of metal shavings and chips.

9   After all the oil has drained, wipe off the drain plug with a clean rag. Even minute metal particles clinging to the plug would immediately contaminate the new oil.

10   Clean the area around the drain plug opening, reinstall the plug and tighten it securely, but do not strip the threads.

11   Move the drain pan into position under the oil filter.

12   Remove all tools, rags, etc. from under the vehicle, being careful not to spill the oil in the drain pan, then lower the vehicle.

13   The oil filter is visible from underneath the engine **(see illustration)**. Loosen the oil filter by turning it counterclockwise with an oil filter wrench. On most engines you will have to use the type of wrench that slips over the bottom of the filter and is turned with a ratchet. Just as the filter is detached from the block, immediately tilt the open end up to prevent the oil inside the filter from spilling out. **Warning:** *The engine exhaust manifold may still be hot, so be careful.* Make sure that the old filter gasket does not remain stuck to the block.

14   With a clean rag, wipe off the mounting surface on the block. If a residue of old oil

is allowed to remain, it will smoke when the block is heated up. It will also prevent the new filter from seating properly. Also make sure that none of the old gasket remains stuck to the mounting surface. It can be removed with a scraper if necessary.

15   Compare the old filter with the new one to make sure they are the same type. Smear some engine oil on the rubber gasket of the new filter and screw it into place **(see illustration)**. Overtightening the filter will damage the gasket, so don't use a filter wrench. Most filter manufacturers recommend tightening the filter by hand only. Normally they should be tightened 3/4-turn after the gasket contacts the block, but be sure to follow the directions on the filter or container.

16   Add new oil to the engine through the oil filler cap in the valve cover. Use a funnel to prevent oil from spilling onto the top of the engine. Pour three quarts of fresh oil into the engine. Wait a few minutes to allow the oil to drain into the pan, then check the level on the oil dipstick (see Section 4 if necessary). If the oil level is at or near the F mark, install the

6.13 Typical oil filter location with lower engine splash shield removed for clarity; the filter is accessible without removing the shield

6.15 Lubricate the oil filter gasket with clean engine oil before installing the filter on the engine

7.1 Tools and materials required for battery maintenance

1 *Face shield/safety goggles* - *When removing corrosion with a brush, the acidic particles can easily fly up into your eyes*
2 *Baking soda* - *A solution of baking soda and water can be used to neutralize corrosion*
3 *Petroleum jelly* - *A layer of this on the battery posts will help prevent corrosion*
4 *Battery post/cable cleaner* - *This wire brush cleaning tool will remove all traces of corrosion from the battery posts and cable clamps*
5 *Treated felt washers* - *Placing one of these on each post, directly under the cable clamps, will help prevent corrosion*
6 *Puller* - *Sometimes the cable clamps are very difficult to pull off the posts, even after the nut/bolt has been completely loosened. This tool pulls the clamp straight up and off the post without damage*
7 *Battery post/cable cleaner* - *Here is another cleaning tool that is a slightly different version of number 4 above, but it does the same thing*
8 *Rubber gloves* - *Another safety item to consider when servicing the battery; remember that's acid inside the battery*

filler cap hand tight, start the engine and allow the new oil to circulate.

17 Allow the engine to run for about a minute. While the engine is running, look under the vehicle and check for leaks at the oil pan drain plug and around the oil filter. If either is leaking, stop the engine and tighten the plug or filter slightly.

18 Wait a few minutes to allow the oil to trickle down into the pan, then recheck the level on the dipstick and, if necessary, add enough oil to bring the level to the F mark.

19 During the first few trips after an oil change, make it a point to check frequently for leaks and proper oil level.

20 The old oil drained from the engine cannot be reused in its present state and should be disposed of. Check with your local auto parts store, disposal facility or environmental agency to see if they will accept the oil for recycling. After the oil has cooled it can be drained into a container (capped plastic jugs, topped bottles, milk cartons, etc.) for transport to one of these disposal sites. Don't dispose of the oil by pouring it on the ground or down a drain!

---

7 Battery check, maintenance and charging (every 5000 miles [8000 km] or 6 months)

Refer to illustrations 7.1, 7.6a, 7.6b, 7.7a and 7.7b

Warning: *Certain precautions must be followed when checking and servicing the battery. Hydrogen gas, which is highly flammable, is always present in the battery cells, so keep lighted tobacco and all other open flames and sparks away from the battery. The electrolyte inside the battery is actually dilute sul-*

furic acid, which will cause injury if splashed on your skin or in your eyes. It will also ruin clothes and painted surfaces. When removing the battery cables, always detach the negative cable first and hook it up last!

Maintenance

1 A routine preventive maintenance program for the battery in your vehicle is the only way to ensure quick and reliable starts. But before performing any battery maintenance, make sure that you have the proper equipment necessary to work safely around the battery **(see illustration).**

2 There are also several precautions that should be taken whenever battery maintenance is performed. Before servicing the battery, always turn the engine and all accessories off and disconnect the cable from the negative terminal of the battery.

3 The battery produces hydrogen gas, which is both flammable and explosive. Never create a spark, smoke or light a match around the battery. Always charge the battery in a ventilated area.

4 Electrolyte contains poisonous and corrosive sulfuric acid. Do not allow it to get in your eyes, on your skin or on your clothes. Never ingest it. Wear protective safety glasses when working near the battery. Keep children away from the battery.

5 Note the external condition of the battery. If the positive terminal and cable clamp on your vehicle's battery is equipped with a rubber protector, make sure that it's not torn or damaged. It should completely cover the terminal. Look for any corroded or loose connections, cracks in the case or cover or loose hold-down clamps. Also check the entire length of each cable for cracks and frayed conductors.

6 If corrosion, which looks like white, fluffy

deposits **(see illustration)** is evident, particularly around the terminals, the battery should be removed for cleaning. Loosen the cable clamp bolts with a wrench, being careful to remove the ground cable first, and slide them off the terminals **(see illustration).** Then disconnect the hold-down clamp bolt and nut, remove the clamp and lift the battery from the engine compartment.

7 Clean the cable clamps thoroughly with a battery brush or a terminal cleaner and a solution of warm water and baking soda **(see illustration).** Wash the terminals and the top of the battery case with the same solution but make sure that the solution doesn't get into the battery. When cleaning the cables, terminals and battery top, wear safety goggles and rubber gloves to prevent any solution from coming in contact with your eyes or hands. Wear old clothes too - even diluted, sulfuric acid splashed onto clothes will burn holes in them. If the terminals have been extensively corroded, clean them up with a terminal cleaner **(see illustration).** Thoroughly wash all cleaned areas with plain water.

8 Make sure that the battery tray is in good condition and the hold-down clamp bolts are tight. If the battery is removed from the tray, make sure no parts remain in the bottom of the tray when the battery is reinstalled. When reinstalling the hold-down clamp bolts, do not overtighten them.

9 Any metal parts of the vehicle damaged by corrosion should be covered with a zinc-based primer, then painted.

10 Information on removing and installing the battery can be found in Chapter 5. Information on jump starting can be found at the front of this manual. For more detailed battery checking procedures, refer to the *Haynes Automotive Electrical Manual.*

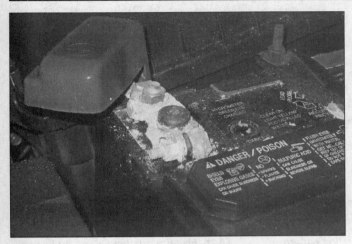

7.6a Battery terminal corrosion usually appears as light, fluffy powder

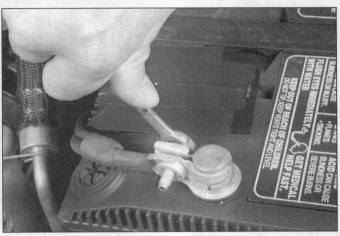

7.6b Removing a cable from the battery post with a wrench - sometimes a pair of special battery pliers are required for this procedure if corrosion has caused deterioration of the nut hex (always remove the ground (-) cable first and hook it up last!)

Charging

Warning: *When batteries are being charged, hydrogen gas, which is very explosive and flammable, is produced. Do not smoke or allow open flames near a battery. Wear eye protection when near the battery during charging. Also, make sure the charger is unplugged before connecting or disconnecting the battery from the charger.*

Note: *The manufacturer recommends the battery be removed from the vehicle for charging because the gas that escapes during this procedure can damage the paint. Fast charging with the battery cables connected can result in damage to the electrical system.*

11   Slow-rate charging is the best way to restore a battery that's discharged to the point where it will not start the engine. It's also a good way to maintain the battery charge in a vehicle that's only driven a few miles between starts. Maintaining the battery charge is particularly important in the winter when the battery must work harder to start the engine and electrical accessories that drain the battery are in greater use.

12   It's best to use a one or two-amp battery charger (sometimes called a "trickle" charger). They are the safest and put the least strain on the battery. They are also the least expensive. For a faster charge, you can use a higher amperage charger, but don't use one rated more than 1/10th the amp/hour rating of the battery. Rapid boost charges that claim to restore the power of the battery in one to two hours are hardest on the battery and can damage batteries not in good condition. This type of charging should only be used in emergency situations.

13   The average time necessary to charge a battery should be listed in the instructions that come with the charger. As a general rule, a trickle charger will charge a battery in 12 to 16 hours.

14   Remove all the cell caps (if equipped) and cover the holes with a clean cloth to prevent spattering electrolyte. Disconnect the negative battery cable and hook the battery charger cable clamps up to the battery posts (positive to positive, negative to negative), then plug in the charger. Make sure it is set at 12-volts if it has a selector switch.

15   If you're using a charger with a rate higher than two amps, check the battery regularly during charging to make sure it doesn't overheat. If you're using a trickle charger, you can safely let the battery charge overnight after you've checked it regularly for the first couple of hours.

16   If the battery has removable cell caps, measure the specific gravity with a hydrometer every hour during the last few hours of the charging cycle. Hydrometers are available inexpensively from auto parts stores - follow the instructions that come with the hydrometer. Consider the battery charged when there's

7.7a When cleaning the cable clamps, all corrosion must be removed (the inside of the clamp is tapered to match the taper on the post, so don't remove too much material)

7.7b Regardless of the type of tool used to clean the battery posts, a clean, shiny surface should be the result

no change in the specific gravity reading for two hours and the electrolyte in the cells is gassing (bubbling) freely. The specific gravity reading from each cell should be very close to the others. If not, the battery probably has a bad cell(s).

17   Some batteries with sealed tops have built-in hydrometers on the top that indicate the state of charge by the color displayed in the hydrometer window. Normally, a bright-colored hydrometer indicates a full charge and a dark hydrometer indicates the battery still needs charging.

18   If the battery has a sealed top and no built-in hydrometer, you can hook up a voltmeter across the battery terminals to check the charge. A fully charged battery should read 12.6 volts or higher after the surface charge has been removed.

19   Further information on the battery and jump starting can be found in Chapter 5 and at the front of this manual.

8   Tire rotation (every 5000 miles [8000 km] or 6 months)

Refer to illustrations 8.2a and 8.2b

1   The tires should be rotated at the specified intervals and whenever uneven wear is noticed. Since the vehicle will be raised and the tires removed anyway, check the brakes (see Section 12) at this time.

2   Radial tires must be rotated in a specific pattern **(see illustrations)**.

3   Refer to the information in *Jacking and towing* at the front of this manual for the proper procedures to follow when raising the vehicle and changing a tire. If the brakes are to be checked, do not apply the parking brake as stated. Make sure the tires are blocked to prevent the vehicle from rolling.

4   Preferably, the entire vehicle should be raised at the same time. This can be done on a hoist or by jacking up each corner and then lowering the vehicle onto jackstands placed under the frame rails. Always use four

RADIAL TIRE ROTATION
1-AJ HAYNES

8.2a Four-tire rotation pattern

1-AJa HAYNES

8.2b Five-tire rotation pattern (to be used only if the spare tire is the same as the other four)

jackstands and make sure the vehicle is firmly supported.

5   After rotation, check and adjust the tire pressures as necessary and be sure to check the lug nut tightness.

6   For further information on the wheels and tires, refer to Chapter 10.

9   Windshield wiper blade inspection and replacement (every 5000 miles [8000 km] or 6 months)

Refer to illustrations 9.5a and 9.5b

1   The windshield wiper and blade assembly should be inspected periodically for damage, loose components and cracked or worn blade elements.

2   Road film can build up on the wiper blades and affect their efficiency, so they should be washed regularly with a mild detergent solution.

3   The action of the wiping mechanism can loosen bolts, nuts and fasteners, so they

should be checked and tightened, as necessary, at the same time the wiper blades are checked.

4   If the wiper blade elements are cracked, worn or warped, or no longer clean adequately, they should be replaced with new ones.

5   Lift the arm assembly away from the glass for clearance, press the release lever, then slide the wiper blade assembly out of the hook at the end of the arm **(see illustrations)**.

6   Attach the new wiper to the arm. Connection can be confirmed by an audible click.

10   Underhood hose check and replacement (every 5000 miles [8000 km] or 6 months)

Warning: *Replacement of air conditioning hoses must be left to a dealer service department or air conditioning shop that has the*

9.5a To release the blade holder, push the release pin . . .

9.5b . . . and pull the wiper blade in the direction of the arrow to separate it from the arm

equipment to depressurize the system safely. Never remove air conditioning components or hoses until the system has been evacuated and the refrigerant recovered by a dealer service department or air conditioning shop.

General

1   High temperatures in the engine compartment can cause the deterioration of the rubber and plastic hoses used for engine, accessory and emission systems operation. Periodic inspection should be made for cracks, loose clamps, material hardening and leaks.

2   Information specific to the cooling system hoses can be found in Section 11.

3   Some, but not all, hoses are secured to the fittings with clamps. Where clamps are used, check to be sure they haven't lost their tension, allowing the hose to leak. If clamps aren't used, make sure the hose has not expanded and/or hardened where it slips over the fitting, allowing it to leak.

Vacuum hoses

4   It's quite common for vacuum hoses, especially those in the emissions system, to be color coded or identified by colored stripes molded into them. Various systems require hoses with different wall thickness, collapse resistance and temperature resistance. When replacing hoses, be sure the new ones are made of the same material.

5   Often the only effective way to check a hose is to remove it completely from the vehicle. If more than one hose is removed, be sure to label the hoses and fittings to ensure correct installation.

6   When checking vacuum hoses, be sure to include any plastic T-fittings in the check. Inspect the fittings for cracks and the hose where it fits over the fitting for distortion, which could cause leakage.

7   A small piece of vacuum hose (1/4-inch inside diameter) can be used as a stethoscope to detect vacuum leaks. Hold one end of the hose to your ear and probe around vacuum hoses and fittings, listening for the "hissing" sound characteristic of a vacuum leak. **Warning:** *When probing with the vacuum hose stethoscope, be very careful not to come into contact with moving engine components such as the drivebelts, cooling fan, etc.*

Fuel hose

Warning: *Gasoline is extremely flammable, so take extra precautions when you work on any part of the fuel system. Don't smoke or allow open flames or bare light bulbs near the work area, and don't work in a garage where a gas-type appliance (such as a water heater or a clothes dryer) is present. Since gasoline is carcinogenic, wear fuel resistant gloves when there's a possibility of being exposed to fuel, and, if you spill any fuel on your skin, rinse it off immediately with soap and water. Mop up any spills immediately and do not store fuel-soaked rags where they could ignite. The fuel system is under constant pressure, so, if*

any fuel lines are to be disconnected, the fuel pressure in the system must be relieved first. When you perform any kind of work on the fuel system, wear safety glasses and have a Class B type fire extinguisher on hand.

8   Check all rubber fuel lines for deterioration and chafing. Check especially for cracks in areas where the hose bends and just before fittings, such as where a hose attaches to the fuel filter.

9   High quality fuel line should be used for fuel line replacement. Never, under any circumstances, use unreinforced vacuum line, clear plastic tubing or water hose for fuel lines.

10   Spring-type clamps are commonly used on fuel lines. These clamps often lose their tension over a period of time, and can be "sprung" during removal. Replace all spring-type clamps with screw clamps whenever a hose is replaced.

Metal lines

11   Sections of metal line are often used for fuel line between the fuel pump and fuel injection unit. Check carefully to be sure the line has not been bent or crimped and that cracks have not started in the line.

12   If a section of metal fuel line must be replaced, only seamless steel tubing should be used, since copper and aluminum tubing don't have the strength necessary to withstand normal engine vibration.

13   Check the metal brake lines where they enter the master cylinder and brake proportioning unit (if used) for cracks in the lines or loose fittings. Any sign of brake fluid leakage calls for an immediate thorough inspection of the brake system.

---

11   Cooling system check (every 5000 miles [8000 km] or 6 months)

Refer to illustration 11.4

1   Many major engine failures can be attributed to a faulty cooling system. If the vehicle is equipped with an automatic transaxle, the cooling system also cools the transaxle fluid and thus plays an important role in prolonging transaxle life.

2   The cooling system should be checked with the engine cold. Do this before the vehicle is driven for the day or after the engine has been shut off for at least three hours. **Warning:** *Never remove the cooling system pressure cap when the engine is running or has just been shut down, because the cooling system is hot. Escaping steam and scalding liquid could cause serious injury.*

3   Remove the surge tank pressure cap by turning it to the left until it reaches a stop. If you hear a hissing sound (indicating there is still pressure in the system), wait until it stops. Now press down on the cap with the palm of your hand and continue turning to the left until the cap can be removed. Thoroughly clean

Check for a chafed area that could fail prematurely.

Check for a soft area indicating the hose has deteriorated inside.

Overtightening the clamp on a hardened hose will damage the hose and cause a leak.

Check each hose for swelling and oil-soaked ends. Cracks and breaks can be located by squeezing the hose.

11.4 Hoses, like drivebelts, have a habit of failing at the worst possible time - to prevent the inconvenience of a blown radiator or heater hose, inspect them carefully as shown here

---

the cap, inside and out, with clean water. Also clean the filler neck on the tank. All traces of corrosion should be removed. The coolant inside should be relatively transparent. If it's rust colored, the system should be drained and refilled (see Section 24). If the coolant level isn't up to the top, add additional antifreeze/coolant mixture (see Section 4).

4   Carefully check the large upper and lower radiator hoses along with the smaller diameter heater hoses which run from the engine to the firewall. Inspect each hose along its entire length, replacing any hose that is cracked, swollen or shows signs of deterioration. Cracks may become more apparent if the hose is squeezed (**see illustration**). Regardless of condition, it's a good idea to replace hoses with new ones every two years.

12.7a You'll find an inspection hole like this in each caliper through which you can view the inner brake pad lining

12.7b The outer pad is more easily checked at the edge of the caliper

5   Make sure that all hose connections are tight. A leak in the cooling system will usually show up as white or rust colored deposits on the areas adjoining the leak. If wire-type clamps are used at the ends of the hoses, it may be a good idea to replace them with more secure screw-type clamps.

6   Use compressed air or a soft brush to remove bugs, leaves, etc. from the front of the radiator or air conditioning condenser. Be careful not to damage the delicate cooling fins or cut yourself on them.

7   Every other inspection, or at the first indication of cooling system problems, have the cap and system pressure tested. If you don't have a pressure tester, most gas stations and garages will do this for a minimal charge.

12   Brake check (every 5000 miles [8000 km] or 6 months)

Warning: *The dust created by the brake system is harmful to your health. Never blow it out with compressed air and don't inhale any of it. An approved filtering mask should be worn when working on the brakes. Do not, under any circumstances, use petroleum-based solvents to clean brake parts. Use brake system cleaner only!*

Note: *For detailed photographs of the brake system, refer to Chapter 9.*

1   In addition to the specified intervals, the brakes should be inspected every time the wheels are removed or whenever a defect is suspected.

2   Any of the following symptoms could indicate a potential brake system defect: The vehicle pulls to one side when the brake pedal is depressed; the brakes make squealing or dragging noises when applied; brake pedal travel is excessive; the pedal pulsates; or brake fluid leaks, usually onto the inside of the tire or wheel.

3   Loosen the wheel lug nuts.

4   Raise the vehicle and place it securely on jackstands.

5   Remove the wheels (see *Jacking and towing* at the front of this book, or your owner's manual, if necessary).

Disc brakes

Refer to illustrations 12.7a and 12.7b

6   There are two pads (an outer and an inner) in each caliper. The pads are visible with the wheels removed. The vehicles covered by this manual have disc brakes front and rear, with a mechanical, drum-type parking brake mechanism inside the rear discs.

7   Check the pad thickness by looking at each end of the caliper and through the inspection window in the caliper body **(see illustrations)**. If the lining material is less than the thickness listed in this Chapter's Specifications, replace the pads. **Note:** *Keep in mind that the lining material is riveted or bonded to a metal backing plate and the metal portion is not included in this measurement.*

8   If it is difficult to determine the exact thickness of the remaining pad material by the above method, or if you are at all concerned about the condition of the pads, remove the caliper(s), then remove the pads from the calipers for further inspection (see Chapter 9).

9   Once the pads are removed from the calipers, clean them with brake cleaner and re-measure them with a ruler or a vernier caliper.

10   Measure the disc thickness with a micrometer to make sure that it still has service life remaining. If any disc is thinner than the specified minimum thickness, replace it (see Chapter 9). Even if the disc has service life remaining, check its condition. Look for scoring, gouging and burned spots. If these conditions exist, remove the disc and have it resurfaced (see Chapter 9).

11   Before installing the wheels, check all brake lines and hoses for damage, wear, deformation, cracks, corrosion, leakage, bends and twists, particularly in the vicinity of the rubber hoses at the calipers. Check the clamps for tightness and the connections for leakage. Make sure that all hoses and lines are clear of sharp edges, moving parts and the exhaust system. If any of the above conditions are noted, repair, reroute or replace the lines and/or fittings as necessary (see Chapter 9).

Brake booster check

12   Sit in the driver's seat and perform the following sequence of tests.

13   With the brake fully depressed, start the engine - the pedal should move down a little when the engine starts.

14   With the engine running, depress the brake pedal several times - the travel distance should not change.

15   Depress the brake, stop the engine and hold the pedal in for about 30 seconds - the pedal should neither sink nor rise.

16   Restart the engine, run it for about a minute and turn it off. Then firmly depress the brake several times - the pedal travel should decrease with each application.

17   If your brakes do not operate as described, the brake booster has failed. Refer to Chapter 9 for the replacement procedure.

Parking brake

18   One method of checking the parking brake is to park the vehicle on a steep hill with the parking brake set and the transmission in Neutral (be sure to stay in the vehicle for this check). If the parking brake cannot prevent the vehicle from rolling, it's in need of attention (see Chapter 9).

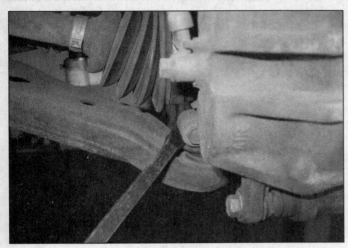

13.7 To check the balljoints, attempt to move the control arm up and down with a prybar to make sure there is no play in the balljoint (if there is, replace it)

13.8 Push on the balljoint boot to check for tears and grease leaks

13 Steering, suspension and driveaxle boot check (every 15,000 miles [24,000 km] or 18 months)

Steering check

Note: *For detailed illustrations of the steering and suspension components, refer to Chapter 10.*

1 With the vehicle on the ground and the front wheels pointed straight ahead, rock the steering wheel gently back and forth. If free-play is excessive, a front wheel bearing, main shaft yoke, intermediate shaft yoke, lower arm balljoint or steering system joint is worn or the steering gear is out of adjustment or broken. Steering wheel freeplay is the amount of travel (measured at the rim of the steering wheel) between the initial steering input and the point at which the front wheels begin to turn (indicated by slight resistance). Refer to Chapter 10 for the appropriate repair procedure.

2 Other symptoms, such as excessive vehicle body movement over rough roads, swaying (leaning) around corners and binding as the steering wheel is turned, may indicate faulty steering and/or suspension components.

Suspension check

Refer to illustrations 13.7 and 13.8

3 Check the shock absorbers by pushing down and releasing the vehicle several times at each corner. If the vehicle does not come back to a level position within one or two bounces, the shocks/struts are worn and must be replaced. When bouncing the vehicle up and down, listen for squeaks and noises from the suspension components. Additional information on suspension components can be found in Chapter 10.

4 Raise the vehicle with a floor jack and support it securely on jackstands. See *Jacking and towing* at the front of this book for the proper jacking points.

5 Check the tires for irregular wear patterns and proper inflation. See Section 5 in this Chapter for information regarding tire wear and Chapter 10 for the wheel bearing replacement procedures.

6 Inspect the universal joint between the steering shaft and the steering gear housing. Check the steering gear housing for lubricant leakage or oozing. Make sure that the dust seals and boots are not damaged and that the boot clamps are not loose. Check the steering linkage for looseness or damage. Check the track rod ends for excessive play. Look for loose bolts, broken or disconnected parts and deteriorated rubber bushings on all suspension and steering components. While an assistant turns the steering wheel from side to side, check the steering components for free movement, chafing and binding. If the steering components do not seem to be reacting with the movement of the steering wheel, try to determine where the slack is located.

7 Check the balljoints for wear by trying to move each control arm up and down with a prybar **(see illustration)** to ensure that its balljoint has no play. If any balljoint does have play, replace it. See Chapter 10 for the front balljoint replacement procedure.

8 Inspect the balljoint boots for damage and leaking grease **(see illustration)**. Replace the balljoints with new ones if they are damaged (see Chapter 10).

Driveaxle boot check

Refer to illustration 13.10

9 The driveaxle boots are very important because they prevent dirt, water and foreign material from entering and damaging the constant velocity (CV) joints. Oil and grease can cause the boot material to deteriorate prematurely, so it's a good idea to wash the boots with soap and water.

10 Inspect the boots for tears and cracks as well as loose clamps **(see illustration)**. If there is any evidence of cracks or leaking lubricant, they must be replaced as described in Chapter 8.

13.10 Flex the driveaxle boots by hand to check for tears, cracks and leaking grease

14.2 Check the exhaust system rubber hangers for damage

15.1 Release the latches securing the air filter housing lid

14 Exhaust system check (every 15,000 miles [24,000 km] or 18 months)

Refer to illustration 14.2

1   With the engine cold (at least three hours after the vehicle has been driven), check the complete exhaust system from its starting point at the engine to the end of the tailpipe. Preferably this should be done on a hoist where unrestricted access is available.
2   Check the pipes and connections for evidence of leaks, severe corrosion or damage. Make sure that all brackets and hangers are in good condition and tight **(see illustration)**.
3   At the same time, inspect the underside of the body for holes, corrosion, open seams, etc. that may allow exhaust gases to enter the passenger compartment. Seal all body openings with silicone or body putty.
4   Rattles and other noises can often be traced to the exhaust system, especially the mounts and hangers. Try to move the pipes, silencer and catalytic converter. If the components can come in contact with the body or

suspension parts, secure the exhaust system with new mounts.
5   Check the running condition of the engine by inspecting inside the end of the tailpipe. The exhaust deposits here are an indication of engine state-of-tune. If the pipe is black and sooty or coated with white deposits, the engine is in need of a tune-up, including a thorough fuel system inspection.

15 Air filter replacement (every 30,000 miles [48,000 km] or 36 months)

Refer to illustrations 15.1 and 15.2

1   The air filter is located inside a housing at the side of the engine compartment. To remove the air filter, release the clamps retaining the two halves of the air filter housing **(see illustration)**. Disconnect the wiring from the mass airflow sensor in order to get enough clearance to raise the lid.
2   Lift the cover up and remove the air filter element **(see illustration)**.

3   Inspect the outer surface of the filter element. If it is dirty, replace it. If it is only moderately dusty, it can be reused by blowing it clean from the back to the front surface with compressed air. **Warning:** *Always wear eye protection when using compressed air!* Because it is a pleated paper type filter, it cannot be washed or oiled. If it cannot be cleaned satisfactorily with compressed air, discard and replace it. **Caution:** *Never drive the vehicle with the air cleaner removed. Excessive engine wear could result and backfiring could even cause a fire under the hood.*
4   Installation is the reverse of removal. Make sure the hinge tabs on the housing cover engage properly with the lower part of the housing.

16 Fuel system check (every 30,000 miles [48,000 km] or 36 months)

Warning: *Gasoline is extremely flammable, so take extra precautions when you work on any part of the fuel system. Don't smoke or allow open flames or bare light bulbs near the work area, and don't work in a garage where a gas-type appliance (such as a water heater or a clothes dryer) is present. Since gasoline is carcinogenic, wear fuel resistant gloves when there's a possibility of being exposed to fuel, and, if you spill any fuel on your skin, rinse it off immediately with soap and water. Mop up any spills immediately and do not store fuel-soaked rags where they could ignite. The fuel system is under constant pressure, so, if any fuel lines are to be disconnected, the fuel pressure in the system must be relieved first. When you perform any kind of work on the fuel system, wear safety glasses and have a Class B type fire extinguisher on hand.*

1   If you smell fuel while driving or after the vehicle has been sitting in the sun, inspect the fuel system immediately.
2   Remove the fuel filler cap and inspect it

15.2 Lift the cover up, remove the filter element and install the new one

17.2 Detach the cable from the side of the glove box

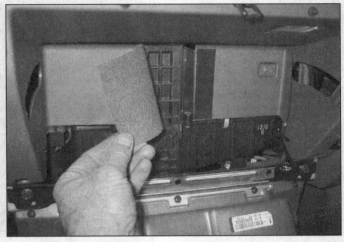

17.4 There is a small flap that covers the filter cover - it's held in place by Velcro

for damage and corrosion. The gasket should have an unbroken sealing imprint. If the gasket is damaged or corroded, remove it and install a new one.

3   Inspect the fuel feed and return lines for cracks. Make sure that the threaded flare nut type connectors which secure the metal fuel lines to the fuel injection system and the fittings on the in-line fuel filter are tight.

4   Since some components of the fuel system - the fuel tank and part of the fuel feed and return lines, for example - are underneath the vehicle, they can be inspected more easily with the vehicle raised on a hoist. If that's not possible, raise the vehicle and support it securely on jackstands.

5   With the vehicle raised and safely supported, inspect the fuel tank and filler neck for punctures, cracks and other damage. The connection between the filler neck and the tank is particularly critical. Sometimes a rubber filler neck will leak because of loose clamps or deteriorated rubber. These are problems a home mechanic can usually rectify. **Warning:**

Do not, under any circumstances, try to repair a fuel tank (except rubber components). A welding torch or any open flame can easily cause fuel vapors inside the tank to explode.

6   Carefully check all rubber hoses and metal lines leading away from the fuel tank. Check for loose connections, deteriorated hoses, crimped lines and other damage. Carefully inspect the lines from the tank to the fuel injection system. Repair or replace damaged sections as necessary (see Chapter 4).

17   Interior ventilation filter replacement (every 30,000 miles [48,000 km] or 36 months)

Refer to illustrations 17.2, 17.4, 17.5 1 and 17.6

1   There is an air filter in the blower housing that cleans the air before it enters the passenger's compartment.

2   To remove the air filter, open the glove box and release the assist cord at the right side **(see illustration)**.

3   Lower the glove box door by pushing inward on both sides of the box.

4   Pull back the trim panel **(see illustration)**.

5   Turn the filter door knob counterclockwise to release it **(see illustration)**.

6   Lift the cover off and remove the upper air filter element **(see illustration)**.

7   Lift out the lower element.

8   Installation is the reverse of removal. Be sure to align the grooves with the lugs in the edges of the filters.

18   Positive Crankcase Ventilation (PCV) valve check and replacement (every 30,000 miles [48,000 km] or 36 months)

Refer to illustration 18.2

1   The PCV valve and hose is located in

17.5 Turn the filter cover knob to release it

17.6 Remove the filter cover to service both inner filters

18.2 The PCV valve is located in the valve cover - unscrew it to remove it

the valve cover.

2   Disconnect the hose, unscrew the PCV valve from the cover, and then reconnect the hose **(see illustration)**.

3   With the engine idling at normal operating temperature, place your finger over the valve opening. If there's no vacuum at the valve, check for a plugged hose or valve. Replace any plugged or deteriorated hoses.

4   Turn off the engine. Remove the PCV valve from the hose. Blow through the valve from the valve cover (cylinder head) end. If air will not pass through the valve in this direction, replace it with a new one.

5   When purchasing a replacement PCV valve, make sure it's for your particular vehicle and engine size. Compare the old valve with the new one to make sure they're the same.

19   Brake fluid change (every 30,000 miles [48,000 km] or 36 months)

Warning: *Brake fluid can harm your eyes and damage painted surfaces, so use extreme caution when handling or pouring it. Do not use brake fluid that has been standing open or is more than one year old. Brake fluid absorbs moisture from the air. Excess moisture can cause a dangerous loss of braking effectiveness.*

1   At the specified intervals, the brake fluid should be drained and replaced. Since the brake fluid may drip or splash when pouring it, place plenty of rags around the master cylinder to protect any surrounding painted surfaces.

2   Before beginning work, purchase the specified brake fluid (see *Recommended lubricants and fluids* at the beginning of this Chapter).

3   Remove the cap from the master cylinder reservoir.

4   Using a hand suction pump or similar device, withdraw the fluid from the master cylinder reservoir.

5   Add new fluid to the master cylinder until it rises to the base of the filler neck.

6   Bleed the brake system as described in Chapter 9 at all four brakes until new and uncontaminated fluid is expelled from the bleeder screw. Be sure to maintain the fluid level in the master cylinder as you perform the bleeding process. If you allow the master cylinder to run dry, air will enter the system.

7   Refill the master cylinder with fluid and check the operation of the brakes. The pedal should feel solid when depressed, with no sponginess. **Warning:** *Do not operate the vehicle if you are in doubt about the effectiveness of the brake system.*

20   Drivebelt check, adjustment and replacement (60,000 miles [96,000 km] or 72 months

Check

Refer to illustrations 20.3 and 20.4

1   The drivebelt(s) are located at the front of the engine. The good condition and proper adjustment of the belts is critical to the operation of the engine. Because of their composition and the high stresses to which they are subjected, drivebelts stretch and deteriorate as they get older. They must therefore be periodically inspected.

2   On four-cylinder models, one belt drives the alternator and water pump and another drives the power steering and air conditioning. On 2.7L V6 models, one belt transmits power to all accessories (the water pump is driven by the timing belt on V6 engines). On 3.5L engines, the inner belt drives the power steering pump and the outer drives the alternator and air conditioning compressor.

3   With the engine off, open the hood and locate the drivebelts. With a flashlight, check each belt for separation of the adhesive rubber on both sides of the core, core separation from the belt side, a severed core, separation of the ribs from the adhesive rubber, cracking or separation of the ribs, and torn or worn ribs or cracks in the inner ridges of the ribs **(see illustration)**. Also check for fraying and glaz-

20.3   Check a multi-ribbed belt for signs like these - if the belt looks worn, replace it

20.4 Measuring drivebelt deflection with a straightedge and ruler

ing, which gives the belt a shiny appearance. Both sides of the belt should be inspected, which means you will have to twist the belt to check the underside. Use your fingers to feel the belt where you can't see it. If any of the above conditions are evident, replace the belt.

4   The tension of each belt is checked by pushing on the belt at a distance halfway between the pulleys. Push firmly with your thumb and see how much the belt moves (deflects) **(see illustration)**. The belt should deflect approximately 1/4-inch.

Adjustment
2.4L four-cylinder engines

Alternator belt
5   Loosen the lower alternator mounting bolt and the upper tension bolts.
6   Carefully tension the belt by prying on the alternator housing. Tighten the upper tension and lock bolts and then the lower bolt.

Power steering pump and air conditioning compressor belt
7   Loosen the lock bolt on the belt tensioner assembly. Use the adjacent adjustment bolt to adjust the tension on the belt.
8   Tighten the tensioner lock bolt.

3.5L V6 engine
9   Both belts are adjusted in the same manner although each has its own tensioner. The adjustment bolts are located at the bottom of each tensioner assembly and face upwards.
10   Turn the tensioner adjustment bolts in or out to achieve the proper belt tension. There are no locking fasteners as parts of the tensioner units.

Replacement
11   Remove any interfering components such as engine covers and engine brackets.

2.4L four-cylinder and 3.5L V6 engines
12   Release tension on the belt(s). Refer to

the adjustment procedures above. Loosen the tension so that the belt will slip off the pulleys.

2.7L V6 engine
13   This engine uses a self-adjusting spring-loaded tensioner. Use a breaker bar or a long-handle ratchet to rotate the tensioner and release tension on the belt. Slip the belt from the pulleys while the tension is released.

All engines
14   Take the old belts to the parts store in order to make a direct comparison for length, width and design.
15   After replacing the drivebelt, make sure that it fits properly in the ribbed grooves in the pulleys. It is essential that the belt be properly centered.
16   To replace a belt, follow the procedures for drivebelt adjustment, but slip the belt off the crankshaft pulley and remove it. Because belts tend to wear out more or less together, it is a good idea to replace both belts at the same time. Mark each belt and its appropriate pulley groove so the replacement belts can be

fitted in their proper positions.
17   Adjust the belt(s) in accordance with the procedures outlined earlier in this Section. **Note:** *The self-adjusting tensioner used on 2.7L V6 engines has a scale that indicates minimum and maximum allowable positions. If the belt has stretched enough to be more than the maximum length, replace it with a new one.*

21   Automatic transaxle fluid change (60,000 miles [96,000 km] or 72 months)

Refer to illustration 21.7
1   At the specified time intervals, the automatic transaxle and differential fluid should be drained and replaced. **Note:** *Although the manufacturer doesn't specify it, it is a good idea to replace the transaxle fluid filter periodically to remove accumulated dirt and metal particles.*
2   Before beginning work, purchase the specified transaxle fluid (see *Recommended lubricants and fluids* at the front of this Chapter).
3   Other tools necessary for this job include jackstands to support the vehicle in a raised position, an appropriate wrench, a drain pan, newspapers and clean rags.
4   The fluid should be drained immediately after the vehicle has been driven. Hot fluid is more effective than cold fluid at removing built up sediment. **Warning:** *Fluid temperature can exceed 350-degrees F in a hot transaxle. Wear protective gloves.*
5   After the vehicle has been driven to warm up the fluid, raise it and place it on jackstands for access to the transaxle and differential drain plugs.
6   Move the necessary equipment under the vehicle, being careful not to touch any of the hot exhaust components.
7   Place the drain pan under the transaxle drain plug and remove the drain plug **(see illustration)**. Once the fluid is drained, rein-

21.7 Remove the automatic transaxle drain plug

24.4 The radiator drain is accessible through this hole in the front radiator support

24.5 The V6 engine has a coolant drain like this located on both the front and rear sides of the block

stall the drain plug and tighten it to the torque listed in this Chapter's Specifications.

8　Lower the vehicle.

9　Early-production 2001 models have a cartridge-type transmission fluid filter located on top of the transaxle case; remove the air filter housing for access (see Chapter 4). Using an oil filter wrench, unscrew the filter. Lubricate the O-ring of the new filter with clean transmission fluid, then install the new filter, tightening it hand-tight.

10　Add new fluid to the transaxle through the dipstick tube (see *Recommended lubricants and fluids* for the recommended fluid type and capacity). Use a funnel to prevent spills. It is best to add a little fluid at a time, continually checking the level with the dipstick (see Section 4). **Caution:** *It's important not to overfill the transaxle.*

11　Start the engine and shift into all positions from P through L, then shift into N and apply the parking brake.

12　With the engine idling, check the fluid level. Add fluid up to the Cool (or lower) level mark on the dipstick.

13　Drive the vehicle to warm up the transaxle to normal operating temperature, then recheck the fluid level.

22 Transfer case (AWD models) and manual transaxle lubricant change (60,000 miles [96,000 km] or 72 months)

1　Raise the vehicle and support it securely on jackstands.

2　Remove the check/fill plug, then remove the drain plug and drain the lubricant.

3　Reinstall the drain plug and tighten it securely.

4　Add new lubricant until it is even with the lower edge of the filler hole. See *Recommended lubricants* and fluids for the specified lubricant type.

5　Reinstall the check/fill plug and tighten it securely.

23 Rear differential lubricant change (AWD models) (60,000 miles [96,000 km] or 72 months)

1　Raise the rear of the vehicle and support it securely on jackstands.

2　Remove the check/fill plug, then remove the drain plug and drain the lubricant.

3　Reinstall the drain plug and tighten it securely.

4　Add new lubricant until it is even with the lower edge of the filler hole (see Section 4). See *Recommended lubricants and fluids* for the specified lubricant type.

5　Reinstall the check/fill plug and tighten it securely.

24 Cooling system servicing (draining, flushing and refilling) (at 100,000 miles [160,000 km] or 120 months and every 50,000 miles [80,500 km] or 60 months thereafter)

Warning 1: *Wait until the engine is completely cool before beginning this procedure.*
Warning 2: *Do not allow engine coolant (antifreeze) to come in contact with your skin or painted surfaces of the vehicle. Rinse off spills immediately with plenty of water. Antifreeze is highly toxic if ingested. Never leave antifreeze lying around in an open container or in puddles on the floor; children and pets are attracted by its sweet smell and may drink it. Check with local authorities about disposing of used antifreeze. Many communities have collection centers that will see that antifreeze is disposed of safely.*

1　Periodically, the cooling system should be drained, flushed and refilled to replenish

the antifreeze mixture and prevent formation of rust and corrosion, which can impair the performance of the cooling system and cause engine damage. When the cooling system is serviced, all hoses and the radiator cap should be checked and replaced if necessary.

Draining

Refer to illustrations 24.4 and 24.5

2　Apply the parking brake and block the wheels. If the vehicle has just been driven, wait several hours to allow the engine to cool down before beginning this procedure.

3　Once the engine is completely cool, remove the surge tank cap.

4　Move a large container under the radiator drain to catch the coolant. Attach a 3/8-inch inner diameter hose to the drain fitting to direct the coolant into the container (some models are already equipped with a hose), then open the drain fitting **(see illustration)**.

5　After the coolant stops flowing out of the radiator, move the container under the engine block drain plug(s). Loosen the plug(s) and allow the coolant in the block to drain. On four-cylinder models, the block drain plug is on the front side of the engine block. On V6 models, there's one on each side of the block **(see illustration)**.

6　While the coolant is draining, check the condition of the radiator hoses, heater hoses and clamps (refer to Section 11 if necessary).

7　Replace any damaged clamps or hoses (see Chapter 3).

Flushing

Refer to illustration 24.10

8　Once the system is completely drained, remove the thermostat from the engine (see Chapter 3). Then reinstall the thermostat housing temporarily without the thermostat. This will allow the system to be flushed.

9　Reinstall the engine block drain plug(s) and tighten the radiator drain plug. Turn your

Garden hose

Upper hose expels water

Radiator

36025-1-22.08 HAYNES

24.10 With the thermostat removed, disconnect the upper radiator hose and flush the radiator and engine block with a garden hose

heating system controls to Hot, so that the heater core will be flushed at the same time as the rest of the cooling system.

10   Disconnect the upper radiator hose from the radiator. Place a garden hose in the upper radiator inlet, turn the water on and flush the system until the water runs clear out of the upper radiator hose **(see illustration)**.

11   In severe cases of contamination or clogging of the radiator, remove the radiator (see Chapter 3) and have a radiator repair facility clean and repair it if necessary. Many deposits can be removed by the chemical action of a cleaner available at auto parts stores. Follow the procedure outlined in the manufacturer's instructions. **Note:** *When the coolant is regu-larly drained and the system refilled with the correct antifreeze/water mixture, there should be no need to use chemical cleaners or des-calers.*

12   After flushing, drain the radiator and remove the block drain plugs once again to drain the water from the system.

Refilling

13   Close and tighten the radiator drain. Install and tighten the block drain plug(s). Replace the thermostat (refer to Chapter 3).

14   Place the heater temperature control in the maximum heat position.

15   Slowly add new coolant to the radiator until it's full. Add coolant to the reservoir up to the lower mark.

16   Leave the surge tank cap off and run the engine in a well-ventilated area until the thermostat opens (coolant will begin flowing through the radiator and the upper radiator hose will become hot).

17   Turn the engine off and let it cool. Add more coolant mixture to bring the level back up to the lip on the radiator filler neck.

18   Squeeze the upper radiator hose to expel air, then add more coolant mixture if necessary. Replace the surge tank cap.

19   Start the engine, allow it to reach normal operating temperature and check for leaks.

25   Spark plug check and replacement (every 120,000 miles [193,000 km] or 144 months)

Refer to illustrations 25.1, 25.6, 25.8, 25.10a and 25.10b

Note: *Do not adjust the gap on platinum or iridium spark plugs. Using a gapping tool on them could damage the plating on the elec-trodes. These spark plugs are pre-gapped by the manufacturer.*

1   Spark plug replacement requires a spark plug socket that fits onto a ratchet. This socket is lined with a rubber grommet to protect the porcelain insulator of the spark plug and to hold the plug while you insert it into the spark plug hole **(see illustration)**.

2   If you are replacing the plugs, purchase the new plugs and replace each plug one at a time. **Note:** *When buying new spark plugs, it's essential that you obtain the correct plugs for your specific vehicle. This information can be found in the Specifications Section at the beginning of this Chapter, on the Vehicle Emissions Control Information (VECI) label located on the underside of the hood or in the owner's manual. If these sources specify different plugs, purchase the spark plug type specified on the VECI label because that information is provided specifically for your engine.*

25.1 Tools required for changing spark plugs

1   *Spark plug socket - This will have special padding inside to protect the spark plug's porcelain insulator*

2   *Torque wrench - Although not mandatory, using this tool is the best way to ensure the plugs are tightened properly*

3   *Ratchet - Standard hand tool to fit the spark plug socket*

4   *Extension - Depending on model and accessories, you may need special extensions and universal joints to reach one or more of the plugs*

25.6 The 3.5L V6 engine uses a combination of ignition coil-on-plug on the front three spark plugs and conventional spark plug wires on the rear three

25.8 Because they are deeply recessed, the proper spark plug socket and an extension will be required when removing or installing the spark plugs

3   Inspect each of the new plugs for defects. If there are any signs of cracks in the porcelain insulator of a plug, don't use it.

4   Remove the engine cover(s) and disconnect any hoses or components that would interfere with access and move them out of the way.

5   On V6 engines, it will be necessary to remove the upper intake manifold to get access to the rear spark plugs. Refer to Chapter 2B for this procedure.

6   Some spark plugs have a conventional spark plug wire attached. On these, pull the spark plug wires from the spark plugs, grasping the wires by the boots, not the wire itself **(see illustration)**. On those that have a coil directly over the spark plugs, disconnect the coil wiring and then unbolt and remove each coil (refer to Chapter 5).

7   If compressed air is available, blow any dirt or foreign material away from the spark plug area before proceeding. **Warning:**

Always wear eye protection when using compressed air!

8   Remove the spark plug **(see illustration)**.

9   Whether you are replacing the plugs at this time or intend to re-use the old plugs, compare each old spark plug with those shown on the inside of the back cover to determine the overall running condition of the engine.

10   Apply a small amount of anti-seize compound to the spark plug threads **(see illustration)**. It's often difficult to insert spark plugs into their holes without cross-threading them. To avoid this possibility, fit a short piece of rubber hose over the end of the spark plug **(see illustration)**. The flexible hose acts as a universal joint to help align the plug with the spark plug hole. Should the plug begin to cross-thread, the hose will slip on the spark plug, preventing thread damage. Tighten the plug to the torque listed in this Chapter's Specifications.

11   Attach the plug wires to the spark plugs, making sure that they're securely snapped in place.

12   Reinstall the removed interfering components.

26 Ignition system component check and replacement (every 120,000 miles [193,000 km] or 144 months)

Note: *Some models don't use spark plug wires; instead they use an ignition coil mounted on each spark plug. 3.5L V6 models use spark plug wires on the rear three cylinders and direct-mounted ignition coils on the front three.*

1   The spark plug wires should be checked whenever new spark plugs are installed.

2   Begin this procedure by making a visual check of the spark plug wires while the engine is running. In a darkened garage (make sure there is adequate ventilation) start the engine and observe each plug wire. Be careful not to come into contact with any moving engine parts. If there is a break in the wire, you will see arcing or a small spark at the damaged area. If arcing is noticed, make a note to obtain new wires, then allow the engine to cool and check the ignition coil packs.

3   The spark plug wires should be inspected one at a time to prevent mixing up the order, which is essential for proper engine operation.

25.10a A light coat of anti-seize compound applied to the threads of the spark plugs will keep the threads in the cylinder head from being damaged the next time the plugs are removed

25.10b A section of rubber hose will aid in getting the spark plug threads started

Each original plug wire should be numbered to help identify its location. If the number is illegible, a piece of tape can be marked with the correct number and wrapped around the plug wire.

4   Disconnect the plug wire from the spark plug. Grasp the rubber boot, twist the boot half a turn and pull the boot free. Do not pull on the wire itself.

5   Check inside the boot for corrosion, which will look like a white crusty powder. Light corrosion can be removed with a small wire brush, but replace the wires if corrosion is heavy.

6   Push the wire and boot back onto the end of the spark plug. It should fit tightly onto the end of the plug. If it doesn't, remove the wire and use pliers to carefully crimp the metal connector inside the wire boot until the fit is snug.

7   Using a clean rag, wipe the entire length of the wire to remove built-up dirt and grease. Once the wire is clean, check for burns, cracks and other damage. Do not bend the wire sharply, because the conductor might break.

8   Disconnect the wire from the ignition coil pack. Pull only on the rubber boot. Check for corrosion and a tight fit. Replace the wire in the coil pack.

9   Inspect the remaining spark plug wires, making sure that each one is securely fastened at the coil pack and spark plug when the check is complete.

10   If new spark plug wires are required, purchase a set for your specific engine model. Remove and replace the wires one at a time to avoid mix-ups in the firing order.

11   Clean the coil pack with a dampened cloth and dry it thoroughly.

12   Inspect the coil pack for cracks, damage and carbon tracking. Carbon tracks can usually be removed. If damage exists, refer to Chapter 5 for the replacement procedure.

27   Fuel filter replacement (every 50,000 miles [80, 500 km] or 60 months)

Warning: *Gasoline is extremely flammable, so take extra precautions when you work on any part of the fuel system. Don't smoke or allow open flames or bare light bulbs near the work area, and don't work in a garage where a gas-type appliance (such as a water heater or a clothes dryer) is present. Since gasoline is carcinogenic, wear fuel resistant gloves when there's a possibility of being exposed to fuel,* *and, if you spill any fuel on your skin, rinse it off immediately with soap and water. Mop up any spills immediately and do not store fuel-soaked rags where they could ignite. The fuel system is under constant pressure, so, if any fuel lines are to be disconnected, the fuel pressure in the system must be relieved first (see Chapter 4, Section 2). When you perform any kind of work on the fuel system, wear safety glasses and have a Class B type fire extinguisher on hand.*

1   Relieve the fuel system pressure (see Chapter 4, Section 2), then disconnect the cable from the negative terminal of the battery (see Chapter 5, Section 1).

2   Raise the rear of the vehicle and support it securely on jackstands. **Note:** *The fuel filter is mounted on a frame rail, near the left front corner of the fuel tank.*

3   Remove the fitting nuts from the fuel lines.

4   Remove the bolt securing the filter mounting strap, then remove the filter.

5   Installation is the reverse of the removal procedure. Use new sealing washers and tighten the fitting nuts to the torque listed in this Chapter's Specifications.

6   Reconnect the battery, turn the ignition key to the On position, then check for leaks.

Notes

Chapter 2 Part A
Four-cylinder engine

Contents

Specifications

General
Engine type .... Dual overhead camshaft
Displacement .... 144 cubic inches (2.35 liters)
Cylinder numbers (drivebelt end-to-transaxle end) 1-2-3-4
Firing order 1-3-4-2

FRONT OF VEHICLE 1 2 3 4 1-3-4-2

Cylinder numbering

Cylinder head
Warpage limits
 Block surface .... 0.008 inch (0.2 mm)
 Intake manifold surface .... 0.012 inch (0.3 mm)

Camshaft and lifters
Journal diameter .... 1.02 inches (26 mm)
Bearing oil clearance .... 0.002 to 0.003 inch (0.040 to 0.076 mm)
Thrust clearance (endplay) .... 0.004 to 0.006 inch (0.10 to 0.15 mm)
Cam lobe height (standard)
 Intake camshaft .... 1.3974 inches (35.493 mm)
 Exhaust camshaft .... 1.3904 inches (35.317 mm)
Cam lobe height wear limit
 Intake .... 1.378 inches (34.99 mm)
 Exhaust .... 1.371 inches (34.82 mm)

Intake manifold
Surface warpage limit.. 0.008 inch (0.2 mm)

Exhaust manifold
Surface warpage limit.. 0.012 inch (0.3 mm)

Oil pump
Tip clearance wear limit

Drive gear... 0.010 inch (0.25 mm)

Driven gear... 0.010 inch (0.25 mm)

Side clearance wear limit

Drive gear... 0.010 inch (0.25 mm)

Driven gear... 0.010 inch (0.25 mm)

Timing belt
Tensioner plunger protrusion, installed

(dimension "A" in **illustration 5.35**) .... 0.22 to 0.35 inch (5.5 to 9 mm)

Torque specifications

Ft-lbs (unless otherwise indicated) **Nm**

Note: *One foot-pound (ft-lb) of torque is equivalent to 12 inch-pounds (in-lbs) of torque. Torque values below approximately 15 ft-lbs are expressed in inch-pounds, since most foot-pound torque wrenches are not accurate at these smaller values.*

	Ft-lbs (unless otherwise indicated)	Nm
Camshaft bearing cap bolts	15	20
Camshaft sprocket bolt	58 to 72	80 to 100
Crankshaft pulley/vibration damper bolt	120	165
Cylinder head bolts (in sequence)		
If any of the block, head or head bolts have been replaced with new ones		
Step 1	46	63
Step 2	Loosen all bolts completely	
Step 3	14	20
Step 4	Tighten an additional 90 degrees	
Step 5	Tighten an additional 90 degrees	
If the block, head and head bolts are all previously used		
Step 1	14	20
Step 2	Tighten an additional 90 degrees	
Step 3	Tighten an additional 90 degrees	
Exhaust manifold nuts, small	20	25 to 30
Exhaust manifold nuts, large	25 to 40	35 to 55
Exhaust manifold heat shield bolts	10	13
Exhaust pipe to manifold-converter nuts	25	35
Flywheel or driveplate bolts	100	135
Intake manifold nuts	22 to 30	30 to 42
Intake manifold bolts	132 to 168 in-lbs	15 to 20
Oil pump cover bolts	144 in-lbs	17
Oil pump sprocket nut	40	55
Oil pan bolts	96 in-lbs	11
Timing belt cover bolts	52 to 84 in-lbs	9
Timing belt rear cover bolts	96 in-lbs	11
Timing belt tensioner pulley bolt	31 to 40	43 to 55
Valve cover fasteners **(see illustration 4.8)**		
"A" fasteners	52 to 84 in-lbs	8 to 10
"B" fasteners	36 to 48 in-lbs	4 to 5

3.5 A compression gauge can be used in the number one spark plug hole to assist in finding TDC

3.8 Align the mark on the damper with the "0" mark on the timing belt cover

1 General information

This Part of Chapter 2 is devoted to in-vehicle repair procedures for the four-cylinder engine. Information concerning engine removal, installation and overhaul can be found in Part C of this Chapter.

The following repair procedures are based on the assumption that the engine is installed in the vehicle. If the engine has been removed from the vehicle and mounted on a stand, many of the steps outlined in this Part of Chapter 2 will not apply. The Specifications included in this Part of Chapter 2 apply only to the in-vehicle procedures contained in this Part.

This engine incorporates a cast iron cylinder block. The aluminum cylinder head utilizes dual overhead camshafts (DOHC). The camshafts are driven from a single timing belt off the crankshaft.

2 Repair operations possible with the engine in the vehicle

Many major repair operations can be accomplished without removing the engine from the vehicle.

Clean the engine compartment and the exterior of the engine with some type of degreaser before any work is done. It will make the job easier and help keep dirt out of the internal areas of the engine.

Depending on the components involved, it may be helpful to remove the hood to improve access to the engine as repairs are performed (refer to Chapter 11 if necessary). Cover the fenders to prevent damage to the paint. Special pads are available, but an old bedspread or blanket will also work.

If vacuum, exhaust, oil or coolant leaks develop, indicating a need for gasket or seal replacement, the repairs can generally be made with the engine in the vehicle. The intake and exhaust manifold gaskets, oil pan gasket, crankshaft oil seals and cylinder head gasket are all accessible with the engine in place.

Exterior engine components, such as the intake and exhaust manifolds, the oil pan, the oil pump, the water pump, the starter motor, the alternator and the fuel system components can be removed for repair with the engine in place.

Since the cylinder head can be removed without pulling the engine, camshaft and valve component servicing can also be accomplished with the engine in the vehicle. Replacement of the timing belt and sprockets is also possible with the engine in the vehicle.

3 Top Dead Center (TDC) for number one piston - locating

Refer to illustrations 3.5 and 3.8

1 Top Dead Center (TDC) is the highest point in the cylinder that each piston reaches as it travels up the cylinder bore. Each piston reaches TDC on the compression stroke and again on the exhaust stroke, but TDC generally refers to piston position on the compression stroke.

2 Positioning the piston(s) at TDC is an essential part of certain procedures such as camshaft and timing belt/sprocket removal.

3 Before beginning this procedure, be sure to place the transmission in Neutral and apply the parking brake or block the rear wheels. Also, disable the fuel injection system by relieving the fuel pressure (see Chapter 4) and the ignition system by disconnecting and removing the ignition coils (see Chapter 5).

4 In order to bring any piston to TDC, the crankshaft must be turned using one of the methods outlined below. When looking at the front of the engine, normal crankshaft rotation is clockwise.

a) *The preferred method is to turn the crankshaft with a socket and ratchet attached to the bolt threaded into the front of the crankshaft. Turn the bolt in a clockwise direction.*

b) *If an assistant is available to turn the ignition switch to the Start position in short bursts, you can get the piston close to TDC without a remote starter switch. Make sure your assistant is out of the vehicle, away from the ignition switch, then disconnect the cable from the negative terminal of the battery and use a socket and ratchet as described in Paragraph (a) to complete the procedure.*

5 Remove the spark plugs (see Chapter 1) and install a compression gauge in the number one spark plug hole. It should be a gauge with a screw-in fitting and a hose at least six inches long **(see illustration)**.

6 Rotate the crankshaft using one of the methods described above while observing for pressure on the compression gauge. The moment the gauge shows pressure indicates that the number one cylinder has begun the compression stroke.

7 Once the compression stroke has begun, TDC for the compression stroke is reached by bringing the piston to the top of the cylinder.

8 Continue turning the crankshaft until the timing marks on the crankshaft pulley and the timing belt cover are aligned **(see illustration)**. **Note:** *If there are no marks on the crankshaft pulley, align the marks on the camshaft pulleys with the marks on the valve cover (see Section 5). At this point, the number one cylinder is at TDC on the compression stroke. If the marks are aligned but there was no compression, the piston was on the exhaust stroke; continue rotating the crankshaft 360-degrees (1-turn).* **Note:** *If a compression gauge is not available, you can simply place a blunt object over the spark plug hole and listen for compression as the engine is rotated. Once compression at the No. 1 spark plug hole is noted, the remainder of the Step is the same.*

9 After the number one piston has been positioned at TDC on the compression stroke,

4.8 The valve cover uses two types of bolts; refer to the Specifications for the correct torque for each

43050-2A-4.8 HAYNES

TDC for any of the remaining cylinders can be located by turning the crankshaft 180-degrees and following the firing order (refer to the Specifications). For example, rotating the engine 180-degrees past TDC #1 will put the engine at TDC compression for cylinder #3.

4   Valve cover - removal and installation

Removal

1   Disconnect the cable from the negative terminal of the battery (see Chapter 5, Section 1).
2   Remove the ignition coils (see Chapter 5).
3   Detach the PCV hoses from the valve cover.
4   Disconnect any other interfering components. Be sure to label hoses and wires so you can connect them later with no confusion.
5   Remove the valve cover mounting bolts and nuts, then detach the valve cover and gasket from the cylinder head. If the valve cover is stuck to the cylinder head, bump the end with a wood block and a hammer to jar it loose. If that doesn't work, try to slip a flexible putty knife between the cylinder head and valve cover to break the seal. **Caution:** *Don't pry at the valve cover-to-cylinder head joint or damage to the sealing surfaces may occur, leading to oil leaks after the valve cover is reinstalled.*

Installation

Refer to illustration 4.8

6   Remove the valve cover gasket from the valve cover and clean the mating surfaces with brake system cleaner. Install a new rubber gasket, pressing it evenly into the grooves around the underside of the valve cover. **Note:** *Make sure the spark plug tube seals are in place on the bottom of the valve cover before reinstalling it.* The mating surfaces of the timing belt cover, the cylinder head and valve cover must be perfectly clean when the valve cover is installed. If there's residue or oil on the mating surfaces when the valve cover is installed, oil leaks may develop.

7   Apply RTV sealant at the sharp corners of the timing belt cover-to-cylinder head joint and also around the semi-circular rubber rear seal, then install the valve cover and fasteners.
8   Tighten the nuts/bolts to the torque listed in this Chapter's Specifications in three or four equal steps **(see illustration)**.
9   Reinstall the remaining parts, run the engine and check for oil leaks.

5   Timing belts and sprockets - removal, inspection and installation

Warning: *Wait until the engine is completely cool before beginning this procedure.*

Removal

Refer to illustration 5.9

1   Detach the cable from the negative terminal of the battery (see Chapter 5, Section 1). Position the number one piston at TDC on the compression stroke (see Section 3). The marks on the camshafts and the valve cover should be aligned. The dowels on the camshaft sprockets should be facing upward.
2   Remove the drivebelts (see Chapter 1) and the alternator (see Chapter 5).
3   Remove the valve cover (see Section 4).
4   Refer to Section 10 and remove the

crankshaft damper and pulley. Also remove the water pump pulley.
5   Remove the timing belt cover. **Note:** *If you intend to reuse the timing belt, use white paint or chalk to make a mark indicating the front of the belt. If a used timing belt is reinstalled with the wear pattern in the opposite direction, noise and increased wear may occur.*
6   Confirm that the engine is still at TDC on the compression stroke for cylinder number one. **Caution:** *If the crankshaft is rotated while the timing belt is removed, the pistons may contact the valves and bend them.*
7   Remove the timing belt tensioner and then the timing belt. Mark the pulley flange so it can be installed with the same side facing outward.
8   The camshaft sprockets can be removed at this time if necessary. To remove the camshaft sprockets, loosen the bolts while holding the lug on the camshaft with a wrench, on the hex portion of the camshaft only. Note the identification marks on the camshaft sprockets before removal, then remove the bolts. Pull the sprockets by hand until they slip off the dowels.
9   Remove the plug on the left side of the block and insert a screwdriver into the hole **(see illustration)**. This will lock the left balance shaft.
10   Remove the oil pump sprocket nut and lift off the sprocket.
11   Remove the plug from the right side of the block, then loosen the right balance shaft sprocket bolt using the same technique as in Step 9.
12   Remove the tensioner and the inner timing belt. Mark the pulley flange so it can be installed with the same side facing outward.

Inspection

13   Visually inspect all parts for wear and damage. Check the timing belt for any signs of wear if there is any doubt, replace it now.
14   If the timing belt is to be replaced, replace the inner belt at the same time.
15   Check all pulleys for rough operation, grease leakage and damage. Check sprockets for cracks. Check the tensioner for leakage and wear. Replace all components as necessary.

5.9 Remove the plug on the side of the block and insert a screwdriver to lock the balance shaft in position - it will engage with a flat area when it is properly aligned

Balance shaft

Cylinder block

43050-2A-5.9 HAYNES

5.18 The sprockets of the inner belt have timing marks located at about the ten o'clock position

5.30 The camshaft sprockets must be positioned so that the dowel pins are up and the sprocket timing marks are aligned with the marks on the valve cover

Installation

Refer to illustrations 5.18, 5.30, 5.32 and 5.35

16 Install the inner crankshaft pulley if it was removed. Make sure to put the flange on the engine side of the belt and with the sharp edge facing toward the rear of the engine if you didn't mark it previously.

17 Install the spacer to the right balance shaft if it was removed. Apply oil to the outside of the spacer and be sure to place the chamfered end facing toward the engine. Place the right balance shaft sprocket onto the shaft and tighten the bolt by hand.

18 Align the timing slot on the front of the engine with the mark on the right balance shaft sprocket. Align the timing mark on the crankshaft sprocket with the mark on the front of the engine. Both marks are at approximately the ten o'clock position **(see illustration)**.

19 Install the inner tensioner. The pulley should be on the left of the mounting bolt.

20 Check the timing marks for the right balance shaft as well as the crankshaft sprocket.

21 Lift the tensioner to tighten the tension side of the timing belt and then tighten the bolt. **Caution:** *Be careful to avoid turning the shaft as the bolt is tightened. This will cause the belt to become overly tight.*

22 Confirm that all of the timing marks are still lined up.

23 Press in on the upper right side of the timing belt with your index finger. The belt should move no more than a quarter inch (7 mm).

24 Install the outer crankshaft sprocket and flange. Use the marks you made previously to avoid installing the flange backward. Tighten the sprocket bolt to the torque listed in this Chapter's Specifications.

25 Make sure the screwdriver is still inserted in the hole in the left side of the block (to hold the balance shaft from turning).

26 Install the oil pump sprocket and tighten the nut to the torque listed in this Chapter's Specifications.

27 Install the camshaft sprockets if they were removed and tighten the bolts to the

torque listed in this Chapter's Specifications.

28 Place the tensioner in a vise with cushioned jaws. If there is a plug on the bottom of the tensioner, use a large washer under it. Compress the tensioner very slowly until you can insert a piece of wire in the small hole to lock the tensioner in the collapsed position.

29 Install the tensioner. Tighten the tensioner pulley bolt to the torque listed in this Chapter's Specifications.

30 Align the camshaft pulley marks with the marks on the valve cover **(see illustration)**.

Make sure that the dowels are facing upward. Align the timing mark on the oil pump sprocket with the corresponding mark on the engine.

31 Install the timing belt by routing it over the pulleys in this order: Crankshaft sprocket, oil pump sprocket, idler pulley, exhaust camshaft sprocket, intake camshaft sprocket and tensioner pulley.

32 Verify that the timing marks of all sprockets are correctly aligned. This includes the oil pump sprocket, the crankshaft sprocket and both camshaft sprockets **(see illustration)**.

5.32 The outer timing belt is installed when the marks on all the sprockets are lined up properly; the oil pump sprocket, the camshaft sprockets and the crankshaft sprocket must all have their respective marks aligned

5.35 The tensioner plunger for the outer timing belt must protrude a specified distance (A) - rotate the engine and allow it to sit for a few minutes before measuring it

6.10 Mount a dial indicator as shown to measure camshaft endplay - pry the camshaft forward and back and read the endplay on the dial

33   Check that the screwdriver can still be inserted into the hole on the left side of the engine at least 2-1/2 inches. This verifies that the oil pump/balance shaft is in the correct position. Remove the screwdriver and reinstall the plug.

34   Remove the wire from the tensioner.

35   Rotate the engine two turns by hand and then let it sit for a few minutes. **Caution:** *If you feel any resistance, stop and find out what is causing it.* Check the protrusion of the tensioner plunger **(see illustration)**. It should be within the Specifications shown in this Chapter. Verify that all sprockets are aligned correctly.

36   The remainder of the procedure is the reverse of disassembly.

6   Camshafts - removal, inspection and installation

Note: *The camshafts should always be thoroughly inspected before installation and camshaft endplay should always be checked prior to camshaft removal (see Step 10).*

Removal

1   Disconnect the cable from the negative terminal of the battery (see Chapter 5, Section 1).

2   Refer to Section 3 and place the engine on TDC for number 1 cylinder. Visually confirm the engine is at TDC on the compression stroke by verifying that the timing mark on the crankshaft pulley/vibration damper is aligned with the "0" mark on the timing belt cover and the camshaft sprocket TDC marks are aligned with the valve cover marks.

3   Remove the valve cover (see Section 4).

4   With the TDC marks aligned, apply a dab of paint to the timing belt and the camshaft sprockets for alignment later. Also put match marks on the other sprockets so the original alignment will not be lost.

5   Refer to Section 5 and remove the timing belt from the camshaft sprockets.

6   Using a large wrench (on the hex portion of the camshaft only) to hold the camshaft from turning, loosen the camshaft sprocket bolts several turns. If the camshaft sprockets have rotated during the bolt loosening process, rotate the engine clockwise until the "TDC" marks on the cam sprockets are realigned. If necessary, remove the camshaft position sensor. Make match marks to record its position before you remove it.

7   Remove the camshaft sprockets. Loosen the camshaft cap bolts in two or three steps starting with the outer camshaft caps and work toward the center (opposite of the tightening sequence). Remove the cap bolts and the camshafts from the cylinder head. **Caution:** *Keep the caps in order. They must go back in the same location from which they were removed. It is very important that the camshafts are returned to their original locations during installation. The exhaust camshaft has a slot in its end to drive the camshaft position sensor.*

8   Remove the lash adjusters and the rocker arms. **Caution:** *Keep the components in order. They must go back in the positions from which they were removed and facing the same direction.*

9   Inspect the camshafts, camshaft bearings, adjusters and rocker arms as described below. Also inspect the camshaft sprockets for wear on the teeth. Inspect the belts for cracks or excessive wear of the rollers, and for stretching. If any of the components show signs of excessive wear they must be replaced.

Inspection

Refer to illustrations 6.10, 6.12 and 6.13

10   Before the camshafts are removed from the engine, check the camshaft endplay by placing a dial indicator with the stem in line with the camshaft and touching the snout **(see**

illustration). Push the camshaft all the way to the rear and zero the dial indicator. Next, pry the camshaft to the front as far as possible and check the reading on the dial indicator. The distance it moves is the endplay. If the endplay for either camshaft is greater than the Specifications listed in this Chapter, the camshaft or the cylinder head (or both) may need to be replaced.

11   With the camshafts removed, visually check the camshaft bearing surfaces in the cylinder head for pitting, score marks, galling and abnormal wear. If the bearing surfaces are damaged, the cylinder head or the journal bearings of the camshafts may have to be replaced.

12   Measure the outside diameter of each camshaft bearing journal and record your measurements **(see illustration)**. Compare them to the journal outside diameter specified in this Chapter, then measure the inside diameter of each corresponding camshaft bearing and record the measurements. Subtract each cam journal outside diameter from its respective cam bearing bore inside diameter to determine the oil clearance for each bearing. Compare the results to the specified journal-to-bearing clearance. If any of the measurements fall outside the standard specified wear limits in this Chapter, either the camshaft or the cylinder head, or both, must be replaced. **Note:** *If precision measuring tools are not available, Plastigage may be used to determine the bearing journal oil clearance.*

13   Using a micrometer, measure the height of each camshaft lobe **(see illustration)**. Compare your measurements with this Chapter's Specifications. If the height for any one lobe is less than the specified minimum, replace the camshaft.

14   Check the camshaft runout by placing the camshaft back into the cylinder head and set up a dial indicator on the center journal. Zero the dial indicator. Turn the camshaft

6.12 Measure each journal diameter with a micrometer - if any journal measures less than the specified limit, replace the camshaft

6.13 Measure the lobe heights on each camshaft - if any lobe height is less than the specified allowable minimum, replace that camshaft

slowly and note the dial indicator readings. Runout should not exceed 0.0012 inch (0.03 mm). If the measured runout exceeds the specified runout, replace the camshaft.

15 Inspect each hydraulic adjuster for scuffing and score marks. Check each roller rocker for smooth bearing operation and damage to either end.

Installation

Refer to illustration 6.18

16 Apply moly-based engine assembly lubricant to the camshaft lobes and journals and install the camshaft into the cylinder head with the dowel pins facing upward. If the old camshafts are being used, make sure they're installed in the same location from which they came. Don't install the rocker arms or adjusters at this time.

17 Install the bearing caps and bolts and tighten them hand tight. Each cap is marked with either an "I" or an "E," indicating if it is for the intake or exhaust side. They are also numbered.

18 Tighten the bearing cap bolts in several equal steps, to the torque listed in this Chapter's Specifications, using the proper tightening sequence (see illustration). If a camshaft oil seal needs to be replaced, do it at this time. Oil the outside of the seal and use a large socket to drive the new seal flush.

19 Turn the camshafts by hand to ensure that they operate smoothly. If they don't, release the bearing caps one at a time to determine which is causing the problem.

20 Remove the camshafts, then reinstall them along with the rocker arms and adjusters. Tighten the rocker arms evenly. Again tighten the bearing cap bolts in several equal steps, to the torque listed in this Chapter's Specifications, using the proper tightening sequence.

21 Engage the camshaft sprocket teeth with the timing belt so that the match marks made during removal align with the upper timing marks on the sprockets. Position the sprock-

ets over the dowels on the camshaft hubs and install the camshaft sprocket bolts finger tight. At this point, all of the sprocket paint marks should be lined up with the paint marks on the belt. Refer to Section 5 and verify that all of the sprockets are also aligned with their respective marks on the engine. Install the camshaft position sensor and its support, aligning the match marks previously made.

22 The remainder of installation is the reverse of removal. Refer to Sections 4 and 5.

7 Intake manifold - removal and installation

Warning: *Wait until the engine is completely cool before beginning this procedure.*

Removal

1 Relieve the fuel system pressure (see Chapter 4), then disconnect the negative cable from the battery (see Chapter 5, Section 1).

2 Remove the engine cover.

3 Remove the air intake duct and resonator (see Chapter 4).

4 Remove the vent hose from the throttle body.

5 Disconnect the throttle cable. Disconnect the wiring from the MAP and IAT sensors.

6 Clamp off the coolant hoses connected to the throttle body, then disconnect them.

7 Disconnect the brake booster hose and the PCV hose.

8 Refer to Chapter 4, relieve the fuel system pressure, then disconnect the fuel supply hose from the fuel rail.

9 Refer to Chapter 4 and remove the fuel rail along with the injectors.

10 Remove the intake manifold brace.

11 Remove the intake manifold with the throttle body.

Installation

12 Clean the mating surfaces of the intake manifold and the cylinder head mounting surface with brake system cleaner. If the gasket shows signs of leaking, check the manifold for warpage with a straightedge and feeler gauges. Compare your readings with those listed in this Chapter's Specifications. If the

6.18 Camshaft bearing cap bolt TIGHTENING sequence

◄ **Camshaft sprocket side**

43050-2A-6.21 HAYNES

← **FRONT**

```
  8      6      1      3      9
```

9.22 Cylinder head bolt TIGHTENING sequence

```
  10     4      2      5      7
```

43050-2A-9.22 HAYNES

manifold is warped it must be surfaced or replaced.

13 Install the manifold and gasket over the studs on the cylinder head.

14 Tighten the manifold-to-cylinder head nuts/bolts in three or four equal steps to the torque listed in this Chapter's Specifications. Work from the middle bolts out to avoid flexing the manifold.

15 Install the remaining parts in the reverse order of removal. Check the coolant level, adding as necessary (see Chapter 1).

16 Run the engine and check for coolant and vacuum leaks.

17 Road test the vehicle and check for proper operation of all accessories, including the cruise control system, if equipped.

8   Exhaust manifold - removal and installation

Warning: *The engine must be completely cool before beginning this procedure.*

Removal

1 Disconnect the negative cable from the battery (see Chapter 5, Section 1).

2 Raise the front of the vehicle and support it securely on jackstands.

3 Apply penetrating oil to the nuts and springs retaining the catalytic converter to the manifold. After the nuts have soaked, remove the nuts retaining the converter to the manifold. Separate the converter from the manifold, being careful not to damage the oxygen sensors.

4 Working in the engine compartment, remove the upper heat shield from the manifold.

5 Remove the nuts and detach the manifold and gasket.

Installation

6 Use a scraper to remove all traces of old gasket material and carbon deposits from the manifold and cylinder head mating surfaces. If the gasket shows signs of leaking, check the manifold for warpage with a straightedge and compare your readings with those listed in this Chapter's Specifications. If the manifold is warped it must be resurfaced or replaced.

7 Position a new gasket over the cylinder head studs, noting any directional marks or arrows on the gasket that may be present.

8 Install the manifold and thread the mounting nuts into place.

9 Working from the center out, tighten the nuts/bolts to the torque listed in this Chapter's Specifications in three or four equal steps.

10 Reinstall the remaining parts in the reverse order of removal.

11 Run the engine and check for exhaust leaks.

9   Cylinder head - removal, inspection and installation

Warning: *The engine must be completely cool before beginning this procedure.*

Removal

1 Relieve the fuel system pressure (see Chapter 4), then disconnect the cable from the negative terminal of the battery (see Chapter 5, Section 1).

2 Drain the engine coolant (see Chapter 1).

3 Refer to Section 7 and perform all the Steps for removing the intake manifold. However, the manifold itself can be left in place if desired.

4 Detach the coolant hoses from the cylinder head (see Chapter 3).

5 Refer to Section 5 and remove the timing belt from the camshaft sprockets.

6 Raise the vehicle and support it securely on jackstands, then disconnect the catalytic converter from the exhaust manifold.

7 Label and detach the electrical connections from the cylinder head.

8 Loosen the cylinder head bolts in 1/4-turn increments until they can be removed by hand. Loosen the cylinder head bolts in the reverse order of the recommended tightening sequence **(see illustration 9.22)** to avoid warping or cracking the cylinder head.

9 With the help of an assistant, lift the cylinder head off the engine block. If it's stuck, very carefully pry up at the transaxle end, beyond the gasket surface.

10 Remove any remaining external components from the cylinder head to allow for thorough cleaning and inspection.

Inspection

11 Use a precision straightedge to check the gasket surfaces of each head. Try to insert a feeler gauge of the correct size between the straightedge and the head surface. If the clearance is more than that listed in this Chapter's Specifications, the head must be surface or replaced. Check the intake and exhaust manifold surfaces as well as the block surface.

12 Examine all areas of each head for signs of cracks and coolant leakage, especially around the valve seats.

Installation

Refer to illustration 9.22

13 The mating surfaces of the cylinder head and block must be perfectly clean when the cylinder head is installed.

14 Use a gasket scraper to remove all traces of carbon and old gasket material, then clean the mating surfaces with brake system cleaner. If there's oil on the mating surfaces when the cylinder head is installed, the gasket may not seal correctly and leaks could develop. When working on the block, stuff the cylinders with clean shop rags to keep out debris. Use a vacuum cleaner to remove material that falls into the cylinders. **Caution:** *The cylinder head is made of aluminum. It is very easy to scratch it, so use care.*

15 Check the block and cylinder head mating surfaces for nicks, deep scratches and other damage. If damage is slight, it can be removed with a file; if it's excessive, machining may be the only alternative.

16 Use a tap of the correct size to chase the threads in the cylinder head bolt holes, then clean the holes with compressed air - make sure that nothing remains in the holes. **Warning:** *Wear eye protection when using compressed air!*

17 Using a wire brush, clean the threads on each bolt to remove corrosion and restore the threads. Dirt, corrosion, sealant and damaged threads will affect torque readings. If the bolts are damaged in any way, replace them with new cylinder head bolts.

18 Install the components that were removed from the cylinder head.

19 Position the new gasket over the dowel pins in the block. Examine it carefully to verify that is installed in the correct orientation.

20 Carefully set the cylinder head on the block without disturbing the gasket.

21 Before installing the cylinder head bolts, apply a small amount of clean engine oil to the threads and under the bolt heads.

22 Install the bolts in their original locations and tighten them finger tight. Following the recommended sequence, tighten the bolts to the torque listed in this Chapter's Specifications **(see illustration)**. Later Steps in the tightening sequence require each bolt to be tightened an additional 90-degrees. If you don't have an angle-torque attachment for your torque wrench, simply apply a paint mark

10.4 Remove the side engine splash shield for access to the crankshaft pulley (3.5L V6 engine shown)

10.6 Use a large wrench to keep the crankshaft from turning as you remove the crankshaft pulley bolt, then the pulley itself

on the socket you'll be using and tighten the bolt until that mark is 90-degrees (1/4-turn) from where you started.

23 If you have replaced either the head bolts, the head itself or the block with new, unused parts, be sure to follow the torque sequence for this application.

24 The remaining installation steps are the reverse of removal. Refer to Section 5 to ensure correct installation of the timing belt.

25 Change the engine oil and filter (see Chapter 1).

26 Refill the cooling system (see Chapter 1), run the engine and check for leaks.

10 Crankshaft pulley/vibration damper - removal and installation

Refer to illustrations 10.4, 10.6 and 10.7

1 Disconnect the cable from the negative terminal of the battery (see Chapter 5, Section 1).

2 Remove the drivebelt (see Chapter 1).

3 With the parking brake applied and the shifter in Park (automatic) or in gear (manual), loosen the lug nuts from the right front wheel, then raise the front of the vehicle and support it securely on jackstands. Remove the engine splash shield (if installed), the front wheel and the splash shield from the right wheelwell.

4 Remove all other interfering components that are installed on your particular vehicle (see illustration).

5 Remove the bolt from the front of the crankshaft. A breaker bar will probably be necessary, since the bolt is very tight. Use a strap wrench to hold the crankshaft from turning. If one is not available, have an assistant lock the flywheel in place with a prybar.

6 Using a puller that bolts to the crankshaft hub, remove the crankshaft pulley from the crankshaft (see illustration). Caution: *Do not use a jaw-type puller - it will damage the pulley/damper assembly. Also, be sure to use the proper adapter to prevent damage to the end of the crankshaft.*

7 To install the crankshaft pulley, slide the pulley onto the crankshaft as far as it will slide

on, then use a vibration damper installation tool to press the pulley onto the crankshaft. Note that the slot (keyway) in the hub must be aligned with the Woodruff key in the end of the crankshaft and that the crankshaft bolt can also be used to press the crankshaft pulley into position (see illustration).

8 Tighten the crankshaft bolt to the torque listed in this Chapter's Specifications.

9 The remaining installation steps are the reverse of removal.

11 Crankshaft front oil seal - replacement

Refer to illustrations 11.2, 11.3 and 11.4

1 Remove the crankshaft pulley (see Section 10).

2 Note how the seal is installed - the new one must be installed to the same depth and facing the same way. Carefully pry the oil seal out of the cover with a seal puller or a large screwdriver (see illustration). Be very careful

10.7 Align the keyway in the crankshaft pulley hub with the Woodruff key in the crankshaft

11.2 Carefully pry the old seal out of the timing belt cover - don't damage the crankshaft in the process

11.3 Drive the new seal into place with a seal driver or a large socket and hammer

11.4 If the sealing surface of the pulley hub has a wear groove from contact with the seal, repair sleeves are available at most auto parts stores

not to distort the cover or scratch the crankshaft! Wrap electrician's tape around the tip of the screwdriver to avoid damage to the crankshaft.

3   Apply clean engine oil or multi-purpose grease to the outer edge of the new seal, then install it in the cover with the lip (spring side) facing IN. Drive the seal into place with a seal driver or a large socket and a hammer **(see illustration)**. Make sure the seal enters the bore squarely and stop when the front face is at the proper depth.

4   Check the surface on the pulley hub that the oil seal rides on. If the surface has been grooved from long-time contact with the seal, a press-on sleeve may be available to renew the sealing surface **(see illustration)**. This sleeve is pressed into place with a hammer and a block of wood and is commonly available at auto parts stores for various applications.

5   Lubricate the pulley hub with clean engine oil and reinstall the crankshaft pulley (see Section 10).

6   Install the crankshaft pulley retaining bolt and tighten it to the torque listed in this Chapter's Specifications.

7   The remainder of installation is the reverse of the removal.

12 Oil pan - removal and installation

Removal

Refer to illustration 12.6

1   Disconnect the cable from the negative terminal of the battery (see Chapter 5, Section 1).

2   Set the parking brake and block the rear wheels. Raise the front of the vehicle and support it securely on jackstands.

3   Remove the engine splash shield, if so equipped

4   Drain the engine oil and remove the oil filter (see Chapter 1). Remove the oil dipstick.

5   Remove any interfering components. The oil pan has two parts: an upper cast section and a lower section made of stamped steel. Remove the lower oil pan now.

6   Remove the upper bolts and detach the oil pan. Two different bolt lengths are used, so note their locations. If it's stuck, pry it loose very carefully with a small screwdriver or putty knife **(see illustration)**. Don't damage the mating surfaces of the pan and block or oil leaks could develop. **Note:** *The lower oil pan can be removed independently of the upper oil pan.*

Installation

7   Use a scraper to remove all traces of old sealant from the block and oil pan. Clean the mating surfaces with lacquer thinner or acetone.

8   Make sure the threaded bolt holes in the block are clean.

9   Check the oil pan flange for distortion, particularly around the bolt holes. Remove any nicks or burrs as necessary.

10   Apply a 3/16-inch wide bead of RTV sealant to the mating surface of the oil pan, following the groove but going to the inside where the bolt holes are located. Install the

pan within 15 minutes.

11   Carefully position the oil pan on the engine block and install the oil pan-to-engine block bolts loosely.

12   Working from the center out, tighten the oil pan-to-engine block bolts to the torque listed in this Chapter's Specifications in three or four steps.

13   Install the lower oil pan, tightening the bolts evenly in several steps to the torque listed in this Chapter's Specifications. The remainder of installation is the reverse of removal

14   Run the engine and check for oil pressure and leaks.

13 Oil pump - removal and installation

Removal

1   Refer to Section 5 and remove the timing belt.

2   Refer to Section 12 and remove the oil pan to remove the oil pickup and its gasket.

3   Remove the access plug on the left side of the engine block and insert a screwdriver

12.6 Pry the oil pan loose with a screwdriver or putty knife - be careful not to damage the mating surfaces of the pan and block or oil leaks may develop

at least 2-1/2 inches to lock the balance shaft into position **(see illustration 5.9)**.
4   Remove the left balance shaft and oil pump sprocket bolt.
5   Remove the front case/oil pump housing.
6   Remove the oil pump cover from the case and then lift out the oil pump gears.
7   Use a scraper to remove all traces of sealant and old gasket material from the pump body and engine block, then clean the mating surfaces with brake system cleaner.
8   Inspect the oil pump for wear and damage. If the oil pump shows signs of wear or you're in doubt about its condition, it is best to simply replace it. The clearances can be measured using a feeler gauge. Compare your readings to those listed in this Chapter's Specifications.

Installation

9   Lubricate the pump cavity by pouring a small amount of clean engine oil into the inlet side of the oil pump and turning the drive gear shaft.
10 Position the oil pump gears and align the two timing marks so they are facing each other.
11 Install new oil seals at this time, if necessary. Also be sure to use new gaskets. There is an O-ring in the front case that should also be replaced.
12 Tighten the bolts to the torque listed in this Chapter's Specifications in several steps. Follow a criss-cross pattern to avoid warping the body.
13 Tighten the lower drive sprocket retaining bolt to the torque listed in this Chapter's Specifications.
14 Reinstall the timing belts by referring to Section 5.
15 Add oil to the proper level, start the engine and check for oil pressure and leaks.

14 Flywheel/driveplate - removal and installation

Removal

1   Disconnect the cable from the negative terminal of the battery (see Chapter 5, Section 1).

2   Remove the transaxle (see Chapter 7).
3   Using a center-punch or paint, apply alignment marks on the crankshaft flange and driveplate to ensure correct alignment on installation.
4   Remove the bolts retaining the driveplate to the crankshaft. Use a driveplate holding tool (available at auto parts stores) or wedge a screwdriver or prybar through one of the holes in the driveplate to keep it from turning while you loosen the bolts.
5   Remove the driveplate, taking note of spacers used and on which side of the driveplate they were installed.

Installation

6   Inspect the driveplate. Look for any fractures in the driveplate. Inspect the driveplate carefully for any other type of damage.
7   Position the driveplate on the crankshaft flange, aligning the marks made during removal. Align the bolt holes; note that some models may have a staggered bolt pattern to ensure correct installation.
8   Apply non-hardening thread locking compound to the threads of the bolts. Install the bolts and tighten them in a criss cross pattern to the torque listed in this Chapter's Specifications. Work up to the final torque in several steps.
9   Install the transaxle (see Chapter 7).

15 Rear main oil seal - replacement

1   Remove the transaxle (see Chapter 7).
2   Remove the driveplate or flywheel (see Section 14).
3   Pry the oil seal from the rear of the engine with a seal removal tool or a screwdriver. Be careful not to nick or scratch the crankshaft or the seal bore. Thoroughly clean the seal bore in the block with a shop towel. Remove all traces of oil and dirt.
4   Lubricate the outside diameter of the seal and install the seal over the end of the crankshaft. Make sure the lip of the seal points toward the engine. Preferably, a seal installation tool (available at most auto parts stores) should be used to press the new seal back into place. **Note:** *There is a small oil drain in the separator that must be in the lowest*

position. If the proper seal installation tool is unavailable, use a large socket and carefully drive the new seal squarely into the seal bore and flush with the edge of the engine block.
5   Install the driveplate or flywheel (see Section 14).
6   Install the transaxle (see Chapter 7).

16 Powertrain mounts - check and replacement

1   Powertrain mounts seldom require attention, but broken or deteriorated mounts should be replaced immediately or the added strain placed on driveline components may cause damage and wear.

Check

2   During the check, the engine (or transaxle) must be raised slightly to remove the weight from the mounts.
3   Raise the vehicle and support it securely on jackstands, then remove the engine splash shield (if so equipped) and position a jack under the engine oil pan. Place a large block of wood between the jack and the oil pan, then carefully raise the engine just enough to take the weight off the mounts. Do not position the wood block under the oil drain plug. **Warning:** *DO NOT place any part of your body under the engine when only a jack supports it!*
4   Check the mounts to see if the rubber is cracked, hardened or separated from the bushing in the center of the mount.
5   Check for relative movement between the mount plates and the engine or frame, (use a large screwdriver or pry bar to attempt to move the mounts).
6   If movement is noted, lower the engine and tighten the mount fasteners.

Replacement

7   All engine mounts are replaced in the same manner. Use the jack to securely support the weight of the engine, then use it to remove all force from the mount in question.
8   Remove the bolts from both sides of the mount, then remove the mount.
9   Install the replacement mount and tighten all fasteners securely.

Notes

Chapter 2 Part B
V6 engines

Contents

Specifications

General
Displacement
  2.7L .... 162 cubic inches (2,656 cc)
  3.5L .... 213 cubic inches (3,497 cc)
Cylinder numbers (timing belt end-to-transaxle end)
  Right (firewall) side 1-3-5
  Left (radiator) side 2-4-6
  Firing order 1-2-3-4-5-6

Cylinder numbering

Cylinder head
Warpage limits
  Block surface .... 0.002 inch (0.05 mm)
  Intake surface .... 0.006 inch (0.15 mm)
  Exhaust surface .... 0.006 inch (0.15 mm)

Camshaft and related components
Bearing journal diameter .... 1.022 to 1.023 inches (25.95 to 25.98 mm)
Bearing oil clearance .... 0.0007 to 0.0024 inch (0.02 to 0.06 mm)
Lobe height minimum allowable, 2.7L .... 1.711 inches (43.45 mm)
Lobe height, 3.5L (standard)
  Intake .... 1.382 to 1.390 inches (35.10 to 35.30 mm)
  Exhaust .... 1.371 to 1.378 inches (34.81 to 35.01 mm)
Thrust clearance (endplay) limit
  2.7L .... 0.005 inch (0.12 mm)
  3.5L .... 0.006 inch (0.15 mm)

Intake manifold

Surface warpage limit.. 0.008 inch (0.2 mm)

Exhaust manifold

Surface warpage limit.. 0.012 inch (0.3 mm)

Oil pump

Driven rotor-to-pump body clearance .... 0.004 to 0.007 inch (0.10 to 0.18 mm)
Rotor side clearance.. 0.0016 to 0.0037 inch (0.040 to 0.096 mm)
Rotor tip clearance .... 0.0024 to 0.0071 inch (0.06 to 0.18 mm)

Timing belt tensioner

Tensioner rod protrusion (installed)
2.7L .... 0.27 to 0.31 inch (7 to 9 mm)
3.5L .... 0.150 to 0.177 inch (3.8 to 4.5 mm)

Torque specifications

	Ft-lbs (unless otherwise indicated)	Nm

Note: One foot-pound (ft-lb) of torque is equivalent to 12 inch-pounds (in-lbs) of torque. Torque values below approximately 15 ft-lbs are expressed in inch-pounds, since most foot-pound torque wrenches are not accurate at these smaller values.

	Ft-lbs	Nm
Crankshaft pulley bolt	135	185
Camshaft bearing cap bolts		
2.7L		
36 mm bolts	108 in-lbs	12
50 mm bolts	144 in-lbs	16
3.5L		
End bolts	168 in-lbs	20
Center bolts	108 in-lbs	12
Camshaft sprocket bolt	75	95
Cylinder head bolts		
2.7L		
Step 1	18	25
Step 2	Tighten an additional 60-degrees	
Step 3	Tighten an additional 45-degrees	
3.5L	80	110
Driveplate/flywheel bolts	55	75
Exhaust manifold nuts		
2.7L	25	35
3.5L	30	45
Exhaust manifold heat shield bolts	120 in-lbs	15
Intake manifold bolts		
2.7L	15	20
3.5L	120 in-lbs	12 to 15
Oil pan bolts		
Lower oil pan	108 in-lbs	12
Upper oil pan		
2.7L		
10 mm x 38 mm	22 to 30	30 to 42
8 mm x 22 mm	14 to 20	19 to 28
Long bolts	60 in-lbs	7
3.5L		
10 mm bolts	22 to 30	30 to 42
6 mm bolts	60 in-lbs	7
Oil pump case bolt	132 in-lbs	15
Oil pump cover screw	108 in-lbs	12
Oil relief valve plug	35	50
Oil pick-up tube mounting bolts, 2.7L	72 in-lbs	8
Timing belt cover bolts	108 in-lbs	12
Timing belt automatic tensioner fixed bolt	20	27
Timing belt automatic tensioner arm bolt	40	55
Timing belt idler pulley bolt	43	60
Timing belt tensioner pulley bolt	40	55
Rear crankshaft oil seal retainer mounting bolts	72 in-lbs	8
Valve cover bolts	84 in-lbs	9

3.5 A compression gauge can be used in the number one plug hole to assist in finding TDC

4.2 The engine cover is secured with screws - use a nut driver or a small socket, an extension and a ratchet to remove them

1   General information

Both the 2.7L and the 3.5L are DOHC (dual overhead cam) with aluminum heads, four valves per cylinder and a two-piece oil pan.

This Part of Chapter 2 is devoted to in-vehicle repair procedures for the V6 engine. Information concerning engine removal and installation and engine overhaul can be found in Part C of this Chapter.

The following repair procedures are based on the assumption that the engine is installed in the vehicle. If the engine has been removed from the vehicle and mounted on a stand, many of the steps outlined in this Part of Chapter 2 will not apply.

2   Repair operations possible with the engine in the vehicle

Many major repair operations can be accomplished without removing the engine from the vehicle.

Clean the engine compartment and the exterior of the engine with some type of degreaser before any work is done. It will make the job easier and help keep dirt out of the internal areas of the engine.

Depending on the components involved, it may be helpful to remove the hood to improve access to the engine as repairs are performed (see Chapter 11 if necessary). Cover the fenders to prevent damage to the paint. Special pads are available, but an old bedspread or blanket will also work.

If vacuum, exhaust, oil or coolant leaks develop, indicating a need for gasket or seal replacement, the repairs can generally be made with the engine in the vehicle. The intake and exhaust manifold gaskets, oil pan gasket, crankshaft oil seals and cylinder head gaskets are all accessible with the engine in place.

Exterior engine components, such as the intake and exhaust manifolds, the oil pan, the oil pump, the water pump, the starter motor, the alternator, and the fuel system compo-

nents can be removed for repair with the engine in place.

Since the cylinder heads can be removed without pulling the engine, valve component servicing can also be accomplished with the engine in the vehicle. Replacement of the camshafts, timing belt and sprockets is also possible with the engine in the vehicle.

3   Top Dead Center (TDC) for number one piston - locating

Refer to illustration 3.5

1   Top Dead Center (TDC) is the highest point in the cylinder that each piston reaches as it travels up the cylinder bore. Each piston reaches TDC on the compression stroke and again on the exhaust stroke, but TDC generally refers to piston position on the compression stroke.

2   Positioning the piston(s) at TDC is an essential part of certain procedures such as valve timing and camshaft and timing belt/sprocket removal and distributor removal.

3   Before beginning this procedure, be sure to place the transaxle in Neutral and apply the parking brake or block the rear wheels. Disable the fuel system by relieving the fuel system pressure (see Chapter 4). Disable the ignition system by disconnecting the electrical connector(s) from the coil(s).

4   In order to bring any piston to TDC, the crankshaft must be turned using one of the methods outlined below. When looking at the front of the engine, normal crankshaft rotation is clockwise.

a) *The preferred method is to turn the crankshaft clockwise with a socket and ratchet attached to the bolt threaded into the front of the crankshaft.*

b) *A remote starter switch, which may save some time, can also be used. Follow the instructions included with the switch. Once the piston is close to TDC, use a socket and ratchet as described in the previous paragraph.*

c) *If an assistant is available to turn the*

ignition switch to the Start position in short bursts, you can get the piston close to TDC without a remote starter switch. Make sure your assistant is out of the vehicle, away from the ignition switch, then use a socket and ratchet as described in Paragraph (a) to complete the procedure.

5   Remove the spark plug and install a compression pressure gauge in the number one spark plug hole. It should be a gauge with a screw-in fitting and a hose at least six inches long **(see illustration). Caution:** *It is possible to check the compression on cylinder number 1 on the V6 engine with the upper intake manifold and throttle body installed on the engine. The spark plugs can remain in the cylinder heads (except for number 1) if the ignition system and the fuel pump have been disabled.*

6   Rotate the crankshaft using one of the methods described above while observing the compression gauge. When the compression stroke of the number one cylinder is reached, pressure will begin to show on the gauge; continue to rotate the crankshaft and align the notch on the crankshaft pulley with the 0 mark on the timing plate. If you go past the marks, release the gauge pressure and rotate the crankshaft around two more revolutions.

7   After the number one piston has been positioned at TDC on the compression stroke, TDC for the remaining cylinders can be located by turning the crankshaft 120-degrees (1/3-turn) at a time and following the firing order (see this Chapter's Specifications).

4   Valve covers - removal and installation

Removal

Refer to illustrations 4.2 and 4.3

1   Disconnect the cable from the negative terminal of the battery (see Chapter 5, Section 1).

2   Remove the engine cover **(see illustration)**.

4.3 With the upper intake manifold removed, the rear valve cover is accessible

5.6 The upper intake manifold is removed here to show the rear brackets and the EGR valve that must be disconnected

3   Remove the upper intake manifold if you're working on the rear valve cover (see Section 5) **(see illustration)**.

4   Detach the engine wiring harnesses and pull them out of the way.

5   Disconnect all interfering wiring and hoses. Be sure to label them as you go to prevent confusion later.

6   Remove the retaining bolts, then detach the cover(s). If the cover is stuck to the head, bump the end with a wood block and a hammer to jar it loose. If that doesn't work, try to slip a flexible putty knife between the head and cover to break the seal. **Caution:** *Don't pry at the cover-to-head joint or damage to the sealing surfaces may occur, leading to oil leaks after the cover is reinstalled.*

Installation

7   The mating surfaces of the cylinder head and cover must be clean when the cover is installed. Use a gasket scraper to remove all traces of sealant and old gasket material, then clean the mating surfaces with brake system cleaner. If there's residue or oil on the mating surfaces when the cover is installed, oil leaks may develop.

8   Install new spark plug tube seals.

9   Apply RTV sealant to the gasket/seal joints at the front and rear camshaft-to-head mounts and install the valve cover with a new gasket.

10   Tighten the bolts a little at a time to the torque listed in this Chapter's Specifications.

11   Reinstall the remaining parts, run the engine and check for oil leaks.

---

5   Intake manifold - removal and installation

Warning: *Wait until the engine is completely cool before beginning this procedure.*

Removal

1   Relieve the fuel system pressure (see Chapter 4), then disconnect the cable from the negative terminal of the battery (see Chapter 5, Section 1).

2   Remove the engine cover and the air intake duct (see Chapter 4).

Upper intake manifold

Refer to illustrations 5.6 and 5.8

3   Disconnect the PCV hose.

4   Disconnect the ground strap, the electrical connectors and the vacuum lines from the upper intake manifold. Label each connector using tape and a marker to ensure correct reassembly. Pull the wiring harnesses aside.

5   Refer to Chapter 4 and disconnect the throttle body. **Note:** *Clamp-off the coolant hoses before detaching them, or plug them as soon as they are detached. Be prepared for coolant spillage.* The throttle body can be removed completely or left attached to the upper intake manifold.

6   Unbolt the upper intake manifold brace(s) at the back of the upper intake manifold assembly **(see illustration)**. Also remove the bolts from the EGR valve at the rear of the intake manifold. Pull the EGR valve away.

7   Remove the bolts mounting the upper intake manifold to the lower intake manifold, following the reverse of the tightening sequence **(see illustration 5.16)**.

8   Move the upper intake manifold to the side and separate it from the throttle body and lower intake manifold **(see illustration)**.

Lower intake manifold

9   Drain the cooling system (see Chapter 1).

10   Disconnect the electrical connectors from the fuel injectors (see Chapter 4). Also detach the fuel line from the fuel rail (see Chapter 4). **Note:** *The intake manifold can be removed with the injectors and fuel rails in place or removed, depending on the work to be done.* Pull the wiring harness aside.

11   Disconnect any remaining components from the lower manifold.

12   Remove the mounting bolts following the reverse of the tightening sequence **(see illustration 5.15)**, then detach the lower intake manifold from the engine. If the manifold is stuck, don't pry between the gasket mating surfaces or damage may result.

5.8 The upper manifold is more easily removed if the various brackets are removed first, rather than disconnecting all of the hoses and wiring harnesses from the brackets

5.15 Lower intake manifold bolt tightening sequence

5.16 Upper intake manifold bolt TIGHTENING sequence

13   Check the manifold's surface with a precision straightedge and compare your readings with those listed in this Chapter's Specifications. If it's excessively deformed it must be replaced.

Installation

Refer to illustrations 5.15 and 5.16

14   Use a scraper to remove all traces of old gasket material and sealant from the lower intake manifold and cylinder heads, then clean the mating surfaces with brake system cleaner.

15   Install new gaskets, then position the lower intake manifold on the engine. Make sure the gaskets haven't shifted, then install the bolts. Tighten the bolts in three or four equal steps to the torque listed in this Chapter's Specifications. Tighten the bolts in the correct sequence **(see illustration)**.

16   Install a new gasket between the lower intake manifold and the upper intake manifold. Place the upper intake manifold on the lower intake manifold. Install the bolts and tighten them, in the proper sequence, to the torque listed in this Chapter's Specifications **(see illustration)**.

17   Remove the radiator cap and check the coolant level, adding if necessary to bring it up to the bottom of the radiator opening, then reinstall the cap. Run the engine and check for fuel, vacuum and coolant leaks.

6   Exhaust manifold/catalytic converter assemblies - removal and installation

Refer to illustration 6.4

Warning: *The engine must be completely cool before beginning this procedure.*

Note: *2.7L engines are equipped with exhaust manifold/catalytic converter assemblies while 3.5L engines are equipped with catalytic con-*

verters that can be unbolted from the exhaust manifolds.

1   Disconnect the cable from the negative terminal of the battery (see Chapter 5, Section 1).

2   Spray penetrating oil on the exhaust manifold fasteners and allow it to soak in.

3   If you're removing the rear (firewall side) exhaust manifold, raise the front of the vehicle and support it securely on jackstands, then remove the engine splash shield.

4   Disconnect or remove the heated oxygen sensors from the manifold(s) (see Chapter 6) **(see illustration)**.

5   Remove the bolts and the heat shield over the exhaust manifold.

6   Remove the exhaust manifold brace, if equipped.

7   Remove the nuts retaining the exhaust pipe(s) to the exhaust manifold(s) or catalytic converter(s).

8   Unbolt the exhaust manifold(s) from the cylinder head(s), working from the ends toward the middle. Slip the manifold(s) off the mounting studs.

9   Carefully inspect the manifold(s) and fasteners for cracks and damage.

10   Use a scraper to remove all traces of old gasket material and carbon deposits from the manifold and cylinder head mating surfaces. If the gasket was leaking, check the manifold for warpage on the cylinder head mounting surface by placing a straightedge over the surface and trying to insert a feeler gauge. If the clearance exceeds the limit listed in this Chapter's Specifications, have the manifold resurfaced at an automotive machine shop.

11   Position a new gasket over the cylinder head studs.

12   Install the manifold(s) and thread the mounting nuts into place.

13   Working from the center out, tighten the nuts to the torque listed in this Chapter's Specifications in three or four equal steps.

14   Reinstall the remaining parts in the reverse order of removal. Use new gaskets when connecting the exhaust pipes.

15   Run the engine and check for exhaust leaks.

6.4 There is an oxygen sensor immediately before and after each catalytic converter (downstream sensor shown)

7.9 If the camshaft sprockets are to be removed, hold the hex portion of the camshaft with a wrench while removing the sprocket bolt

7   Timing belt and sprockets - removal, inspection and installation

Removal

Refer to illustration 7.9

1   Disconnect the cable from the negative terminal of the battery (see Chapter 5, Section 1).
2   Remove the engine cover.

2.7L engine

3   Refer to Chapter 1 and release the tension on the drivebelt and lift it from the pulleys.
4   Remove the pulleys from the power steering pump, the idler, the belt tensioner and the crankshaft (see Chapter 2A).
5   Remove both timing belt covers.
6   Refer to Section 3 and set the engine at TDC on the number one cylinder. Make absolutely sure that all of the timing marks are aligned.
7   If you intend to reuse the belt, mark it with an arrow indicating direction of travel and put match marks from the belt to the sprockets so it can be realigned easily.
8   Remove the timing belt tensioner assembly.
9   The camshaft sprockets can be removed now **(see illustration)**. Remove the valve covers and hold the hex area of the camshaft securely with a wrench while removing the bolts.

3.5L engine

10   Loosen the lug nuts on the right front wheel, but don't remove them yet.
11   Raise the front of the vehicle and support it securely on jackstands. Apply the parking brake and block the rear wheels. Remove the right front wheel.
12   Remove the right front inner fender apron (see Chapter 11).
13   Support the engine from below, using a jack and a block of wood under the oil pan. Disconnect the power steering hose from the engine mount, then remove the mount.
14   Remove the upper timing belt cover.

15   Refer to Chapter 1 and remove the drivebelt. Refer to Chapter 2A and remove the crankshaft pulley.
16   Loosen the alternator nuts and disconnect the wiring from the alternator. Loosen all the bolts of the engine mount bracket.
17   Lift the engine mount bracket upwards and off of the engine. You may have to rock the engine by hand to do so.
18   Refer to Section 3 and set the engine at TDC on the number one cylinder. Verify that all timing marks are aligned before proceeding.
19   If you intend to reuse the belt, mark it with an arrow indicating direction of travel and put match marks from the belt to the sprockets so it can be realigned easily.
20   Remove the tensioner and the timing belt.
21   The camshaft sprockets can be removed now. Remove the valve covers and hold the hex area of the camshaft securely with a wrench while removing the bolts.

Inspection

Refer to illustrations 7.22 and 7.24

22   Check the belt for the presence of oil or dirt, and inspect for visible defects **(see illustration)**.
23   Check the belt tensioner for visible oil leakage. If there's only a faint trace of oil on the pushrod side, the tensioner seal is in satisfactory condition.
24   Hold the tensioner in both hands and push it forcefully against an immovable object **(see illustration)**. If the pushrod moves, replace the tensioner.
25   Check that the idler pulleys turn smoothly.

Installation

Refer to illustrations 7.30, 7.32 and 7.37

26   Remove all dirt, oil and grease from the timing belt area at the front of the engine.
27   Install the camshaft sprocket(s) (if they were removed) on the camshaft(s). Align the pin hole in the sprocket with the pin in the end of the camshaft.
28   Install the camshaft sprocket bolt(s) and tighten it to the torque listed in this Chapter's Specifications.
29   Carefully align all of the camshaft sprocket marks with the marks on the engine.

2.7L engine

30   Using a press or vise, compress the timing belt tensioner pushrod extremely slowly. Insert a metal pin, drill bit or Allen wrench through the holes in the pushrod and housing. Remove the tensioner from the press or vise **(see illustration)**.
31   Install the timing belt tensioner and tighten the bolts to the torque listed in this Chapter's Specifications.
32   Align all of the timing marks and place

7.22 Check the timing belt for cracked or missing teeth - if the belt is cracked or worn, also check the pulleys for nicks or burrs - wear on one side of the belt indicates pulley misalignment problems

7.24 Check the tensioner for signs of leakage and test for leakdown by forcing it against an immovable object

7.30 Restrain the tensioner pushrod by compressing the unit in a vise and inserting a pin approximately 0.060-inch (1.5 mm) in diameter

the timing belt around the sprockets and pulleys in this order (**see illustration**):

Crankshaft
Idler
Front (left) camshaft
Water pump
Rear (right) camshaft
Tensioner

3.5L engine

33   Install all the sprockets and pulleys if they were removed. Verify that the engine is still at TDC.
34   Make sure that the crankshaft sprocket is installed with the spacer first, then the sensor

blade between the spacer and the sprocket.
35   Align the marks on the front (left) camshafts with the marks on the engine. The right camshafts may have to be rotated counterclockwise about 50 degrees before final positioning.
36   Using a press or vise, compress the timing belt tensioner pushrod extremely slowly. Insert a metal pin, drill bit or Allen wrench through the holes in the pushrod and housing. Remove the tensioner from the press or vise and install it on the engine with the pin in place.
37   Align all of the timing marks and place the timing belt around the sprockets and pul-

leys in this order (**see illustration**):

Crankshaft
Idler
Camshafts
Tensioner

All engines

38   Again verify that all timing marks are aligned, then pull the pin from the tensioner, allowing it to snap into position.
39   Using a socket and breaker bar on the crankshaft pulley bolt, turn the crankshaft slowly (clockwise) through two complete revolutions (720-degrees). Recheck the timing marks. **Caution:** *If the timing marks are*

7.32 Timing belt alignment marks - 2.7L V6 engine

7.37 Timing belt alignment marks - 3.5L V6 engine

9.11 Camshaft sprocket/ timing chain alignment marks (2.7L V6 engine)

43050-2B-9.11 HAYNES

not aligned exactly as shown in **illustration 7.32 (2.7L) or 7.37 (3.5L)**, repeat the timing belt installation procedure. DO NOT start the engine until you're absolutely certain that the timing belt is installed correctly. Serious and costly engine damage could occur if the belt is installed incorrectly. Stop turning the crankshaft immediately if you feel solid resistance; the valves could be contacting the pistons.

40   Let the engine sit for five minutes at TDC, then check the protrusion of the tensioner rod. Compare your measurement to that listed in this Chapter's Specifications. If it isn't correct, replace the tensioner or determine if there's another problem.

41   Reinstall the remaining parts in the reverse order of removal.

8   Oil seals - replacement

Crankshaft front oil seal

1   Remove the timing belt and crankshaft sprocket (see Section 7). Slip off the sensor ring and the spacer behind it.

2   Carefully pry the seal out of the engine with a screwdriver or seal removal tool. If you use a screwdriver, wrap tape around the tip - don't scratch the housing bore or damage the crankshaft (if the crankshaft is damaged, the new seal will end up leaking).

3   Clean the bore in the engine and coat the outer edge of the new seal with engine oil or multi-purpose grease. Apply the same grease to the seal lip.

4   Using a seal driver or a socket with an outside diameter slightly smaller than the outside diameter of the seal, carefully drive the new seal into place with a hammer. Make sure it's installed squarely and driven in to the same depth as the original. Check the seal after installation to make sure the spring didn't pop out of place.

5   Reinstall the crankshaft timing sprocket and timing belt (see Section 7).

6   Run the engine and check for oil leaks at the front seal.

Camshaft oil seals

7   Remove the timing belt and camshaft sprocket(s) (see Section 7).

8   Remove the bolts and detach the rear timing belt cover.

9   Note how far the seal is seated in the bore, then carefully pry it out with a screwdriver. Wrap the screwdriver tip with tape - don't scratch the bore or damage the camshaft (if the camshaft is damaged, the new seal will end up leaking).

10   Clean the bore and coat the outer edge of the new seal with engine oil or multi-purpose grease. Apply multi-purpose grease to the seal lip.

11   Using a seal driver or a socket with an outside diameter slightly smaller than the outside diameter of the seal, carefully drive the new seal into place with a hammer. Make sure it's installed squarely and driven in to the same depth as the original.

12   Reinstall the rear timing belt cover and tighten the bolts.

13   Reinstall the camshaft sprocket(s) and timing belt (see Section 7). **Caution:** Verify that all timing marks are aligned as shown in Section 7. Major engine damage can occur if they are not.

14   Run the engine and check for oil leaks at the camshaft seal.

9   Camshafts and valvetrain - removal, inspection and installation

Removal

1   Position the engine at TDC (see Section 3), then remove the valve covers (see Section 4), the timing belt and the camshaft sprockets (see Section 7).

2   The following steps apply to the removal of each of the four camshafts.

3   Make sure the cam timing marks on the sprockets and engine are in alignment.

4   The camshafts are not interchangeable.

Mark them clearly to avoid confusion later.

5   Loosen the camshaft bearing cap bolts in 1/4-turn increments until they can be removed by hand. Start with the outer caps and work inward.

6   The bearing caps are marked I and E for intake and exhaust and numbered. Mark the caps with your own numbers if necessary. Remove the bearing caps and gently lift out the camshaft. **Note:** On 2.7L engines, the camshafts in each head must be removed together because they are connected by a timing chain.

7   Store the bearing caps in the correct order. If necessary, the valve hydraulic adjusters and rocker arms can now be removed. Be sure to store them separately so they can be reinstalled in their original locations.

Inspection

8   Refer to Chapter 2, Part A for camshaft, lifter and related component inspection procedures. Be sure to use the Specifications in this Part of Chapter 2 for the V6 engines.

Installation

Refer to illustration 9.11

9   Apply camshaft installation lubricant to the camshaft lobes and bearing journals.

10   Install the lash adjusters (and the rocker arms on 3.5L engines) in their original positions.

11   On 2.7L engines, install the timing chains around the sprockets of each pair of camshafts and set them in their journals. Make sure that the timing marks on the sprockets are aligned with the marks on the timing chains **(see illustration)**.

12   On 3.5L engines, simply place each camshaft in its original position and verify that the timing marks on the sprockets are lined up with the marks on the engine. The left (front cylinder bank) intake camshaft is marked "I," the left (front cylinder bank) exhaust camshaft is marked "E," the right (rear cylinder bank) intake camshaft is marked "J," the right (rear cylinder bank) exhaust camshaft is marked "H."

13   Install the bearing caps in numerical order with the arrows pointing toward the timing belt end of the engine.

14   Tighten the bearing cap bolts in 1/4-turn increments to the torque listed in this Chapter's Specifications. Start with the center cap and work your way out to the ends.

15   Refer to Section 8 and install a new camshaft oil seal if necessary.

16   Reinstall the remaining components in the reverse order of removal.

17   The remainder of the installation is the reverse of the disassembly sequence. **Caution:** Verify that all timing marks are aligned as shown in Section 7. Major engine damage can occur if they are not.

18   Run the engine, then check for leaks and proper operation. If the hydraulic valve adjusters have been somewhat drained, it may take several minutes for valvetrain noise to disappear.

10.18 Be sure the new head gaskets are positioned right side up (check all holes and coolant passages for correct alignment) and over the block dowels

10 Cylinder heads - removal, inspection and installation

Warning: *Wait until the engine is completely cool before beginning this procedure.*

Removal

1   Relieve the fuel system pressure (see Chapter 4), then disconnect the cable from the negative terminal of the battery (see Chapter 5, Section 1).

2   Drain the cooling system, including the engine block (see Chapter 1).

3   Remove the upper and lower intake manifolds (see Section 5).

4   Remove the exhaust manifold(s) (see Section 6).

5   Disconnect the timing belt from the camshaft sprocket(s) (see Section 7).

6   Remove the bolts holding the rear timing belt cover and remove it from the engine block and cylinder head(s) if it interferes on your engine.

7   Disconnect any remaining sensors or hoses.

8   Loosen the cylinder head bolts in 1/4-turn increments until they can be removed by hand, along with their hardened washers. Follow the reverse order of the recommended tightening sequence **(see illustration 10.21).**

9   Lift the cylinder head off the engine block. If the head is stuck, place a wood block against it and strike the wood with a hammer. **Caution:** *Don't pry between the head and block. The gasket surfaces may be damaged and leaks could result.*

10   Repeat the procedure for the other head if necessary.

Inspection

11   Use a precision straightedge to check the gasket surfaces of each head. Try to insert a feeler gauge of the maximum specified size between the straightedge and the head surface. If the clearance is more than that listed in this Chapter's Specifications, the head must be surface or replaced. Check the intake and exhaust manifold surfaces as well as the block surface.

12   Examine all areas of each head for signs of cracks and coolant leakage, especially around the valve seats.

Installation

Refer to illustrations 10.18 and 10.21

13   The mating surfaces of the cylinder heads and block must be perfectly clean when the heads are installed.

14   Use a gasket scraper to remove all traces of carbon and old gasket material, then clean the mating surfaces with brake cleaner. If there's oil on the mating surfaces when the head is installed, the gasket may not seal correctly and leaks could develop. When working on the block, stuff the cylinders with clean shop rags to keep out debris. Use a vacuum cleaner to remove material that falls into the cylinders.

15   Check the block and head mating surfaces for nicks, deep scratches and other damage. If damage is slight, it can be removed with a file; if it's excessive, machining may be the only alternative.

16   Use a tap of the correct size to chase the threads in the cylinder head bolt holes, then clean the holes with compressed air - make sure that nothing remains in the holes. **Warning:** *Wear eye protection when using compressed air!*

17   Mount each bolt in a vise and run a die down the threads to remove corrosion and restore the threads. Dirt, corrosion, sealant and damaged threads will affect torque readings. Replace any bolts that have been worn or damaged.

18   Position the new gaskets over the dowel pins in the block **(see illustration)**. The side of the gasket with the identification mark must face upward.

19   Carefully set the head on the block without disturbing the gasket.

20   Before installing the head bolts, apply a small amount of clean engine oil to the threads.

21   Install the bolts and tighten them finger tight. Following the recommended sequence, tighten the bolts to the torque listed in this Chapter's Specifications **(see illustration)**. If you don't have a torque angle gauge attachment, simply apply a paint mark to the socket you will be using to act as a reference point.

22   The remaining installation steps are the reverse of removal.

23   Refill the cooling system, change the oil and filter (see Chapter 1), run the engine and check for leaks.

11 Oil pan - removal and installation

Removal

Refer to illustration 11.9

1   Disconnect the cable from the negative terminal of the battery (see Chapter 5, Section 1).

2   Raise the vehicle and support it securely on jackstands

3   Remove the engine splash shields if so equipped.

10.21 V6 cylinder head bolt TIGHTENING sequence

43050-2B-10.23 HAYNES

11.9 There are two oil pans: an upper cast aluminum pan and a lower stamped steel pan

11.18 Upper oil pan bolt TIGHTENING sequence

4   Drain the engine oil and remove the oil filter. The oil pan is a two-part assembly, with an aluminum casting attached to the block and transaxle, and a lower stamped-steel pan section at the bottom.

5   Disconnect the exhaust pipe from both exhaust manifolds.

6   Disconnect the oxygen sensors (if necessary) and support the pipe temporarily. Unbolt the pipe at the rear, disconnect it from the hangers and remove it from the vehicle.

7   On 3.5L engines, remove the two lower bolts holding the upper aluminum oil pan section to the transaxle.

8   Remove any interfering components. These components vary by year and model; be sure you have enough clearance for oil pan removal.

9   Remove the bolts and detach the lower steel pan **(see illustration)**. If it's stuck, pry it loose very carefully with a small screwdriver or putty knife. Don't damage the mating surfaces of the pan or oil leaks could develop.

10   Remove the lower baffle (if equipped) and the oil pump strainer/pickup if necessary.

11   Remove the bolts securing the aluminum oil pan to the block. **Note:** *Some bolts are within the area formerly covered by the steel pan.*

Installation

Refer to illustrations 11.18 and 11.21

12   Use a scraper to remove all traces of old sealant from the block and oil pan. Clean the mating surfaces with lacquer thinner or acetone.

13   Make sure the threaded bolt holes in the block are clean.

14   Check the flange of the steel pan section for distortion, particularly around the bolt holes. If necessary, place the pan on a wood block and use a hammer to flatten and restore the gasket surface.

15   If the baffle had been removed, reinstall it now.

16   Clean the mating surfaces of the engine

block and aluminum pan section, being careful not to gouge the soft metal, which could lead to leaks.

17   Apply a 3/16-inch wide bead of RTV sealant to the aluminum pan section.

18   Install the aluminum pan section within five minutes and uniformly tighten the bolts to the torque listed in this Chapter's Specifications in several passes. Follow the tightening sequence shown **(see illustration)**.

19   Inspect the oil pump pick-up/strainer assembly for cracks and a blocked strainer. If the pick-up was removed, clean it with solvent or thinner and install it now, using a new gasket (see Section 12). Tighten the fasteners to the torque listed in this Chapter's Specifications.

20   Apply a 3/16-inch wide bead of RTV sealant to the flange of the steel oil pan section. **Note:** *The steel pan section must be installed within five minutes once the sealant has been applied.*

21   Carefully position the steel pan on the aluminum section and install the bolts, tightening them to the torque listed in this Chapter's Specifications in three or four steps. Follow

the tightening sequence shown **(see illustration)**.

22   The remainder of installation is the reverse of removal. Allow the sealant to set for at least two hours before adding new oil and a new oil filter.

23   Run the engine and check for oil pressure and leaks.

12   Oil pump - removal, inspection and installation

Removal

1   Disconnect the cable from the negative battery terminal (see Chapter 5, Section 1).

2   Refer to Section 7 and remove the timing belt.

3   Remove the oil filter. On 2.7L engines, remove the oil filter bracket and its gasket.

4   Remove the crankshaft sprocket.

5   On 3.5L engines, remove the sensor ring and the spacer behind it.

6   Remove the oil pressure relief plug, the spring and the valve plunger.

11.21 Lower oil pan bolt TIGHTENING sequence

12.13a Measure the driven rotor-to-body clearance with a feeler gauge

12.13b Measure the rotor side clearance with a precision straightedge and feeler gauge

7   Remove the oil pump case from the front of the engine.
8   Remove the cover from the oil pump and lift out the inner and outer gears.
9   Lift the cover off and remove the pump rotors.
10   Use a scraper to remove all traces of sealant and old gasket material from the pump body and engine block, then clean the mating surfaces with brake cleaner.

Inspection

Refer to illustrations 12.13a, 12.13b and 12.13c

11   Clean all components with solvent, then inspect them for wear and damage.
12   Check the oil pressure relief valve sliding surface and valve spring. If either the spring or the valve is damaged, they must be replaced as a set.
13   Check the clearance of the following components with a feeler gauge and compare the measurements to this Chapter's Specifications (see illustrations):

   a) *Driven rotor-to-oil pump body clearance*
   b) *Rotor side clearance*
   c) *Rotor tip clearance*

Installation

14   Pry the old crankshaft seal out with a screwdriver.
15   Apply multi-purpose grease or engine oil to the outer edge of the new seal and carefully drive it into place with a seal driver and a hammer. Also apply multi-purpose grease to the seal lip.
16   Place the drive and driven rotors into the pump body.
17   Pack the pump cavity with white grease and install the cover using either a new gasket or RTV sealant. Tighten the screws securely following a criss-cross pattern to the torque listed in this Chapter's Specifications.
18   Lubricate the oil pressure relief valve with engine oil and install the valve compo-

12.13c Measure the rotor tip clearance with a feeler gauge - note the rotor marks are facing out (when the pump body cover is installed, the marks will be against the cover)

nents in the pump body.
19   Use brake cleaner and a clean rag to remove all traces of oil from the case gasket surfaces.
20   Install the oil pump case with a new gasket. Install the mounting bolts and tighten them to the torque listed in this Chapter's Specifications in a criss-cross pattern.
21   Using a new gasket, install the oil pick-up tube and tighten the fasteners to the torque listed in this Chapter's Specifications.
22   Reinstall the remaining parts in the reverse order of removal. Pay special attention to aligning the timing belt marks (see Section 7).
23   Add oil, start the engine and check oil pressure and leaks.
24   Recheck the engine oil level.

13   Driveplate - removal and installation

Refer to Chapter 2, Part A for this procedure, but be sure to use the torque speci-

fications in this Part of Chapter 2 for the V6 engine. On automatic transaxle vehicles, there is an adapter plate used on the rear of the driveplate.

14   Rear main oil seal - replacement

Refer to Chapter 2, Part A for this procedure. Note that the V6 engine doesn't have a gasket between the seal retainer and the engine block. Instead, apply a 2 to 3 mm wide bead of RTV sealant to the retainer flange before attaching the retainer to the block. Also, be sure to use the torque specifications in this Part of Chapter 2 for the V6 engine.

15   Powertrain mounts - check and replacement

Refer to Chapter 2, Part A; the V6 engine mounts are slightly different in ways that don't significantly affect the check and replacement procedures.

Notes

Chapter 2 Part C
General engine overhaul procedures

Contents

Specifications

General
Displacement
- 2.4L four-cylinder ... 144 cubic inches (2,351 cc)
- 2.7L V6 ... 162 cubic inches (2,656 cc)
- 3.5L V6 ... 213 cubic inches (3,497 cc)

Minimum compression pressure (all models) ... 140 psi
Variation between cylinders (all models) ... 14 psi

Minimum oil pressure at curb idle, engine warm
- 2.4L engine ... 12 psi or more
- 2.7L engine ... 7 psi or more
- 3.5L engine ... 11 psi or more

Connecting rod side clearance
- Standard ... 0.004 to 0.010 inch (0.1 to 0.25 mm)
- Limit ... 0.016 inch (0.4 mm)

Torque specifications

Note: *One foot-pound (ft-lb) of torque is equivalent to 12 inch-pounds (in-lbs) of torque. Torque values below approximately 15 ft-lbs are expressed in inch-pounds, since most foot-pound torque wrenches are not accurate at these smaller values.*

	Ft-lbs (unless otherwise indicated)	Nm
Connecting rod bearing cap bolts		
2.4L 4 cylinder and 2.7L V6 engines		
Step 1	168 in-lbs	20
Step 2	Tighten an additional 90 degrees	
3.5L V6 engine		
Step 1	26	34
Step 2	Tighten an additional 90 degrees	
Main bearing cap bolts		
2.4L engine		
Step 1	168 in-lbs	20
Step 2	Tighten an additional 90 degrees	
2.7L engine		
M8 bolts		
Step 1	144 in-lbs	16
Step 2	Tighten an additional 90 degrees	
M10 bolts		
Step 1	22	30
Step 2	Tighten an additional 90 degrees	
3.5L engine	52 to 59	70 to 80

1.2 An engine block being bored - an engine rebuilder will use special machinery to recondition the cylinder bores

1.3 If the cylinders are bored, the machine shop will normally hone the engine on a machine like this

1   General information - engine overhaul

Refer to illustrations 1.2, 1.3, 1.4, 1.5, 1.6 and 1.7

Included in this portion of Chapter 2 are general information and diagnostic testing procedures for determining the overall mechanical condition of your engine.

The information ranges from advice concerning preparation for an overhaul and the purchase of replacement parts and/or components to detailed, step-by-step procedures covering removal and installation.

The following Sections have been written to help you determine whether your engine needs to be overhauled and how to remove and install it once you've determined it needs to be rebuilt. For information concerning in-vehicle engine repair, see Chapter 2A or 2B.

The Specifications included in this Part are general in nature and include only those necessary for testing the oil pressure, check-ing the engine compression, and bottom-end torque specifications. Refer to Chapter 2A or 2B for additional engine Specifications.

It's not always easy to determine when, or if, an engine should be completely overhauled, because a number of factors must be considered.

High mileage is not necessarily an indication that an overhaul is needed, while low mileage doesn't preclude the need for an overhaul. Frequency of servicing is probably the most important consideration. An engine that's had regular and frequent oil and filter changes, as well as other required maintenance, will most likely give many thousands of miles of reliable service. Conversely, a neglected engine may require an overhaul very early in its service life.

Excessive oil consumption is an indication that piston rings, valve seals and/or valve guides are in need of attention. Make sure that oil leaks aren't responsible before deciding that the rings and/or guides are bad. Per-form a cylinder compression check to determine the extent of the work required (see Section 3). Also check the vacuum readings under various conditions (see Section 4).

Check the oil pressure with a gauge installed in place of the oil pressure sending unit and compare it to this Chapter's Specifications (see Section 2). If it's extremely low, the bearings and/or oil pump are probably worn out.

Loss of power, rough running, knocking or metallic engine noises, excessive valve train noise and high fuel consumption rates may also point to the need for an overhaul, especially if they're all present at the same time. If a complete tune-up doesn't remedy the situation, major mechanical work is the only solution.

An engine overhaul involves restoring the internal parts to the specifications of a new engine. During an overhaul, the piston rings are replaced and the cylinder walls are reconditioned (rebored and/or honed) **(see**

1.4 A crankshaft having a main bearing journal ground

1.5 A machinist checks for a bent connecting rod, using specialized equipment

illustrations 1.2 and 1.3). If a rebore is done by an automotive machine shop, new oversize pistons will also be installed. The main bearings, connecting rod bearings and camshaft bearings are generally replaced with new ones and, if necessary, the crankshaft may be reground to restore the journals **(see illustration 1.4)**. Generally, the valves are serviced as well, since they're usually in less-than-perfect condition at this point. While the engine is being overhauled, other components, such as the distributor, starter and alternator, can be rebuilt as well. The end result should be a like-new engine that will give many trouble-free miles. **Note:** *Critical cooling system components such as the hoses, drivebelts, thermostat and water pump should be replaced with new parts when an engine is overhauled. The radiator should be checked carefully to ensure that it isn't clogged or leaking (see Chapter 3). If you purchase a rebuilt engine or short block, some rebuilders will not warranty their engines unless the radiator has*

been professionally flushed. Also, we don't recommend overhauling the oil pump - always install a new one when an engine is rebuilt.

Overhauling the internal components on today's engines is a difficult and time-consuming task which requires a significant amount of specialty tools and is best left to a professional engine rebuilder **(see illustrations 1.5, 1.6 and 1.7)**. A competent engine rebuilder will handle the inspection of your old parts and offer advice concerning the reconditioning or replacement of the original engine. Never purchase parts or have machine work done on other components until the block has been thoroughly inspected by a professional machine shop. As a general rule, time is the primary cost of an overhaul, especially since the vehicle may be tied up for a minimum of two weeks or more. Be aware that some engine builders only have the capability to rebuild the engine you bring them while other rebuilders have a large inventory of rebuilt exchange engines in stock. Also be

aware that many machine shops could take as much as two weeks time to completely rebuild your engine depending on shop workload. Sometimes it makes more sense to simply exchange your engine for another engine that's already rebuilt to save time.

2   Oil pressure check

Refer to illustrations 2.2 and 2.3

1   Low engine oil pressure can be a sign of an engine in need of rebuilding. A "low oil pressure" indicator (often called an "idiot light") is not a test of the oiling system. Such indicators only come on when the oil pressure is dangerously low. Even a factory oil pressure gauge in the instrument panel is only a relative indication, although much better for driver information than a warning light. A better test is with a mechanical (not electrical) oil pressure gauge.

1.6 A bore gauge being used to check the main bearing bore

1.7 Uneven piston wear like this indicates a bent connecting rod

2.2 On 3.5L V6 models, the oil pressure sending unit is located at the front of the engine at the oil filter

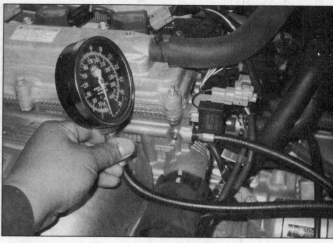

2.3 The oil pressure can be checked by removing the sending unit and installing a pressure gauge in its place

2   Locate the oil pressure indicator sending unit on the engine block **(see illustration)**.

3   Unscrew and remove the oil pressure sending unit, then screw in the hose for your oil pressure gauge **(see illustration)**. If necessary, install an adapter fitting. Use Teflon tape or thread sealant on the threads of the adapter and/or the fitting on the end of your gauge's hose.

4   Check the oil pressure with the engine running (normal operating temperature) at idle, and compare it to this Chapter's Specifications. If it's extremely low, the bearings and/or oil pump are probably worn out.

3   Cylinder compression check

Refer to illustration 3.6

1   A compression check will tell you what mechanical condition the upper end of your engine (pistons, rings, valves, head gaskets) is in. Specifically, it can tell you if the compression is down due to leakage caused by worn piston rings, defective valves and seats or a blown head gasket. **Note:** *The engine must be at normal operating temperature and the battery must be fully charged for this check.*

2   Begin by cleaning the area around the spark plugs before you remove them (compressed air should be used, if available). The idea is to prevent dirt from getting into the cylinders as the compression check is being done.

3   Disable the fuel pump circuit by relieving the fuel pressure (see Chapter 4, Section 2).

4   Disconnect the wires from the spark plugs (see Chapter 5), then remove all of the spark plugs from the engine (see Chapter 1). Disconnect the primary (low voltage) electrical connector(s) from the coil pack(s) (V6 engines).

5   Block the throttle wide open.

6   Install a compression gauge in the spark plug hole **(see illustration)**.

7   Crank the engine over at least seven compression strokes and watch the gauge. The compression should build up quickly in a healthy engine. Low compression on the first stroke, followed by gradually increasing pressure on successive strokes, indicates worn piston rings. A low compression reading on the first stroke, which doesn't build up during successive strokes, indicates leaking valves or a blown head gasket (a cracked head could also be the cause). Deposits on the undersides of the valve heads can also cause low compression. Record the highest gauge reading obtained.

8   Repeat the procedure for the remaining cylinders and compare the results to this Chapter's Specifications.

9   Add some engine oil (about three squirts from a plunger-type oil can) to each cylinder, through the spark plug hole, and repeat the test.

10   If the compression increases after the oil is added, the piston rings are definitely worn. If the compression doesn't increase significantly, the leakage is occurring at the valves or head gasket. Leakage past the valves may be caused by burned valve seats and/or faces or warped, cracked or bent valves.

11   If two adjacent cylinders have equally very low compression, there's a strong possibility that the head gasket between them is blown. The appearance of coolant in the combustion chambers or the crankcase would verify this condition.

12   If one cylinder is slightly lower than the others, and the engine has a slightly rough idle, a worn lobe on the camshaft could be the cause.

13   If the compression is unusually high, the combustion chambers are probably coated with carbon deposits. If that's the case, the cylinder head(s) should be removed and decarbonized.

14   If compression is way down or varies greatly between cylinders, it would be a good idea to have a leak-down test performed by an automotive repair shop. This test will pinpoint exactly where the leakage is occurring and how severe it is.

3.6 Use a compression gauge with a threaded fitting for the spark plug hole, not the type that requires hand pressure to maintain the seal - be sure to open the throttle valve as far as possible during the test

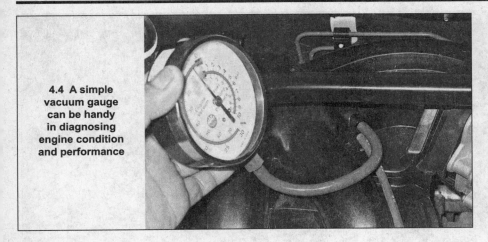

4.4 A simple vacuum gauge can be handy in diagnosing engine condition and performance

4   Vacuum gauge diagnostic checks

Refer to illustrations 4.4 and 4.6

A vacuum gauge provides inexpensive but valuable information about what is going on in the engine. You can check for worn rings or cylinder walls, leaking head or intake manifold gaskets, incorrect carburetor adjust-

ments, restricted exhaust, stuck or burned valves, weak valve springs, improper ignition or valve timing and ignition problems.

Unfortunately, vacuum gauge readings are easy to misinterpret, so they should be used in conjunction with other tests to confirm the diagnosis.

Both the absolute readings and the rate of needle movement are important for accu-

rate interpretation. Most gauges measure vacuum in inches of mercury (in-Hg). The following references to vacuum assume the diagnosis is being performed at sea level. As elevation increases (or atmospheric pressure decreases), the reading will decrease. For every 1,000-foot increase in elevation above approximately 2000 feet, the gauge readings will decrease about one inch of mercury.

Connect the vacuum gauge directly to the intake manifold vacuum, not to ported (throttle body) vacuum **(see illustration)**. Be sure no hoses are left disconnected during the test or false readings will result.

Before you begin the test, allow the engine to warm up completely. Block the wheels and set the parking brake. With the transmission in Park, start the engine and allow it to run at normal idle speed. **Warning:** *Keep your hands and the vacuum gauge clear of the fans and drivebelts.*

Read the vacuum gauge; an average, healthy engine should normally produce about 17 to 22 in-Hg with a fairly steady needle **(see illustration)**. Refer to the following vacuum gauge readings and what they indicate about the engine's condition:

1   A low steady reading usually indicates a

Low, steady reading   Low, fluctuating needle   Regular drops

Irregular drops   Rapid vibration

Large fluctuation   Slow fluctuation

STD-O-OBR HAYNES

4.6 Typical vacuum gauge readings

6.1 After tightly wrapping water-vulnerable components, use a spray cleaner on everything, with particular concentration on the greasiest areas, usually around the valve cover and lower edges of the block. If one section dries out, apply more cleaner

6.2 Depending on how dirty the engine is, let the cleaner soak in according to the directions, then hose off the grime and cleaner. Get the rinse water down into every area you can get at, then dry important components with a hair dryer or paper towels

leaking gasket between the intake manifold and cylinder head(s) or throttle body, a leaky vacuum hose, late ignition timing or incorrect camshaft timing. Check ignition timing with a timing light and eliminate all other possible causes, utilizing the tests provided in this Chapter before you remove the timing belt cover to check the timing marks.

2   If the reading is three to eight inches below normal and it fluctuates at that low reading, suspect an intake manifold gasket leak at an intake port or a faulty fuel injector.

3   If the needle has regular drops of about two-to-four inches at a steady rate, the valves are probably leaking. Perform a compression check or leak-down test to confirm this.

4   An irregular drop or down-flick of the needle can be caused by a sticking valve or an ignition misfire. Perform a compression check or leak-down test and read the spark plugs.

5   A rapid vibration of about four in-Hg vibration at idle combined with exhaust smoke indicates worn valve guides. Perform a leak-down test to confirm this. If the rapid vibration occurs with an increase in engine speed, check for a leaking intake manifold gasket or head gasket, weak valve springs, burned valves or ignition misfire.

6   A slight fluctuation, say one inch up and down, may mean ignition problems. Check all the usual tune-up items and, if necessary, run the engine on an ignition analyzer.

7   If there is a large fluctuation, perform a compression or leak-down test to look for a weak or dead cylinder or a blown head gasket.

8   If the needle moves slowly through a wide range, check for a clogged PCV system, incorrect idle fuel mixture, throttle body or intake manifold gasket leaks.

9   Check for a slow return after revving the engine by quickly snapping the throttle open until the engine reaches about 2,500 rpm and

let it shut. Normally the reading should drop to near zero, rise above normal idle reading (about 5 in-Hg over) and then return to the previous idle reading. If the vacuum returns slowly and doesn't peak when the throttle is snapped shut, the rings may be worn. If there is a long delay, look for a restricted exhaust system (often the muffler or catalytic converter). An easy way to check this is to temporarily disconnect the exhaust ahead of the suspected part and redo the test.

5   Engine rebuilding alternatives

The do-it-yourselfer is faced with a number of options when purchasing a rebuilt engine. The major considerations are cost, warranty, parts availability and the time required for the rebuilder to complete the project. The decision to replace the engine block, piston/connecting rod assemblies and crankshaft depends on the final inspection results of your engine. Only then can you make a cost effective decision whether to have your engine overhauled or simply purchase an exchange engine for your vehicle.

Some of the rebuilding alternatives include:

Individual parts - If the inspection procedures reveal that the engine block and most engine components are in reusable condition, purchasing individual parts and having a rebuilder rebuild your engine may be the most economical alternative. The block, crankshaft and piston/connecting rod assemblies should all be inspected carefully by a machine shop first.

Short block - A short block consists of an engine block with a crankshaft and piston/ connecting rod assemblies already installed. All new bearings are incorporated and all clearances will be correct. The existing camshafts, valve train components, cylinder head

and external parts can be bolted to the short block with little or no machine shop work necessary.

Long block - A long block consists of a short block plus an oil pump, oil pan, cylinder head, valve cover, camshaft and valve train components, timing sprockets and belt or gears and timing cover. All components are installed with new bearings, seals and gaskets incorporated throughout. The installation of manifolds and external parts is all that's necessary.

Low mileage used engines - Some companies now offer low mileage used engines that are a very cost effective way to get your vehicle up and running again. These engines often come from vehicles that have been in totaled in accidents or come from other countries that have a higher vehicle turn over rate. A low mileage used engine also usually has a similar warranty like the newly remanufactured engines.

Give careful thought to which alternative is best for you and discuss the situation with local automotive machine shops, auto parts dealers and experienced rebuilders before ordering or purchasing replacement parts.

6   Engine removal - methods and precautions

Refer to illustrations 6.1, 6.2, 6.3 and 6.4

If you've decided that an engine must be removed for overhaul or major repair work, several preliminary steps should be taken. Read all removal and installation procedures carefully prior to committing this job. These engines are removed by lowering to the floor, then raising the vehicle sufficiently to slide it out; this will require a vehicle hoist.

Locating a suitable place to work is extremely important. Adequate work space,

6.3 Get an engine hoist that's strong enough to easily lift your engine in and out of the engine compartment; an adapter, like the one shown here, can be used to change the angle of the engine as it's being removed or installed

6.4 Get an engine stand sturdy enough to firmly support the engine while you're working on it. Stay away from three-wheeled models - they have a tendency to tip over more easily, so get a four-wheeled unit

along with storage space for the vehicle, will be needed. If a shop or garage isn't available, at the very least a flat, level, clean work surface made of concrete or asphalt is required. Cleaning the engine compartment and engine before beginning the removal procedure will help keep tools clean and organized **(see illustrations 6.1 and 6.2)**.

An engine hoist or A-frame will also be necessary. Make sure the equipment is rated in excess of the combined weight of the engine and transmission. Safety is of primary importance, considering the potential hazards involved in lifting the engine out of the vehicle.

If you're a novice at engine removal, get at least one helper. One person cannot easily do all the things you need to do to lower a big heavy engine out of the engine compartment. Also helpful is to seek advice and assistance from someone who's experienced in engine removal.

Plan the operation ahead of time. Arrange for or obtain all of the tools and equipment you'll need prior to beginning the job **(see illustrations 6.3 and 6.4)**. Some of the equipment necessary to perform engine removal and installation safely and with relative ease are a heavy duty floor jack, complete sets of wrenches and sockets as described in the front of this manual, wooden blocks, plenty of rags and cleaning solvent for mopping up spilled oil, coolant and gasoline. If the hoist must be rented, make sure that you arrange for it in advance and have everything disconnected and/or removed before bringing

the hoist home. This will save you money and time.

Plan for the vehicle to be out of use for quite a while. A machine shop can do the work that is beyond the scope of the home mechanic. Machine shops often have a busy schedule, so before removing the engine, consult the shop for an estimate of how long it will take to rebuild or repair the components that may need work.

7   Engine - removal and installation

Warning: *The engine must be completely cool before beginning this procedure.*
Note 1: *Engine removal on these vehicles is a difficult job, especially for the do-it-yourself mechanic working at home. Because of the vehicle's design, the manufacturer states that the engine and transaxle have to be removed as a unit from the bottom of the vehicle, not the top. With a floor jack and jackstands, the vehicle can't be raised high enough or supported safely enough for the engine/transaxle assembly to slide out from underneath. The manufacturer recommends that removal of the engine/transaxle assembly only be performed with the use of a frame-contact type vehicle hoist.*
Note 2: *Keep in mind that during this procedure you'll have to adjust the height of the vehicle with the vehicle hoist to perform certain operations.*

Removal

Refer to illustrations 7.4 and 7.21

1   Park the vehicle on a frame-contact type vehicle hoist, then engage the arms of the hoist with the jacking points of the vehicle. Raise the hoist arms until they contact the vehicle, but not so much that the wheels come off the ground. Loosen the front wheel lug nuts and the driveaxle/hub nuts.

2   Relieve the fuel system pressure (see Chapter 4).
3   Remove the battery (see Chapter 5). Remove the air inlet assembly and air filter housing (see Chapter 4).
4   Clearly label and disconnect all vacuum lines, emissions hoses, electrical connectors and ground straps connecting the engine and transaxle to the vehicle. Masking tape and/or a touch up paint applicator work well for marking items **(see illustration)**. Take instant photos or sketch the locations of components and brackets, if necessary.
5   Drain the coolant, transaxle fluid and the engine oil (see Chapter 1).
6   Disconnect the cooler hoses from the automatic transaxle. Plug the hose ends to prevent leakage and contamination.
7   Refer to Chapter 3 and remove the entire radiator assembly.
8   Disconnect both heater hoses.
9   Disconnect the accelerator cable (on models so equipped).
10   Disconnect the fuel lines at the fuel rail (see Chapter 4).

7.4 Label both ends of each wire or hose before disconnecting it

7.21 The four main subframe bolts support the entire engine and transaxle assembly

b) *Attach the transaxle to the engine following the procedure described in Chapter 7.*
c) *When installing the subframe, tighten the subframe mounting bolts to the torque listed in the Chapter 10 Specifications.*
d) *Tighten the driveaxle/hub nuts to the torque listed in the Chapter 8 Specifications. Tighten all steering and suspension fasteners to the torque listed in the Chapter 10 Specifications. Tighten the wheel lug nuts to the torque listed in the Chapter 1 Specifications.*
e) *Refill the engine coolant, oil, power steering and transaxle fluids (see Chapter 1).*
f) *Reconnect the battery (see Chapter 5, Section 1).*
g) *Run the engine and check for proper operation and leaks. Shut off the engine and recheck fluid levels.*

11   If you're working on a model with a manual transaxle, remove the clutch release cylinder and support it out of the way with a piece of wire. Don't disconnect the hose from the release cylinder. **Caution:** *Do not depress the clutch pedal while the release cylinder is removed.*
12   Detach the shift cable(s) from the transaxle.
13   Disconnect the power steering hoses from the pump. Plug the hose ends to prevent leakage and contamination.
14   Disconnect the steering shaft U-joint after pulling back the plastic cover and making match marks with dabs of paint (see Chapter 10).
15   Raise the vehicle on the hoist and remove the front wheels.
16   Remove the driveaxles (see Chapter 8).
17   Remove the front section of the exhaust system.
18   Support the engine/transaxle assembly from above with a hoist. Attach the hoist chain to the lifting brackets. If no lifting brackets or hooks are present, lifting hooks may be available from your local auto parts store or dealer parts department. If not, you will have to fasten the chain to some substantial parts of the engine - ones that are strong enough to take the weight, but in locations that will provide good balance. If you're attaching a chain to a stud on the engine, or are using a bolt passing through the chain and into a threaded hole, place a washer between the nut or bolt head and the chain and tighten the nut or bolt securely. **Warning:** *Do not place any part of your body under the engine/transaxle when it's supported only by a hoist or other lifting device.*
19   Take up the slack until there is slight tension on the hoist. Position the chain on the hoist so it balances the engine and the transaxle level with the vehicle. **Note 1:** *Depending on the design of the engine hoist, it may be helpful to position the hoist from the side of the vehicle, so that when the engine/transaxle assembly is lowered, it will*

fit between the legs of the hoist. **Note 2:** *The chain or sling must be long enough to allow the engine hoist to lower the engine/transaxle assembly to the ground, without letting the hoist arm contact the vehicle.*
20   Recheck to be sure nothing is still connecting the engine or transaxle to the vehicle. Disconnect and label anything still remaining.
21   Remove the subframe mounting bolts **(see illustration)**. Remove the two lower brackets that attach the engine and transaxle to the body. Leave the two upper "roll stop" mounts connected at this time.
22   Lower the engine and transaxle assembly with the hoist and then disconnect the remaining front and rear engine mounts.
23   Lower the engine/transaxle assembly completely. Once the engine/transaxle assembly is on the floor, disconnect the engine hoist and raise the vehicle until it clears the engine/transaxle assembly.
24   Reconnect the belt or sling to support the engine and transaxle.
25   Raise the engine/transaxle assembly, then support the engine with blocks of wood or another floor jack, while leaving the chain or sling attached. Support the transaxle with another floor jack, preferably one with a transaxle jack head adapter. At this point the transfer case can be unbolted and removed (4WD models - see Chapter 7C). Be very careful to ensure that the components are supported securely so they won't topple off their supports during disconnection.
26   Remove the transaxle-to-engine bolts and separate the transaxle from the engine.
27   Reconnect the lifting chain to the engine, then raise the engine and attach it to an engine stand.

Installation

28   Installation is the reverse of removal, noting the following points:

a) *Check the engine/transaxle mounts. If they're worn or damaged, replace them.*

8   Engine overhaul - disassembly sequence

1   It's much easier to disassemble the engine if it's mounted on a portable engine stand. A stand can often be rented quite cheaply from an equipment rental yard. Before the engine is mounted on a stand, the driveplate should be removed from the engine.
2   If a stand isn't available, it's possible to remove the external engine components with it blocked up on the floor. Be extra careful not to tip or drop the engine when working without a stand.
3   If you're going to obtain a rebuilt engine, all external components must come off first, to be transferred to the replacement engine. These components include:

   Driveplate
   Ignition system components
   Emissions-related components
   Engine mounts and mount brackets
   Fuel injection components
   Intake/exhaust manifolds
   Oil filter
   Thermostat and housing assembly
   Water pump

Note: *When removing the external components from the engine, pay close attention to details that may be helpful or important during installation. Note the installed position of gaskets, seals, spacers, pins, brackets, washers, bolts and other small items.*
4   If you're going to obtain a short block (assembled engine block, crankshaft, pistons and connecting rods), then you should remove the timing belt, cylinder head, oil pan, oil pump pick-up tube, oil pump and water pump from your engine so that you can turn in your old short block to the rebuilder as a core. See *Engine rebuilding alternatives* for additional information regarding the different possibilities to be considered.

10.1 Before you try to remove the pistons, use a ridge reamer to remove the raised material (ridge) from the top of the cylinders

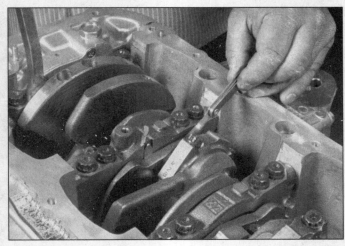

10.3 Checking the connecting rod endplay (side clearance)

9   Balance shafts (four-cylinder models) - removal and installation

Note: *This procedure assumes that the engine has been removed from the vehicle and the driveplate, timing belt and oil pan have also been removed (see Chapter 2A).*

Removal

1   The balance shafts are located in the lower section of the engine block. The right balance shaft is driven from the crankshaft by its own small inner belt which has its own tensioner. The left balance shaft is connected to the rear of the oil pump that is driven by the main timing belt. The shafts counterbalance moving masses within the engine and result in an engine with less vibration.

2   Remove the timing belt and tensioner from the engine block (see Chapter 2A). Remove the inner timing belt and its tensioner.

3   Remove the oil pump (see Chapter 2A).

4   Remove both balance shafts by sliding them straight out the front of the block. Take care to avoid damaging the balance shaft bearings.

Cleaning and inspection

5   Clean all components with solvent and dry thoroughly. Inspect all components for damage and wear. Pay close attention to the belt, sprocket teeth and the bearing surfaces of the balance shafts. Replace defective parts as necessary.

Installation

6   Lubricate the balance shafts with clean engine oil; install them into the lower block.

7   The remainder of installation is the reverse of removal.

10   Pistons and connecting rods - removal and installation

Removal

Refer to illustrations 10.1, 10.3 and 10.4

Note: *Prior to removing the piston/connecting rod assemblies, remove the cylinder head, oil pan, and the upper (aluminum) oil pan (see Chapter 2A or 2B). Also, on four-cylinder engines, remove the balance shafts (see Section 9).*

1   Use your fingernail to feel if a ridge has formed at the upper limit of ring travel (about 1/4-inch down from the top of each cylinder). If carbon deposits or cylinder wear have produced ridges, they must be completely removed with a special tool **(see illustration)**. Follow the manufacturer's instructions provided with the tool. Failure to remove the ridges before attempting to remove the piston/connecting rod assemblies may result in piston breakage.

2   After the cylinder ridges have been removed, turn the engine so the crankshaft is facing up.

3   Before the pistons and connecting rods are removed, check the connecting rod endplay with feeler gauges. Slide them between the first connecting rod and the crankshaft throw until the play is removed **(see illustration)**. Repeat this procedure for each connecting rod. The endplay is equal to the thickness of the feeler gauge(s). Check with an automotive machine shop for the endplay service limit. If the play exceeds the service limit, new connecting rods will be required. If new rods (or a new crankshaft) are installed, the endplay may fall under the minimum allowable clearance. If it does, the rods will have to be machined to restore it. If necessary, consult an automotive machine shop for advice.

4   Check the connecting rods and caps for identification marks **(see illustration)**. If

they aren't plainly marked, use a small center-punch to make the appropriate number of indentations on each rod and cap (1, 2, 3, etc., depending on the cylinder they're associated with).

5   Loosen each of the connecting rod cap bolts 1/2-turn at a time until they can be removed by hand. Remove the number one connecting rod cap and bearing insert. Don't drop the bearing insert out of the cap.

6   Remove the bearing insert and push the connecting rod/piston assembly out through the top of the engine. Use a wooden or plastic hammer handle to push on the upper bearing surface in the connecting rod. Be careful to avoid scratching the crankshaft bearing journals with the rod bolts. **Note:** *Slip a sort section of rubber hose over the rod bolts before pushing the piston/rod assemblies out to make sure the crankshaft isn't damaged.*

10.4 If the connecting rods and caps are not marked, use a center punch or numbered impression stamps to mark the caps to the rods by cylinder number - do not confuse the markings shown here with rod numbers; these are bearing size identifications

10.13 Install the piston ring into the cylinder, then push it down into position using a piston so the ring will be square in the cylinder

10.14 With the ring square in the cylinder, measure the ring end gap with a feeler gauge

7   If resistance is felt, double-check to make sure that the entire ridge was removed from the cylinder.

8   Repeat the procedure for the remaining cylinders.

9   After removal, reassemble the connecting rod caps and bearing inserts in their respective connecting rods and install the cap bolts finger tight. Leaving the old bearing inserts in place until reassembly will help prevent the connecting rod bearing surfaces from being accidentally nicked or gouged.

10   The pistons and connecting rods are now ready for inspection and overhaul at an automotive machine shop.

Piston ring installation

Refer to illustrations 10.13, 10.14, 10.15, 10.19a, 10.19b and 10.22

11   Before installing the new piston rings, the ring end gaps must be checked. It's assumed that the piston ring side clearance has been checked and verified correct. **Note:** *Pistons and rods can only be installed after the crankshaft has been installed (see Section 11).*

12   Lay out the piston/connecting rod assemblies and the new ring sets so the ring sets will be matched with the same piston and cylinder during the end gap measurement and engine assembly.

13   Insert the top (number one) ring into the first cylinder and square it up with the cylinder walls by pushing it in with the top of the piston **(see illustration)**. The ring should be near the bottom of the cylinder, at the lower limit of ring travel.

14   To measure the end gap, slip feeler gauges between the ends of the ring until a gauge equal to the gap width is found **(see illustration)**. The feeler gauge should slide between the ring ends with a slight amount of drag. Check with an automotive machine shop for the correct end gap for your engine. If the gap is larger or smaller than specified, double-check to make sure you have the cor-

rect rings before proceeding.

15   If the gap is too small, it must be enlarged or the ring ends may come in contact with each other during engine operation, which can cause serious damage to the engine. The end gap can be increased by filing the ring ends very carefully with a fine file. Mount the file in a vise equipped with soft jaws, slip the ring over the file with the ends contacting the file face and slowly move the ring to remove material from the ends. When performing this operation, file only by pushing the ring from the outside end of the file towards the vise **(see illustration)**.

16   Excess end gap isn't critical unless it's greater than approximately 0.030-inch. Again, double-check to make sure you have the correct ring type.

17   Repeat the procedure for each ring that will be installed in the first cylinder and for each ring in the remaining cylinders. Remember to keep rings, pistons and cylinders matched up.

18   Once the ring end gaps have been checked/corrected, the rings can be installed on the pistons.

19   The oil control ring (lowest one on the piston) is usually installed first. It's composed of three separate components. Slip the spacer/expander into the groove **(see illustration)**. If an anti-rotation tang is used, make sure it's inserted into the drilled hole in the ring groove. Next, install the upper side rail in the same manner **(see illustration)**. Don't use a piston ring installation tool on the oil ring side rails, as they may be damaged. Instead, place one end of the side rail into the groove between the spacer/expander and the ring land, hold it firmly in place and slide a finger around the piston while pushing the rail into the groove. Finally, install the lower side rail.

20   After the three oil ring components have been installed, check to make sure that both the upper and lower side rails can be rotated smoothly inside the ring grooves.

21   The number two (middle) ring is installed next. It's usually stamped with a mark that must face up, toward the top of the piston. Do not mix up the top and middle rings, as they have different cross-sections. **Note:** *Always follow the instructions printed on the ring package or box - different manufacturers may*

10.15 If the ring end gap is too small, clamp a file in a vise as shown and file the piston ring ends - be sure to file the ends squarely and finish by removing all raised material or burrs with a fine stone

10.19a Installing the spacer/expander in the oil ring groove

10.19b DO NOT use a piston ring installation tool when installing the oil control side rails

require different approaches.

22 Use a piston ring installation tool and make sure the identification mark is facing the top of the piston, then slip the ring into the middle groove on the piston **(see illustration)**. Don't expand the ring any more than necessary to slide it over the piston.

23 Install the number one (top) ring in the same manner. Make sure the mark is facing up. Be careful not to confuse the number one and number two rings.

24 Repeat the procedure for the remaining pistons and rings.

Installation

25 Before installing the piston/connecting rod assemblies, the cylinder walls must be perfectly clean, the top edge of each cylinder bore must be chamfered, and the crankshaft must be in place.

26 Remove the cap from the end of the number one connecting rod (refer to the marks made during removal - the bearing locating tangs must be together).

27 Remove the original bearing inserts and wipe the bearing surfaces of the connecting rod and cap with a clean, lint-free cloth. They must be kept spotlessly clean.

Connecting rod bearing oil clearance check

Refer to illustrations 10.30, 10.35, 10.37 and 10.41

28 Clean the rear of the new upper bearing insert, then lay it in place in the connecting rod. Make sure the tab on the bearing fits into the recess in the rod. Don't hammer the bearing insert into place and be very careful not to nick or gouge the bearing face. Don't lubricate the bearing at this time.

29 Clean the back of the other bearing insert and install it in the rod cap. Again, make sure the tab on the bearing fits into the recess in the cap, and don't apply any lubricant. It's critically important that the mating surfaces of the bearing and connecting rod are perfectly clean and oil free when they're assembled.

30 Position the piston ring gaps around the piston as shown **(see illustration)**.

31 Lubricate the piston and rings with clean engine oil and attach a piston ring compressor to the piston. Leave the skirt protruding about 1/4-inch to guide the piston into the cylinder. The rings must be compressed until they're flush with the piston. **Note:** *Slip pieces of rubber hose about 6 inches long over each rod bolt. These will guide the connecting rod into position and keep the rod bolts from damaging the crankshaft.*

32 Rotate the crankshaft until the number

10.22 Use a piston ring installation tool to install the number 2 and the number 1 (top) rings - be sure the directional mark on the piston ring(s) is facing toward the top of the piston

10.30 Position the piston ring end gaps as shown here before installing the piston/connecting rod assemblies into the engine

A Top compression ring gap and oil ring spacer gap
B Second compression ring
C Upper oil ring gap
D Lower oil ring gap

ENGINE BEARING ANALYSIS

Debris

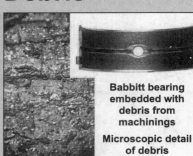

Babbitt bearing embedded with debris from machinings

Microscopic detail of debris

Microscopic detail of gouges

Overplated copper alloy bearing gouged by cast iron debris

Aluminum bearing embedded with glass beads

Microscopic detail of glass beads

Damaged lining caused by dirt left on the bearing back

Misassembly

Result of a lower half assembled as an upper - blocking the oil flow

Excessive oil clearance is indicated by a short contact arc

Polished and oil-stained backs are a result of a poor fit in the housing bore

Result of a wrong, reversed, or shifted cap

Overloading

Damage from excessive idling which resulted in an oil film unable to support the load imposed

Damaged upper connecting rod bearings caused by engine lugging; the lower main bearings (not shown) were similarly affected

The damage shown in these upper and lower connecting rod bearings was caused by engine operation at a higher-than-rated speed under load

Misalignment

A warped crankshaft caused this pattern of severe wear in the center, diminishing toward the ends

A poorly finished crankshaft caused the equally spaced scoring shown

A bent connecting rod led to the damage in the "V" pattern

A tapered housing bore caused the damage along one edge of this pair

Lubrication

Result of dry start: The bearings on the left, farthest from the oil pump, show more damage

Result of a low oil supply or oil starvation

Severe wear as a result of inadequate oil clearance

Corrosion

Microscopic detail of corrosion

Corrosion is an acid attack on the bearing lining generally caused by inadequate maintenance, extremely hot or cold operation, or inferior oils or fuels

Microscopic detail of cavitation

Example of cavitation - a surface erosion caused by pressure changes in the oil film

Damage from excessive thrust or insufficient axial clearance

Bearing affected by oil dilution caused by excessive blow-by or a rich mixture

10.35 Use a plastic or wooden hammer handle to push the piston into the cylinder

10.37 Place Plastigage on each connecting rod bearing journal parallel to the crankshaft centerline

one connecting rod journal is at BDC (bottom dead center) and apply a liberal coat of engine oil to the cylinder walls.

33   With the mark on top of the piston facing the front (timing belt end) of the engine, gently insert the piston/connecting rod assembly into the number one cylinder bore and rest the bottom edge of the ring compressor on the engine block. **Note:** *The connecting rod also has a mark on it that must face the correct direction.*

34   Tap the top edge of the ring compressor to make sure it's contacting the block around its entire circumference.

35   Gently tap on the top of the piston with the end of a wooden or plastic hammer handle **(see illustration)** while guiding the end of the connecting rod into place on the crankshaft journal. The piston rings may try to pop out of the ring compressor just before entering the cylinder bore, so keep some downward pressure on the ring compressor. Work slowly, and if any resistance is felt as the piston enters the cylinder, stop immediately. Find out what's hanging up and fix it before proceeding. Do not, for any reason, force the piston into the cylinder - you might break a ring and/or the piston.

36   Once the piston/connecting rod assembly is installed, the connecting rod bearing oil clearance must be checked before the rod cap is permanently installed.

37   Cut a piece of the appropriate size Plastigage slightly shorter than the width of the connecting rod bearing and lay it in place on the number one connecting rod journal, parallel with the journal axis **(see illustration)**.

38   Clean the connecting rod cap bearing face and install the rod cap. Make sure the mating mark on the cap is on the same side as the mark on the connecting rod.

39   Install the rod bolts and tighten them to the torque listed in this Chapter's Specifications in two steps. **Note:** *Use a thin-wall socket to avoid erroneous torque readings that can result if the socket is wedged between the rod*

cap and the bolt. If the socket tends to wedge itself between the fastener and the cap, lift up on it slightly until it no longer contacts the cap. DO NOT rotate the crankshaft at any time during this operation.

40   Remove the fasteners and detach the rod cap, being very careful not to disturb the Plastigage.

41   Compare the width of the crushed Plastigage to the scale printed on the Plastigage envelope to obtain the oil clearance **(see illustration)**. The connecting rod oil clearance is usually about 0.001 to 0.002 inch. Consult an automotive machine shop for the clearance specified for the rod bearings on your engine.

42   If the clearance is not as specified, the bearing inserts may be the wrong size (which means different ones will be required). Before deciding that different inserts are needed, make sure that no dirt or oil was between the bearing inserts and the connecting rod or cap when the clearance was measured. Also, recheck the journal diameter. If the Plastigage was wider at one end than the other, the journal may be tapered. If the clearance still exceeds the limit specified, the bearing will have to be replaced with an undersize bear-

ing. **Caution:** *When installing a new crankshaft always use a standard size bearing.*

Final installation

43   Carefully scrape all traces of the Plastigage material off the rod journal and/or bearing face. Be very careful not to scratch the bearing - use your fingernail or the edge of a plastic card.

44   Make sure the bearing faces are perfectly clean, then apply a uniform layer of clean moly-base grease or engine assembly lube to both of them. You'll have to push the piston into the cylinder to expose the face of the bearing insert in the connecting rod.

45   Slide the connecting rod back into place on the journal, install the rod cap and bolts, tightening them to the torque listed in this Chapter's Specifications in two steps.

46   Repeat the entire procedure for the remaining pistons/connecting rods.

47   The important points to remember are:

a) *Keep the back sides of the bearing inserts and the insides of the connecting rods and caps perfectly clean when assembling them.*

10.41 Use the scale on the Plastigage package to determine the bearing oil clearance - be sure to measure the widest part of the Plastigage and use the correct scale; it comes with both standard and metric scales

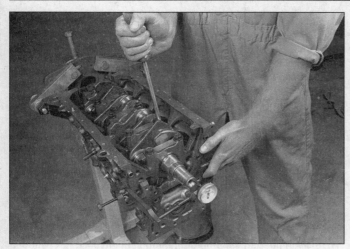

11.1 Checking crankshaft endplay with a dial indicator

11.3 Checking crankshaft endplay with feeler gauges at the thrust bearing journal

b) *Make sure you have the correct piston/ rod assembly for each cylinder.*

c) *The mark on the piston must face the front (timing belt end) of the engine.*

d) *Lubricate the cylinder walls liberally with clean oil.*

e) *Lubricate the bearing faces when installing the rod caps after the oil clearance has been checked.*

48   After all the piston/connecting rod assemblies have been correctly installed, rotate the crankshaft a number of times by hand to check for any obvious binding.

49   As a final step, check the connecting rod endplay again. If it was correct before disassembly and the original crankshaft and rods were reinstalled, it should still be correct. If new rods or a new crankshaft were installed, the endplay may be inadequate. If so, the rods will have to be removed and taken to an automotive machine shop for resizing.

11   Crankshaft - removal and installation

Removal

Refer to illustrations 11.1 and 11.3

Note: *The crankshaft can be removed only after the engine has been removed from the vehicle. It's assumed that the driveplate, crankshaft pulley, timing belt, oil pan, oil pump body, oil filter and piston/connecting rod assemblies have already been removed. The rear main oil seal retainer must be unbolted and separated from the block before proceeding with crankshaft removal.*

1   Before the crankshaft is removed, measure the endplay. Mount a dial indicator with the indicator in line with the crankshaft and touching the end of the crankshaft **(see illustration)**.

2   Pry the crankshaft all the way to the rear and zero the dial indicator. Next, pry the crankshaft to the front as far as possible and check the reading on the dial indicator. The distance traveled is the endplay. A typical crankshaft endplay will fall between 0.003 to 0.010-inch. If it's greater than that, check the crankshaft thrust surfaces for wear after it's removed. If no wear is evident, new main bearings should correct the endplay.

3   If a dial indicator isn't available, feeler gauges can be used. Gently pry the crankshaft all the way to the front of the engine. Slip feeler gauges between the crankshaft and the front face of the thrust bearing or washer to determine the clearance **(see illustration)**.

4   Loosen the main bearing cap bolts 1/4-turn at a time each, until they can be removed by hand. On 2.7L V6 engines, loosen the bolts in the reverse order of the tightening sequence **(see illustration 11.19)**.

5   Gently tap the main bearing caps with a soft-face hammer. Pull the main bearing cap straight up and off the cylinder block. Try not to drop the bearing inserts if they come out with the cap. **Note:** *2.7L V6 engine uses a main bearing cap support that must be removed prior to removing the main caps.*

6   Carefully lift the crankshaft out of the engine. It may be a good idea to have an assistant available, since the crankshaft is quite heavy and awkward to handle. With the bearing inserts in place inside the engine block and main bearing caps, reinstall the main bearing caps onto the engine block and tighten the bolts finger tight. Make sure you install the main bearing cap(s) with the arrow facing the front end of the engine.

Installation - main bearing oil clearance check

Refer to illustrations 11.17, 11.19 and 11.21

7   Crankshaft installation is the first step in engine reassembly. It's assumed at this point that the engine block and crankshaft have been cleaned, inspected and repaired or reconditioned.

8   Position the engine block with the bottom facing up.

9   Remove the mounting bolts and lift off the main bearing cap(s).

10   If they're still in place, remove the original bearing inserts from the block and from the main bearing caps. Wipe the bearing surfaces of the block and main bearing caps with a clean, lint-free cloth. They must be kept spotlessly clean. This is critical for determining the correct bearing oil clearance.

11   Without mixing them up, clean the backs of the new upper main bearing inserts (with grooves and oil holes) and lay one in each main bearing saddle in the block. Each upper bearing has an oil groove and oil hole in it. **Caution:** *The oil holes in the block must line up with the oil holes in the upper bearing inserts.* Install the thrust washers with the grooved side facing out. Clean the back sides of the lower main bearing inserts (without grooves) and lay them in the corresponding caps. Make sure the tab on the bearing insert fits into the recess in the block or main bearing cap. **Caution:** *Do not hammer the bearing insert into place and don't nick or gouge the bearing faces. DO NOT apply any lubrication at this time.*

12   Clean the faces of the bearing inserts in the block and the crankshaft main bearing journals with a clean, lint-free cloth.

13   Check or clean the oil holes in the crankshaft, as any dirt here can go only one way - straight through the new bearings.

14   Once you're certain the crankshaft is clean, carefully lay it in position in the cylinder block.

15   Before the crankshaft can be permanently installed, the main bearing oil clearance must be checked.

16   Cut several strips of the appropriate size of Plastigage (they must be slightly shorter than the width of the main bearing journal).

11.17 Place the Plastigage onto the crankshaft bearing journal as shown

43050-2C-11.19 HAYNES

11.19 Main bearing cap bolt tightening sequence - 2.7L V6 models only (other models require only that the main bearing caps be tightened evenly)

17   Place one piece on each crankshaft main bearing journal, parallel with the journal axis (see illustration).
18   Clean the faces of the bearing inserts in the main bearing caps. Hold the bearing inserts in place and install the caps onto the crankshaft and cylinder block. DO NOT disturb the Plastigage. Make sure you install the main bearing cap with the arrow facing the front of the engine.
19   Apply clean engine oil to all bolt threads prior to installation, then install all bolts finger-tight. Tighten the main bearing cap bolts in the sequence shown (see illustration), progressing in two steps, to the torque listed in this Chapter's Specifications. DO NOT rotate the crankshaft at any time during this operation.
20   Remove the bolts in the reverse order of the tightening sequence and carefully lift the main bearing cap straight up and off the block. Do not disturb the Plastigage or rotate the crankshaft. If the main bearing cap is difficult to remove, tap it gently from side-to-side with a soft-face hammer to loosen it.
21   Compare the width of the crushed Plastigage on each journal to the scale printed on the Plastigage envelope to determine the main bearing oil clearance (see illustration). A typical main bearing oil clearance should fall between 0.0015 to 0.0023-inch. Check with an automotive machine shop for the clearance specified for your engine.
22   If the clearance is not as specified, the bearing inserts may be the wrong size (which means different ones will be required). Before deciding if different inserts are needed, make sure that no dirt or oil was between the bearing inserts and the cap or block when the clearance was measured. If the Plastigage was wider at one end than the other, the crankshaft journal may be tapered. If the clearance still exceeds the limit specified, the bearing insert(s) will have to be replaced with an undersize bearing insert(s). Caution: When installing a new crankshaft, always

install a standard bearing insert set.
23   Carefully scrape all traces of the Plastigage material off the main bearing journals and/or the bearing insert faces. Be sure to remove all residue from the oil holes. Use your fingernail or the edge of a plastic card - don't nick or scratch the bearing faces.

Final installation

24   Carefully lift the crankshaft out of the cylinder block.
25   Clean the bearing insert faces in the cylinder block, then apply a thin, uniform layer of moly-base grease or engine assembly lube to each of the bearing surfaces. Be sure to coat the thrust faces as well as the journal face of the thrust bearing. Note: The thrust bearings are installed in the no. 3 main cap/saddle position (counting from the front) on all engines covered by this manual.
26   Make sure the crankshaft journals are clean, then lay the crankshaft back in place in the cylinder block.
27   Clean the bearing insert faces and apply the same lubricant to them.

28   Hold the bearing inserts in place and install the main bearing caps on the crankshaft and cylinder block. Tap the bearing caps into place with a brass punch or a soft-face hammer. On 2.7L V6 engines, install the bearing support.
29   Apply clean engine oil to the bolt threads, wipe off any excess oil and install the bolts finger-tight.
30   Tighten the main bearing cap bolts, in sequence (see illustration 11.19), to 10 or 12 foot-pounds. Note: The 2.7L V6 engine is the only one that uses a specific sequence.
31   Push the crankshaft forward using a screwdriver or prybar to seat the thrust bearing. Once the crankshaft is pushed fully forward to seat the thrust bearing, leave the screwdriver in position so that force stays on the crankshaft until after all main bearing cap bolts have been tightened.
32   Tighten the main bearing cap bolts in two steps, in sequence (see illustration 11.19) and to the torque and angle listed in this Chapter's Specifications.
33   Recheck crankshaft endplay with a feeler

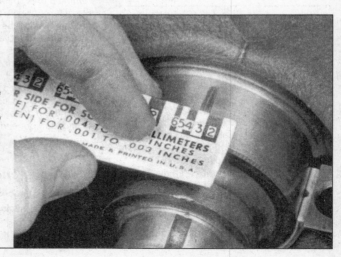

11.21 Use the scale on the Plastigage package to determine the bearing oil clearance - be sure to measure the widest part of the Plastigage and use the correct scale; it comes with both standard and metric scales gauge or a dial indicator. The endplay should be correct if the crankshaft thrust faces aren't worn or damaged and if new bearings have been installed.

34 Rotate the crankshaft a number of times by hand to check for any obvious binding. It should rotate with a running torque of 50 in-lbs or less. If the running torque is too high, correct the problem at this time.

35 Install a new rear main oil seal (see Chapter 2A or 2B).

12 Engine overhaul - reassembly sequence

1 Before beginning engine reassembly, make sure you have all the necessary new parts, gaskets and seals as well as the following items on hand:

Common hand tools
A 1/2-inch drive torque wrench
New engine oil
Gasket sealant
Thread locking compound

2 If you obtained a short block, it will be necessary to install the cylinder head, the oil pump and pick-up tube, the oil pan, the water pump, the timing belt and timing cover, and the valve cover (see Chapter 2A or 2B). In order to save time and avoid problems, the external components must be installed in the following general order:

Thermostat and housing cover
Water pump
Intake and exhaust manifolds
Fuel injection components
Emission control components
Spark plugs
Ignition coils
Oil filter
Engine mounts and mount brackets
Flywheel and clutch (manual transaxle)
Driveplate (automatic transaxle)

13 Initial start-up and break-in after overhaul

Warning: *Have a fire extinguisher handy when starting the engine for the first time.*

1 Once the engine has been installed in the vehicle, double-check the engine oil and coolant levels.

2 With the spark plugs out of the engine and the ignition system and fuel pump disabled (see Section 3 to disable the ignition system and Chapter 4, Section 2 to disable the fuel pump), crank the engine until oil pressure registers on the gauge or the light goes out.

3 Install the spark plugs and ignition coils and restore the fuel pump and ignition functions.

4 Start the engine. It may take a few moments for the fuel system to build up pressure, but the engine should start without a great deal of effort.

5 After the engine starts, it should be allowed to warm up to normal operating temperature. While the engine is warming up, make a thorough check for fuel, oil and coolant leaks.

6 Shut the engine off and recheck the engine oil and coolant levels.

7 Drive the vehicle to an area with minimum traffic, accelerate from 30 to 50 mph, then allow the vehicle to slow to 30 mph with the throttle closed. Repeat the procedure 10 or 12 times. This will load the piston rings and cause them to seat properly against the cylinder walls. Check again for oil and coolant leaks.

8 Drive the vehicle gently for the first 500 miles (no sustained high speeds) and keep a constant check on the oil level. It is not unusual for an engine to use oil during the break-in period.

9 At approximately 500 to 600 miles, change the oil and filter.

10 For the next few hundred miles, drive the vehicle normally. Do not pamper it or abuse it.

11 After 2,000 miles, change the oil and filter again and consider the engine broken in.

COMMON ENGINE OVERHAUL TERMS

B

Backlash - The amount of play between two parts. Usually refers to how much one gear can be moved back and forth without moving the gear with which it's meshed.

Bearing Caps - The caps held in place by nuts or bolts which, in turn, hold the bearing surface. This space is for lubricating oil to enter.

Bearing clearance - The amount of space left between shaft and bearing surface. This space is for lubricating oil to enter.

Bearing crush - The additional height which is purposely manufactured into each bearing half to ensure complete contact of the bearing back with the housing bore when the engine is assembled.

Bearing knock - The noise created by movement of a part in a loose or worn bearing.

Blueprinting - Dismantling an engine and reassembling it to EXACT specifications.

Bore - An engine cylinder, or any cylindrical hole; also used to describe the process of enlarging or accurately refinishing a hole with a cutting tool, as to bore an engine cylinder. The bore size is the diameter of the hole.

Boring - Renewing the cylinders by cutting them out to a specified size. A boring bar is used to make the cut.

Bottom end - A term which refers collectively to the engine block, crankshaft, main bearings and the big ends of the connecting rods.

Break-in - The period of operation between installation of new or rebuilt parts and time in which parts are worn to the correct fit. Driving at reduced and varying speed for a specified mileage to permit parts to wear to the correct fit.

Bushing - A one-piece sleeve placed in a bore to serve as a bearing surface for shaft, piston pin, etc. Usually replaceable.

C

Camshaft - The shaft in the engine, on which a series of lobes are located for operating the valve mechanisms. The camshaft is driven by gears or sprockets and a timing chain. Usually referred to simply as the cam.

Carbon - Hard, or soft, black deposits found in combustion chamber, on plugs, under rings, on and under valve heads.

Cast iron - An alloy of iron and more than two percent carbon, used for engine blocks and heads because it's relatively inexpensive and easy to mold into complex shapes.

Chamfer - To bevel across (or a bevel on) the sharp edge of an object.

Chase - To repair damaged threads with a tap or die.

Combustion chamber - The space between the piston and the cylinder head, with the piston at top dead center, in which air-fuel mixture is burned.

Compression ratio - The relationship between cylinder volume (clearance volume) when the piston is at top dead center and cylinder volume when the piston is at bottom dead center.

Connecting rod - The rod that connects the crank on the crankshaft with the piston. Sometimes called a con rod.

Connecting rod cap - The part of the connecting rod assembly that attaches the rod to the crankpin.

Core plug - Soft metal plug used to plug the casting holes for the coolant passages in the block.

Crankcase - The lower part of the engine in which the crankshaft rotates; includes the lower section of the cylinder block and the oil pan.

Crank kit - A reground or reconditioned crankshaft and new main and connecting rod bearings.

Crankpin - The part of a crankshaft to which a connecting rod is attached.

Crankshaft - The main rotating member, or shaft, running the length of the crankcase, with offset throws to which the connecting rods are attached; changes the reciprocating motion of the pistons into rotating motion.

Cylinder sleeve - A replaceable sleeve, or liner, pressed into the cylinder block to form the cylinder bore.

D

Deburring - Removing the burrs (rough edges or areas) from a bearing.

Deglazer - A tool, rotated by an electric motor, used to remove glaze from cylinder walls so a new set of rings will seat.

E

Endplay - The amount of lengthwise movement between two parts. As applied to a crankshaft, the distance that the crankshaft can move forward and back in the cylinder block.

F

Face - A machinist's term that refers to removing metal from the end of a shaft or the face of a larger part, such as a flywheel.

Fatigue - A breakdown of material through a large number of loading and unloading cycles. The first signs are cracks followed shortly by breaks.

Feeler gauge - A thin strip of hardened steel,

ground to an exact thickness, used to check clearances between parts.

Free height - The unloaded length or height of a spring.

Freeplay - The looseness in a linkage, or an assembly of parts, between the initial application of force and actual movement. Usually perceived as slop or slight delay.

Freeze plug - See Core plug.

G

Gallery - A large passage in the block that forms a reservoir for engine oil pressure.

Glaze - The very smooth, glassy finish that develops on cylinder walls while an engine is in service.

H

Heli-Coil - A rethreading device used when threads are worn or damaged. The device is installed in a retapped hole to reduce the thread size to the original size.

I

Installed height - The spring's measured length or height, as installed on the cylinder head. Installed height is measured from the spring seat to the underside of the spring retainer.

J

Journal - The surface of a rotating shaft which turns in a bearing.

K

Keeper - The split lock that holds the valve spring retainer in position on the valve stem.

Key - A small piece of metal inserted into matching grooves machined into two parts fitted together - such as a gear pressed onto a shaft - which prevents slippage between the two parts.

Knock - The heavy metallic engine sound, produced in the combustion chamber as a result of abnormal combustion - usually detonation. Knock is usually caused by a loose or worn bearing. Also referred to as detonation, pinging and spark knock. Connecting rod or main bearing knocks are created by too much oil clearance or insufficient lubrication.

L

Lands - The portions of metal between the piston ring grooves.

Lapping the valves - Grinding a valve face and its seat together with lapping compound.

Lash - The amount of free motion in a gear train, between gears, or in a mechanical assembly, that occurs before movement can begin. Usually refers to the lash in a valve train.

Lifter - The part that rides against the cam to transfer motion to the rest of the valve train.

M

Machining - The process of using a machine to remove metal from a metal part.

Main bearings - The plain, or babbit, bearings that support the crankshaft.

Main bearing caps - The cast iron caps, bolted to the bottom of the block, that support the main bearings.

O

O.D. - Outside diameter.

Oil gallery - A pipe or drilled passageway in the engine used to carry engine oil from one area to another.

Oil ring - The lower ring, or rings, of a piston; designed to prevent excessive amounts of oil from working up the cylinder walls and into the combustion chamber. Also called an oil-control ring.

Oil seal - A seal which keeps oil from leaking out of a compartment. Usually refers to a dynamic seal around a rotating shaft or other moving part.

O-ring - A type of sealing ring made of a special rubberlike material; in use, the O-ring is compressed into a groove to provide the sealing action.

Overhaul - To completely disassemble a unit, clean and inspect all parts, reassemble it with the original or new parts and make all adjustments necessary for proper operation.

P

Pilot bearing - A small bearing installed in the center of the flywheel (or the rear end of the crankshaft) to support the front end of the input shaft of the transmission.

Pip mark - A little dot or indentation which indicates the top side of a compression ring.

Piston - The cylindrical part, attached to the connecting rod, that moves up and down in the cylinder as the crankshaft rotates. When the fuel charge is fired, the piston transfers the force of the explosion to the connecting rod, then to the crankshaft.

Piston pin (or wrist pin) - The cylindrical and usually hollow steel pin that passes through the piston. The piston pin fastens the piston to the upper end of the connecting rod.

Piston ring - The split ring fitted to the groove in a piston. The ring contacts the sides of the ring groove and also rubs against the cylinder wall, thus sealing space between piston and wall. There are two types of rings: Compression rings seal the compression pressure in the combustion chamber; oil rings scrape excessive oil off the cylinder wall.

Piston ring groove - The slots or grooves cut in piston heads to hold piston rings in position.

Piston skirt - The portion of the piston below the rings and the piston pin hole.

Plastigage - A thin strip of plastic thread, available in different sizes, used for measuring clearances. For example, a strip of plastigage is laid across a bearing journal and mashed as parts are assembled. Then parts are disassembled and the width of the strip is measured to determine clearance between journal and bearing. Commonly used to measure crankshaft main-bearing and connecting rod bearing clearances.

Press-fit - A tight fit between two parts that requires pressure to force the parts together. Also referred to as drive, or force, fit.

Prussian blue - A blue pigment; in solution, useful in determining the area of contact between two surfaces. Prussian blue is commonly used to determine the width and location of the contact area between the valve face and the valve seat.

R

Race (bearing) - The inner or outer ring that provides a contact surface for balls or rollers in bearing.

Ream - To size, enlarge or smooth a hole by using a round cutting tool with fluted edges.

Ring job - The process of reconditioning the cylinders and installing new rings.

Runout - Wobble. The amount a shaft rotates out-of-true.

S

Saddle - The upper main bearing seat.

Scored - Scratched or grooved, as a cylinder wall may be scored by abrasive particles moved up and down by the piston rings.

Scuffing - A type of wear in which there's a transfer of material between parts moving against each other; shows up as pits or grooves in the mating surfaces.

Seat - The surface upon which another part rests or seats. For example, the valve seat is the matched surface upon which the valve face rests. Also used to refer to wearing into a good fit; for example, piston rings seat after a few miles of driving.

Short block - An engine block complete with crankshaft and piston and, usually, camshaft assemblies.

Static balance - The balance of an object while it's stationary.

Step - The wear on the lower portion of a ring land caused by excessive side and back-clearance. The height of the step indicates the ring's extra side clearance and the length of the step projecting from the back wall of the groove represents the ring's back clearance.

Stroke - The distance the piston moves when traveling from top dead center to bottom dead center, or from bottom dead center to top dead center.

Stud - A metal rod with threads on both ends.

T

Tang - A lip on the end of a plain bearing used to align the bearing during assembly.

Tap - To cut threads in a hole. Also refers to the fluted tool used to cut threads.

Taper - A gradual reduction in the width of a shaft or hole; in an engine cylinder, taper usually takes the form of uneven wear, more pronounced at the top than at the bottom.

Throws - The offset portions of the crankshaft to which the connecting rods are affixed.

Thrust bearing - The main bearing that has thrust faces to prevent excessive endplay, or forward and backward movement of the crankshaft.

Thrust washer - A bronze or hardened steel washer placed between two moving parts. The washer prevents longitudinal movement and provides a bearing surface for thrust surfaces of parts.

Tolerance - The amount of variation permitted from an exact size of measurement. Actual amount from smallest acceptable dimension to largest acceptable dimension.

U

Umbrella - An oil deflector placed near the valve tip to throw oil from the valve stem area.

Undercut - A machined groove below the normal surface.

Undersize bearings - Smaller diameter bearings used with re-ground crankshaft journals.

V

Valve grinding - Refacing a valve in a valve-refacing machine.

Valve train - The valve-operating mechanism of an engine; includes all components from the camshaft to the valve.

Vibration damper - A cylindrical weight attached to the front of the crankshaft to minimize torsional vibration (the twist-untwist actions of the crankshaft caused by the cylinder firing impulses). Also called a harmonic balancer.

W

Water jacket - The spaces around the cylinders, between the inner and outer shells of the cylinder block or head, through which coolant circulates.

Web - A supporting structure across a cavity.

Woodruff key - A key with a radiused backside (viewed from the side).

Notes

Chapter 3
Cooling, heating and air conditioning systems

Contents

Specifications

General
Radiator cap pressure rating .... 13.9 to 18.1 psi (86 to 125 kPa)
Thermostat rating
Opens .... 176 to 183-degrees F (80 to 84-degrees C)
Fully open... 203-degrees F (95-degrees C)

Torque specifications
Note: *One foot-pound (ft-lb) of torque is equivalent to 12 inch-pounds (in-lbs) of torque. Torque values below approximately 15 ft-lbs are expressed in inch-pounds, since most foot-pound torque wrenches are not accurate at these smaller values.*

	Ft-lbs (unless otherwise indicated)	Nm
Receiver/drier Allen plug..	15 to 18	20 to 32
Thermostat housing bolts		
Four-cylinder engine	84 to 132 in-lbs	10 to 15
V6 engine	144 to 168 in-lbs	17 to 20
Water pump bolts/nuts		
Four-cylinder engine	15 to 20	20 to 27
2.7L V6 engine	16	22
3.5L engine		
M8 bolts	16	22
M10 bolts	24 to 36	33 to 50

1.1 Typical cooling system component locations (3.5L V6 shown, other models similar)

1	Coolant reservoir	4	Cooling fans	6	Thermostat (vicinity shown)
2	Radiator cap	5	Radiator	7	Fuse and relay box
3	Upper radiator hose				

1   General information

Engine cooling system

Refer to illustrations 1.1 and 1.2

All vehicles covered by this manual employ a pressurized engine cooling system with thermostatically controlled coolant circulation **(see illustration)**. An impeller type water pump mounted on the front of the block pumps coolant through the engine. The coolant flows around each cylinder and toward the rear of the engine. Cast-in coolant passages direct coolant around the intake and exhaust ports, near the spark plug areas and in proximity to the exhaust valve guides.

A wax pellet-type thermostat is located in the thermostat housing near the front of the engine **(see illustration)**. During warm up, the closed thermostat prevents coolant from circulating through the radiator. When the engine reaches normal operating temperature, the thermostat opens and allows hot coolant to travel through the radiator, where it is cooled before returning to the engine.

There are two types of cooling systems used on these models. In the most common

type, the radiator is sealed by a pressure cap. This raises the boiling point of the coolant and this higher boiling point increases the efficiency of the radiator. If the system pressure exceeds the cap's pressure relief value, then the excess pressure in the system forces the spring-loaded valve in the cap off its seat and allows the coolant to escape through the overflow tube and into the coolant reservoir. When the system cools, the coolant is drawn from the reservoir back into the radiator. This type of system is known as a closed design because coolant that escapes past the pressure cap is saved and reused.

In the second type of system, the cooling system is sealed by a pressure-type cap on the surge tank/reservoir. The radiator is connected directly to the reservoir by a hose. If the system pressure exceeds the cap pressure relief value, the excess pressure in the system forces the spring-loaded valve inside the cap off its seat and allows coolant to escape through the overflow tube.

The coolant reservoir serves as both the point at which fresh coolant is added to the cooling system to maintain the proper fluid level and as a holding tank for heated coolant.

Heating system

The heating system consists of a blower fan and heater core located within the heater box, the inlet and outlet hoses connecting the heater core to the engine cooling system and the heater/air conditioning control head on the dashboard. Hot engine coolant is circulated through the heater core. When the heater mode is activated, a flap door opens to expose the heater box to the passenger compartment. A fan switch on the control head activates the blower motor, which forces air through the core, heating the air.

Air conditioning system

The air conditioning system consists of a condenser mounted in front of the radiator, an evaporator mounted adjacent to the heater core under the dashboard, a compressor mounted on the engine, a receiver-drier which contains a high pressure relief valve and the plumbing connecting all of the above.

A blower fan forces the warmer air of the passenger compartment through the evaporator core (sort of a radiator-in-reverse), transferring the heat from the air to the refrigerant. The liquid refrigerant boils off into low-

1.2 A typical thermostat

1	*Flange*	5	*Valve seat*
2	*Piston*	6	*Valve*
3	*Jiggle valve*	7	*Frame*
4	*Main coil spring*	8	*Secondary coil spring*

2.4 An inexpensive hydrometer can be used to test the condition of your coolant

pressure vapor, taking the heat with it when it leaves the evaporator. The compressor keeps refrigerant circulating through the system, pumping the warmed coolant through the condenser where it is cooled and then circulated back to the evaporator.

Some models are equipped with an optional automatic temperature control air conditioning system. With this system, the driver selects the desired interior temperature with the controls, similar to setting the temperature on a home heating/cooling thermostat, and the system automatically adds the right blend of cool or warm air to maintain this temperature. The system has sensors that detect both the interior and outside temperature.

2 Antifreeze - general information

Refer to illustration 2.4

Warning: *Do not allow antifreeze to come in contact with your skin or painted surfaces of the vehicle. Rinse off spills immediately with plenty of water. Antifreeze is highly toxic if ingested. Never leave antifreeze lying around in an open container or in puddles on the floor; children and pets are attracted by its sweet smell and may drink it. Check with local authorities on disposing of used antifreeze. Many communities have collection centers that will see that antifreeze is disposed of safely. Never dump used antifreeze on the ground or into drains.*
Note: *Non-toxic coolant is available at local auto parts stores. Although the coolant is non-toxic when fresh, proper disposal of used coolant is still required.*

The cooling system should be filled with a water/ethylene-glycol based antifreeze solution, which will prevent freezing down to at least -20 degrees F, or lower if local climate requires it. It also provides protection against

corrosion and increases the coolant boiling point.

The cooling system should be drained, flushed and refilled at least every other year (see Chapter 1). The use of antifreeze solutions for periods of longer than two years is likely to cause damage and encourage the formation of rust and scale in the system. If your tap water is hard (it contains a lot of dissolved minerals), use distilled water with the antifreeze.

Before adding antifreeze to the system, check all hose connections, because antifreeze tends to leak through very minute openings. Engines do not normally consume coolant. Therefore, if the level goes down, find the cause and correct it.

The exact mixture of antifreeze-to-water that you should use depends on the relative weather conditions. The mixture should contain at least 40-percent antifreeze, but should never contain more than 70-percent antifreeze. Consult the mixture ratio chart on the antifreeze container before adding coolant. Hydrometers are available at most auto parts stores to test the ratio of antifreeze to water **(see illustration)**. Use antifreeze that meets the vehicle manufacturer's specifications.

3 Thermostat - check and replacement

Warning: *Do not attempt to remove the surge tank cap, coolant or thermostat until the engine has cooled completely.*

General check

1   Before assuming the thermostat is responsible for a cooling system problem, check the coolant level (see Chapter 1), drive-belt tension (see Chapter 1) and temperature gauge (or light) operation.

2   If the engine takes a long time to warm up (as indicated by the temperature gauge or heater operation), the thermostat is probably stuck open. Replace the thermostat with a new one.
3   If the engine runs hot, use your hand to check the temperature of the lower radiator hose. If the hose is not hot, but the engine is, the thermostat is probably stuck in the closed position, preventing the coolant inside the engine from escaping to the radiator. Replace the thermostat. **Caution:** *Do not drive the vehicle without a thermostat. The computer may stay in open loop and emissions and fuel economy will suffer.*
4   If the lower radiator hose is hot, it means that the coolant is flowing and the thermostat is open. Consult the *Troubleshooting* Section at the front of this manual for further diagnosis.

Thermostat test

5   A more thorough test of the thermostat can only be made when it is removed from the vehicle (see below). If the thermostat remains in the open position at room temperature, it is faulty and must be replaced.
6   To test it fully, suspend the (closed) thermostat on a length of string or wire in a container of cold water, with a thermometer (cooking type that reads beyond 212-degrees F). A clear Pyrex cooking container is easiest to use.
7   Heat the water on a stove while observing the temperature and the thermostat. Neither should contact the sides of the container.
8   Note the temperature when the thermostat begins to open and when it is fully open. Compare the temperatures to the Specifications in this Chapter. The number stamped into the thermostat is generally the fully-open temperature.
9   If the thermostat doesn't open and close as specified, or sticks in any position, replace it.

3.11 Both radiator hoses attach to the 3.5L engine in the same area - the thermostat is in the housing at the end of the lower hose

3.14 The thermostat seal fits around the edge of the thermostat

Replacement

Refer to illustrations 3.11, 3.14 and 3.15

10   Drain the cooling system (see Chapter 1).

11   Follow the radiator hose to the thermostat housing cover and disconnect the hose **(see illustration)**.

12   Remove the thermostat housing cover mounting fasteners and remove it from the cylinder block. Be prepared for some coolant to spill as the gasket seal is broken.

13   Remove the thermostat, noting the direction in which it was installed in the housing, and thoroughly clean the sealing surfaces.

14   Fit a new gasket onto the thermostat. Make sure it is evenly fitted all the way around **(see illustration)**.

15   Install the thermostat and housing, positioning the jiggle pin at the highest point **(see illustration)**.

16   Tighten the housing cover fasteners to the torque listed in this Chapter's Specifications and reinstall the remaining components in the reverse order of removal.

17   Refill the cooling system (see Chapter 1). Run the engine and check for leaks and proper operation.

4   Engine cooling fans - removal and installation

Refer to illustrations 4.3a, 4.3b, 4.4 and 4.5

Warning 1: *Do not start this procedure until the engine is completely cool.*

Warning 2: *The models covered by this manual are equipped with Supplemental Restraint Systems (SRS), more commonly known as airbags. Always disarm the airbag system before working in the vicinity of any airbag system component to avoid the possibility of accidental deployment of the airbag, which*

3.15 Note the position of the thermostat - the "jiggle pin" should be installed at the highest point

4.3a Disconnect the wiring harnesses to the cooling fans and remove the wiring mounting bracket

4.3b Rear engine cooling fan/shroud upper mounting nuts

4.4 Remove the fan from the motor

4.5 Remove the screws and separate the motor from the shroud

could cause personal injury (see Chapter 12).
Note: The manufacturer's procedure for engine cooling fan removal involves removing the radiator and fan assemblies together and separating them afterwards. It is possible to remove the engine cooling fans without removing the radiator.

1   Disconnect the cable from the negative terminal of the battery (see Chapter 5, Section 1). Drain the cooling system (see Chapter 1).

2   If you're removing the rear fan, drain the engine coolant (see Chapter 1) and detach the radiator hose from the top of the radiator. If you're removing the front fan, remove the bumper cover (see Chapter 11).

3   Disconnect the electrical connector, then remove the fan/shroud mounting fasteners **(see illustrations)**.

4   Hold the fan blades and remove the fan retaining nut **(see illustration)**.

5   Unbolt the fan motor from the shroud **(see illustration)**.

6   Installation is the reverse of removal. Refill the cooling system (see Chapter 1).

5   Radiator and coolant reservoir - removal and installation

Warning 1: Do not start this procedure until the engine is completely cool. Do not allow antifreeze to come in contact with your skin or painted surfaces of the vehicle. Rinse off spills immediately with plenty of water. Antifreeze is highly toxic if ingested. Never leave antifreeze lying around in an open container or in puddles on the floor; children and pets are attracted by its sweet smell and may drink it. Check with local authorities on disposing of used antifreeze. Many communities have collection centers, which will see that antifreeze is disposed of safely. Never dump used antifreeze on the ground or into drains.

Warning 2: The models covered by this manual are equipped with Supplemental Restraint Systems (SRS), more commonly known as airbags. Always disarm the airbag system before working in the vicinity of any airbag system component to avoid the possibility of accidental deployment of the airbag, which could cause personal injury (see Chapter 12).

Note: Non-toxic coolant is available at local auto parts stores. Although the coolant is non-toxic when fresh, proper disposal of used coolant is still required.

Radiator

Removal

Refer to illustrations 5.6a, 5.6b, 5.7a and 5.7b

1   Disconnect the negative battery cable (see Chapter 5, Section 1).

2   Remove the engine splash shield(s) from beneath the radiator and any covers for the engine, if equipped (see Chapter 2).

3   Disconnect the wiring to both fan motors **(see illustration 4.3a)**.

4   Drain the cooling system (see Chapter 1).

5   Detach the upper and lower radiator hoses from the radiator and the reservoir hose from the radiator filler neck. Be sure to mark the exact positions of the hoses and clamps with a dab of white paint or something similar.

6   On vehicles equipped with automatic transaxles, disconnect the transaxle oil cooler lines from the radiator **(see illustrations)**.

5.6a There is a cooler hose at the left side of the lower radiator tank . . .

5.6b . . . and at the right

5.7a Remove this plastic cover from the hood latch

5.7b The upper radiator core support can now be removed; the radiator can then be slid upward

Place a drip pan to catch the fluid and cap the fittings to prevent leakage and contamination.

7   Unbolt the radiator top mounts and carefully remove the radiator and fans as an assembly **(see illustrations).**

8   Remove the cooling fans from the radiator (see Section 4).

9   With the radiator removed, it can be inspected for leaks, damage and internal blockage. If in need of repairs, have a professional radiator shop perform the work, as special techniques are required.

10   Bugs and dirt can be cleaned from the radiator with compressed air and a soft brush. Don't bend the cooling fins as this is done. **Warning:** *Wear eye protection.*

Installation

11   Installation is the reverse of the removal procedure. Be sure the rubber mounts are correctly in place.

12   After installation, fill the cooling system with the proper mixture of antifreeze and water. Refer to Chapter 1 if necessary.

13   Start the engine and check for leaks. Allow the engine to reach normal operating temperature, indicated by the upper radiator hose becoming hot. Recheck the coolant level and add more if required.

14   Be sure to check the automatic transaxle

fluid level and add fluid as needed (see Chapter 1).

Coolant reservoir

Refer to illustration 5.15

15   The coolant reservoir is bolted to the right fenderwell **(see illustration)**.

16   Use a small clamp to pinch the hose connecting the reservoir to the radiator.

17   Place a drain pan under the reservoir and then disconnect the hose.

18   Remove the mounting screws and lift the reservoir out.

19   Pour any remaining coolant into the container. Wash out and inspect the reservoir for cracks and chafing. Replace it if it's damaged.

20   Installation is the reverse of removal. Refill the reservoir to the lower level line.

---

6   Water pump - check

1   A failure in the water pump can cause serious engine damage due to overheating.

2   Water pumps are equipped with weep or vent holes. If a failure occurs in the pump seal, coolant will leak from this hole.

3   The water pumps on these models are

located behind the timing belt covers. If you suspect water pump leakage, remove this cover (see Chapter 2A or 2B).

4   In most cases it will be necessary to use a flashlight to find the hole in the water pump by looking through the space behind the pulley just below the water pump shaft. A slight gray discoloration around the weep hole is normal, while dark brown stains indicate a problem.

5   If the water pump shaft bearings fail, there may be a howling sound at the front of the engine while it is running. Bearing wear can be felt if the water pump pulley can be rocked up and down. Do not mistake drivebelt slippage, which causes a squealing sound, for water pump failure. Spray automotive drivebelt dressing on the belts to eliminate the belt as a possible cause of the noise.

---

7   Water pump - removal and installation

Warning: *Do not start this procedure until the engine is completely cool. Do not allow antifreeze to come in contact with your skin or painted surfaces of the vehicle. Rinse off spills immediately with plenty of water. Antifreeze is highly toxic if ingested. Never leave antifreeze lying around in an open container or in puddles on the floor; children and pets are attracted by its sweet smell and may drink it. Check with local authorities on disposing of used antifreeze. Many communities have collection centers, which will see that antifreeze is disposed of safely. Never dump used antifreeze on the ground or into drains.*

Note: *Non-toxic coolant is available at local auto parts stores. Although the coolant is non-toxic when fresh, proper disposal of used coolant is still required.*

1   Disconnect the negative battery cable (see Chapter 5, Section 1) and drain the cooling system (see Chapter 1).

2   Remove the drivebelt (see Chapter 1) and the alternator (see Chapter 5).

5.15 The coolant reservoir is a pressurized component on some early models - if it's fitted with a pressure cap, don't try to remove it until the engine has cooled

9.3 Release the support cord to allow the glove box to open completely

9.5 Remove the four screws to remove the glove box inner shell - this will expose the blower motor cover

3   On 2.4L four-cylinder engines, remove the water inlet pipe.

4   Remove the water pump pulley on 2.4L four-cylinder and 2.7L V6 engines using a strap wrench or pin spanner wrench to hold the pulley while you loosen the bolts.

5   Remove the timing belt covers (see Chapter 2A or 2B).

6   Paint each sprocket with alignment marks onto the timing belt so that the belt can be installed in exactly the same position. **Caution:** *Every sprocket must maintain its position on the timing belt or severe engine damage can occur! If the marks are not legible later, it will be necessary to follow the timing belt installation procedure outlined in Chapter 2A or 2B to ensure correct alignment.* **Note:** *The belt can be secured to the pulleys with plastic zip-ties or a similar device to prevent them from coming off.*

7   Remove the timing belt tensioner (see Chapter 2A or 2B). **Caution:** *Don't rotate the crankshaft with the timing belt disconnected!*

8   Remove the fasteners and pry the water pump off. If necessary, tap the pump loose with a soft-face hammer.

9   To install, clean the water pump and block of any old gasket material or sealant, then clean with lacquer thinner.

10   Install a new gasket and install the water pump. Install the water pump bolts and nuts and tighten them to the torque listed in this Chapter's Specifications.

11   Install the remaining parts in the reverse order of removal. Make sure to follow the procedure in Chapter 2A or 2B for retracting the timing belt tensioner. **Caution:** *Verify that all sprocket marks are aligned with the marks you made on the timing belt before starting the engine!*

12   Refill the cooling system (see Chapter 1), then run the engine and check for leaks and proper operation.

8   Coolant temperature indicator - check

Warning: *Wait until the engine is completely cool before beginning this procedure.*

1   The coolant temperature indicator system consists of a temperature gauge on the dash and a sensor mounted on the engine. On all models, the Engine Coolant Temperature sensor gives information to the Powertrain Control Module (PCM) that then controls the coolant temperature gauge in addition to controlling engine operation. Refer to Chapter 6 for more information on this sensor.

2   If an overheating indication has occurred, first check the coolant level in the system (see Chapter 1) and that the coolant mixture is correct (see Section 2). Also, refer to the *Troubleshooting* Section at the beginning of this book before assuming that the temperature indicator is faulty.

3   Start the engine and warm it up for 10 minutes. If the temperature gauge has not moved from the C position, check the wiring harness connections going to the instrument cluster.

9   Blower motor - removal and installation

Refer to illustrations 9.3, 9.5, 9.7 and 9.8

Warning: *The models covered by this manual are equipped with Supplemental Restraint Systems (SRS), more commonly known as airbags. Always disarm the airbag system before working in the vicinity of any airbag system component to avoid the possibility of accidental deployment of the airbag, which could cause personal injury (see Chapter 12).*

1   Disconnect the cable from the negative terminal of the battery (see Chapter 5, Section 1).

2   The blower unit is located under the dash and behind the glove box.

3   Open the glove compartment and disconnect the support cord **(see illustration)**. Push inward on its sides to lower the door fully.

4   Remove the dash panel at the right of the glove compartment by removing the screw, then pulling it rearward.

5   Remove the glove compartment inner frame screws and the screw to the right of the glove compartment opening **(see illustration)**.

6   Remove the glove compartment door screws and remove the door.

7   Remove the blower/evaporator mounting bolts and remove the blower motor **(see illustration)**.

9.7 Location of blower motor housing; the blower motor is at the right lower portion of the unit, mounted vertically and accessible from the bottom, the resistor is at the wiring terminal to the right

9.8 Use pliers to release and remove the clip, then lift the blower fan off the motor shaft

10.2 Press down on the inside lever to remove the ashtray, then remove the two screws behind it

8   If the motor is being replaced, transfer the fan to the new motor prior to installation **(see illustration)**.

9   Installation is the reverse of removal. Check for proper operation.

10   Heater and air conditioning control assembly - removal and installation

Refer to illustrations 10.2 and 10.3

Warning: *The models covered by this manual are equipped with Supplemental Restraint Systems (SRS), more commonly known as airbags. Always disarm the airbag system before working in the vicinity of any airbag system component to avoid the possibility of accidental deployment of the airbag, which could cause personal injury (see Chapter 12).*

1   Disconnect the negative cable from the battery (see Chapter 5, Section 1).

2   Remove the ashtray, then remove the two screws behind it **(see illustration)**.

3   Use a plastic trim tool or a screwdriver wrapped with electrical tape to pry the top of the panel out. Pull the assembly out slightly and disconnect all electrical connectors for the control assembly **(see illustration)**.

4   The heater control can be separated from its panel by removing the screws that are accessible from the rear of the panel.

5   Installation is the reverse of the removal procedure.

6   Run the engine and check for proper functioning of the heater and air conditioning.

11   Heater core - removal and installation

Refer to illustrations 11.6 and 11.7

Warning 1: *The models covered by this manual are equipped with Supplemental Restraint Systems (SRS), more commonly known as airbags. Always disarm the airbag system before working in the vicinity of any airbag system component to avoid the possibility of accidental deployment of the airbag, which could cause personal injury (see Chapter 12).*

Warning 2: *Do not allow antifreeze to come in contact with your skin or painted surfaces of the vehicle. Rinse off spills immediately with plenty of water. Antifreeze is highly toxic if*

ingested. Never leave antifreeze lying around in an open container or in puddles on the floor; children and pets are attracted by its sweet smell and may drink it. Check with local authorities on disposing of used antifreeze. Many communities have collection centers that will see that antifreeze is disposed of safely. Never dump used antifreeze on the ground or into drains.

Warning 3: *Wait until the engine is completely cool before beginning this procedure.*

Note 1: *Non-toxic coolant is available at local auto parts stores. Although the coolant is non-toxic when fresh, proper disposal of used coolant is still required.*

Note 2: *Removal of the heater core is a difficult procedure for the home mechanic. There are numerous fasteners involved, some of which can be difficult to access. We recommend that you have considerable mechanical experience before performing a heater core replacement.*

1   Take the vehicle to a dealer service department or automotive air conditioning shop and have the air conditioning system discharged and the refrigerant recovered.

2   Disconnect the cable from the negative terminal of the battery (see Chapter 5, Section 1).

3   Refer to Chapter 1 and drain the cooling system.

4   The procedure for removal of the heater core involves removal of the heater/evaporator housing, which requires complete removal of the instrument panel and its support tube. Refer to Chapter 11 to remove the instrument panel assembly.

5   Unbolt and remove the cross-cowl support tube.

6   Disconnect both air conditioner lines at the firewall **(see illustration)**. Seal the openings to prevent contamination.

7   Raise the front of the vehicle and support it securely on jackstands. Disconnect the heater hoses at the firewall **(see illustration)**.

8   Disconnect the wiring from the heater unit.

10.3 Disconnect the wiring harnesses from the heater controls and the lighter - there is no need to remove the knobs before prying the heater control unit out, but be careful to avoid scratching the plastic trim

11.6 After having the air conditioning system evacuated, disconnect the refrigerant lines at the firewall - the heater hoses must also be disconnected after draining the coolant

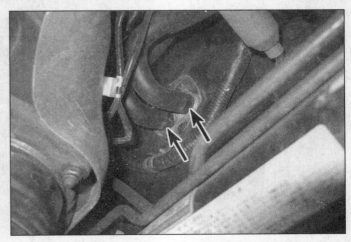

11.7 The heater hoses are accessible from under the car

9 Disconnect any air ducts that are attached directly to the unit.

10 Remove the mounting fasteners from the unit. Carefully pull it rearward until the tubes are free of the firewall openings.

11 Remove the screws and separate the halves of the heater housing, then remove the heater core from the housing.

12 Installation is the reverse order of removal. Use new O-rings to seal the evaporator refrigerant connections. Make sure all of the cross-cowl support tube mounting fasteners are tightened securely before installing the instrument panel pad.

13 Refill the cooling system (see Chapter 1). Have the air conditioning system serviced at the station that discharged it.

12 Air conditioning and heating system - check and maintenance

Air conditioning system

Warning: *The air conditioning system is under high pressure. Do not loosen any hose fittings or remove any components until the system has been discharged. Air conditioning refrigerant must be properly discharged into an EPA-approved recovery/recycling unit by a dealer service department or an automotive air conditioning repair facility. Always wear eye protection when disconnecting air conditioning system fittings.*

1 The following maintenance checks should be performed on a regular basis to ensure that the air conditioner continues to operate at peak efficiency.

a) *Inspect the condition of the compressor drivebelt. If it is worn or deteriorated, replace it (see Chapter 1).*

b) *Check the drivebelt tension and, if necessary, adjust it (see Chapter 1).*

c) *Inspect the system hoses. Look for cracks, bubbles, hardening and deterio-*

ration. Inspect the hoses and all fittings for oil bubbles or seepage. If there is any evidence of wear, damage or leakage, replace the hose(s).

d) *Inspect the condenser fins for leaves, bugs and any other foreign material that may have embedded itself in the fins. Use a fin comb or compressed air to remove debris from the condenser.*

e) *Make sure the system has the correct refrigerant charge.*

2 It's a good idea to operate the system for about ten minutes at least once a month. This is particularly important during the winter months because long-term non-use can cause hardening, and subsequent failure, of the seals.

3 Because of the complexity of the air conditioning system and the special equipment necessary to service it, in-depth troubleshooting and repairs are beyond the scope of this manual. However, simple component replacement procedures are provided in this Chapter.

4 The most common cause of poor cooling is simply a low system refrigerant charge. If a noticeable drop in system cooling ability occurs, one of the following quick checks will help you determine whether the refrigerant level is low.

Check

Refer to illustration 12.8

5 Warm the engine up to normal operating temperature.

6 Place the air conditioning temperature selector at the coldest setting and put the blower at the highest setting. Open the doors (to make sure the air conditioning system doesn't cycle off as soon as it cools the passenger compartment).

7 After the system reaches operating temperature, feel the two pipes connected to the evaporator at the firewall.

8 The pipe (thinner tubing) leading from the condenser outlet to the evaporator should be cold, and the evaporator outlet line (the thicker tubing that leads back to the compressor) should be slightly colder (3 to 10 degrees F). If the evaporator outlet is considerably warmer than the inlet, the system needs a charge. Insert a thermometer in the center air distribution duct **(see illustration)** while operating the air conditioning system - the temperature of the output air should be 35 to 40 degrees F below the ambient air temperature (down to approximately 40 degrees F). If the ambient (outside) air temperature is very high, say 110-degrees F, the duct air temperature may be as high as 60 degrees F, but generally the air conditioning is 35 to 40 degrees F cooler than the ambient air. If the air isn't as cold as it used to be, the system probably needs a charge. Further inspection or testing of the system is beyond the scope of the home mechanic and should be left to a professional.

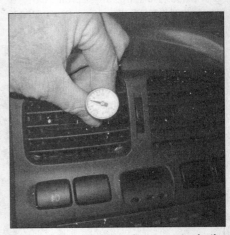

12.8 Place an accurate thermometer in the center dash vent, turn the air conditioning on and check the output temperature

12.10 A basic charging kit for R-134a systems is available at most auto parts stores - it must say R-134a (not R-12) and so must the can of refrigerant

12.13a The low pressure fitting cap is clearly marked "L"

Adding refrigerant

Refer to illustrations 12.10, 12.13a and 12.13b

9   **Note:** *All models covered by this manual use the refrigerant R-134a. When recharging or replacing air conditioning components, use only refrigerant, refrigerant oil and seals compatible with this system. The seals and compressor oil used with older, conventional R-12 refrigerant are not compatible with the components in this system.*

10   Buy an automotive charging kit at an auto parts store. A charging kit includes a 12-ounce can of R-134a refrigerant, a tap valve and a short section of hose that can be attached between the tap valve and the system low side service valve **(see illustration)**.

11   Connect the charging kit by following the manufacturer's instructions.

12   Back off the valve handle on the charging kit and screw the kit onto the refrigerant can, first making sure that the O-ring or rubber seal inside the threaded portion of the kit is in place. **Warning:** *Wear protective eyewear when dealing with pressurized refrigerant cans.*

13   Remove the dust cap from the low-side charging port and attach the quick-connect fitting on the kit hose **(see illustrations)**. **Warning:** *DO NOT hook the charging kit hose to the system high side! The fittings on the charging kit are designed to fit **only** on the low side of the system.*

14   Warm the engine to normal operating temperature and turn on the air conditioning. Keep the charging kit hose away from the fan and other moving parts. In some cases, if the refrigerant charge is low enough, the air conditioning system pressure switch may prevent the compressor from operating. **Note:** *The charging process requires that the compressor be running. If the clutch cycles off, you can switch the A/C controls to High and leave the vehicle's doors open to keep the clutch on the compressor working.*

15   Turn the valve handle on the kit until the stem pierces the can, then back the handle out to release the refrigerant. You should be able to hear the rush of gas. Add refrigerant to the low side of the system until both the outlet and the evaporator inlet pipe feel about the same temperature. Allow stabilization time

between each addition. **Warning:** *Never add more than two cans of refrigerant to the system.* The can may tend to frost up, slowing the procedure. Wet a shop towel with hot water and wrap it around the bottom of the can to keep it from frosting.

16   Put your thermometer back in the center register and check that the output air is getting colder.

17   When the can is empty, turn the valve handle to the closed position and release the connection from the low-side port. Reinstall the dust cap.

18   Remove the charging kit from the can and store the kit for future use with the piercing valve in the UP position, to prevent inadvertently piercing the can on the next use.

Heating systems

19   If the air coming out of the heater vents isn't hot, the problem could stem from any of the following causes:

a) *The thermostat is stuck open, preventing the engine coolant from warming up enough to carry heat to the heater core. Replace the thermostat (see Section 3).*

b) *A heater hose is blocked, preventing the flow of coolant through the heater core. Feel both heater hoses at the firewall. They should be hot. If one of them is cold, there is an obstruction in one of the hoses or in the heater core, or the heater control valve is shut. Detach the hoses and back flush the heater core with a water hose. If the heater core is clear but circulation is impeded, remove the two hoses and flush them out with a garden hose.*

c) *If flushing fails to remove the blockage from the heater core, the core must be replaced (see Section 11).*

20   If the blower motor speed does not correspond to the setting selected on the blower switch, the problem could be a bad fuse, circuit, blower relay, speed switch or blower resistor.

12.13b Add R-134a only to the low side port - the procedure is easier if you wrap the can with a warm, wet towel to prevent icing

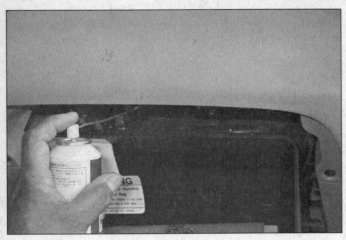

12.27 Remove the cabin air filter, then insert the disinfectant spray nozzle

13.4 After the system has been discharged, remove the Allen plug and pull the drier from the tube on the condenser

21   If there isn't any air coming out of the vents:

a) *Turn the ignition ON and activate the fan control. Place your ear at the heating/air conditioning register (vent) and listen. Most motors are audible. Can you hear the motor running?*

b) *If you can't (and have already verified that the blower switch and the blower motor resistor are good), the blower motor itself is probably bad (see Section 9).*

22   If the carpet under the heater core is damp, or if antifreeze vapor or steam is coming through the vents, the heater core is leaking. Remove it (see Section 11) and install a new unit (most radiator shops will not repair a leaking heater core).

23   Inspect the drain hose from the heater/evaporator, which exits the body under the floor. If there is a humid mist coming from the system ducts, this hose may be plugged with leaves or road debris.

Eliminating air conditioning odors

Refer to illustration 12.27

24   Unpleasant odors that often develop in air conditioning systems are caused by the growth of a fungus, usually on the surface of the evaporator core. The warm, humid environment there is a perfect breeding ground for mildew to develop.

25   The evaporator core on most vehicles is difficult to access, and factory dealerships have a lengthy, expensive process for eliminating the fungus by opening up the evaporator case and using a powerful disinfectant and rinse on the core until the fungus is gone. You can service your own system at home, but it takes something much stronger than basic household germ-killers or deodorizers.

26   Aerosol disinfectants for automotive air-conditioning systems are available in most auto parts stores, but remember when shopping for them that the most effective treatments are also the most expensive. The basic procedure for using these sprays is to start by running the system in the RECIRC mode for ten minutes with the blower on its highest speed. Use the highest heat mode to dry out the system and keep the compressor from engaging by disconnecting the wiring connector at the compressor (see Section 14).

27   The disinfectant can usually comes with a long spray hose. Remove the cabin air filter (see Chapter 1), point the nozzle inside the hole and spray according to the manufacturer's recommendations **(see illustration)**. Follow the manufacturer's recommendations for the length of spray and waiting time between applications.

28   Once the evaporator has been cleaned, the best way to prevent the mildew from coming back again is to make sure your evaporator housing drain tube is clear and to run the defrost cycle briefly to dry the evaporator out after a long drive with the air conditioning on.

13   Air conditioning receiver/drier - removal and installation

Refer to illustration 13.4

Warning: *The air conditioning system is under high pressure. Do not loosen any hose fittings or remove any components until the system has been discharged. Air conditioning refrigerant must be properly discharged into an EPA-approved recovery/recycling unit by a dealer service department or an automotive air conditioning repair facility. Always wear eye protection when disconnecting air conditioning system fittings.*

1   Have the refrigerant discharged by an air conditioning technician. **Note:** *The receiver/drier is a part of the condenser and is not serviceable by itself.*

2   Disconnect the negative battery cable (see Chapter 5, Section 1).

3   Refer to Section 15 and remove the condenser from the vehicle.

4   Using an Allen wrench, detach the end plug **(see illustration)** and remove the desiccant from the condenser with a pair of needle-nose pliers.

5   Use new O-rings and a new bottom cap when installing the new desiccant and tighten the end plug to the torque listed in this Chapter's Specifications. Be sure to lubricate the O-rings with R-134a compatible refrigerant oil.

6   Installation is the reverse of removal.

7   Have the system evacuated, charged and leak tested by the shop that discharged it.

14   Air conditioning compressor - removal and installation

Refer to illustration 14.6

Warning: *The air conditioning system is under high pressure. Do not loosen any hose fittings or remove any components until the system has been discharged. Air conditioning refrigerant must be properly discharged into an EPA-approved recovery/recycling unit by a dealer service department or an automotive air conditioning repair facility. Always wear eye protection when disconnecting air conditioning system fittings.*

Caution: *The receiver/drier should be serviced whenever the compressor is replaced.*

1   Have the refrigerant discharged by an automotive air conditioning technician.

2   Disconnect the negative cable from the battery (see Chapter 5, Section 1).

14.6 The air conditioning compressor is mounted on the front side of the block (3.5L V6 engine shown)

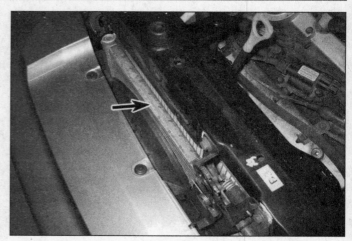

15.2 The condenser is mounted between the condenser cooling fan and the radiator

3   Raise the vehicle and support it securely on jackstands.

4   Remove the drivebelt from the compressor (see Chapter 1).

5   Disconnect the electrical connector.

6   Disconnect the refrigerant lines **(see illustration)**. Seal the ends to prevent contamination.

7   Unbolt the compressor and lower it from the vehicle.

8   If a new or rebuilt compressor is being installed, follow the directions, which come with it regarding the proper level of oil prior to installation.

9   Installation is the reverse of removal. Replace any O-rings with new ones specifically made for the purpose and lubricate them with refrigerant oil.

10   Have the system evacuated, recharged and leak tested by the shop that discharged it.

15 Air conditioning condenser - removal and installation

Refer to illustration 15.2

Warning: *The air conditioning system is under high pressure. Do not loosen any hose fittings or remove any components until the system has been discharged. Air conditioning refrigerant must be properly discharged into an EPA-approved recovery/recycling unit by a dealer service department or an automotive air conditioning repair facility. Always wear eye protection when disconnecting air conditioning system fittings.*

Caution: *The receiver/drier should be replaced whenever the condenser is replaced.*

1   Have the refrigerant discharged by an air conditioning technician.

2   Refer to Section 5 and remove the radiator supports **(see illustration)**. Pull the radia-

tor upward and rearward for access to the condenser.

3   Disconnect the inlet and outlet fittings. Cap the open fittings immediately to keep moisture and dirt out of the system.

4   Remove the mounting fasteners. Push the radiator back toward the engine, then push the condenser rearward until it's free of the radiator support and can be pulled up and out of the vehicle.

5   Install the condenser, brackets and bolts, making sure the rubber cushions fit on the mounting points properly.

6   Reconnect the refrigerant lines, using new O-rings where needed.

7   Reinstall the remaining parts in the reverse order of removal.

8   Have the system evacuated, charged and leak tested by the shop that discharged it.

Chapter 4
Fuel and exhaust systems

Contents

Specifications

General

Fuel system pressure (at idle)
With pressure regulator vacuum hose connected ... 35 to 39 psi (240 to 270 kPa)
With pressure regulator vacuum hose disconnected ... 46 to 49 psi (320 to 340 kPa)
Fuel injector resistance (approximate) ... 13 to 16 ohms

Torque specifications

Note: One foot-pound (ft-lb) of torque is equivalent to 12 inch-pounds (in-lbs) of torque. Torque values below approximately 15 ft-lbs are expressed in inch-pounds, since most foot-pound torque wrenches are not accurate at these smaller values.

	Ft-lbs (unless otherwise indicated)	Nm
Fuel rail mounting bolts or nuts		
Four-cylinder models	15	20
V6 models	84 in-lbs	10
Pulsation damper		
Four-cylinder models (mounting bolts)	80 in-lbs	9
V6 models (damper unscrews from fuel rail)	24	33
Fuel crossover pipe banjo bolt (V6 engine)	24	33
Throttle body mounting bolts/nuts		
Four-cylinder engines	22	30
V6 engines		
1999 through 2003	180 in-lbs	20
2004 on	96 in-lbs	11

1   General information

The fuel system consists of the fuel tank, the electric in-tank fuel pump, the fuel pressure regulator, the fuel rail, the fuel injectors and the fuel lines connecting the pump to the fuel rail. The injectors are energized by the Powertrain Control Module (PCM). The fuel system electrical circuits are protected by the EFI fuse and the circuit opening relay (fuel pump relay). The air intake system consists of the air filter housing, the air intake duct, the throttle body and the intake manifold. (The intake manifold is covered in Chapter 2.)

Electronic Fuel Injection (EFI) system

Hyundai refers to the fuel injection systems used on these vehicles as Electronic Fuel Injection (EFI). The system uses timed impulses to inject the fuel directly into the intake port of each cylinder. The Powertrain Control Module (PCM) controls the injectors. The PCM monitors various engine parameters and delivers the exact amount of fuel required into the intake ports. The throttle body controls the amount of air drawn into the engine.

Fuel pump and lines

Fuel is circulated from the in-tank fuel pump to the fuel rail through fuel lines running along the underside of the vehicle. Various sections of the fuel line are either rigid metal or nylon, or flexible fuel hose. The various sections of the fuel hose are connected by quick-connect fittings. An electric fuel pump/fuel level sending unit is located inside the fuel tank.

The circuit opening relay (fuel pump relay) is equipped with a primary and secondary voltage circuit. The primary circuit is controlled by the PCM and the secondary circuit is linked directly to the EFI main relay from the ignition switch. With the ignition switch ON (engine not running), the PCM will ground the relay for two seconds. During cranking, the PCM grounds the fuel pump relay as long as the Camshaft Position (CMP) sensor sends its position signal. If there are no reference pulses, the fuel pump will shut off after two seconds.

Exhaust system

The exhaust system consists of the exhaust manifold(s), the exhaust pipe(s), the catalytic converters, mufflers, and a tail pipe. On all models, there are multiple catalytic converters, an upstream catalyst just below each exhaust manifold and a downstream catalyst underneath the vehicle.

2   Fuel pressure relief procedure

Warning: *Gasoline is extremely flammable, so take extra precautions when you work on any part of the fuel system. Don't smoke or*

3.4 This fuel pressure testing kit contains all the necessary fittings and adapters, along with the fuel pressure gauge, to test most automotive fuel systems

allow open flames or bare light bulbs near the work area, and don't work in a garage where a gas-type appliance (such as a water heater or a clothes dryer) is present. Since gasoline is carcinogenic, wear fuel resistant gloves when there's a possibility of being exposed to fuel, and, if you spill any fuel on your skin, rinse it off immediately with soap and water. Mop up any spills immediately and do not store fuel-soaked rags where they could ignite. The fuel system is under constant pressure, so, if any fuel lines are to be disconnected, the fuel pressure in the system must be relieved first. When you perform any kind of work on the fuel system, wear safety glasses and have a Class B type fire extinguisher on hand.

1   Remove the gas cap to release any pressure in the fuel tank.
2   Remove the rear seat cushion (see Chapter 11).
3   Remove the fuel pump/sending unit floor service hole cover **(see illustration 5.4a)**.
4   Disconnect the fuel pump electrical connector **(see illustration 5.4b)**.
5   Start the engine and allow it to run until it stops, then turn the ignition key to OFF.
6   Disconnect the cable from the negative battery terminal before working on the fuel system (see Chapter 5, Section 1).
7   The fuel system pressure is now relieved, and you can now safely open fuel line fittings anywhere in the system. But even though there is no longer any pressure in the system, it's still a good idea to wrap a shop rag around a fitting before opening it to soak up any fuel that leaks out.

3   Fuel pump/fuel pressure - check

Warning: *Gasoline is extremely flammable, so take extra precautions when you work on any part of the fuel system. See the* **Warning** *in Section 2.*

General checks

1   Make sure that there is adequate fuel in the fuel tank.
2   Verify the fuel pump actually runs. Have

an assistant turn the ignition switch to ON - you should hear a brief whirring noise for about two seconds as the pump comes on and pressurizes the system. **Note:** *The fuel pump is easy to hear through the fuel filler neck.* If the fuel pump makes no sound, check the EFI fuse and the circuit opening or EFI relay, both of which are located in the fuse and relay box. Refer to Section 15 and check the fuel pump cut switch (this is especially important if the vehicle has recently had any kind of impact that may have tripped the switch). If the fuse and relay are OK, check the wiring back to the fuel pump. If voltage is present at the fuel pump electrical connector for a couple of seconds when the ignition key is turned on, the fuel pump is defective. If no voltage is present, the PCM might be defective. Have the vehicle checked at a dealer service department.

Fuel pump pressure check

Refer to illustrations 3.4 and 3.5

3   Relieve the fuel system pressure (see Section 2).
4   To test the fuel pressure you will need a fuel pressure gauge capable of measuring the fuel pressure in the range listed in this Chapter's Specifications, and you'll need a T-fitting that fits the inside diameter of the fuel hoses. Fuel pressure gauge kits **(see illustration)** are available at many auto parts stores.
5   Disconnect the fuel supply line from the fuel rail (if you're unfamiliar with quick-connect fittings, see Section 4), then hook up your fuel pressure test rig between the fuel supply line and the fuel rail. Make sure that the clamps are tight on the hoses **(see illustration)**.

Return-type fuel systems (four-cylinder, 2.7L V6 and some 3.5L V6 engines)

6   Turn off all accessories and turn the ignition switch key to ON. The fuel pump should run for about two seconds to pressurize the system. Note the reading on the gauge. After the pump stops running, the pressure should hold steady. After five minutes it should not

3.5 Connect the pressure gauge to the hose you've spliced into the fuel supply line

drop below the minimum listed in this Chapter's Specifications.

7   Start the engine, allow it to warm up to its normal operating temperature, then measure the fuel pressure and compare your readings to the system pressure listed in this Chapter's Specifications.

a) *If the pressure is high, disconnect the vacuum hose from the fuel pressure regulator and connect a vacuum gauge to the hose. Make sure there is 12 in-Hg or more vacuum present at the hose. If there isn't, check the hose for a restriction or leak.*

b) *If there is adequate vacuum to the regulator but the pressure is high, check for a restricted fuel return hose or line. If the return hose and line are clear, replace the pressure regulator.*

c) *If the pressure is low, pinch the fuel return hose. If the pressure goes up, replace the fuel pressure regulator. If the pressure does not increase, replace the fuel filter (see Chapter 1) and recheck the pressure. If it's still low, check the fuel supply hose and line for a restriction. If there is no restriction, replace the fuel pump (see Section 6).* **Note:** *As the fuel pump is removed, check the inlet strainer on the bottom of the pump for clogging.*

d) *Another possibility of low fuel pressure is a leaking fuel injector, but that would most likely set a trouble code and turn on the CHECK ENGINE light (because the fuel mixture would be too rich).*

8   To check the operation of the fuel pressure regulator, disconnect the vacuum hose from the regulator with the engine idling and watch the fuel pressure gauge - the fuel pressure should increase 3 to 10 psi as soon as the hose is disconnected. If it doesn't, check for vacuum at the hose (see Step 7a). If vacuum is present, replace the fuel pressure regulator.

9   Turn the key off and observe the pressure for five minutes. If the pressure drops substantially, then there is either a leaking injector or a faulty check valve in the fuel pump.

10   Relieve the system fuel pressure (see Section 2), then disconnect the cable from the negative battery terminal (see Chapter 5, Section 1). Remove the fuel pressure gauge and test hoses, then reconnect the fuel supply hose to the fuel rail. Reconnect the cable to the negative battery terminal (see Chapter 5, Section 1), then start the engine and check for leaks.

Returnless fuel systems (some 2005 and all 2006 3.5L V6 engines)

11   Start the engine and let it warm up until it's idling at its normal operating temperature, then measure the fuel pressure and compare your reading to the fuel pressure listed in this Chapter's Specifications.

a) *If the indicated fuel pressure is low, inspect the fuel supply hose and line for an obstruction. If the hose and line are clear, replace the fuel filter, then recheck the fuel pressure. If the indicated fuel pressure is still low, replace the fuel pump/fuel pressure regulator, then recheck the fuel pressure.* **Note:** *At the time of writing, the fuel pressure regulator was not available separately. Check with your local auto parts store or dealer parts department to see if the pressure regulator can be purchased separately.*

b) *If the indicated fuel pressure is high, replace the fuel pump/fuel pressure regulator, then recheck the fuel pressure. If the fuel pressure is still high, have the fuel system diagnosed by a dealer service department or other qualified repair shop.*

12   After the test is complete, relieve the system fuel pressure (see Section 2), then disconnect the cable from the negative battery terminal (see Chapter 5, Section 1).

13   Remove the fuel pressure gauge.

14   Reconnect the cable to the negative battery terminal (see Chapter 5, Section 1).

15   Start the engine and check for fuel leaks.

4   Fuel lines and fittings - general information

Warning: *Gasoline is extremely flammable, so take extra precautions when you work on any part of the fuel system. See the* **Warning** *in Section 2.*

Fuel lines

1   Before servicing fuel lines or fittings, relieve the fuel pressure (see Section 2) and disconnect the cable from the negative battery terminal (see Chapter 5, Section 1).

2   The fuel line extends from the fuel tank to the engine compartment. The fuel line is secured to the underbody with plastic clips. Inspect these clips and the fuel line whenever you're working under the vehicle.

3   Look for leaks, kinks and dents in the fuel line. If you find any sign of damage, replace the fuel line immediately. Make sure that the metal fuel lines don't chafe against the pan or against any under-vehicle components. There must be a minimum of 1/4-inch clearance around the metal fuel lines to prevent chafing.

4   Some of the fuel line clips are bolted to the underside of the vehicle. To detach a bolted clip, simply remove the retaining bolt. Most of the clips, however, are pushed onto threaded studs welded to the pan. This type of clip is secured to the stud by ratchet teeth that grip the threads on the stud.

5   To install a new fuel line clip:

a) *Push the fuel and EVAP lines into their guides in the clip.*

b) *Align the clip with the threaded stud.*

c) *Push the clip onto the threaded stud until it seats firmly against the underside of the vehicle.*

6   If you're replacing a damaged metal fuel line, replace the damaged line with factory replacement metal fuel line tubing or use equivalent grade steel tubing that meets the manufacturer's specifications. An unapproved line might fail when subjected to the high pressure of the fuel system. Don't use copper or aluminum tubing to replace steel tubing. These materials cannot withstand normal vehicle vibration.

7   Some fuel lines use banjo fittings with banjo bolts and sealing washers. Replace the two sealing washers every time that you open one of these fittings.

Fuel hoses

Warning: *Use only original equipment replacement hoses or their equivalent. Unapproved hoses might fail when pressurized.*

8   Never route flexible fuel hose within four inches of any part of the exhaust system or within ten inches of the catalytic converter. Rubber hoses must never be allowed to chafe against the frame. A minimum of 1/4-inch clearance must be maintained around a hose to prevent contact with the frame.

4.11 To remove the protective cover from the quick-connect fitting, simply push it off to the side

4.12 To disconnect a quick-connect fitting, depress the two buttons on opposite sides of the fitting, then pull the fitting off the end of the fuel line

Nylon fuel lines

9   Some fuel lines are nylon, and use quick-connect fittings to connect them to the fuel pump, metal fuel lines and the fuel rail. These nylon fuel lines and quick-connect fittings cannot be serviced separately from one another. If any part of one of these lines or fittings is damaged, replace the entire assembly. Do not attempt to repair them.

10   Read through the following procedure for disconnecting and reconnecting a quick-connect fitting before trying to disconnect it.

Quick-connect fittings

Button-type quick-connects

Refer to illustrations 4.11, 4.12 and 4.13

11   Some button-type quick-connect fittings are protected by a plastic cover **(see illustration)** that surrounds the fitting on three sides. To remove the cover, simply pull it off.

12   To disconnect a button-type quick-con-

nect fitting, depress the two buttons on either side of the fitting and pull the fitting off the fuel line **(see illustration)**.

13   Inspect the condition of the O-ring inside the fitting **(see illustration)**. If it's damaged, replace it.

14   Installation is the reverse of removal. To reconnect a button-type quick-connect fitting, push it onto the fuel line until both retaining pawls lock with a clicking sound.

15   Before installing the plastic cover over the fitting, reconnect the cable to the negative battery terminal, start the engine and check for leaks.

Clamp-type quick-connects

Refer to illustrations 4.16a and 4.16b

16   To unlock the clamp, press the locking tab and turn the clamp clockwise to unlock the fitting **(see illustrations)**.

17   Pull the two halves of the fitting apart.

18   Installation is the reverse of removal. Make sure that the raised ridge on the fuel

line clicks into the fitting.

19   To verify that the fitting is securely connected, try to pull the two sides of the fitting apart.

20   Reconnect the cable to the negative battery terminal, start the engine and check for leaks.

---

5   Fuel pump/fuel level sending unit - removal and installation

Refer to illustrations 5.2, 5.3, 5.4a and 5.4b

Warning: *Gasoline is extremely flammable, so take extra precautions when you work on any part of the fuel system. See the* **Warning** *in Section 2.*

1   Remove the rear seat (see Chapter 11).

2   Cut the carpet where it is slotted to make a flap **(see illustration)**.

3   Likewise cut the padding below the carpet and pull it back **(see illustration)**

4.13 Inspect the O-ring inside the quick-connect fitting. If it's damaged, replace it

4.16a To unlock a clamp-type quick-connect fitting, push this locking tab to unlock the clamp . . .

4.16b . . . then rotate the clamp in a clockwise direction to unlock the fitting

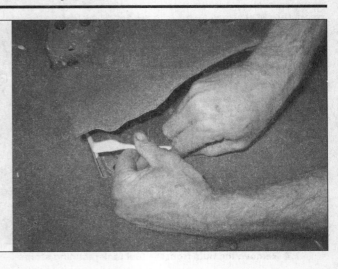

5.3 There is carpet padding that must also be cut free to reach the fuel tank access cover

5.2 Use a sharp razor to connect the slits in the carpet under the left rear seat

4   Remove the fuel pump/sending unit floor service hole cover (see illustrations).
5   Disconnect the fuel pump electrical connector.
6   Relieve the fuel system pressure (see Section 2) and remove the fuel tank cap.
7   Disconnect the cable from the negative battery terminal (see Chapter 5, Section 1).
8   Disconnect the fuel lines from the top of the fuel pump unit.
9   Remove the retaining bolts from the fuel pump/fuel level sending unit mounting flange.
10   Carefully lift the fuel pump/fuel level sending unit assembly from the fuel tank.
11   Inspect the fuel pump inlet strainer for contamination. If it's dirty, try cleaning the strainer with some clean solvent and an old toothbrush. If the strainer is too dirty to be cleaned while it's installed, remove it from the fuel pump/fuel level sending unit (see Section 6) and try cleaning it again. If you still can't clean it adequately, replace it.
12   Installation is the reverse of removal.

6 Fuel pump/fuel level sending unit - component replacement

Warning: *Gasoline is extremely flammable, so take extra precautions when you work on any part of the fuel system. See the* **Warning** *in Section 2.*
Note: *Once you have removed the fuel pump/fuel level sending unit from the fuel tank, you can replace the entire assembly, or you can disassemble it and replace the fuel inlet strainer, the fuel pump or the fuel level sending unit.*
1   Remove the fuel pump/fuel level sending unit assembly from the fuel tank (see Section 5).
2   Drain any residual gasoline from the fuel pump/fuel level sending unit, then place the fuel pump/fuel level sending unit on a clean workbench. Make sure that the work area is well ventilated, because there will be gasoline evaporating from the pump/sending unit for a while.
3   Check the strainer for clogging. If in doubt, replace it.

4   Unclip the fuel pump from the filter/sender assembly.
5   Reassembly is the reverse of disassembly.
6   Install the fuel pump/fuel level sending unit in the fuel tank (see Section 5).

7 Fuel tank - removal and installation

Refer to illustration 7.7
Warning: *Gasoline is extremely flammable, so take extra precautions when you work on any part of the fuel system. See the* **Warning** *in Section 2.*
1   Relieve the fuel system pressure (see Section 2). Remove the fuel filler cap to relieve fuel tank pressure.
2   Disconnect the cable from the negative battery terminal (see Chapter 5, Section 1).
3   Remove the fuel pump/fuel level sending unit assembly from the fuel tank (see Section 5).

5.4a This cover provides access to the top of the fuel tank

5.4b Disconnect the wiring, remove the bolts and carefully withdraw the fuel pump and sender

7.7 Remove the nuts from the fuel tank retaining straps

9.7 Remove the air filter for access to these three retaining bolts

4   Remove the drain plug and drain the fuel into an approved container.

5   Raise the vehicle and place it securely on jackstands. **Note:** *Some models have fuel tank protection plates or other components that interfere with tank removal. Remove all interfering items at this time.*

6   Place a floor jack (with a block of wood on it) under the fuel tank.

7   Remove the nuts from the tank retaining straps **(see illustration)**.

8   Lower the tank to gain access to the top of it.

9   Disconnect the remaining hoses from the tank.

10   Carefully lower the tank.

11   Installation is the reverse of removal. Be sure to tighten the fuel tank strap bolts securely.

---

8   Fuel tank cleaning and repair - general information

1   Any repairs to the fuel tank or filler neck should be done by a professional with experience in this critical and potentially dangerous work. Even after cleaning and flushing of the fuel system, explosive fumes can remain and ignite during repair of the tank.

2   If the fuel tank is removed from the vehicle, it should not be placed in an area where sparks or open flames could ignite the fumes coming out of the tank. Be especially careful inside garages where a gas-type appliance is located, because it could cause an explosion.

---

9   Air filter housing - removal and installation

Air intake duct and resonators

1   Remove the engine cover (see *Intake manifold - removal and installation* in Chapter 2).

10.2 To disconnect the accelerator cable from the throttle cam, align the cable with the slot in the side of the cam, then slide the cable end plug out of the cam

2   Disconnect the electrical connector at the airflow sensor.

3   Loosen the hose clamps at both ends of the air intake duct and remove the duct.

4   If you're replacing the air intake duct, remove the resonators (2.4L and 2.7L engines only) and install them on the new intake duct.

5   Installation is the reverse of removal.

Air filter housing

Refer to illustration 9.7

6   Remove the air filter housing cover and remove the filter element (see Chapter 1).

7   Remove the three air filter housing mounting bolts **(see illustration)**.

8   Remove the air filter housing.

9   Installation is the reverse of removal.

---

10   Accelerator cable - removal and installation

Refer to illustrations 10.2 and 10.4

1   Remove the engine cover (see *Intake manifold - removal and installation* in Chapter 2).

2   Disengage the accelerator cable from the throttle lever **(see illustration)**. **Note:** *The throttle lever is located on the throttle body on 2.4L four-cylinder and 2.7L V6 engines. On 3.5L V6 engines it is on the accelerator pedal position sensor in the left side of the engine compartment, near the brake master cylinder.*

3   Trace the accelerator cable back to the firewall, note the routing of the cable and detach any cable clips or guides.

4   Inside the vehicle, disengage the cable from the accelerator pedal **(see illustration)**.

5   Remove the bolts and detach the cable from the firewall. Pull the cable through the firewall from the engine compartment side.

6   Installation is the reverse of removal. Apply a dab of white grease to the nylon ball at the accelerator pedal end of the cable.

---

11   Electronic Fuel Injection (EFI) system - general information

The EFI system consists of the fuel tank, the electric in-tank fuel pump, the fuel pressure regulator, the EFI main relay, the circuit opening relay (fuel pump relay), the fuel rail

10.4 To disconnect the cable from the accelerator pedal, pull the cable end (A) out of the pedal, then guide the cable out the slot on the left (B)

12.7 Using a stethoscope, listen to each fuel injector and verify that it's making a clicking sound when the engine is running

and the fuel injectors. The induction system consists of the air filter housing, the air intake duct and the throttle body. The throttle bodies on all models are conventional, cable-operated units. The EFI system is easy to understand if you divide it into three sub-systems: the air intake system, the electronic control system and the fuel delivery system.

Air intake system

The air intake system consists of the air filter housing, the air intake duct, the resonators, the throttle body and the intake manifold The resonators are oddly shaped appendages clamped to the air intake duct. They function as accumulators, or reservoirs, that help to quiet the flow of air through the air intake duct. The replacement procedures for all of these components are covered in this Chapter except the intake manifolds, which are covered in Chapter 2A or 2B.

The throttle body on all models is a conventional single-barrel design. The lower portion of the throttle body is heated by engine coolant to prevent icing in cold weather. The Throttle Position (TP) sensor is attached to the throttle shaft to monitor changes in the throttle opening. The Idle Air Control (IAC) valve is attached to the side of the throttle body on all 2.4L four-cylinder and 2.7L V6 engines. For information about the TP sensor and the IAC valve, refer to Chapter 6.

2.4L four-cylinder and 2.7L V6 engines

When the engine is idling, the air/fuel ratio is controlled by the Idle Speed Control (ISC) system. The ISC system consists of the Engine Coolant Temperature (ECT) sensor, the Intake Air Temperature (IAT) sensor the Throttle Position (TP) sensor, the Mass Air Flow (MAF) sensor, various other sensors, the Powertrain Control Module (PCM) and the ISC valve. The ISC valve is activated by the PCM under certain conditions, such as cold temperature during cranking, or loads imposed on

the engine by power steering demand at low vehicle speeds or by turning on the air conditioning. The ISC valve regulates the amount of airflow bypassing the throttle plate and into the intake manifold. For more information about the ISC valve and the ISC system, refer to Chapter 6.

3.5L V6 engines

The throttle on these models is electrically controlled by the PCM in response to signals from the accelerator position sensor as well as other sensors. The electronic throttle motor is mounted on the rear of the throttle body; the throttle position sensor and idle switch are on the front. The air/fuel ratio is controlled as with the two other engines.

Electronic control system

The information sensors, Powertrain Control Module (PCM) and output actuators, and the various emission control systems employed on these vehicles, are described in Chapter 6.

Fuel delivery system

The fuel delivery system consists of the fuel pump, the fuel pressure regulator, the fuel filter, the fuel lines, the pulsation damper, the fuel rail and the fuel injectors. The in-tank fuel pump is an electric in-line type. Fuel is drawn through an inlet strainer into the pump, passes through the fuel filter and is delivered to the injectors. The fuel pressure regulator adjusts the fuel pressure to the injectors.

The injectors are solenoid-actuated, constant stroke, pintle types consisting of a solenoid, plunger, needle valve and housing. When current is applied to the solenoid coil, the needle valve is raised off its seat and pressurized fuel squirts out of the injector body through the nozzle. The injection quantity is determined by the pulse width (the length of time that the pintle valve is open), which is controlled by the length of time during which current is supplied to the solenoid coil.

The EFI main relay, located in the instrument panel relay/fuse box, supplies power to the fuel pump relay (circuit opening relay) from the ignition key. The PCM controls the grounding signal to the fuel pump in response to the starting and camshaft position signals at start-up.

12 Fuel injection system - check

Refer to illustrations 12.7, 12.8 and 12.9
Warning: *Gasoline is extremely flammable, so take extra precautions when you work on any part of the fuel system. See the* **Warning** *in Section 2.*

1   Check all electrical connectors, especially ground connections, for the system. Loose connectors and poor grounds can cause many engine control system problems.

2   Verify that the battery is fully charged, because the Powertrain Control Module (PCM) and sensors cannot operate properly without an adequate voltage supply.

3   Refer to Chapter 1 and check the air filter element. A dirty or partially blocked filter will reduce performance and economy.

4   Check fuel pump operation (see Section 3). If the fuel pump fuse is blown, replace it and see if it blows again. If it does, look for a short in the wiring harness to the fuel pump.

5   Inspect the vacuum hoses connected to the intake manifold for damage, deterioration and leakage.

6   Remove the air intake duct from the throttle body and check for dirt, carbon, varnish, or other residue in the throttle body, particularly around the throttle plate. If it's dirty, refer to Chapter 6 and troubleshoot the PCV and EGR systems for the cause of excessive varnish buildup.

7   With the engine running, place an automotive stethoscope against each injector, one at a time, and listen for a clicking sound that indicates operation **(see illustration)**. If you don't have a stethoscope, you can place the

12.8 Plug the "noid" light into the electrical connector for each fuel injector and verify that it blinks with the engine running

12.9 Turn the mode knob on your digital multimeter to the appropriate resistance range, touch the probes of the meter to the two terminals on each injector and measure the resistance, which should be within the range listed in this Chapter's Specifications

tip of a long screwdriver against the injector and listen through the handle.

8   If an injector does not seem to be operating electrically (not clicking), purchase a special injector test light (sometimes called a "noid" light) and install it into the injector wiring harness connector **(see illustration)**. Start the engine and see if the noid light flashes. If it does, the injector is receiving proper voltage. If it doesn't flash, further diagnosis is necessary. You might want to have it checked by a dealership service department or other qualified repair shop.

9   With the engine off and the fuel injector electrical connectors disconnected, measure the resistance of each injector with an ohmmeter **(see illustration)**. If any injector differs from the average of the others by more than 15-percent, replace it.

10   Refer to Chapter 6 for other system checks.

---

13 Throttle body - check, removal and installation

Check

Refer to illustration 13.2

1   On 2.4L four-cylinder and 2.7L V6 models, verify that the throttle cable operates smoothly.

2   Remove the air intake duct from the throttle body and check for carbon and residue build-up. If it is dirty, clean it with aerosol carburetor cleaner (make sure the can specifically states that it is safe with oxygen sensor systems and catalytic converters) and a toothbrush **(see illustration)**. **Caution:** *Do not clean the Throttle Position (TP) sensor or the Idle Speed Control (ISC) valve with the solvent.*

Removal and installation

Refer to illustrations 13.5a, 13.5b and 13.12

Warning: *Wait until the engine is completely cool before beginning this procedure.*

3   Disconnect the cable from the negative battery terminal (see Chapter 5, Section 1).

4   Remove the air intake duct (see Section 9).

5   Disconnect the electrical connector from the Throttle Position (TP) sensor **(see illustrations)**.

6   Disconnect the electrical connector from the Idle Speed Control (ISC) valve on 2.4L four-cylinder and 2.7L V6 models.

7   Disconnect the wiring from the throttle control motor on 3.5L V6 models.

8   Disconnect the accelerator cable/cruise control cable from the throttle body on 2.4L four-cylinder and 2.7L V6 models.

9   Disconnect the vacuum hoses from the throttle body.

10   Clamp off the coolant hoses to the throttle body to minimize coolant loss.

11   Remove the throttle body mounting fas-

teners and remove the throttle body.

12   Disconnect the coolant hoses from the throttle body **(see illustration)**.

13   Remove and discard the old throttle body gasket.

14   Installation is the reverse of removal. Be sure to tighten the throttle body mounting nuts to the torque listed in this Chapter's Specifications. Check the coolant level, adding as necessary (see Chapter 1).

---

14 Fuel rail and injectors - removal and installation

Refer to illustrations 14.7, 14.9 and 14.10

Warning: *Gasoline is extremely flammable, so take extra precautions when you work on any part of the fuel system. See the* **Warning** *in Section 2.*

Note: *We recommend replacing all injector O-rings even when only one injector O-ring or seal is leaking. On most fuel rails you have to remove the entire assembly anyway, so*

13.2 With the engine off, use aerosol carburetor cleaner, a toothbrush and a shop rag to clean the throttle body bore. Open the throttle plate so that you can clean behind it. (Make sure that the carb cleaner won't damage catalysts and oxygen sensors)

13.5a The 3.5L V6 throttle body is equipped with electronic throttle control; there is no cable attached to the throttle body - all operation is done by a small electric motor

13.5b Disconnect all electrical connectors from the throttle body

replace all of the O-rings/seals at one time to avoid having to remove the fuel rail later to replace another O-ring and/or seal.

1   Relieve the fuel pressure (see Section 2).
2   Disconnect the cable from the negative battery terminal (see Chapter 5, Section 1).
3   Remove the engine cover, if equipped.
4   Remove the air intake duct (see Section 9).
5   On V6 models, refer to Chapter 2B and remove the upper intake manifold.
6   Disconnect the electrical connectors from the fuel injectors and set the injector harness aside.
7   Remove the fuel rail mounting bolts (see illustration).
8   Remove the fuel rail and the fuel injectors as a single assembly.
9   Remove the fuel injectors from the fuel rail (see illustration).
10 If you intend to re-use the same injec-

13.12 Pinch off the two coolant hoses to avoid spillage prior to detaching them from the throttle body

14.7 Fuel rail mounting bolts (3.5L V6 engine)

14.9 To remove each fuel injector from the fuel rail, simultaneously twist and pull it out of the fuel rail

14.10 If you plan to reinstall the original injectors, remove and discard the old O-rings and grommets and replace them with new ones

15.1 The fuel cut switch (inertia switch) may be activated in an accident and shut off power to the fuel pump - push in the top button to reset it

tors, replace the grommets and O-rings **(see illustration)**.

11   Installation is the reverse of removal. Be sure to use new injector O-rings and tighten the fuel rail mounting bolts to the torque listed in this Chapter's Specifications.

15   Fuel cut switch - description

Refer to illustration 15.1

The fuel cut switch is an electrical switch mounted in the engine compartment near the brake master cylinder **(see illustration)**. In the event of a vehicle impact, such as in a severe accident, the fuel cut switch interrupts the fuel pump circuit. This stops the fuel pump from discharging fuel through a damaged fuel system component and possibly causing a fire or explosion. Check the fuel cut switch if the vehicle won't start. Simply push down on the button on top of it to reset it.

16   Fuel pressure regulator - replacement

Return-type fuel systems (four-cylinder, 2.7L V6 and some 3.5L V6 engines)

Refer to illustration 16.5

1   Relieve the fuel system pressure (see Section 2).
2   Disconnect the cable from the negative terminal of the battery.
3   Disconnect the vacuum hose from the fuel pressure regulator.
4   Detach the fuel return line from the regulator.
5   Remove the two bolts and detach the fuel pressure regulator from the fuel rail **(see illustration)**.

6   If you're installing the same regulator, check the condition of the O-ring, replacing it if necessary.
7   Installation is the reverse of the removal procedure.

Returnless fuel systems (some 2005 and all 2006 3.5L V6 engines)

8   At the time of writing, the fuel pressure regulator was not available separately, necessitating replacement of the fuel pump assembly. Check with your local auto parts store or dealer parts department to see if the pressure regulator can be purchased separately.

17   Exhaust system servicing - general information

Refer to illustration 17.1

Warning: *Inspect and repair exhaust system components only after the system components have cooled down.*

1   The exhaust system consists of the exhaust manifold(s), the catalytic converters, the muffler, the tailpipe and the exhaust pipes that connect these components together, as well as the brackets, hangers and clamps that support and secure these components. The exhaust system is attached to the body with mounting brackets and rubber hangers **(see illustration)**. If any of these parts are damaged or deteriorated, excessive noise and vibration will be transmitted to the body. The exhaust system is divided into various sections, which are bolted together. Some of these sections consist of several components welded together into one assembly. For example, the center part of the exhaust system, which is also the longest single section, includes the downstream catalytic converter and the pre-muffler. If either of these components are damaged, you will have to replace the entire assembly, or have the old catalyst or muffler cut off and a new unit welded in. You'll also have to remove the center exhaust pipe assembly in order to remove the fuel tank.

16.5 Fuel pressure regulator mounting bolts (3.5L V6 engine shown, others similar)

2   Conducting regular inspections of the exhaust system will keep it safe and quiet. Look for damaged or bent parts, open seams, holes, loose connections, excessive corrosion or other damage that could allow exhaust fumes to enter the vehicle. Do not repair deteriorated exhaust system components - replace them.

3   If the exhaust system components are extremely corroded or rusted together, they will probably have to be cut from the exhaust system. The convenient way to accomplish this is to have a muffler repair shop remove the corroded sections with a cutting torch. If, however, you want to save money by doing it yourself and you don't have an oxy/acetylene welding outfit with a cutting torch, simply cut off the old components with a hacksaw. If you have compressed air, you can also use special pneumatic cutting chisels. If you do decide to tackle the job at home, be sure to wear eye protection to protect your eyes from metal chips, and wear work gloves to protect your hands.

4   Here are some simple guidelines to apply when repairing the exhaust system:

a) *Work from the back to the front when removing exhaust system components.*

b) *Apply penetrating oil to the exhaust system component fasteners to make them easier to remove.*

c) *Use new gaskets, hangers and clamps*

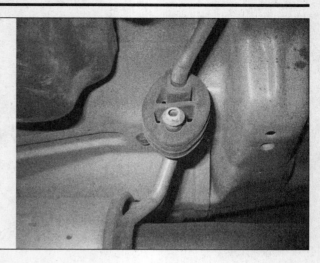

17.1 The rubber exhaust system hangers can deteriorate and break - they should be checked periodically

when installing exhaust system components. Unless the fasteners are in good condition, it's also a good idea to replace them as well. Even if you're successful in unscrewing rusted fasteners, they will be even more difficult to unscrew the next time that you need to do so, and they might break the next time that they're loosened or tightened.

d) *Apply anti-seize compound to the threads of all exhaust system fasteners during reassembly. Be sure to allow suf-ficient clearance between newly installed parts and all points on the underbody to avoid overheating the floor pan and possibly damaging the interior carpet and insulation. Pay particularly close attention to the catalytic converter and its heat shield.* **Warning:** *The catalytic converter operates at very high temperatures and takes a long time to cool. Wait until it's completely cool before attempting to remove the converter. Failure to do so could result in serious burns.*

Notes

Chapter 5
Engine electrical systems

Contents

Specifications

Charging system
Battery voltage	12.5 to 12.9 volts
Charging voltage	14.0 to 15.0 volts

Ignition system
Ignition coil resistance (approximate)
- 2.4L four-cylinder engine
  - Primary: Not available
  - Secondary: 17.0 to 23.0 k-ohms
- 2.7L V6 engine
  - Primary: 0.67 to 0.82 ohms
  - Secondary: 11.3 to 15.3 k-ohms
- 3.5L V6 engine
  - Primary: 1.3 ohms
  - Secondary: 10.3 to 15.0 k-ohms

Torque specifications
	Ft-lbs	Nm
Alternator mounting bolts		
Upper (adjustment)	15 to 18	20 to 25
Lower (pivot)	26 to 40	34 to 54

3.2 To test the open circuit voltage of the battery, touch the black probe of the voltmeter to the negative terminal and the red probe to the positive terminal of the battery. A fully charged battery should read between 12.6 and 12.9 volts, depending on the ambient temperature

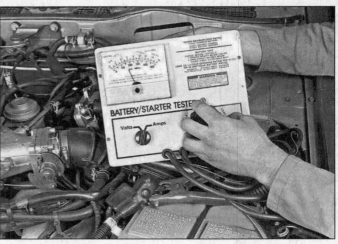

3.3 Some battery load testers are equipped with an ammeter that enables you to dial in the battery load (shown). Less expensive testers only have a load switch and voltmeter

1   General information, precautions and battery disconnection

The engine electrical systems include all ignition, charging and starting components. Because of their engine-related functions, these components are discussed separately from body electrical devices such as the lights, the instruments, etc. (which are included in Chapter 12).

Precautions

Always observe the following precautions when working on the electrical system:

a) *Be extremely careful when servicing engine electrical components. They are easily damaged if checked, connected or handled improperly.*

b) *Never leave the ignition switched on for long periods of time when the engine is not running.*

c) *Never disconnect the battery cables while the engine is running.*

d) *Maintain correct polarity when connecting battery cables from another vehicle during jump starting - see the "Booster battery (jump) starting" Section at the front of this manual.*

e) *Always disconnect the negative battery cable from the battery before working on the electrical system, but read the following battery disconnection procedure first.*

It's also a good idea to review the safety-related information regarding the engine electrical systems located in the "Safety first!" Section at the front of this manual, before beginning any operation included in this Chapter.

Battery disconnection

Several systems - such as the alarm system, radio, power door locks or power windows - require continuous battery power, either to ensure their continued operation or to maintain control unit memory, such as the Powertrain Control Module (PCM), which will be lost if the battery is disconnected. Therefore, whenever the battery is to be disconnected, first note the following to ensure that there are no unforeseen consequences of this action:

a) *The engine management system's PCM will eventually lose some data stored in its memory when the battery is disconnected. This could include idling and operating values, detected fault codes and the system monitors required for emissions testing. Whenever the battery is disconnected, the computer may require a certain period of time to re-learn the operating values.*

b) *On any vehicle with power door locks, it is a wise precaution to remove the key from the ignition and to keep it with you, so that it does not get locked inside if the power door locks should engage accidentally when the battery is reconnected!*

Devices known as "memory-savers" can be used to avoid some of the above problems. Typically, a memory-saver is plugged into the cigarette lighter and connected to another voltage source. The vehicle battery is then disconnected from the electrical system, and the memory-saver provides current levels sufficient to maintain audio unit security codes and PCM memory values, and to power always-on circuits such as the clock and radio memory, all the while isolating the battery in the event that a short-circuit occurs while servicing the vehicle. **Warning 1:** *Some of these devices allow a considerable amount of current to pass, which can mean that many of the vehicle's systems are still operational when the main battery is disconnected. So if you're using a memory-saver, make sure that a circuit is actually open before touching it.* **Warning 2:** *If you're working around*

an airbag, disconnect the battery and do not use a memory saver. If you use a memory-saver device to keep up power while working around an airbag, remember that the airbag is capable of accidental deployment.

The battery on all models is located in the engine compartment. To disconnect the battery for service procedures requiring power to be cut from the vehicle, loosen the negative cable clamp nut and detach the negative cable from the negative battery post. Isolate the cable end to prevent it from accidentally coming into contact with the battery post.

2   Battery - emergency jump starting

Refer to the *Booster battery (jump) starting procedure* at the front of this manual.

3   Battery - check and replacement

Check

Refer to illustrations 3.2 and 3.3

1   Disconnect the negative battery cable, then the positive cable from the battery.

2   Check the battery state of charge. Perform an open voltage circuit test using a digital voltmeter **(see illustration)**. **Note:** *The battery's surface charge must be removed before accurate voltage measurements can be made. Turn on the high beams for ten seconds, then turn them off, and let the vehicle stand for two minutes.* With the engine and all accessories turned off, touch the negative probe of the voltmeter to the negative terminal of the battery and the positive probe to the positive terminal of the battery. The battery voltage should be about 12.6 to 12.9 volts. If the battery is less than the specified voltage,

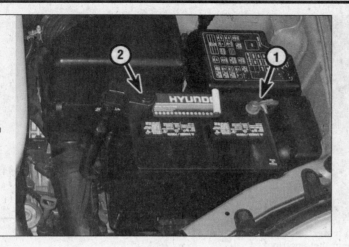

3.4 To remove the battery, disconnect the cable from the negative battery terminal first (1), then disconnect the cable from the positive terminal (2)

charge the battery before proceeding to the next test. Do not proceed with the battery load test unless the battery charge is correct.

3   Perform a battery load test. An accurate check of the battery condition can only be performed with a load tester (available at most auto parts stores). This test evaluates the ability of the battery to operate the starter and other accessories during periods of heavy load (current draw). Install a battery load-testing tool onto the terminals **(see illustration)**. Load test the battery according to the manufacturer's instructions for the particular tool. This tool increases the load demand (amperage draw) on the battery. Maintain the load on the battery for 15 seconds or less and observe that the battery voltage does not drop below 9.6 volts. If the battery condition is weak or defective, the tool will indicate this condition immediately. **Note:** *Cold temperatures will cause the minimum voltage reading to drop slightly. Follow the chart given in the manufacturer's instructions to compensate for cold climates. Minimum load voltage for freezing temperatures (32-degrees F) should be approximately 9.1 volts.*

Replacement
Refer to illustrations 3.4 and 3.5

4   Disconnect the negative battery cable, then the positive cable from the battery **(see illustration)**.
5   Remove the battery hold-down clamp **(see illustration)**.
6   Lift out the battery. Be careful - it's heavy.
Note: *Battery straps and handlers are available at most auto parts stores for a reasonable price. They make it easier to remove and carry the battery.*
7   While the battery is out, remove the battery tray and inspect it for corrosion.
8   If there's corrosion on the battery tray, wash the tray thoroughly in clean water. If the tray is cracked or damaged, replace it.
9   If you are replacing the battery, make sure you get one that's identical, with the same dimensions, amperage rating, cold cranking rating, etc.
10   Installation is the reverse of removal.

4   Battery cables - check and replacement

1   Periodically, inspect the entire length of each battery cable for damage, cracked or burned insulation and corrosion. Poor battery cable connections can cause starting problems and decreased engine performance.
2   Inspect the cable-to-terminal connections at the ends of the cables for cracks, loose wire strands and corrosion (see Chapter 1). The presence of white, fluffy deposits under the insulation at the cable terminal connection are a sign that the cable is corroded and should be replaced. Check the terminals for distortion, missing mounting bolts and corrosion.
3   When removing the cables, always disconnect the negative cable first and hook it up last or you might accidentally short the battery with the tool that you're using to loosen the cable clamps. Even if only the positive cable is being replaced, be sure to disconnect the negative cable from the battery first.
4   Disconnect the old cables from the battery, then trace each of them to their opposite ends and detach them from the starter solenoid and ground terminals. Note the routing of each cable to ensure correct installation.
5   If you are replacing either or both of the

old cables, take them with you when buying new cables. It is vitally important that you replace the cables with identical parts. Cables have characteristics that make them easy to identify. Positive cables are usually red and larger in cross-section; ground cables are usually black and smaller in cross section.
6   Clean the threads of the solenoid or ground connection with a wire brush to remove rust and corrosion. Apply a light coat of battery terminal corrosion inhibitor, or petroleum jelly, to the threads to prevent future corrosion.
7   Attach the cable to the solenoid or ground connection and tighten the mounting nut/bolt securely.
8   Before connecting a new cable to the battery, make sure that it reaches the battery post without having to be stretched.
9   Connect the positive cable first, followed by the negative cable.

5   Ignition system - general information and precautions

1   All models covered by this manual are equipped with a computer-controlled electronic ignition system. The ignition system includes the Camshaft Position (CMP) sensor, the Crankshaft Position (CKP) sensor, various other information sensors, the Powertrain Control Module (PCM), and the spark plugs; there is no distributor. 2.7L V6 engines use a conventional coil pack that fires the spark plugs via six spark plug wires. 2.4L four-cylinder and 3.5L V6 engines use a coil-on-plug system. On the 3.5L V6, there are coils on the front cylinder bank only. Each of these coils has a spark plug wire attached that also fires a spark plug on the other side of the engine simultaneously. This is called a "waste spark" system. The cylinder that is being fired while on its exhaust stroke consumes very little spark energy.
2   When working on the ignition system, take the following precautions:
a) *Do not keep the ignition switch on for more than 10 seconds if the engine will not start.*

3.5 The battery is secured on its tray by a clamp at the base; check it for acid corrosion and replace damaged components

6.2 To use this type of calibrated ignition tester, unbolt and remove the ignition coil (don't disconnect the electrical connector), plug the tester into the boot at the lower end of the coil, clip the tester to a convenient ground and operate the starter with the ignition turned to ON. If there's enough power to fire the plug, sparks will be visible between the electrode tip and the tester body

7.2 Connect the ohmmeter to the coil as shown to check the winding insulation

b) *Always connect a tachometer in accordance with the manufacturer's instructions. Some tachometers may be incompatible with this ignition system. Consult an auto parts counterperson before buying a tachometer for use with this vehicle.*

c) *Never allow the ignition coil terminals to touch ground. Grounding the coil could result in damage to the igniter and/or the ignition coil.*

d) *Do not disconnect the battery when the engine is running.*

6   Ignition system - check

Refer to illustration 6.2

Warning: *Because of the high voltage generated by the ignition system, be extremely cautious when servicing or checking ignition components. This not only includes the igni-*

tion coils and spark plugs but test equipment as well.

1   Relieve the fuel system pressure (see Chapter 4). Keep the fuel system disabled while performing the ignition system checks.
2   If the engine turns over but won't start, disconnect each ignition coil (or spark plug wire) from its corresponding spark plug (see Section 7) and attach it to a calibrated ignition tester **(see illustration)**. Calibrated ignition testers are available at most auto parts stores. Make sure that the spark plug is well grounded.
3   Crank the engine and watch the tester to see if bright blue, well-defined sparks occur.
4   If sparks occur, sufficient voltage is reaching the spark plug to fire it. Repeat this test at each spark plug to verify that all the ignition coils are functioning. If there is no spark at a plug, the ignition coil for that plug is probably bad. However, the plug itself might be fouled, so remove and check the plug as described in Chapter 1. If a number of plugs

are fouled, it's a good idea to install a set of new spark plugs so that the plug gaps are uniform and the electrodes are all in the same condition.
5   Use a code-reading tool or a scan tool to check for any stored Diagnostic Trouble Codes (DTCs) related to the ignition system, the Camshaft Position (CMP) sensor, the Crankshaft Position (CKP) sensor, other sensors or and/or the Powertrain Control Module (PCM).

7   Ignition coils - check and replacement

Check

Refer to illustrations 7.2, 7.3 and 7.8

2.4L four-cylinder and 3.5L V6 models

1   Remove the coils from the engine (see Steps 11 through 15).
2   Connect the ohmmeter between terminal number one in the connector and the spark plug terminal **(see illustration)**. This will check the insulation between the two windings. The reading should be very high or infinity. If it's substantially out of range, replace the coil.
3   Measure the secondary resistance by connecting the ohmmeter between the two high voltage terminals of the coil **(see illustration)**. Compare your readings to those listed in this Chapter's Specifications. If the reading is close, then the coil is probably good. If it's far out of range, replace it.
4   If you're in doubt about a coil, try swapping it to another cylinder. If a PCM trouble code indicated a misfire on the old cylinder, the problem will transfer to the new cylinder if the coil is bad.

7.3 Connect the ohmmeter between the spark plug terminal and spark plug wire terminal to check the secondary resistance

7.8 On 2.7L V6 engines, unplug the wiring harness from the coil pack and probe terminals 1 and 2, then 2 and 4, then 2 and 3, with an ohmmeter

7.13 Each ignition coil is secured by two bolts (3.5L V6 shown)

2.7L V6 models

5   Disconnect the spark plug wires from the coil pack. Also disconnect the primary wiring connector.

6   Connect an ohmmeter between the first two spark plug terminals. This is the secondary resistance. Compare your reading with that listed in this Chapter's Specifications. If it's substantially out of range, replace the coil.

7   Repeat this procedure for the next two terminals, then the last two.

8   Connect the ohmmeter between terminals 1 and 2 of the wiring connector **(see illustration)**. This is the primary resistance for cylinders 3 and 6. Compare your reading with that listed in this Chapter's Specifications. If it's substantially out of range, replace the coil.

9   Repeat this procedure between terminals 2 and 4. This will give the primary resistance for cylinders 1 and 4.

10   Repeat it again between terminals 2 and 3. This will give the primary resistance for cylinders 2 and 5.

Replacement

Refer to illustrations 7.13 and 7.15

11   Disconnect the cable from the negative battery terminal (see Sections 1 and 3).

12   Remove the engine cover (see *Intake manifold - removal and installation* in Chapter 2).

2.4L four-cylinder and 3.5L V6 models

13   Disconnect the electrical connector from the ignition coil, then remove the mounting bolts **(see illustration)**.

14   On 3.5L V6 models, disconnect the spark plug wire. Pull on the boot only - not on the wire.

15   Pull the coil straight up and out of the valve cover **(see illustration)**.

16   Installation is the reverse of removal.

2.7L V6 models

17   The coil pack on these engines is mounted to the front cylinder head.

18   Mark the positions of the spark plug wires, then detach them from the coil pack.

19   Disconnect the electrical connector from the ignition coil, then remove the mounting bolts.

20   Lift the coil pack from the cylinder head.

21   Installation is the reverse of removal.

8   Charging system - general information and precautions

The charging system includes the alternator with an internal voltage regulator, the discharge warning light, the battery, a fusible link and the wiring between all the components. The charging system supplies electrical power for the ignition system, the lights, the radio, etc. The alternator is driven by a drivebelt at the front of the engine. The voltage regulator limits the alternator's voltage to a preset value to prevent power surges and circuit overloads during peak voltage output.

The discharge warning light on the instrument cluster should come on when the ignition key is turned to START, then it should go off immediately. If it remains on, or if it comes on during vehicle operation, there is a malfunction in the charging system.

The charging system doesn't ordinarily require periodic maintenance. However, the drivebelt, battery and wires and connections should be inspected at the intervals outlined in Chapter 1. Be very careful when making electrical circuit connections to a vehicle equipped with an alternator and note the following:

a)   *When reconnecting wires to the alternator from the battery, be sure to note the polarity.*

b)   *Before using arc-welding equipment to repair any part of the vehicle, disconnect the wires from the alternator and the battery terminals.*

c)   *Never start the engine with a battery charger connected.*

d)   *Always disconnect both battery leads before using a battery charger.*

7.15 After removing the screws, pull the coil straight up and out. Make sure the boot (A) is in good condition

9.3 To check charging voltage, connect a voltmeter to the battery terminals and check the battery voltage with the engine running

e) *The alternator is driven by an engine drivebelt that could cause serious injury if your hand, hair or clothes become entangled in it with the engine running.*

f) *Because the alternator is connected directly to the battery, it could arc or cause a fire if overloaded or shorted out.*

g) *Wrap a plastic bag over the alternator and secure it with rubber bands before steam cleaning the engine.*

9   Charging system - check

Refer to illustration 9.3

1   If a malfunction occurs in the charging circuit, do not immediately assume that the alternator is causing the problem. First, check the following items:

a) *Make sure the battery cable clamps are clean and tightly secured to the battery terminals.*

b) *Test the condition of the battery (see Section 3). If it does not pass all the tests, replace it.*

c) *Check the external alternator wiring and connections.*

d) *Check the drivebelt condition and tension (see Chapter 1).*

e) *Check the alternator mounting bolts for tightness.*

f) *Run the engine and check the alternator for abnormal noise.*

g) *Check the fusible link (see Chapter 12). If it's burned, determine the cause and repair the circuit.*

h) *Check the discharge warning indicator light on the instrument cluster. It should illuminate when the ignition key is turned to ON (engine not running). If it doesn't, check the circuit between the alternator and the discharge warning indicator light (see the Wiring Diagrams at the end of Chapter 12).*

i) *Check the fuses that are in series with the charging system circuit (see the Wiring Diagrams at the end of Chapter 12).*

2   With the ignition key off, check the battery voltage with no accessories operating. It should be approximately 12.6 to 12.9 volts

(see illustration 3.2). It may be slightly higher if the engine had been operating within the last hour.

3   Connect an ammeter to the charging system following the tool manufacturer's instructions. Start the engine, and check the battery voltage and amperage. It should now be approximately 13.2 to 14.8 volts **(see illustration)**.

4   Load the battery by turning on the high beam headlights and the air conditioning system and place the blower fan on HIGH. Raise the engine speed to 2,000 rpm and check the voltage and amperage. If the charging system is working properly the voltage should stay above 13.5 volts and the amperage should be 30 amps or more (depending on the condition of the battery, it could be less than 30 amps).

5   If the voltage rises above 15.0 volts in either test, the regulator is defective.

6   If the indicated voltage reading is less than the specified charge voltage, the alternator is probably defective. Have the charging system checked at a dealer service department or other properly equipped repair facility. **Note:** *Many auto parts stores will bench test an alternator off the vehicle. Refer to your local auto parts store regarding their policy (many stores will perform this service free of charge).*

10   Alternator - removal and installation

Removal

1   Disconnect the cable from the negative battery terminal (see Sections 1 and 3).

Four-cylinder models

2   Disconnect the electrical connectors from the alternator.

3   Loosen the lock bolt on the upper alternator adjusting mount and the lower mount bolt.

4   Turn the adjusting bolt counterclockwise to release tension on the drivebelt.

5   Remove the drivebelt.

6   Remove the two alternator mounting bolts and remove the alternator.

V6 models

7   Remove the drivebelt (see Chapter 1). **Note:** *Access is very limited on these models. It will be necessary to remove various components to gain access. These components vary from model to model.*

8   Disconnect the electrical connectors from the alternator.

9   Remove the mounting bolts and remove the alternator.

Installation

10   If you're replacing the alternator, take the old alternator with you when purchasing a replacement unit. Make sure that the new/rebuilt unit is identical to the old alternator. Look at the terminals - they should be the same in number, size and locations as the terminals on the old alternator. Finally, look at the identification markings - they will be stamped in the housing or printed on a tag or plaque affixed to the housing. Make sure that these numbers are the same on both alternators.

11   If the replacement alternator doesn't have a pulley installed, you might have to switch the pulley from the old unit to the replacement unit. When buying a new or rebuilt alternator, ask about the shop's policy regarding pulley swapping. Some shops will perform this service for free.

12   Installation is the reverse of removal. After the alternator is installed, adjust the drivebelt tension on 2.4L four-cylinder models (see Chapter 1), then check the charging voltage to verify that the alternator is operating correctly (see Section 9).

11   Starting system - general information and precautions

The starting system consists of the battery, the starter motor, the starter solenoid and the electrical circuit connecting the components. The solenoid is mounted directly on the starter motor. The solenoid/starter motor assembly is installed on the upper part of the transaxle bellhousing.

When the ignition key is turned to the START position, the starter solenoid is actuated through the starter control circuit. The starter solenoid then connects the battery to the starter. The battery supplies the electrical energy to the starter motor, which does the actual work of cranking the engine.

Always observe the following precautions when working on the starting system:

a) *Excessive cranking of the starter motor can overheat it and cause serious damage. Never operate the starter motor for more than 15 seconds at a time without pausing to allow it to cool for at least two minutes.*

b) *The starter is connected directly to the battery and could arc or cause a fire if mishandled, overloaded or short-circuited.*

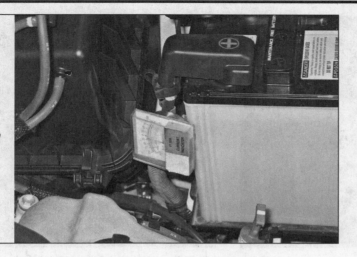

12.3 To use an inductive ammeter, simply hold the ammeter over the positive or negative cable (whichever is more accessible)

c) *Always detach the cable from the negative terminal of the battery before working on the starting system.*

12 Starter motor and circuit - check

Refer to illustrations 12.3 and 12.4

1　If a malfunction occurs in the starting circuit, do not immediately assume that the starter is causing the problem. First, check the following items:

a) *Make sure the battery cable clamps, where they connect to the battery, are clean and tight.*

b) *Check the condition of the battery cables (see Section 4). Replace any defective battery cables with new parts.*

c) *Test the condition of the battery (see Section 3). If it does not pass all the tests, replace it with a new battery.*

d) *Check the starter solenoid wiring and connections. Refer to the wiring diagrams at the end of Chapter 12.*

e) *Check the starter mounting bolts for tightness.*

f) *Check the fusible link (see Chapter 12). If it's burned, determine the cause and repair the circuit.*

g) *Check the operation of the Park/Neutral switch. Make sure the shift lever is in PARK or NEUTRAL. Refer to Chapter 7 for the Park/Neutral switch check and adjustment procedure. Refer to Chapter 12 wiring diagrams, if necessary, when performing circuit checks. These systems must operate correctly to provide battery voltage to the ignition solenoid.*

h) *Check the operation of the starter relay. The starter relay is located in the fuse/relay box inside the engine compartment. Refer to Chapter 12 for the relay testing procedure.*

2　If the starter does not actuate when the ignition switch is turned to the start position, check for battery voltage to the solenoid. This will determine if the solenoid is receiving the correct voltage signal from the ignition switch. Connect a test light or voltmeter to the starter solenoid positive terminal and while an assistant turns the ignition switch to the start position. If voltage is not available, refer to the wiring diagrams in Chapter 12 and check all the fuses and relays in series with the starting system. If voltage is available but the starter motor does not operate, remove the starter (see Section 13) and bench test it (see Step 4).

3　If the starter turns over slowly, check the starter cranking voltage and the current draw from the battery. This test must be performed with the starter assembly on the engine. Crank the engine over (for 10 seconds or less) and observe the battery voltage. It should not drop below 8.0 volts on manual transaxle models or 8.5 volts on automatic transaxle models. Also, observe the current draw using an ammeter **(see illustration)**. It should not exceed 400 amps or drop below 250 amps. If the starter motor cranking amp values are not within the correct range, replace it with a new unit. There are several conditions that may affect the starter cranking potential. The battery must be in good condition and the battery cold-cranking rating must not be under-rated for the particular application. Be sure to check the battery specifications carefully. The battery terminals and cables must be clean and not corroded. Also, in cases of extreme cold temperatures, make sure the battery and/or engine block is warmed before performing the tests.

4　If the starter is receiving voltage but does not activate, remove and check the starter/solenoid assembly on the bench **(see illustration)**. Most likely the solenoid is defective. In some rare cases, the engine may be seized, so be sure to try and rotate the crankshaft pulley (see Chapter 2A or 2B) before proceeding. With the starter/solenoid assembly mounted in a vise on the bench, install one jumper cable from the negative battery terminal to the body of the starter. Install the other jumper cable from the positive battery terminal to the B+ terminal on the starter. Install a starter switch and apply battery voltage to the solenoid S terminal (for 10 seconds or less) and see if the solenoid plunger, shift lever and overrunning clutch extends and rotates the pinion drive. If the pinion drive extends but does not rotate, the solenoid is operating but the starter motor is defective. If there is no movement but the solenoid clicks, the solenoid and/or the starter motor is defective. If the solenoid plunger extends and rotates the pinion drive, the starter/solenoid assembly is working properly.

12.4 Starter motor bench testing details

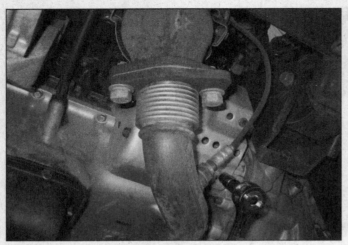

13.3 The starter is covered with a heat shield; on some models the shield may be disconnected and moved aside - on others the exhaust must be lowered to allow it to be removed

13.5 The starter is retained by two bolts - make sure the battery and the starter wiring are disconnected before removing it

13   Starter motor - removal and installation

Refer to illustrations 13.3 and 13.5

1   Disconnect the cable from the negative battery terminal (see Sections 1 and 3).

2   Detach the electrical connectors from the starter/solenoid assembly.

3   Remove the starter heat shield if so equipped **(see illustration).**

4   On some V6 models it will be necessary to unbolt the front section of the exhaust system from the exhaust manifolds, disconnect the front exhaust system hanger and lower the exhaust pipes for access.

5   Remove the starter motor mounting bolts and remove the starter **(see illustration).**

6   Installation is the reverse of removal.

Chapter 6
Emissions and engine control systems

Contents

Specifications

Torque specifications

	Ft-lbs	Nm
Oxygen sensors	35	44

1 General information

Refer to illustration 1.6

To prevent pollution of the atmosphere from incompletely burned and evaporating gases, and to maintain good driveability and fuel economy, a number of emission control systems are incorporated. They include the:

Catalytic converter
Electronic Throttle Control System
Evaporative Emissions Control
     (EVAP) system
Exhaust Gas Recirculation
     (EGR) system
Positive Crankcase Ventilation
     (PCV) system
Electronic Fuel Injection
     (EFI) system

The Sections in this Chapter include general descriptions, general inspection procedures within the scope of the home mechanic and component replacement procedures, where possible, for the components used in each of the systems listed above. You'll also find a general description of each information sensor and output actuator used in the engine management system, including its function and location, and a brief description of how it works (see Section 2). We have also included replacement procedures for all sensors and actuators.

Before assuming that an emissions control system is malfunctioning, check the fuel and ignition systems carefully. Diagnosis of many emission control devices requires specialized tools, equipment and training. If a service procedure is beyond the scope of this

book, or your ability, consult a dealer service department or other repair shop. But keep in mind that the most frequent cause of emissions problems is simply a loose connector, a broken wire or a disconnected vacuum hose, so always check the hoses, wiring and connections first.

Emission control systems are not, however, particularly difficult to maintain and repair. You can quickly and easily perform many checks and do most of the regular maintenance at home with common tune-up and hand tools. **Note:** *Because of a Federally mandated warranty that covers the emissions control system components, check with your dealer about warranty coverage before working on any emissions-related systems. Once the warranty has expired, you may wish to perform some of the component checks and/*

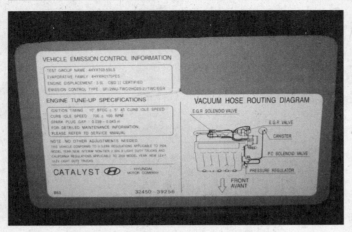

1.6 The Vehicle Emission Control Information (VECI) label contains such essential information as the types of emission control systems installed on the engine, certain tune-up specifications and a vacuum hose routing diagram (3.5L V6 model shown)

2.1 Simple code readers are an economical way to extract trouble codes when the CHECK ENGINE light comes on

or replacement procedures in this Chapter to save money.

Pay close attention to any special precautions outlined in this Chapter. It should be noted that the illustrations of the various systems might not exactly match the system installed on your vehicle because of changes made by the manufacturer during production or from year-to-year.

A Vehicle Emissions Control Information (VECI) label is attached to the underside of the hood. This label contains important emissions specifications and adjustment information, as well as a vacuum hose routing diagram **(see illustration)** with emissions components identified. When servicing the engine or emissions systems, always refer to the VECI label and the vacuum hose routing diagram on your vehicle for up-to-date information.

2   On Board Diagnostic (OBD) system and trouble codes

Scan tool information

Refer to illustrations 2.1 and 2.2

1   Hand-held scanners are handy for analyzing the engine management systems used on late-model vehicles. Because extracting the Diagnostic Trouble Codes (DTCs) from an engine management system is now the first step in troubleshooting many computer-controlled systems and components, even the most basic generic code readers are capable of accessing a computer's DTCs **(see illustration)**. More powerful scan tools can also perform many of the diagnostics once associated with expensive factory scan tools. If you're planning to obtain a generic scan tool for your vehicle, make sure that it's compatible with OBD-II systems. If you don't plan to purchase a code reader or scan tool and don't have access to one, you can have the codes

extracted by a dealer service department or by an independent repair shop. Some auto parts stores also provide this service.

2   With the advent of the Federally mandated emission control system known as On-Board Diagnostics-II (OBD-II), specially designed scanners were developed. Several tool manufacturers have released OBD-II scan tools for the home mechanic **(see illustration)**.

OBD-II system general description

3   All models are equipped with the second generation On-Board Diagnostic (OBD-II) system. The OBD-II system includes a computer known as the Powertrain Control Module (PCM), information sensors that monitor various functions of the engine and send data to the PCM, and output actuators that carry out the PCM's various control commands. The OBD-II system also incorporates a series of diagnostic monitors that detect and identify fuel injection and emission control system faults and store the information in the com-

puter memory. The system also tests sensors and output actuators, diagnoses drive cycles, freezes data and clears codes.

4   This powerful diagnostic computer must be accessed with an OBD-II scan tool and the 16 pin Data Link Connector (DLC) located under the driver's dash area. The PCM is the brain of the electronically controlled fuel and emissions system. It receives data from a number of sensors and other electronic components (switches, relays, etc.). Based on the information it receives, the PCM generates output signals to control various relays, solenoids (fuel injectors) and other actuators. The PCM is specifically calibrated to optimize the emissions, fuel economy and driveability of the vehicle.

5   It isn't a good idea to attempt diagnosis or replacement of the PCM or emission control components at home while the vehicle is under warranty. Because of a Federally mandated warranty which covers the emissions system components and because any owner-induced damage to the PCM, the sensors and/or the control devices may void this

2.2 Scanners like these from Actron and AutoXray are powerful diagnostic aids - they can tell you just about anything that you want to know about your engine management system

warranty. Take the vehicle to a dealer service department if the PCM or a system component malfunctions.

Information sensors

6   Accelerator Pedal Position (APP) sensor - All 3.5L V6 models covered by this manual are equipped with an electronically operated throttle. This system uses an electronic throttle body instead of a conventional cable-operated throttle body. The Powertrain Control Module (PCM) controls the position of the throttle plate with a solenoid that's located in the throttle body. The PCM's commands are based on the inputs that it receives from the APP sensor, which is located in the engine compartment attached to the throttle cable. Its electrical output signal, which is proportional to the angle of the accelerator pedal, is used by the system to determine the corresponding opening angle of the throttle plate inside the throttle body.

7   Camshaft Position (CMP) sensor - A CMP sensor monitors the position of the camshaft and tells the Powertrain Control Module (PCM) when the piston in the No. 1 cylinder is on its compression stroke. The PCM uses the CMP sensor signal to synchronize the firing of the fuel injectors. On four-cylinder engines, the sensor is located on the driver-side end of the cylinder head. On 2.7L V6 engines it's located near the air filter assembly. On 3.5L V6 engines it's mounted to the side of the front cylinder head directly under the exhaust camshaft sprocket.

The CMP sensor is a *variable reluctance* (pick-up coil) type sensor that generates an analog (sine wave) signal pulse each time that a boss on the timing rotor passes by the sensor. There are bosses on the timing rotor. As the timing rotor rotates with the camshaft, the CMP sensor generates a voltage output each time one of the bosses no the rotor passes by the sensor. The PCM uses these voltage outputs to determine the position of the intake camshaft.

8   Crankshaft Position (CKP) sensor - Like the CMP sensor, the CKP sensor is a *variable reluctance* (pick-up coil) type sensor that generates an analog (sine wave) signal pulse each time that a boss on the timing rotor passes by the sensor. On four-cylinder engines, the CKP sensor is located behind the timing chain cover, and the timing rotor is mounted behind the crankshaft timing sprocket. On V6 engines, the CKP sensor is located on the front of the engine, and the timing rotor is mounted on the back of the crankshaft timing belt sprocket. All timing rotors have evenly spaced teeth, with two missing. As the crankshaft rotates, each tooth on the timing rotor moves past the CKP sensor. As each tooth moves past the sensor, the magnetic flux in the sensor coil changes because the air gap between the sensor and the timing rotor changes. This change in magnetic flux induces a voltage pulse in the sensor, and this pulse is sent to the PCM as an output signal. And the blank space with the missing teeth?

The PCM uses the missing teeth to determine Top Dead Center (TDC).

The CKP sensor is the primary sensor that provides ignition information to the PCM. The PCM uses the CKP sensor to determine crankshaft position (which piston will be at TDC next) and crank speed (rpm), both of which it needs to synchronize the ignition system.

9   Engine Coolant Temperature (ECT) sensor - The ECT sensor measures the temperature of the engine coolant. The ECT sensor is a thermistor; its resistance decreases as the temperature increases, and its resistance increases as the temperature decreases. This type of thermistor is also referred to as a Negative Temperature Coefficient (NTC) thermistor. This variable resistance produces an analogous voltage drop across the sensor terminals, thus providing an electrical signal to the PCM that accurately reflects the engine coolant temperature.

The ECT sensor is a critical sensor because it tells the PCM when the engine is warmed up sufficiently to go into closed loop operation. Once the engine is in closed loop, the PCM also uses the ECT sensor to control fuel injector pulse width and ignition timing. It also uses the ECT sensor signal to determine when to purge the EVAP system.

On four-cylinder engines, the ECT sensor is located near the thermostat housing. On 2.7L V6 models, the ECT sensor is directly below the coil pack. On 3.5L V6 engines it's on the driver's side of the engine, threaded into the coolant passage near the rear bank cylinder head.

10   Intake Air Temperature (IAT) sensor - The IAT sensor is used by the PCM to calculate air density, which is one of the variables that it must know in order to calculate injector pulse width and adjust ignition timing (to prevent spark knock when air intake temperature is high). Like the ECT sensor, the IAT sensor is a Negative Temperature Coefficient (NTC) type thermistor, whose resistance decreases as the temperature increases. The IAT sensor is an integral component of the Mass Air Flow (MAF) sensor, which is located on the air inlet duct. For more information about the MAF sensor, see paragraph 12.

11   Knock sensor - The knock sensor monitors engine vibration caused by detonation. Basically, a knock sensor converts engine vibration to an electrical signal. When the knock sensor detects a knock in one of the cylinders, it signals the PCM so that the PCM can retard ignition timing accordingly. The knock sensor contains a piezoelectric material, a certain type of piezoresistive crystal that has the ability to produce a voltage when subjected to a mechanical stress. The piezoelectric crystal in the knock sensor vibrates constantly and produces an output signal that's proportional to the intensity of the vibration. As the intensity of the vibration increases, so does the voltage of the output signal. When the intensity of the crystal's vibration reaches a specified threshold, the PCM stores that value in its memory and retards ignition timing

in all cylinders (the PCM does not selectively retard timing only at the affected cylinder). The PCM doesn't respond to the knock sensor's input when the engine is idling; it only responds when the engine reaches a specified speed.

On four-cylinder engines, the knock sensor is located on the side of the engine block. There are two knock sensors on 2.7L V6 engines. They are located in the valley between the cylinder heads. On 3.5L V6 engines, the knock sensor(s) is also located in the valley between the cylinder heads. On these models, you must remove the upper and lower intake manifolds to access the knock sensor.

12   Mass Air Flow/Intake Air Temperature (MAF/IAT) sensor - The MAF sensor is the principal means by which the PCM monitors intake airflow. It uses a hot-film sensing element to measure the amount of air entering the engine. Air passing over the hot film causes it to cool down. The hot film's temperature is maintained at a preset level above the ambient temperature by electrical current supplied to the wire and controlled by the PCM. The current required to maintain the specified constant temperature value is used by the PCM as an indicator of airflow.

The functions of the MAF and the Intake Air Temperature (IAT) sensors are combined into one assembly on all models. For more information about the IAT sensor, see paragraph 10. The MAF/IAT sensor is located in the air intake duct.

13   Oxygen sensors - Oxygen sensors generate a voltage signal that varies in accordance with the amount of oxygen in the exhaust stream. The PCM uses the data from the upstream oxygen sensor to calculate the injector pulse width. The downstream oxygen sensor monitors the oxygen content of the exhaust gases as they exit the catalytic converters. This information is used by the PCM to predict catalyst deterioration and/or failure. One job of the catalytic converter is to store excess oxygen. As long as the catalyst is functioning correctly, the downstream sensor should show little activity because there should be little oxygen exiting the catalyst. But as the catalyst deteriorates, its ability to store oxygen is compromised. When the output signal from the downstream sensor starts to look like the output signal from the upstream sensor, the PCM stores a DTC and turns on the MIL to let you know that it's time to replace the catalyst.

On all models there are two oxygen sensors at each exhaust manifold; one immediately before and one after the catalytic converter.

14   Power Steering Pressure (PSP) sensor - The PSP sensor monitors the hydraulic pressure of the power steering fluid in the power steering system. The PSP sensor provides a voltage input to the PCM that varies in accordance with changes in the hydraulic pressure. The PCM uses the input signal from the PSP sensor to elevate the idle speed when the engine is already under some other load, such as the air conditioning compressor, while maneuvering the vehicle at low speed, such as parking or stop-and-go driving. The PSP sensor is located at the power steering pump

15   Throttle Position (TP) sensor - The TP sensor, which is located on the throttle body, is a rotary potentiometer, which is a type of variable resistor that produces a variable voltage signal in proportion to the opening angle of the throttle plate. The PCM sends 5 volts to the TP sensor. As the plate opens and closes, the resistance of the TP sensor changes with it, altering the signal back to the PCM. The output voltage of the TP sensor is about 0.6 volt at idle (closed throttle plate) to 4.8 volts at wide-open throttle. This variable signal enables the PCM to calculate the position (opening angle) of the throttle plate. The PCM uses the TP sensor input, along with other sensor inputs, to adjust fuel injector pulse-width and ignition timing.

16   Transmission Range (TR) sensor - Like the Park/Neutral Position (PNP) switch that it replaces, the TR sensor prevents you from starting the engine unless the automatic transaxle is in Park or Neutral, and it activates the back-up lights when you put the shift lever in Reverse. Unlike a PNP or inhibitor switch, however, the TR sensor also tells the PCM what range the transaxle is in. The PCM uses this information to determine what gear the transaxle *should* be in based on the load, engine speed, vehicle speed, etc. and to determine when to upshift and downshift the transaxle. The TR sensor is mounted on the transaxle.

17   Transmission speed sensors - There are two speed sensors on all transaxles covered by this manual: the **Input Turbine Speed Sensor**, or **Input Shaft RPM Sensor**, and the **Counter Gear Speed Sensor**, or **Counter Gear RPM Sensor**. The speed sensors are variable reluctance (pick-up coil) type sensors that generate an analog (sine wave) signal pulse each time that a boss on a timing rotor passes by the sensor. Both sensors are located on top of the transaxle. The PCM uses the signal from the Input Turbine Speed Sensor to monitor input turbine or input shaft speed. And it uses the signal from the Counter Gear Speed Sensor to monitor counter gear or output shaft speed. The PCM constantly compares these two speeds to its map (program) for the transaxle in order to determine shift scheduling, Torque Converter Clutch (TCC) engagement scheduling and optimal hydraulic pressure for various hydraulically-controlled components inside the transaxle. Both of the speed sensors are located inside of the transaxle.

18   Vapor pressure sensor - The vapor pressure sensor is a component of the Evaporative Emission Control (EVAP) system. It's located on top of the fuel tank. The vapor pressure sensor monitors the pressure of fuel vapors inside the tank. When the vapor pressure exceeds the upper threshold, the vapor

pressure sensor signals the PCM, which opens the Vacuum Switching Valve (VSV) for the pressure switching valve, allowing the fuel vapors to migrate to the EVAP canister, where they are stored until they're purged.

Powertrain Control Module (PCM)

19   Based on the information that it receives from the information sensors described above, the PCM adjusts fuel injector pulse width, idle speed, ignition spark advance, ignition coil dwell, EVAP canister purge operation and many other things. It does so by controlling the *output actuators*. The following list provides a brief description of the function, location and operation of each of the important output actuators.

Output actuators

20   Canister closed valve (CCV) - The canister closed valve is a part of the Evaporative Emissions Control (EVAP) system. The canister closed valve opens and closes the EVAP system's fresh air line (between the air filter housing and the EVAP canister) in response to signals from the Powertrain Control Module (PCM). When commanded by the PCM, the canister closed valve also closes the EVAP canister for monitor testing.

21   Purge control solenoid valve (PCSV) - The canister purge valve is a component of the Evaporative Emission Control (EVAP) system. When the engine is cold or still warming up, no captive fuel vapors are allowed to escape from the EVAP canister. After the engine is warmed up, the PCM energizes the canister purge valve, which regulates the flow of these vapors from the canister to the intake manifold. The rate of vapor flow is regulated by the purge valve in response to commands from the PCM, which controls the duty cycle of the valve. On 2.4L four-cylinder and 2.7L V6 models, the EVAP canister purge valve is located in the center of the engine compartment near the firewall. On 3.5L V6 engines it's on top of the engine at the driver's side. For more information about the EVAP system, see Section 16.

22   Electronic Throttle Body - 3.5L V6 models are equipped with the electronic throttle control system. These vehicles do not have a conventional accelerator cable-actuated throttle body. Instead, they use an electronic throttle body that is controlled by the Powertrain Control Module (PCM). The throttle plate inside the throttle body is opened and closed by a PCM-controlled throttle motor. There is no cruise control cable and no Idle Air Control (IAC) valve. Cruise control and idle speed are handled electronically by the PCM. The electronic throttle body still has a Throttle Position (TP) sensor. The PCM determines the correct throttle plate angle by processing the input signal from the Accelerator Pedal Position (APP) sensor (see *Accelerator Pedal Position sensor* in paragraph 6).

23   Fuel injectors - The PCM activates the

fuel injectors. The PCM also controls the injector *pulse width*, which is the interval of time during which each injector is open. The pulse width of an injector (measured in milliseconds) determines the amount of fuel delivered. For more information on the fuel system and the fuel injectors, including injector replacement, refer to Chapter 4.

24   Fuel pump relay - When grounded by the PCM, the fuel pump relay provides battery voltage to the fuel pump (and to other fuel system components). The location of this relay may change depending on model and year, so if you can't find it, refer to the fuse and relay guide in your owner's manual.

25   Idle Air Control (IAC) valve - The PCM-controlled IAC valve, which is located on the throttle body on 2.4L four-cylinder and 2.7L V6 models, regulates the flow of air that bypasses the throttle plate when the engine is idling. The PCM opens and closes the IAC valve in response to loads - air conditioning and power steering loads, for example - to keep the engine idle speed at its target rpm. The IAC valve also increases the idle speed during the early stages of the warm-up period and functions as a dashpot when the throttle plate is abruptly closed during sudden deceleration conditions. There is no IAC valve on 3.5L V6 models, because electronic throttle bodies do not require an IAC valve to control idle speed.

26   Ignition coil(s) - 2.4L four-cylinder and 3.5L V6 models use a modified coil-on-plug system in which half of the cylinders use an ignition coil mounted directly to the spark plug. These coils have spark plug wires that attach to the other cylinders. Each coil therefore ignites two cylinders at the same time. This is called a "waste spark" system since one cylinder receives a spark that is wasted on its exhaust stroke. 2.7L V6 engines use a three-coil pack mounted to the side of the engine that fires all six cylinders via spark plug wires using the same waste-spark principle. There is no separate ignition control module. The Powertrain Control Module (PCM) handles this function. For more information about the ignition coils, refer to Chapter 5.

27   Fuel tank pressure sensor (FTPS) - The vapor pressure sensor, which is a component of the Evaporative Emission Control (EVAP) system, monitors the pressure inside the fuel tank and sends a signal to the Powertrain Control Module (PCM). When the pressure exceeds the upper threshold, the PCM commands the canister closed valve to send the excessive vapors to the EVAP canister. The vapor pressure sensor is located on top of the fuel tank.

Obtaining trouble codes
Refer to illustrations 2.29a and 2.29b
28   The PCM illuminates the CHECK ENGINE light (also called the Malfunction Indicator Light) on the dash if it recognizes a component fault for two consecutive drive cycles. It will continue to turn on the light until

2.29a The 16-pin Data Link Connector (DLC) is located behind this panel on the left of the dash

2.29b The DLC is at the right side of the opening

the PCM does not detect any malfunction for three or more consecutive drive cycles.

29   To extract the Diagnostic Trouble Codes (DTCs) you will need an OBD-II scan tool **(see illustration 2.2)**. Plug the scan tool into the PCM's data link connector, which is located under the left side of the dash in the fuse and relay center **(see illustrations).**

30   Plug the scan tool into the 16-pin data link connector (DLC), and follow the instructions included with the scan tool to extract all the diagnostic codes.

Diagnostic Trouble Codes

Trouble code	Code identification
P0030	Oxygen sensor heater control circuit (bank 1, sensor 1)
P0031	Oxygen sensor heater control circuit, low voltage (Bank 1, Sensor 1)
P0032	Oxygen sensor heater control circuit, high voltage (Bank 1, Sensor 1)
P0036	Oxygen sensor heater control circuit (Bank 1, Sensor 2)
P0037	Oxygen sensor heater control circuit, low voltage (Bank 1, Sensor 2)
P0038	Oxygen sensor heater control circuit, high voltage (Bank 1, Sensor 2)
P0050	Oxygen sensor heater control circuit (bank 2, sensor 1)
P0051	Oxygen sensor heater control circuit low (bank 2, sensor 1)
P0052	Oxygen sensor heater control circuit high (bank 2, sensor 1)
P0056	Oxygen sensor heater control circuit (bank 2, sensor 2)
P0057	Oxygen sensor heater control circuit low (bank 2, sensor 2)
P0058	Oxygen sensor heater control circuit high (bank 2, sensor 2)
P0101	Mass Air Flow (MAF) sensor, range or performance problem

Diagnostic Trouble Codes (continued)

Trouble code	Code identification
P0102	Mass Air Flow (MAF) sensor, low input voltage
P0103	Mass Air Flow (MAF) sensor, high input voltage
P0110	Intake Air Temperature (IAT) sensor, circuit fault
P0111	Intake air temperature circuit, range or performance problem
P0112	Intake Air Temperature (IAT) sensor circuit, low input voltage
P0113	Intake Air Temperature (IAT) sensor circuit, high input voltage
P0116	Engine Coolant Temperature (ECT) sensor, range or performance problem
P0117	Engine Coolant Temperature (ECT) sensor circuit, low input voltage
P0118	Engine Coolant Temperature (ECT) sensor circuit, high input voltage
P0119	Engine Coolant Temperature (ECT) circuit, Intermittent
P0121	Throttle Position (TP) sensor or Accelerator Pedal Position (APP) sensor circuit, range or performance problem
P0122	Throttle Position (TP) sensor or Accelerator Pedal Position (APP) sensor circuit, low input voltage
P0123	Throttle Position (TP) sensor or Accelerator Pedal Position (APP) sensor circuit, high input voltage
P0125	Insufficient coolant temperature for closed loop fuel control
P0130	Oxygen sensor circuit malfunction (bank 1, sensor 1)
P0131	Oxygen sensor circuit, low voltage (bank 1, sensor 1)
P0132	Oxygen sensor circuit, high voltage (bank 1, sensor 1)
P0133	Oxygen sensor circuit, slow response (bank 1, sensor 1)
P0134	Oxygen sensor circuit - no activity detected (bank 1, sensor 1)
P0136	Oxygen sensor circuit fault (Bank 1, Sensor 2)
P0137	Oxygen sensor circuit, low voltage (Bank 1, Sensor 2)
P0138	Oxygen sensor circuit, high voltage (Bank 1, Sensor 2)
P0139	Oxygen sensor circuit, slow response (bank 1, sensor 2)
P0140	Oxygen sensor circuit - no activity detected (bank 1, sensor 2)
P0150	Oxygen sensor circuit malfunction (bank 2, sensor 1)
P0151	Oxygen sensor circuit, low voltage (bank 2, sensor 1)

Trouble code	Code identification
P0152	Oxygen sensor circuit, high voltage (bank 2, sensor 1)
P0153	Oxygen sensor circuit, slow response (bank 2, sensor 1)
P0154	Oxygen sensor circuit - no activity detected (bank 2, sensor 1)
P0156	Oxygen sensor circuit fault (Bank 2, Sensor 2)
P0157	Oxygen sensor circuit, low voltage (bank 2, sensor 2)
P0158	Oxygen sensor circuit, high voltage (bank 2, sensor 2)
P0159	Oxygen sensor circuit, slow response (bank 2, sensor 2)
P0160	Oxygen sensor circuit - no activity detected (bank 2, sensor 2)
P0170	Fuel trim malfunction (bank 1)
P0171	Fuel injection system, fuel trim too lean (Bank 1)
P0172	Fuel injection system fuel trim too rich (Bank 1)
P0173	Fuel trim malfunction (bank 2)
P0174	Fuel injection system fuel trim too lean (Bank 2)
P0175	Fuel injection system fuel trim too rich (Bank 2)
P0230	Fuel pump primary circuit malfunction
P0261	Cylinder no. 1 injector circuit, low
P0262	Cylinder no. 1 injector circuit, high
P0264	Cylinder no. 2 injector circuit, low
P0265	Cylinder no. 2 injector circuit, high
P0267	Cylinder no. 3 injector circuit, low
P0268	Cylinder no. 3 injector circuit, high
P0270	Cylinder no. 4 injector circuit, low
P0271	Cylinder no. 4 injector circuit, high
P0273	Cylinder no. 5 injector circuit, low
P0274	Cylinder no. 5 injector circuit, high
P0276	Cylinder no. 6 injector circuit, low
P0277	Cylinder no. 6 injector circuit, high

Diagnostic Trouble Codes (continued)

Trouble code	Code identification
P0300	Random or multiple cylinder misfire detected
P0301	Cylinder no. 1 misfire detected
P0302	Cylinder no. 2 misfire detected
P0303	Cylinder no. 3 misfire detected
P0304	Cylinder no. 4 misfire detected
P0305	Cylinder no. 5 misfire detected
P0306	Cylinder no. 6 misfire detected
P0315	Crankshaft position system - variation not learned
P0325	Knock sensor no. 1 circuit malfunction (bank 1 or single sensor)
P0330	Knock sensor no. 2 circuit malfunction (bank 2)
P0335	Crankshaft position sensor "A" circuit malfunction
P0340	Camshaft position sensor "A", circuit malfunction (bank 1)
P0350	Ignition coil primary or secondary circuit malfunction
P0351	Ignition coil A primary or secondary circuit malfunction
P0352	Ignition coil B primary or secondary circuit malfunction
P0353	Ignition coil C primary or secondary circuit malfunction
P0354	Ignition coil D primary or secondary circuit malfunction
P0355	Ignition coil E primary or secondary circuit malfunction
P0356	Ignition coil F primary or secondary circuit malfunction
P0420	Catalyst system efficiency below threshold (Bank 1)
P0430	Catalyst system efficiency below threshold (Bank 2)
P0441	Evaporative Emission Control (EVAP) system, incorrect purge flow
P0442	Evaporative Emission Control (EVAP) system malfunction or small leak detected
P0444	Evaporative emission control system, open purge control valve circuit
P0445	Evaporative emission control system, short in purge control valve circuit
P0447	Evaporative emission control system, open vent control circuit

Trouble code	Code identification
P0448	Evaporative emission control system, shorted vent control circuit
P0449	Evaporative emission control system, vent valve/solenoid circuit malfunction
P0451	Evaporative Emission Control (EVAP) system, pressure sensor range or performance problem
P0452	Evaporative Emission Control (EVAP) system, pressure sensor/switch, low input voltage
P0453	Evaporative Emission Control (EVAP) system, pressure sensor/switch, high input voltage
P0454	Evaporative emission control system, pressure sensor intermittent
P0455	Evaporative Emission Control (EVAP) system, gross leak detected
P0456	Evaporative Emission Control (EVAP) system, small leak detected
P0461	Fuel level sensor circuit, range or performance problem
P0462	Fuel level sensor circuit, low input
P0463	Fuel level sensor circuit, high input
P0464	Fuel level sensor circuit, intermittent
P0501	Vehicle speed sensor, range or performance problem
P0506	Idle control system, rpm lower than expected
P0507	Idle control system, rpm higher than expected
P0551	Power steering pressure sensor circuit, range or performance problem
P0560	System voltage
P0562	System voltage low
P0563	System voltage high
P0605	Internal control module, read only memory (ROM) error
P0630	VIN not programmed or mismatch - ECM/PCM
P0650	Malfunction indicator lamp (MIL), control circuit malfunction
P0700	Transmission control system malfunction
P0703	Torque converter/brake switch B, circuit malfunction
P0707	Transmission range sensor circuit, low input
P0708	Transmission range sensor circuit, high input
P0711	Transmission fluid temperature sensor circuit, range or performance problem

Diagnostic Trouble Codes (continued)

Trouble code	Code identification
P0712	Transaxle fluid temperature sensor circuit, low input voltage
P0715	Input/turbine speed sensor circuit malfunction
P0720	Output speed sensor malfunction
P0731	Incorrect gear ratio, first gear
P0732	Incorrect gear ratio, second gear
P0733	Incorrect gear ratio, third gear
P0734	Incorrect gear ratio, fourth gear
P0736	Incorrect gear ratio, reverse gear
P0741	Torque converter clutch circuit, performance problem or stuck in OFF position
P0750	Transaxle shift solenoid A malfunction, or stuck open or closed
P0753	Transaxle shift solenoid A, electrical malfunction or circuit fault

3 Accelerator Pedal Position (APP) sensor - replacement

Refer to illustration 3.2

Note: *This procedure applies to 3.5L V6 models only.*

1   Disconnect the cable from the negative battery terminal (see Chapter 5, Section 1).
2   Disconnect the APP sensor electrical connector **(see illustration)**.
3   Disconnect the accelerator cable from the sensor.
4   Remove the sensor mounting bolts and remove the sensor.
5   Installation is the reverse of removal.

4 Camshaft Position (CMP) sensor - replacement

2.4L four-cylinder models
Note: *The CMP sensor is located on the driver's end of the cylinder head.*

1   Disconnect the cable from the negative battery terminal (see Chapter 5, Section 1).
2   Remove the air intake duct, if necessary,

to provide more room to work (see *Air filter housing - removal and installation* in Chapter 4).
3   Disconnect the electrical connector from the CMP sensor.
4   Make an alignment mark with a dab of paint so it can be reinstalled in the same position.
5   Remove the CMP sensor mounting bolt(s) and remove the sensor.

6   If you're going to install the same sensor, check the condition of the O-ring. Replace the O-ring if it's damaged.
7   Installation is the reverse of removal.

2.7L V6 models
Note: *The camshaft position sensor is mounted on the driver's end of the cylinder head.*

3.2 The Accelerator Pedal Position sensor is mounted at the end of the throttle cable on the left side of the engine compartment on 3.5L V6 models

6.2a Location of the ECT (engine coolant temperature) sensor (3.5L V6 shown)

6.2b ECT (engine coolant temperature) sensor - 3.5L V6 (upper intake manifold removed for clarity)

8   Disconnect the cable from the negative battery terminal (see Chapter 5, Section 1).
9   Remove the engine cover if necessary for access (see *Intake manifold - removal and installation* in Chapter 2B).
10   Disconnect the sensor electrical connector.
11   Remove the bolt securing the sensor to the side of the cylinder head. Pull the sensor out of its socket.
12   Installation is the reverse of removal.

3.5L V6 models
Note: *The camshaft position sensor is mounted under the timing belt cover near the exhaust camshaft sprocket of the front cylinder head.*
13   Disconnect the cable from the negative battery terminal (see Chapter 5, Section 1).
14   Remove the timing belt cover from the front cylinder head. The sensor is mounted next to the sprocket of the front exhaust camshaft.
15   Disconnect the sensor electrical connector.
16   Remove the two sensor mounting bolts.
17   Installation is the reverse of removal.

---

5   Crankshaft Position (CKP) sensor - replacement

2.4L four-cylinder and 3.5L V6 models
Note: *The CKP sensor is located on the front of the engine, behind the timing belt cover, next to the crankshaft sprocket.*
1   Disconnect the cable from the negative battery terminal (see Chapter 5, Section 1).
2   Refer to Chapter 2 and remove the lower timing belt cover.
3   Disconnect the sensor wiring harness.

4   Remove the two mounting bolts and lift the sensor off.
5   Installation is the reverse of removal.

2.7L V6 models
6   The sensor is mounted to the front on the outside of the engine on these models.
7   Disconnect the sensor wiring harness.
8   Remove the CKP sensor mounting bolt and remove the CKP sensor.
9   Installation is the reverse of removal.

---

6   Engine Coolant Temperature (ECT) sensor - replacement

Refer to illustrations 6.2a and 6.2b
Warning: *Wait until the engine is completely cool before beginning this procedure.*
Caution: *Handle the ECT sensor with care. Damage to the ECT sensor will affect the operation of the entire fuel injection system.*
Note: *The ECT sensor is located at the driver's end of the engine, either in the thermostat housing or in the coolant passage between the cylinder heads.*
1   Disconnect the cable from the negative battery terminal (see Chapter 5, Section 1). Partially drain the cooling system (see Chapter 1).
2   Disconnect the electrical connector from the ECT sensor **(see illustrations)**.
3   Unscrew the ECT sensor from the cylinder head.
4   Don't seal the threads of the new ECT sensor with Teflon tape, as this will interfere with the grounding of the sensor. Apply a small amount of liquid sealer to the threads before installation.
5   Installation is the reverse of removal. Be sure to tighten the ECT sensor securely. Refill the cooling system (see Chapter 1).

7   Knock sensor - replacement

Warning: *Wait until the engine is completely cool before beginning this procedure.*

Four-cylinder models
Note: *The knock sensor is located on the side of the engine block near the coolant transfer pipe.*
1   Disconnect the cable from the negative battery terminal (see Chapter 5, Section 1).
2   Disconnect the knock sensor electrical connector.
3   Unscrew the knock sensor.
4   Installation is otherwise the reverse of removal.

V6 models
Note: *The knock sensors are located in the valley between the cylinder heads. To access them, you have to remove the lower intake manifold.*
5   Disconnect the cable from the negative battery terminal (see Chapter 5, Section 1).
6   Remove the upper and lower intake manifolds (see Chapter 2B).
7   Disconnect the electrical connectors from the knock sensors.
8   Disconnect the wiring harness retainers from the engine block.
9   Unscrew the sensors.
10   Installation is the reverse of removal.

---

8   Mass Air Flow/Intake Air Temperature (MAF/IAT) sensor - replacement

Refer to illustration 8.2
Note: *The MAF/IAT sensor is located in the air inlet duct.*
1   Disconnect the cable from the negative battery terminal (see Chapter 5, Section 1).

8.2 The MAF (mass air flow) sensor is located in the inlet duct; it also incorporates the intake air temperature sensor

9.2 There are two heated oxygen sensors at the outlet of each exhaust manifold - before and after each catalytic converter (this is the downstream sensor for the front cylinder bank)

2   Disconnect the electrical connector from the MAF sensor **(see illustration)**.
3   Loosen the hose clamps and remove the MAF sensor from the air intake ducts.
4   Installation is the reverse of removal.

9   Oxygen sensors - general information and replacement

General information

1   Use special care when servicing an oxygen sensor:

a) *Oxygen sensors have a permanently attached pigtail and electrical connector that can't be removed from the sensor. Damage to or removal of the pigtail or the electrical connector will ruin the sensor.*

b) *Keep grease, dirt and other contaminants away from the electrical connector and the oxygen sensor.*
c) *Do not use cleaning solvents of any kind on an oxygen sensor.*
d) *Do not drop or roughly handle an oxygen sensor.*

Replacement

Refer to illustrations 9.2, 9.4a and 9.4b

Note: *Because it is installed in the exhaust manifold or catalytic converter, both of which contract when cool, an oxygen sensor might be very difficult to loosen when the engine is cold. Rather than risk damage to the sensor, start and run the engine for a minute or two, then shut it off. Be careful not to burn yourself during the following procedure.*

2   The sensors are located at the inlet and outlet of each primary catalytic converter **(see**

illustration). These converters are bolted to the bases of the exhaust manifolds. There are two on four-cylinder models and four on V6 models.
3   If you're working on the sensors on the rear manifold of a V6 model, raise the vehicle and support it securely on jackstands. This may ease things even if you're removing a front lower sensor.
4   Remove any interfering components to provide wrench access to the sensor. These components vary greatly depending on the year and options installed **(see illustrations)**.
5   Disconnect the sensor pigtail.
6   Unscrew the sensor. **Note:** *Special oxygen sensor sockets are available at most auto parts stores.*
7   Installation is the reverse of removal. Be sure to coat the threads of the oxygen sensor with anti-seize compound and tighten it to the torque listed in this Chapter's Specifications.

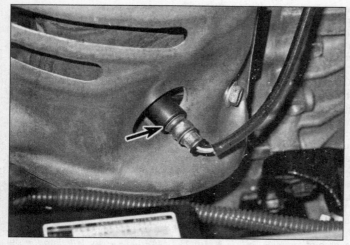

9.4a The primary (upstream) oxygen sensors on some models are accessible through holes in the heat shields

9.4b After disconnecting the wiring, carefully unscrew the sensor with an oxygen sensor socket (shown) or with a large wrench - oxygen sensor sockets are handy where there's no room to turn a wrench

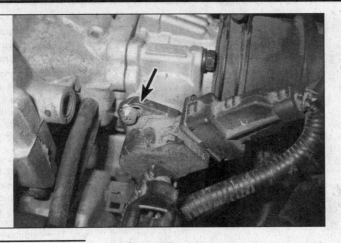

11.3 The Throttle Position sensor has slotted mounting holes to allow for adjustment

3.5L V6 engine

Four-cylinder and 2.7L V6 engine

43059-6-11.12 HAYNES

11.12 TP sensor connector terminal designations (connector face [harness side] shown)

10 Power Steering Pressure (PSP) sensor - replacement

Warning: *Wait until the power steering fluid has cooled completely before beginning this procedure.*

1 Disconnect the cable from the negative battery terminal (see Chapter 5, Section 1).
2 Locate the PSP sensor on the power steering pump, then disconnect the sensor electrical connector.
3 Place a drain pain under the pump, then unscrew the PSP sensor from the pump. Be prepared for some power steering fluid to leak out.
4 Installation is the reverse of removal. After you're done, check the power steering fluid level (see Chapter 1) and add fluid as necessary

11 Throttle Position (TP) sensor - replacement and adjustment

Refer to illustration 11.3

Note: *The TP sensor is located on the throttle body.*

Replacement

1 Disconnect the cable from the negative battery terminal (see Chapter 5, Section 1).
2 Remove the engine cover, if necessary (see *Intake manifold - removal and installation* in Chapter 2).
3 Disconnect the TP sensor electrical connector **(see illustration)**.
4 Mark the position of the sensor if you plan to reinstall the same one.
5 Remove the TP sensor mounting screws and remove the sensor from the throttle body.
6 Install the sensor and rotate it until the mounting holes in the TP sensor are aligned with the mounting holes in the throttle body.
7 Installation is otherwise the reverse of removal.

Adjustment

Using a scan tool

8 Connect a scan tool to the 16-pin Data Link Connector (DLC), then bring up the throt-

tle position sensor values parameter on the screen.
9 Turn the ignition key to the On position.
10 With the throttle fully closed, note the value on the scan tool - it should be as follows:

> 2.4L four-cylinder and 3.5L V6 engines = 300 to 900 millivolts (mV)
>
> 2.7L V6 engine = 250 to 800 millivolts (mV)

11 If the sensor voltage doesn't fall within the specified range, loosen the TP sensor mounting screws and turn the sensor one way or the other until it does, then tighten the screws securely.

Using a voltmeter

Refer to illustration 11.12

Note: *Use only a high-impedance digital voltmeter for this procedure.*

12 Connect the negative lead of a high-impedance digital voltmeter to a good ground and connect the positive lead to the TP sensor signal wire. It will be necessary to backprobe the sensor's connector using a straight-pin to take the voltage reading, or pierce the wire with a pin and connect the lead to it (although the latter method isn't recommended if at all possible to avoid). It may also be necessary to separate the "clamshell" halves of the connector to allow the connector to be back-

probed. The signal wire designations are as follows **(see illustration)**:

> 2.4L four-cylinder engine: Terminal 3 of the TP sensor connector (orange wire)
> 2.7L V6 engine: Terminal 3 of the TP sensor connector (red/orange wire)
> 3.5L V6 engine: Terminal 4 of the TP sensor connector (yellow wire)

13 Follow Steps 9 through 11 to check and, if necessary, adjust the TP sensor.

12 Transmission Range (TR) sensor - replacement

Removal

Refer to illustration 12.2

Note: *The TR sensor is located on the top of the transaxle near the shift cable.*

1 Disconnect the cable from the negative battery terminal (see Chapter 5, Section 1). Detach the fresh air intake duct from the air filter housing.
2 Disconnect the electrical connector from the TR sensor **(see illustration)**.
3 Remove the nut that secures the shift

12.2 Remove the fresh air intake duct for access to the transmission range sensor

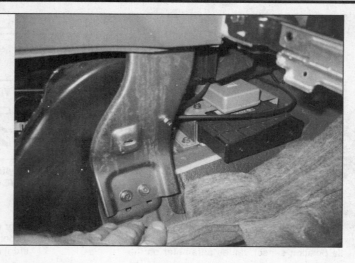

13.3 The PCM is mounted under the center of the instrument panel

control cable to the control shaft lever and disconnect the cable from the lever.

4   Remove the nut and washer that secures the control shaft lever to the manual valve shaft and remove the control shaft lever from the manual valve shaft.

5   Remove the TR sensor mounting bolts and remove the TR sensor.

Installation

6   To install the TR sensor, slide it onto the manual valve shaft, then loosely install the mounting bolts.

7   Install the lever on the manual valve shaft. Install the nut and tighten it securely. Turn the lever through the gears - it will click as it changes to the next gear - until it stops at Park, then turn it two clicks. It's now in the Neutral position.

8   Connect the cable to the manual valve shaft and install the nut, but don't tighten it yet.

9   Align the holes on the manual lever and the sensor; use an appropriately sized drill bit to insert into the holes to ensure alignment, turning the sensor as necessary. When alignment is achieved, tighten the sensor mounting screws securely, being careful to avoid moving the sensor.

10   The remainder of installation is the reverse of removal.

11   Tighten the cable nut and check that the transmission and indicator operate properly. Make sure the engine only starts in Park and Neutral, and make sure the back-up lights come on when the shifter is placed in Reverse.

13   Powertrain Control Module (PCM) - replacement

Refer to illustration 13.3

Warning: *The models covered by this manual are equipped with Supplemental Restraint systems (SRS), more commonly known as airbags. Always disable the airbag system*

before working in the vicinity of any airbag system component to avoid the possibility of accidental deployment of the airbag, which could cause personal injury (see Chapter 12).
Caution: *To avoid electrostatic discharge damage to the PCM, handle the PCM only by its case. Do not touch the electrical terminals during removal and installation. If available, ground yourself to the vehicle with an anti-static ground strap, available at computer supply stores, and use a special anti-static pad to store the PCM on once it is removed.*
Note: *The PCM is located inside the passenger compartment at the center of the instrument panel at the right side of the console.*

1   Disconnect the cable from the negative battery terminal (see Chapter 5, Section 1).

2   Refer to Chapter 11 and remove the console covers and the instrument panel covers to expose the area under and to the right of the audio system.

3   Disconnect the electrical connectors from the PCM **(see illustration)**.

4   Remove the upper and lower PCM mounting bracket fasteners and carefully remove the PCM (see **Caution** above).

5   Installation is the reverse of removal.

14   Idle Air Control (IAC) valve - replacement

Note: *The IAC valve is located below the throttle body on 2.4L four-cylinder and 2.7L V6 models. There is no IAC valve on 3.5L V6 models.*

1   Disconnect the cable from the negative battery terminal (see Chapter 5, Section 1).

2   Remove the throttle body (see Chapter 4). Disconnect the sensor wiring harness.

3   Remove the IAC valve mounting screws and remove the IAC valve.

4   Remove and discard the old IAC valve gasket.

5   Installation is the reverse of removal. Be sure to use a new gasket and tighten the IAC valve mounting screws securely.

15   Catalytic converters - description, check and component replacement

Note: *Because of a Federally mandated extended warranty which covers emissions-related components such as the catalytic converter, check with a dealer service department before replacing the converter at your own expense.*

General description

1   The catalytic converter is an emission control device installed in the exhaust system that reduces pollutants from the exhaust gas stream. There are two types of converters: The oxidation catalyst reduces the levels of hydrocarbon (HC) and carbon monoxide (CO) by adding oxygen to the exhaust stream to produce water vapor (H_2O) and carbon dioxide (CO_2). The reduction catalyst lowers the levels of oxides of nitrogen (NOx) by removing oxygen from the exhaust gases to produce nitrogen (N) and oxygen. These two types of catalysts are combined into a three-way catalyst that reduces all three pollutants.

2   The amount of oxygen entering the catalyst is critical to its operation, because without oxygen it cannot convert harmful pollutants into harmless compounds. The catalyst is most efficient at capturing and storing oxygen when it converts the exhaust gases of an intake charge that's mixed at the ideal (stoichiometric) air/fuel ratio of 14.7:1. If the air/fuel ratio is leaner than stoichiometric for an extended period of time, the catalyst will store even more oxygen. But if the air/fuel ratio is richer than stoichiometric for any length of time, the oxygen content in the catalyst can become totally depleted. If this condition occurs, the catalyst will not convert anything!

3   Because the catalyst's ability to store oxygen is such an important factor in its operation, it can also be considered a factor in the catalyst's eventual inability to do its job. The PCM monitors the oxygen content going into and coming out of the catalyst by comparing the voltage signals from the upstream and downstream oxygen sensors. When the catalyst is functioning correctly, there is very little oxygen to monitor at the outlet end of the catalyst because it's capturing, storing and releasing oxygen as needed to convert HC, CO and NOx into more benign substances. If the catalyst isn't doing its job, the downstream oxygen sensor tells the PCM that the oxygen content in the catalyzed exhaust gases is going up. When the amount of oxygen exiting the catalyst reaches a specified threshold, the PCM stores a Diagnostic Trouble Code (DTC) and turns on the Malfunction Indicator Light (MIL), also known as the CHECK ENGINE light.

Check

4   The test equipment for a catalytic converter is expensive and highly sophisticated. If you suspect that the converter on your vehicle

is malfunctioning, take it to a dealer or authorized emissions inspection facility for diagnosis and repair.

5   Whenever the vehicle is raised for servicing of underbody components, check the converter for leaks, corrosion, dents and other damage. Check the welds/flange bolts that attach the front and rear ends of the converter to the exhaust system. If damage is discovered, the converter should be replaced.

6   Although catalytic converters don't break too often, they can become plugged. The easiest way to check for a restricted converter is to use a vacuum gauge to diagnose the effect of a blocked exhaust on intake vacuum.

a) *Connect a vacuum gauge to an intake manifold vacuum source (see Chapter 2C).*

b) *Warm the engine to operating temperature, place the transaxle in Park (automatic) or Neutral (manual) and apply the parking brake.*

c) *Note and record the vacuum reading at idle.*

d) *Quickly open the throttle to near full throttle and release it shut. Note and record the vacuum reading.*

e) *Perform the test three more times, recording the reading after each test.*

f) *If the reading after the fourth test is more than one in-Hg lower than the reading recorded at idle, the exhaust system may be restricted (the catalytic converter could be plugged or an exhaust pipe or muffler could be restricted).*

Replacement

Warning: *Do NOT service a catalytic converter until it has completely cooled down.*

Manifold catalytic converters

2.4L four-cylinder and 3.5L V6 models

Note: *On these models, the exhaust manifold catalytic converters are located directly below the exhaust manifolds, to which they're bolted.*

7   Raise the vehicle and support it securely on jackstands.

8   Unbolt the exhaust pipe from the bottom of the catalytic converter.

9   Disconnect the rubber exhaust pipe supports under the car and carefully lower the front of the pipe as much as possible for access to the catalytic converters.

10   Disconnect the oxygen sensors from the catalytic converter.

11   Unbolt the converter from the exhaust manifold and remove it from beneath the vehicle.

2.7L V6 models

Note: *On these models, the primary catalytic converters are integral parts of the exhaust manifolds.*

12   Refer to *Exhaust manifold - removal and installation* in Chapter 2B.

Undercar catalytic converter

Refer to illustration 15.15

Note: *The downstream catalytic converter is located underneath the vehicle. It's located*

15.15 A typical downstream catalytic converter; the upstream converters are located at the exhaust manifolds

between the flange at the rear end of the front exhaust pipe and the muffler, to which it's connected by a short pipe. These catalytic converters are usually replaced at muffler shops that are equipped with the proper welding equipment. If you wish to replace the catalytic converter without welding, it will be necessary to replace the section of exhaust pipe that includes the converter from flange to flange.

13   Raise the front of the vehicle and place it securely on jackstands.

14   Support the catalytic converter with a floor jack.

15   Remove the bolts from the flanges at each end of the catalytic converter **(see illustration).**

16   Disconnect the flanges and remove any gaskets.

17   Lower the converter from the vehicle.

---

16   Evaporative emissions control (EVAP) system - description and component replacement

Description

1   The Evaporative Emissions Control (EVAP) system absorbs fuel vapors (unburned hydrocarbons) and, during engine operation, releases them into the intake manifold from which they're drawn into the intake ports where they mix with the incoming air-fuel mixture. The EVAP system consists of the fuel tank filler neck cap, the EVAP canister, the vapor pressure sensor, the canister closed valve, the two-way valve and the purge valve. Everything except the purge valve is located underneath the vehicle.

2   Modern EVAP systems are quite complex, but basically, here's how they work: When the gasoline inside the fuel tank warms up on a hot day, it evaporates and produces fuel vapors. These vapors, which are raw unburned hydrocarbons, elevate the pressure inside the sealed fuel tank. If there were no way to vent them somewhere, the fuel tank

would eventually spring a leak. The **vapor pressure sensor** monitors the pressure inside the tank and keeps the Powertrain Control Module (PCM) informed. The fuel tank vapors enter the canister by flowing through a **two-way valve**. The canister stores these vapors until the PCM energizes the **purge control solenoid valve**, which opens and purges the EVAP system, allowing intake manifold vacuum to pull the vapors from the canister into the intake manifold.

3   The **vapor pressure sensor** is located on top of the fuel tank. The vapor pressure sensor monitors the pressure of fuel vapors inside the tank.

4   After the engine is warmed up (165 degrees F.) the PCM puts the system into closed loop operation. Then it energizes the **canister purge control solenoid valve**, which regulates the flow of vapors from the canister to the intake manifold. The rate of vapor flow is regulated by the purge valve in response to commands from the PCM, which controls the duty cycle of the valve, which means that the valve's opening can be controlled to a fine degree (it's not just open or closed) in order to regulate the volume of the purged vapors in an appropriate way so that the air/fuel mixture doesn't become too rich. On al models the canister purge control solenoid valve is located in the engine compartment.

5   When the EVAP system is being purged and stored vapors are being drawn from the canister by intake manifold vacuum, a vacuum condition would quickly result inside the canister and the fuel tank if they were not vented to atmospheric pressure. So during purging, atmospheric air is drawn through the fresh air line, then into the canister. The **canister closed valve** opens and closes the EVAP system's fresh air line in response to signals from the Powertrain Control Module (PCM). When commanded by the PCM, the canister closed valve also closes the fresh air line to the EVAP canister for monitor testing. The canister closed valve is located on the canister.

16.13 Location of the purge control solenoid valve (3.5L V6 engine shown)

16.19 The EVAP components are mounted in a module in the center tunnel on 2WD models - on 4WD models it is offset to the side at the center of the vehicle

The EVAP system monitor

6   The EVAP system diagnostic monitor is an OBD-II test that the PCM runs to check the EVAP system and the fuel tank for leaks. Before the monitor sequence begins, several things must happen. First, you must start the engine. If the engine is cold, the engine coolant temperature and the intake air temperature are about the same. The PCM watches the progress of the warm-up sequence closely. Once the oxygen sensors and the catalysts have warmed up enough for the PCM to put the system into closed loop operation, the PCM initiates the EVAP purge sequence. The purge valve opens, the canister closed valve opens and the EVAP canister's contents are purged (drawn into the intake manifold). During a fast-idle warm-up, intake vacuum is high and the extra-rich mixture caused by purging the vapors stored inside the EVAP canister actually helps to smooth out the idle.

7   During purging, the pressure inside the EVAP system is neutral because the opened canister closed valve allows atmospheric pressure to be drawn into the canister as vapors are drawn from the canister into the intake manifold. During this initial period of operation, the PCM is also monitoring the fuel tank pressure with the vapor pressure sensor. As soon as the purge sequence is complete, the PCM closes the canister closed valve. When the canister closed valve is first closed, the pressure switching valve and the purge valve are still open, so a (relative) vacuum develops inside the purge line from the air intake to the canister and to the EVAP line from the canister to the fuel tank. The PCM then closes the purge valve to produce a (relative) vacuum in the line between the tank and the purge valve. Then it monitors any change in pressure (through the vapor pressure sensor) to check for EVAP system leaks. If there's a leak, the Malfunction Indicator Light (MIL) or Check Engine light comes on and the PCM stores a

Diagnostic Trouble Code (DTC) that indicates a malfunction in the EVAP system (see Section 2).

8   At a certain point in the monitoring sequence the PCM closes the canister closed valve which causes a pressure drop in the EVAP system. The PCM keeps the purge valve open until the pressure inside the EVAP system drops to a specified threshold, at which point the PCM closes the purge valve. If the pressure doesn't drop, or drops too much, the PCM turns on the MIL or Check Engine light and stores a DTC (see Section 2) that indicates an incorrect purge flow in the EVAP system.

9   Then the PCM monitors the operation of the canister closed valve and the venting (air inlet) function of the system. When vapor pressure rises to a specified threshold, the PCM opens the canister closed valve. The pressure inside the system goes up quickly because of the air drawn into the system. If the PCM detects no increase in pressure or if the pressure is below the specified increase, the PCM concludes that either the canister closed valve is malfunctioning or there's a restriction somewhere in the venting and, again, stores a DTC (see Section 2) and turns on the MIL or Check Engine light.

10   Finally, the PCM closes the pressure switching valve, which prevents atmospheric air from entering the fuel tank side of the system. When the pressure switching valve is operating correctly, this should produce a slight pressure rise inside the tank (because the fuel inside the tank is still slowly getting warmer). But if there's no change in pressure, the PCM concludes that the pressure switching valve isn't closing and, again, stores a DTC (see Section 2) and turns on the MIL or Check Engine light. The monitoring sequence is now completed. The PCM immediately repeats the entire sequence again, conditions permitting, and continues to do so as long as the engine is operating in closed loop.

Replacement

Warning: *Gasoline and gasoline vapor is extremely flammable, so take extra precautions when you work on any part of the fuel system or EVAP system. Don't smoke or allow open flames or bare light bulbs near the work area, and don't work in a garage where a gas-type appliance (such as a water heater or a clothes dryer) is present. Since gasoline is carcinogenic, wear fuel resistant gloves when there's a possibility of being exposed to fuel, and, if you spill any fuel on your skin, rinse it off immediately with soap and water. Mop up any spills immediately and do not store fuel-soaked rags where they could ignite. When you perform any kind of work on the fuel system, wear safety glasses and have a Class B type fire extinguisher on hand.*

Purge control solenoid valve

Refer to illustration 16.13

11   Disconnect the cable from the negative battery terminal (see Chapter 5, Section 1).
12   Remove the engine cover, if applicable (see *Intake manifold - removal and installation* in Chapter 2).
13   Disconnect the electrical connector from the purge valve **(see illustration)**.
14   Disconnect the vacuum hoses from the purge valve.
15   Remove the purge valve mounting fasteners and remove the purge valve.
16   Installation is the reverse of removal.

Other components (under vehicle)

Refer to illustration 16.19

17   Disconnect the cable from the negative battery terminal (see Chapter 5, Section 1).
18   Raise the rear of the vehicle and support it securely on jackstands.
19   Remove the protective cover from the EVAP canister assembly, if so equipped **(see illustration)**.

Two-way valve

Note: *The two-way valve is located in the line between the fuel tank and the canister.*

20   Disconnect the EVAP hoses from the two-way valve.

21   Installation is the reverse of removal. Be sure that the valve is installed facing the correct direction according to the arrow on it.

EVAP canister

Note: *The EVAP canister is mounted to the frame rail near the fuel tank.*

22   Disconnect the hoses from the canister.

23   Disconnect the wiring from the canister closed valve.

24   Remove the EVAP canister mounting bracket bolts and remove the EVAP canister and mounting bracket as a single assembly.

25   Installation is the reverse of removal.

Vapor pressure sensor

26   This sensor is mounted to the rear end of the fuel tank in the line connecting the fuel tank and the canister.

27   Disconnect the wiring harness from the sensor.

28   Disconnect the fuel hoses.

29   Remove the sensor along with its mounting bracket. The bracket can be removed after it is out of the vehicle.

30   Installation is the reverse of removal.

Canister closed valve

31   This valve is connected to the canister.

32   Detach the wiring connector from the valve.

33   Remove the valve from the canister.

34   Installation is the reverse of removal.

---

17   Positive Crankcase Ventilation (PCV) system - general information

---

1   The Positive Crankcase Ventilation (PCV) system reduces hydrocarbon emissions by directing blow-by gases and crankcase vapors into the intake manifold, where they're mixed with intake air before being drawn into the combustion chambers where they're consumed along with the air/fuel mixture. The PCV system does this by circulating fresh air from the air filter housing through a series of hoses into the crankcase, where the fresh air mixes with blow-by gases before being drawn from the crankcase by intake

vacuum, through the PCV valve and then into the intake manifold.

2   During idle and part-throttle conditions, intake manifold vacuum is high. Blow-by gases and crankcase vapors flow from the crankcase through the PCV valve and the crankcase ventilation hose (also known as the PCV hose) into the intake manifold. The strong intake manifold vacuum also pulls fresh air from the air intake duct or the air filter housing through the fresh air inlet hose into the crankcase.

3   There is no scheduled maintenance interval for the PCV valve or the PCV system hoses. But over time the PCV system might become less efficient as an oily residue of sludge builds up inside the PCV valve and the hoses. One symptom of a clogged PCV system is leaking seals. When crankcase vapors can't escape, pressure builds inside the bottom end and eventually causes crankshaft seals to leak. So anytime that you're changing the oil filter, air filter, fuel filter, spark plugs, etc. it's a good idea to pull off the PCV hoses and inspect them. If the hoses are clogged, remove them and clean them out. If they're cracked, torn or deteriorated, replace them.

4   Checking and replacement of the PCV valve is covered in Chapter 1.

---

18   Exhaust Gas Recirculation (EGR) system - description and component replacement

---

General description

Note: *2.7L V6 models do not use an EGR system. They are only used on 2.4L four-cylinder and 3.5L V6 models.*

1   To reduce oxides of nitrogen (NOx) emissions, some of the exhaust gas is recirculated through the EGR valve to the intake manifold to lower combustion temperatures.

2   The EGR system consists of an EGR valve, an EGR vacuum solenoid valve, a MAP (manifold absolute pressure) sensor, the PCM, vacuum hoses and the wiring harnesses. The position of the EGR valve is controlled by vacuum. The vacuum is modulated by the EGR solenoid valve, which in turn is controlled by the PCM. The MAP sensor is used to provide information to the PCM for EGR system operation.

Replacement

EGR valve

3   Remove the engine cover and gain access to the EGR valve. It is identifiable by the large diaphragm housing with the vacuum hose attached. On 2.4L four-cylinder models it is near the throttle body. On 3.5L V6 models it's at the rear center of the intake manifold - refer to Chapter 2B, *Intake manifold - removal and installation.*

4   Disconnect the vacuum hose.

5   Remove the mounting bolts and lift the EGR valve off.

6   Check the EGR valve for sticking and heavy carbon deposits. They can sometimes be cleaned of carbon, but if it's excessive, it must be replaced.

7   Installation is the reverse of removal. Be sure to use a new gasket, and to clean the mounting surfaces thoroughly.

EGR vacuum solenoid valve

8   The EGR vacuum solenoid valve is connected to the EGR valve by a vacuum hose. There is also a vacuum hose connecting it to an engine vacuum source. On 2.4L models it's on the top of the engine near the valve cover. On 3.5L V6 models it's located between the firewall and the upper intake manifold.

9   Disconnect the wiring harness from the valve.

10   Disconnect both vacuum hoses from the valve. Label them if there is any chance they could be confused later.

11   Remove the mounting bolts and take off the solenoid valve.

12   Installation is the reverse of removal.

MAP sensor

13   The MAP sensor is connected directly to the intake manifold. On 2.4L four-cylinder models, its only function is to supply information to the PCM for proper operation of the EGR system. It is not used as a sensor for general engine performance. On 2.4L four-cylinder models, it's located at the passenger-side end of the intake manifold.

14   Disconnect the wiring/vacuum hose connections from the valve.

15   Remove the mounting screws and lift off the sensor.

16   Installation is the reverse of removal.

Notes

Chapter 7 Part A
Manual transaxle

Contents

Specifications

General

Transaxle oil type	See Chapter 1
Transaxle oil capacity	See Chapter 1

Torque specifications

	Ft-lbs	Nm
Roll stopper bracket-to-subframe bolts	29 to 38	40 to 55
Roll stopper insulator nut	36 to 47	50 to 65
Roll stopper bracket-to-transaxle bolts	43 to 58	60 to 80
Rear roll stopper bracket bolts	29 to 38	40 to 55
Transaxle-to-mounting bracket bolts	29 to 38	40 to 55
Transaxle-to-engine mounting bolts	33	45
Crossmember-to-subframe bolts	85	115

1   General information

The vehicles covered by this manual are equipped with either a 5-speed manual or an automatic transaxle. This Part of Chapter 7 contains information on the manual transaxle. Service procedures for the automatic transaxle are contained in Part B. Information on the transfer case used on 4WD models can be found in Part C.

The transaxle is contained in a cast-aluminum alloy casing bolted to the engine's rear end, and consists of the gearbox and final drive differential. The transaxle unit type is stamped on a plate attached to the transaxle.

Transaxle overhaul

Because of the complexity of the assembly, possible unavailability of replacement parts and special tools necessary, internal repair procedures for the transaxle are not recommended for the home mechanic. The bulk of the information in this Chapter is devoted to removal and installation procedures.

2　Shift lever - removal and installation

1　Apply the parking brake. Place the shift lever in Neutral. Unscrew and remove the shift lever knob.
2　Refer to Chapter 11 and remove the center console assembly.
3　Use pliers to remove the shift cable pins and clips. Move the cables aside.
4　Remove the shifter assembly from the mounting bracket.
5　Remove the retainer from the shift lever.
6　Installation is the reverse of removal.

3　Shift cables - removal and installation

1　Apply the parking brake. Place the shift lever in Neutral. Unscrew and remove the shift lever knob.
2　Refer to Chapter 11 and remove the center console assembly.
3　Use pliers to remove the pins from the ends of the shift cables.
4　Pull the cable housing retaining clips out of the shifter base.
5　Locate the shift cables at the transaxle and pull their retaining clips out.
6　Pull the pins out of the transaxle ends of the shift cables.
7　Feed the cables through the firewall grommet to remove them.
8　Check the end bushings for any signs of looseness or damage before replacing the cables.
9　Installation is the reverse of removal.

4　Driveaxle oil seals - replacement

1　Oil leaks frequently occur due to wear of the driveaxle oil seals. Replacement of these seals is relatively easy, since the repair can be performed without removing the transaxle from the vehicle.
2　Driveaxle oil seals are located at the sides of the transaxle/transfer case, where the driveaxles are attached. If leakage at the seal is suspected, raise the vehicle and support it securely on jackstands. If the seal is leaking, lubricant will be found on the sides of the transaxle below the seals.
3　Refer to Chapter 8 and remove the drive-axles.
4　Use a screwdriver or prybar to carefully pry the oil seal out of the transaxle bore.
5　If the oil seal cannot be removed with a screwdriver or prybar, a special oil seal removal tool (available at auto parts stores) will be required.
6　Using a large section of pipe or a large deep socket (slightly smaller than the outside diameter of the seal) as a drift, install the new oil seal. Drive it into the bore squarely and make sure it's completely seated. Coat the seal lip with transaxle lubricant.

7　Install the driveaxle(s). Be careful not to damage the lip of the new seal.

5　Manual transaxle - removal and installation

Note: *If you're working on a 4WD vehicle, refer to Chapter 7C for the removal procedures for the driveshaft and transfer case.*

Removal

1　Loosen the front wheel lug nuts and the driveaxle/hub nuts.
2　Refer to Chapter 5 and remove the battery from the vehicle. Also, remove the battery support tray.
3　Refer to Chapter 4 and remove the entire air cleaner assembly along with the intake duct.
4　Disconnect the wiring from the back-up light switch.
5　Disconnect the wiring from the crankshaft position sensor, the oxygen sensors and the oil pressure sender. Remove their wiring harness mounting bracket.
6　Disconnect the speedometer connection at the transaxle.
7　Loosen the clutch release lever at the bellhousing. Remove the cotter pin and clevis pin from the release lever shaft. Remove the release lever. **Note:** *This Step must be performed because the bearing, pressure plate and fork are secured to one another.*
8　Refer to Section 3 and disconnect both shift cables from the transaxle.
9　Refer to Chapter 10 and disconnect the steering shaft inside the vehicle. Make sure to mark the positions of the sections of the shaft to avoid confusion at reassembly.
10　Disconnect both power steering hoses from the pump and pull the tubing free of its clips. Seal the ends to avoid contamination.
11　Remove the topmost transaxle mounting bolt.
12　Refer to Chapter 5 and remove the starter.
13　Support the engine securely from above with a fixture that mounts between the fenders. These can be rented at most rental yards if you don't own one.
14　Raise the vehicle and support it securely on jackstands. Refer to Chapter 8 and remove both driveaxles.
15　Drain the transaxle lubricant (see Chapter 1).
16　Remove the transaxle mounting bracket and the front and rear lower "roll stopper" mounts.
17　Remove the front section of the exhaust system.
18　Make sure that the engine is solidly supported by the fixture. Remove the subframe mounting bolts and lift the subframe clear with the help of an assistant.
19　Put a transmission jack (or a floor jack with an appropriate saddle) under the

transaxle. Safety chains will help steady the transaxle on the jack.
20　Remove the remaining transaxle-to-engine bolts. Check to make certain that all connections between the transaxle and the vehicle are disconnected.
21　With the help of an assistant, pull the transaxle away from the engine and slowly lower it to the ground, checking that it's not catching on other components as you do so.
22　Pull the transaxle out from beneath the vehicle, remove it from the jack and set it where it can't roll over and become damaged.

Installation

23　Lubricate the input shaft with a light coat of high-temperature grease. With the transaxle secured to the jack, raise it into position behind the engine and carefully slide it forward, engaging the input shaft with the clutch. Do not use excessive force to install the transaxle - if the input shaft won't slide into place, readjust the angle of the transaxle or turn the input shaft so the splines engage properly with the clutch.
24　Once the transaxle is flush with the engine, install the transaxle-to-engine bolts. Tighten the bolts to the torque listed in this Chapter's Specifications. **Caution:** *Don't use the bolts to force the transaxle and engine together.*
25　The remainder of installation is the reverse of removal, but note the following points:
　a) *Tighten the suspension mounting bolts to the torque values listed in the Chapter 10 Specifications.*
　b) *Tighten the driveaxle/hub nuts to the torque value listed in the Chapter 8 Specifications.*
　c) *Tighten the starter mounting bolts to the torque value listed in the Chapter 5 Specifications.*
　d) *If installing the transfer case, refer to Chapter 7, Part C.*
　e) *Tighten the wheel lug nuts to the torque listed in the Chapter 1 Specifications.*
　f) *Fill the transaxle with the correct type and amount of transaxle fluid as described in Chapter 1.*

6　Manual transaxle overhaul - general information

1　Overhauling a manual transaxle is a difficult job for the do-it-yourselfer. It involves the disassembly and reassembly of many small parts. Numerous clearances must be precisely measured and, if necessary, changed with select-fit spacers and snap-rings. As a result, if transaxle problems arise, it can be removed and installed by a competent do-it-yourselfer, but overhaul should be left to a transmission repair shop. Rebuilt transaxles may be available - check with your dealer parts department and auto parts stores. At any rate, the time and money involved in an overhaul is almost sure to exceed the cost of a rebuilt unit.

2   Nevertheless, it's not impossible for an inexperienced mechanic to rebuild a transaxle if the special tools are available and the job is done in a deliberate step-by-step manner so nothing is overlooked.

3   The tools necessary for an overhaul include internal and external snap-ring pliers, a bearing puller, a slide hammer, a set of pin punches, a dial indicator and possibly a hydraulic press. In addition, a large, sturdy workbench and a vise or transaxle stand will be required.

4   During disassembly of the transaxle, make careful notes of how each piece comes off, where it fits in relation to other pieces and what holds it in place.

5   Before taking the transaxle apart for repair, it will help if you have some idea what area of the transaxle is malfunctioning. Certain problems can be closely tied to specific areas in the transaxle, which can make component examination and replacement easier. Refer to the *Troubleshooting* Section at the front of this manual for information regarding possible sources of trouble.

7   Transaxle mount - replacement

1   Insert a large screwdriver or prybar between the mount and the transaxle and pry up.

2   The transaxle should not move excessively away from the mount. If it does, replace the mount.

3   There are two lower mounts (one each at the front and rear of the transaxle) and an upper mount assembly.

4   Support the transaxle from below with a jack, remove the nuts and bolts and remove the mount. It may be necessary to raise the transaxle slightly to provide enough clearance to remove the mount.

5   Installation is the reverse of removal.
Note: *Install all of the mount fasteners before tightening any of them.*

Notes

Chapter 7 Part B
Automatic transaxle

Contents

Specifications

General

Fluid type and capacity.. See Chapter 1

Torque specifications

	Ft-lbs	Nm
Crossmember-to-subframe bolts	85	115
Torque converter-to-driveplate fasteners	27	36
Transaxle-to-engine mounting bolts	30	40
Roll stopper bracket-to-subframe bolts	30 to 38	40 to 55
Roll stopper insulator nut	36 to 47	50 to 65
Roll stopper bracket-to-transaxle bolts	43 to 58	60 to 80
Rear roll stopper bracket bolts	29 to 38	40 to 55
Transaxle-to-mounting bracket bolts	29 to 38	40 to 55
Transaxle-to-engine mounting bolts	33	45

1 General information

All information on the automatic transaxle is included in this Part of Chapter 7. Information for the manual transaxle can be found in Part A of this Chapter.

Because of the complexity of the automatic transaxles and the specialized equipment necessary to perform most service operations, this Chapter contains only those procedures related to general diagnosis, routine maintenance, adjustment and removal and installation.

If the transaxle requires major repair work, it should be left to a dealer service department or an automotive or transmis-sion repair shop. Once properly diagnosed you can, however, remove and install the transaxle yourself and save the expense, even if the repair work is done by a transmis-sion shop.

2 Diagnosis - general

1   Automatic transaxle malfunctions may be caused by five general conditions:

a) *Poor engine performance*
b) *Improper adjustments*
c) *Hydraulic malfunctions*
d) *Mechanical malfunctions*
e) *Malfunctions in the computer or its signal network*

2   Diagnosis of these problems should always begin with a check of the easily repaired items: fluid level and condition (see Chapter 1), shift cable adjustment and shift lever installation. Next, perform a road test to determine if the problem has been corrected or if more diagnosis is necessary. If the problem persists after the preliminary tests and corrections are completed, additional diagnosis should be performed by a dealer service department or other qualified transmission repair shop. Refer to the *Troubleshooting* Section at the front of this manual for information on symptoms of transaxle problems.

3.2 There are two small screws at the front of the shift handle; when replacing the handle, align the pushbutton with the plunger to allow the handle to slip into the correct position, allowing the screws to line up with their holes

Preliminary checks

3   Drive the vehicle to warm the transaxle to normal operating temperature.

4   Check the fluid level as described in Chapter 1:

a) *If the fluid level is unusually low, add enough fluid to bring the level within the designated area of the dipstick, then check for external leaks (see following).*

b) *If the fluid level is abnormally high, drain off the excess, then check the drained fluid for contamination by coolant. The presence of engine coolant in the automatic transmission fluid indicates that a failure has occurred in the internal radiator oil cooler walls that separate the coolant from the transmission fluid (see Chapter 3).*

c) *If the fluid is foaming, drain it and refill the transaxle, then check for coolant in the fluid, or a high fluid level.*

5   Check the engine idle speed. **Note:** *If the engine is malfunctioning, do not proceed with the preliminary checks until it has been repaired and runs normally.*

6   Check and adjust the shift cable, if necessary (see Section 4).

7   If hard shifting is experienced, inspect the shift cable under the steering column and at the manual lever on the transaxle (see Section 4).

Fluid leak diagnosis

8   Most fluid leaks are easy to locate visually. Repair usually consists of replacing a seal or gasket. If a leak is difficult to find, the following procedure may help.

9   Identify the fluid. Make sure it's transmission fluid and not engine oil or brake fluid (automatic transmission fluid is a deep red color).

10   Try to pinpoint the source of the leak. Drive the vehicle several miles, then park it over a large sheet of cardboard. After a minute or two, you should be able to locate the leak by determining the source of the fluid dripping onto the cardboard.

11   Make a careful visual inspection of the suspected component and the area immediately around it. Pay particular attention to gasket mating surfaces. A mirror is often helpful for finding leaks in areas that are hard to see.

12   If the leak still cannot be found, clean the suspected area thoroughly with a degreaser or solvent, then dry it thoroughly.

13   Drive the vehicle for several miles at normal operating temperature and varying speeds. After driving the vehicle, visually inspect the suspected component again.

14   Once the leak has been located, the cause must be determined before it can be properly repaired. If a gasket is replaced but the sealing flange is bent, the new gasket will not stop the leak. The bent flange must be straightened.

15   Before attempting to repair a leak, check to make sure that the following conditions are corrected or they may cause another leak. **Note:** *Some of the following conditions cannot be fixed without highly specialized tools and expertise. Such problems must be referred to a qualified transmission shop or a dealer service department.*

Gasket leaks

16   Check the pan periodically. Make sure the bolts are tight, no bolts are missing, the gasket is in good condition and the pan is flat (dents in the pan may indicate damage to the valve body inside).

17   If the pan gasket is leaking, the fluid level or the fluid pressure may be too high, the vent may be plugged, the pan bolts may be too tight, the pan sealing flange may be warped, the sealing surface of the transaxle housing may be damaged, the gasket may be damaged or the transaxle casting may be cracked or porous. If sealant instead of gasket material has been used to form a seal between the pan and the transaxle housing, it may be the wrong type of sealant.

Seal leaks

18   If a transaxle seal is leaking, the fluid level or pressure may be too high, the vent may be plugged, the seal bore may be damaged, the seal itself may be damaged or improperly installed, the surface of the shaft protruding through the seal may be damaged

or a loose bearing may be causing excessive shaft movement.

19   Make sure the dipstick tube seal is in good condition and the tube is properly seated. Periodically check the area around the sensors for leakage. If transmission fluid is evident, check the seals for damage.

Case leaks

20   If the case itself appears to be leaking, the casting is porous and will have to be repaired or replaced.

21   Make sure the oil cooler hose fittings are tight and in good condition.

Fluid comes out vent pipe or fill tube

22   If this condition occurs, the possible causes are: the transaxle is overfilled, there is coolant in the fluid, the case is porous, the dipstick is incorrect, the vent is plugged or the drain-back holes are plugged.

---

3   Shift lever - replacement

Refer to illustration 3.2

Warning 1: *These models are equipped with a Supplemental Restraint System (SRS), more commonly known as airbags. Always disable the airbag system before working in the vicinity of any airbag system component to avoid the possibility of accidental deployment of the airbag(s), which could cause personal injury (see Chapter 12).*

Warning 2: *Do not use a memory saving device to preserve the PCM or radio memory when working on or near airbag system components.*

1   Disconnect the cable from the negative battery terminal (see Chapter 5, Section 1).

2   Loosen the two small screws at the front of the handle, then remove it **(see illustration)**. If you remove the button and spring from the handle, be sure to note the direction the button is installed.

3   Pry up the indicator panel and disconnect any wiring as you remove it. Remove the center console (see Chapter 11).

4   Remove the electromagnetic switch and the detent assembly if necessary.

5   Remove the long pivot bolt from the passenger side.

6   Lift out the parking brake cable bracket, the pivot sleeve, the cable lever, the shift lever and the switch lever.

7   Installation is the reverse of removal. Depress the button to allow it to engage with the top of the shift mechanism before tightening the screws.

---

4   Shift and interlock cables - replacement and adjustment

Replacement

Refer to illustrations 4.3a and 4.3b

1   Disconnect the cable from the negative battery terminal (see Chapter 5, Section 1).

4.3a The shift cable is secured to the shift mechanism with a clip

4.3b Remove the retainer with pliers to release the shift cable from the lever bracket

2   Disassemble the shifter assembly enough to get access to the end of the shift cable.
3   Remove the retaining pin from the end of the cable and remove the clip that secures the cable housing to the shifter bracket **(see illustrations)**.
4   Feed the cable through the instrument panel area and through the grommet in the firewall.
5   Disconnect the cable from retainers and interfering components.
6   Disconnect the cable from the lever at the transaxle and remove it from the vehicle.
7   Installation is the reverse of removal. Be certain to adjust the new cable after installation.

Adjustment

Refer to illustration 4.9

8   Refer to Chapter 6 to adjust the Transmission Range sensor.
9   Remove the console cover if it hasn't been removed already **(see illustration)**. Loosen the screws securing the interlock cables to the shifter bracket.
10   Shift the lever into the Park position. Verify that the key is in the Off position.
11   Make sure that the key lock cable cam is placed in the correct position by the detent pin. The key lock cable is connected to the key cylinder.
12   Make sure that the shift lock cable cam is in the correct position. The shift lock cable is attached to the brake pedal assembly.
13   Gently push the lower shift lock cable away from the shifter and tighten the self-tapping screw.
14   Gently pull the upper key lock cable toward the shifter and tighten the self-tapping screw.
15   After installing any remaining components, apply the parking brake and operate the vehicle in each gear position to verify the adjustment is correct. Verify that the vehicle

can't be shifted out of Park unless the key is On and the brake pedal is depressed. Check that the key can't be turned to the Lock position unless the shifter is in Park.

5   Automatic transaxle - removal and installation

Refer to illustrations 5.13 and 5.15

Removal

1   Disconnect the cable from the negative terminal of the battery (see Chapter 5).
2   Drain the fluid from the transaxle (see Chapter 1).
3   Refer to Chapter 4 and remove the entire air cleaner assembly including the air duct.
4   Disconnect the wiring harnesses from the speedometer sensor, Transmission Range sensor, solenoid connector and the oil temperature sensor.
5   Disconnect the transmission fluid cooler hoses and seal their ends to prevent leakage and contamination.
6   Disconnect the shift control cable.

7   Disconnect the steering shaft from the steering gear. Make sure to mark the parts so they can be installed in the same positions.
8   Disconnect both power steering hoses and seal their ends.
9   Remove the upper transaxle mounting bolt.
10   Support the engine securely from above with a fixture that mounts between the fenders. These can be rented at most rental yards if you don't own one.
11   Loosen the front wheel lug nuts and the driveaxle/hub nuts. Raise the vehicle and support it securely on jackstands. Remove the driveaxles (see Chapter 8). After the driveaxles have been removed, temporarily reattach the steering knuckles to the struts.
12   Remove the inspection plate, then remove the torque converter-to-driveplate fasteners. This will involve rotating the engine for access to all of the bolts. Have an assistant do this with a ratchet and socket on the end of the crankshaft. This will also hold the engine from rotating as the bolts are loosened. Mark the position of the torque converter on the driveplate with a dab of paint.

4.9 The interlock cables attach to the right side of the shifter - if one is disconnected or misadjusted, it might be possible to shift out of Park without turning the key On and pressing the brake pedal

5.13 Disconnect the roll stopper transaxle mounts

5.15 Subframe mounting bolts

13   Remove the transaxle mounting bracket and the front and rear lower "roll stopper" mounts **(see illustration)**.

14   Remove the front section of the exhaust system.

15   Make sure that the engine is solidly supported by the fixture. Detach the control arms from the steering knuckles and the stabilizer bar links from the control arms. Support the subframe with two floor jacks (one on each side). Remove the subframe mounting bolts and lower the subframe, steering gear and control arms with the help of an assistant **(see illustration)**, then remove it out from under the vehicle.

16   Put a transmission jack (or a floor jack with an appropriate saddle) under the transaxle. Safety chains will help steady the transaxle on the jack.

17   Remove the remaining transaxle-to-engine bolts. Check to make certain that all connections between the transaxle and the vehicle are disconnected.

18   Move the transaxle to the rear to disengage it from the engine block dowel pins and make sure the torque converter is detached from the driveplate. Lower the transaxle with the jack. Clamp a pair of locking pliers on the bellhousing case. The pliers will prevent the torque converter from falling out while you're removing the transaxle.

19   Pull the transaxle out from beneath the vehicle, remove it from the jack and set it where it can't roll over and become damaged.

Installation

20   Installation of the transaxle is a reversal of the removal procedure, but note the following points:

a)   *As the torque converter is reinstalled, ensure that the drive tangs at the center of the torque converter hub engage with the recesses in the automatic transaxle fluid pump inner gear. This can be confirmed by turning the torque converter while pushing it towards the transaxle. If it isn't fully engaged, it will "clunk" into place.*

b)   *When installing the transaxle, make sure the matchmarks you made on the torque converter and driveplate line up.*

c)   *Install all of the driveplate-to-torque converter nuts before tightening any of them.*

d)   *Tighten the driveplate-to-torque converter fasteners to the specified torque.*

e)   *Tighten the transaxle mounting bolts to the specified torque.*

f)   *Tighten the subframe mounting bolts to the torque listed in the Chapter 10 Specifications.*

g)   *Tighten the driveaxle/hub nuts to the torque value listed in the Chapter 8 Specifications.*

h)   *Tighten the wheel lug nuts to the torque listed in the Chapter 1 Specifications.*

i)   *Fill the transaxle with the correct type and amount of automatic transmission fluid as described in Chapter 1.*

j)   *On completion, adjust the shift cable and Transmission Range sensor as described in Section 4.*

6   Automatic transaxle overhaul - general information

In the event of a problem occurring, it will be necessary to establish whether the fault is electrical, mechanical or hydraulic in nature, before repair work can be contemplated. Diagnosis requires detailed knowledge of the transaxle's operation and construction, as well as access to specialized test equipment, and so is deemed to be beyond the scope of this manual. It is therefore essential that problems with the automatic transaxle are referred to a dealer service department or other qualified repair facility for assessment.

Note that a faulty transaxle should not be removed before the vehicle has been diagnosed by a knowledgeable technician equipped with the proper tools, as troubleshooting must be performed with the transaxle installed in the vehicle.

Chapter 7 Part C
Transfer case

Contents

Specifications

Transfer case fluid type .... See Chapter 1

Torque specifications

	Ft-lbs	Nm
Transfer case-to-transaxle bolts/nuts	33	45

1   General information

Due to the complexity of the transfer case covered in this manual and the need for specialized equipment to perform most service operations, this Chapter contains only routine maintenance and removal and installation procedures.

If the transfer case requires major repair work, it should be taken to a dealer service department or an automotive or transmission repair shop. You can, however, remove and install the transfer case yourself and save the expense of that labor, even if the repair work is done by a transmission shop. Note that a faulty transfer case should not be removed before the vehicle has been diagnosed by a knowledgeable technician equipped with the proper tools, as troubleshooting must be performed with the transfer case installed in the vehicle.

2   Transfer case rear output shaft oil seal - removal and installation

1   Raise the vehicle and support it securely on jackstands.
2   Drain the transfer case lubricant (see Chapter 1).
3   Remove the driveshaft (see Chapter 8).
4   Mark the relative positions of the pinion, nut and flange.
5   Use a beam- or dial-type inch-pound torque wrench to determine the torque required to rotate the pinion. Record it for use later.
6   Count the number of threads visible between the end of the nut and the end of the pinion shaft and record it for use later.
7   Remove the flange mounting nut, using a chain wrench to hold the pinion flange while loosening the locknut.
8   Remove the companion flange; a small

puller may be required for removal.
9   Pry out the seal with a screwdriver or a seal removal tool. Don't damage the seal bore.
10   Lubricate the lips of the new seal with multi-purpose grease and tap it evenly into position with a seal installation tool or a large socket. Make sure it enters the housing squarely and is tapped into its full depth.
11   Align the mating marks made before disassembly and install the companion flange. If necessary, tighten the pinion nut to draw the flange into place.
12   Tighten the nut carefully until the original number of threads are exposed and the marks are aligned.
13   Measure the torque required to rotate the pinion and tighten the nut in small increments until it matches the figure recorded in Step 5.
14   Connect the driveshaft, then add the specified lubricant to the transfer case (see Chapter 1).

3 Transfer case driveaxle oil seal - removal and installation

1   Break the right front hub nut loose with a socket and large breaker bar.
2   Loosen the wheel lug nuts, raise the vehicle and support it securely on jackstands. Remove the wheel.
3   Remove the driveaxle assembly (see Chapter 8).
4   Carefully pry out the oil seal with a seal removal tool or a large screwdriver; make sure you don't scratch the seal bore.
5   Using a seal installer or a large deep socket as a drift, install the new oil seal. Drive it into the bore squarely and make sure it's completely seated.
6   Lubricate the lip of the new seal with multi-purpose grease, then install a new dust shield.
7   Install the driveaxle (see Chapter 8).
8   The remainder of installation is the reverse of removal. Check the transfer case lubricant level and add some, if necessary, to bring it to the appropriate level (see Chapter 1).

4 Transfer case - removal and installation

1   Disconnect the cable from the negative battery terminal (see Chapter 5, Section 1).
2   Remove the air inlet hose and the air filter housing cover.
3   Disconnect the oxygen sensor wiring harnesses from the sensors and their brackets on each side of the engine compartment.
4   Remove the oxygen sensor wiring harness mounting bracket.
5   Remove the alternator wire terminal mounting nut.
6   Loosen the nuts on the right front wheel. Raise the vehicle and support it securely on jackstands.
7   Refer to Chapter 8 and remove the right driveaxle from the transfer case.
8   Remove the interfering front section of the exhaust system.
9   Refer to Chapter 5 and remove the alternator.
10   Remove the rear exhaust manifold if you're working on a V6 model.
11   Disconnect the driveshaft from the trans-

fer case (see Chapter 8). Support it temporarily with wire.
12   Remove the transfer case mounting bracket.
13   Remove the four transfer case mounting bolts.
14   Use a screwdriver to pry the transfer case from the transaxle, then remove it.
15   Installation is the reverse of removal, noting the following points:

a) *Install a new O-ring seal to the case if necessary.*
b) *Tighten the exhaust system fasteners to the torque listed in the Chapter 4 Specifications.*
c) *Tighten the driveshaft fasteners to the torque listed in the Chapter 8 Specifications.*
d) *Tighten the transfer case and crossmember fasteners to the torque listed in this Chapter's Specifications.*
e) *Refill the transfer case with the proper type and amount of fluid (see Chapter 1).*
f) *Tighten the wheel lug nuts to the torque listed in the Chapter 1 Specifications.*

Chapter 8
Clutch and driveline

Contents

Specifications

Torque specifications

Clutch cover-to-flywheel bolts	Ft-lbs	Nm
Conventional flywheel	11 to 16	15 to 22
Dual-mass flywheel	14 to 19	20 to 27
Rear wheel bearing flange nut	148 to 192	200 to 260
Differential mount rear bracket bolts	58 to 74	80 to 100
Differential carrier mounting bracket bolts	51 to 58	70 to 80
Differential pinion nut	139 to 183	190 to 250
Driveshaft flange nuts	37 to 44	50 to 60
Driveshaft center bearing mount nuts	29 to 37	40 to 50
Driveshaft center bearing-to-flange mount fasteners	29 to 37	40 to 50
Driveshaft center bearing mount nuts	22 to 29	30 to 40
Driveshaft pinion nut	168 to 183	230 to 250
Driveshaft rear rubber coupling nuts	74 to 89	100 to 120
Driveaxle/hub nut (front or rear)	148 to 192	200 to 260

1   General information

The information in this Chapter deals with the components from the rear of the engine to the wheels, except for the transaxle, which is dealt with in the previous Chapter. For the purposes of this Chapter, these components are grouped into three categories - clutch, driveshaft and driveaxles. Separate Sections within this Chapter offer general descriptions and checking procedures for components in each of the two groups.

Since nearly all the procedures covered in this Chapter involve working under the vehicle, make sure it's securely supported on sturdy jackstands or on a hoist where the vehicle can be easily raised and lowered.

2   Clutch - description and check

1   All vehicles with a manual transaxle use a single dry plate, diaphragm spring type clutch. The clutch disc has a splined hub which allows it to slide along the splines of the transaxle input shaft. The clutch and pressure plate are held in contact by spring pressure exerted by the diaphragm in the pressure plate.

2   The clutch release system is operated by hydraulic pressure. The hydraulic release system consists of the clutch pedal, a master cylinder and fluid reservoir, the hydraulic line, a release (or slave) cylinder which actuates the clutch release lever and the clutch release (or throwout) bearing.

3   When pressure is applied to the clutch pedal to release the clutch, hydraulic pressure is exerted against the outer end of the clutch release lever. As the lever pivots, the shaft fingers push against the release bearing. The bearing pushes against the fingers of the diaphragm spring of the pressure plate assembly, which in turn releases the clutch plate.

4   Terminology can be a problem when discussing the clutch components because common names are in some cases different from those used by the manufacturer. For example, the driven plate is also called the clutch plate or disc, the clutch release bearing is sometimes called a throwout bearing, the release cylinder is sometimes called the operating or slave cylinder.

5   Other than to replace components with obvious damage, some preliminary checks should be performed to diagnose clutch problems.

a) *The first check should be of the fluid level in the clutch master cylinder. If the fluid level is excessively low, add fluid as necessary and inspect the hydraulic system for leaks (fluid level will actually rise as the clutch wears).*

b) *To check clutch spin down time, run the engine at normal idle speed with the shifter in Neutral (clutch pedal*

5.7 Be sure to mark the pressure plate and flywheel in order to ensure proper alignment during installation (this won't be necessary if a new pressure plate is to be installed)

up - engaged). Disengage the clutch (pedal down), wait several seconds and shift into Reverse. No grinding noise should be heard. A grinding noise would most likely indicate a problem in the pressure plate or the clutch disc.

c) *To check for complete clutch release, run the engine (with the parking brake applied to prevent movement) and hold the clutch pedal approximately 1/2 inch from the floor. Shift between First gear and Reverse several times. If the shift is hard or grinds, component failure is indicated. Check the release cylinder pushrod travel. With the clutch pedal depressed completely, the release cylinder pushrod should extend substantially. If it doesn't, check the fluid level in the clutch master cylinder (see Chapter 1).*

d) *Visually inspect the pivot bushing at the top of the clutch pedal to make sure there is no binding or excessive play.*

e) *Crawl under the vehicle and make sure the clutch release lever is solidly mounted on the ball stud.*

3   Clutch release system components - removal and installation

Master cylinder

1   Drain the clutch fluid through the bleeder screw. Be sure to catch the fluid in a container or with rags to prevent it from contacting painted surfaces.

2   Working under the instrument panel, disconnect the clutch pushrod from the pedal by removing the cotter pin, washer and the clevis pin.

3   Disconnect the clutch tubing from the clutch master cylinder.

4   Remove the master cylinder mounting bolts and lift it off. **Note:** *If you need to remove*

the clutch fluid tube or hose, hold the hose nut with a wrench while you turn the flare nut on the tube using a flare nut wrench.

5   Installation is the reverse of removal. Bleed the system (see Section 4)

Release cylinder

6   Raise the vehicle and support it securely on jackstands.

7   Disconnect the clutch fluid hose from the release cylinder and drain the system into a container.

8   Remove the cotter pin from the clevis pin at the end of the shaft. Slide out the clevis pin.

9   Remove the mounting bolts and remove the release cylinder.

10   Installation is the reverse of removal. Replace the copper washers on the hose banjo fitting with new ones.

11   Bleed the system (see Section 4).

4   Clutch hydraulic system - bleeding

1   The hydraulic system should be bled of all air whenever any part of the system has been removed, or if the fluid level has been allowed to fall so low that air has been drawn into the master cylinder. The procedure is very similar to bleeding a brake system.

2   Fill the master cylinder with new brake fluid conforming to DOT 3 specifications. **Caution:** *Do not re-use any of the fluid coming from the system during the bleeding operation or use fluid which has been inside an open container for an extended period of time.*

3   Raise the vehicle and place it securely on jackstands to gain access to the release cylinder, which is located on the left side of the clutch housing.

4   Remove the dust cap that fits over the bleeder valve and push a length of plastic hose over the valve. Place the other end of

the hose into a clear container with about two inches of brake fluid in it. The hose end must be submerged in the fluid.

5   Have an assistant depress the clutch pedal and hold it. Open the bleeder valve on the release cylinder, allowing fluid to flow through the hose. Close the bleeder valve when fluid stops flowing from the hose. Once closed, have your assistant release the pedal.

6   Continue this process until all air is evacuated from the system, indicated by a full, solid stream of fluid being ejected from the bleeder valve each time, and no air bubbles in the hose or container. Keep a close watch on the fluid level inside the clutch master cylinder reservoir; if the level drops too low, air will be sucked back into the system and the process will have to be started all over again.

7   Install the dust cap and lower the vehicle. Check carefully for proper operation before placing the vehicle in normal service.

5   Clutch components - removal, inspection and installation

Warning: *Dust produced by clutch wear and deposited on clutch components is hazardous to your health. DO NOT blow it out with compressed air and DO NOT inhale it. DO NOT use gasoline or petroleum-based solvents to remove clutch dust. Brake system cleaner should be used to flush the dust into a drain pan. After the clutch components are wiped clean with a rag, dispose of the contaminated rags and cleaner in a covered, marked container.*

Removal

Refer to illustration 5.7

1   Access to clutch components is normally accomplished by removing the transaxle from the vehicle. If, of course, the engine is being removed for major overhaul, then check the clutch for wear and replace worn components

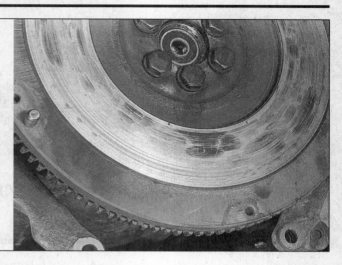

5.11 Check the flywheel for cracks, hot spots and other obvious defects - slight imperfections can be removed by a machine shop

as necessary. However, the relatively low cost of the clutch components compared to the time and trouble spent gaining access to them warrants their replacement any time the engine or transaxle is removed, unless they are nearly new. The following procedures are based on the assumption that the engine will stay in place.

2   Refer to Chapter 7, Part A and remove the transaxle from the vehicle. Support the engine while the transaxle is out. Preferably, an engine hoist or support fixture should be used to support it from above. However, if a jack is used under the engine, make sure a piece of wood is between the jack and the oil pan to spread the load. **Caution:** *The oil pump pickup is located very close to the bottom of the pan. If the pan is bent, engine oil starvation could occur.*

3   The clutch fork can remain attached to the bellhousing.

4   Turn the release bearing to bring the opening of the snap-ring into view.

5   Put snap-ring pliers under the wave washer and engage the snap-ring.

6   Push down on the release bearing and open the snap-ring. Remove the release bearing.

7   Inspect the flywheel and clutch for indexing marks **(see illustration)**. If they can't be found, scribe marks yourself so the pressure plate and flywheel will be in the same alignment during installation (if you're not replacing them).

8   Insert a clutch alignment tool through the disc and into the pilot bushing to support the disc.

9   Turn each pressure plate bolt only 1/4 turn at a time to loosen the pressure plate-to-flywheel bolts. Work in a criss-cross pattern until all spring force is relieved. Hold the pressure plate securely and completely remove the bolts, followed by the pressure plate and clutch disc.

Inspection

Refer to illustrations 5.11, 5.13, 5.15a and 5.15b

10   When a problem occurs in the clutch, it can usually be attributed to wear of the driven plate assembly (clutch disc). However, all components should be checked at this time.

11   Inspect the flywheel for cracks, heat checking, grooves and other obvious defects **(see illustration)**. If the imperfections are small, a machine shop can machine the surface flat and smooth. This is highly recommended regardless of the surface appearance. Refer to Chapter 2 for the flywheel removal and installation procedures.

12   Inspect the pilot bushing (see Section 7).

13   Inspect the lining of the clutch disc **(see illustration)**. There should be at least 1/16 inch of lining above the rivet heads. Check for loose rivets, cracks, distortion, broken springs and other obvious damage. As mentioned above, the clutch disc is routinely replaced, so if in doubt about the condition, replace it with a new one.

14   The release bearing should also be replaced along with the clutch disc (see Section 6).

15   Check the machined surfaces and the spring fingers of the pressure plate **(see**

5.13 The clutch plate

1   *Lining* - This will wear down in use
2   *Rivets* - These secure the lining and will damage the flywheel if allowed to contact the surfaces
3   *Markings* - "Flywheel side" or something similar

NORMAL FINGER WEAR   **EXCESSIVE FINGER WEAR**   **BROKEN OR BENT FINGERS**

EXCESSIVE WEAR

5.15a   Replace the pressure plate if excessive wear is noted

illustrations). If the surface is grooved or otherwise damaged, replace it. Also check for obvious damage, distortion, cracking, etc. Light glazing can be removed with sandpaper or emery cloth. If a new pressure plate is required, new and rebuilt units are available.

Installation

Refer to illustration 5.18

16   Clean the flywheel and pressure plate machined surfaces with brake system cleaner. It's important that no oil or grease is on these surfaces or the lining of the clutch disc. Handle the parts only with clean hands.

17   Position the disc onto the flywheel with the side marked "flywheel" against the flywheel. If there are no marks, install the clutch disc with the springs facing the transaxle.

18   Secure the disc with the alignment tool **(see illustration)**. Make sure the tool engages the pilot bushing.

19   Put the pressure plate into place, aligning the marks you previously made if you're not replacing it. Install the bolts and tighten them finger tight.

20   Tighten the bolts a little at a time, working in a criss-cross pattern to prevent distorting the cover. After all of the bolts are snug, tighten them to the torque listed in this Chapter's Specifications. Remove the alignment tool.

21   Refer to Section 6 for information on the proper installation of the release bearing.

22   The remainder of installation is the reverse of removal.

---

6   Clutch release bearing - removal, inspection and installation

Warning: *Dust produced by clutch wear and deposited on clutch components is hazardous to your health. DO NOT blow it out with compressed air and DO NOT inhale it. DO NOT use gasoline or petroleum-based solvents to remove clutch dust. Brake system cleaner should be used to flush the dust into a drain pan. After the clutch components are wiped clean with a rag, dispose of the contaminated rags and cleaner in a covered, marked container.*

Removal

1   Refer to Chapter 7A and remove the transaxle from the vehicle.

2   Refer to Section 5 for information on disengaging the release bearing from the pressure plate.

Inspection

3   Hold the center of the bearing and apply force while rotating the outer portion. If the bearing doesn't operate smoothly or if it's noisy, replace it with a new one. Wipe the bearing with a clean rag and inspect if for damage, wear and cracks. Don't immerse it in solvent - it's sealed for life and to do so would ruin it. Also check the release fork for wear on the fingertips, cracks and other damage.

4   Check the snap-ring for proper retention.

Installation

5   Apply a small amount of high-temperature grease to the inside of the release bearing and to the area where the fork fingers contact it.

6   Install the bearing onto the input shaft

5.15b   Examine the pressure plate for scoring marks, cracks and evidence of overheating

5.18   Center the clutch disc using an alignment tool

7.5 A small slide-hammer puller is handy for removing the pilot bushing

of the transaxle, engaging it with the fork fingers.

7   Raise the transaxle into position next to the engine.

8   Install the release lever on the fork shaft and connect it to the release cylinder with the clevis pin and cotter pin.

9   Refer to Chapter 7 Part A and bolt the transaxle to the engine.

10   Push the release lever away from the release cylinder about 20 degrees. There should be a click from the snap-ring as the assembly snaps into place. If it doesn't snap into position, start over again. **Note:** *The release lever is only supposed to move a maximum of 3 degrees in normal operation. If it moves more, then the bearing is not engaged properly on the pressure plate. Try pushing the lever forward again.*

11   The rest of the installation is the reverse of removal.

7   Pilot bushing - inspection and replacement

Refer to illustrations 7.5 and 7.6

1   The clutch pilot bushing is pressed into the rear of the crankshaft. It is greased at the factory and does not require additional lubrication. Its primary purpose is to support the front of the transaxle input shaft. The pilot bushing should be inspected whenever the clutch components are removed from the engine. Due to its inaccessibility, if you are in doubt as to its condition, replace it with a new one. **Note:** *If the engine has been removed from the vehicle, disregard the following steps which do not apply.*

2   Remove the transaxle (see Chapter 7 Part A).

3   Remove the clutch components (see Section 5).

4   Inspect for any excessive wear, scoring, lack of grease, dryness or obvious damage. If any of these conditions are noted, the bearing should be replaced. A flashlight will be helpful to direct light into the recess.

5   Removal can be accomplished with a slide hammer fitted with a puller attachment **(see illustration)**, which are available at most auto parts stores or equipment rental yards.

6   To install the new bearing, lightly lubricate the outside surface with multi-purpose grease, then drive it into the recess with a hammer and bearing/bushing driver **(see illustration)**. Make sure the bearing seal faces toward the transmission. If you don't have a bearing driver, carefully tap it into place with a hammer and a socket. **Caution:** *Be careful not to let the bearing become cocked in the bore.*

7   Install the clutch components, transaxle and all other components removed previously, tightening all fasteners properly.

8   Clutch pedal position switch - check and replacement

Check

1   The clutch pedal position switch, which is part of the starter relay circuit, is mounted at the top of the clutch pedal. The switch closes the starter relay circuit only when the clutch pedal is depressed.

2   To test the switch, verify that the engine will not crank over when the clutch pedal is

7.6 The pilot bushing can be driven in with an appropriately sized socket

in the released position and that it does crank over when the pedal is depressed.

3   If the engine can be started without depressing the clutch pedal, replace the switch.

Replacement

4   Slide the driver's seat fully rearward and access the pivot at the top of the clutch pedal.

5   Disconnect the wiring harness from the switch.

6   Make a mental note of the switch's adjustment, then remove it.

7   Installation is the reverse of removal. Position the new switch in the same adjustment range as the original one.

8   Test the new switch (see Step 2).

9   Driveshaft (4WD models) - check, removal and installation

Check

1   Raise the rear of the vehicle and support it securely on jackstands. Block the front wheels to keep the vehicle from rolling off the stands. Release the parking brake and place the transmission in Neutral.

2   Crawl under the vehicle and visually inspect the driveshaft. Look for any dents, bends or cracks in the tubing. If any are found, the driveshaft must be replaced.

3   Check for oil leakage at the front and rear of the driveshaft. Leakage where the driveshaft connects to the transfer case indicates a defective transfer case seal. Leakage where the driveshaft connects to the differential or coupling indicates a defective pinion seal or coupling assembly.

4   While under the vehicle, have an assistant rotate a rear wheel so the driveshaft will rotate. As it does, make sure the universal joint and the rear rubber coupler are operating properly without binding, noise or looseness. Listen for any noise from the center bearing, indicating it's worn or damaged. Also check the rubber portion of the center bearing for cracking or separation.

9.8 Mark the relationship of the driveshaft to the pinion flange and also to the transfer case output shaft

5   The universal joint can also be checked with the driveshaft motionless, by gripping your hands on both sides of the joint and attempting to twist the joint. Any movement at all in the joint is a sign of considerable wear. Lifting up on the shaft will also indicate movement in the universal joint. If the joint is worn, they must be replaced to prevent eventual breakage.

6   Finally, check the driveshaft mounting bolts at the ends and the center bearing to make sure they're tight.

Removal and installation

Refer to illustrations 9.8 and 9.9

7   Raise the rear of the vehicle and support it securely on jackstands. Block the front wheels to prevent the vehicle from rolling. Place the transmission in Neutral with the parking brake off.

8   Make reference marks on the driveshaft flange and the differential pinion flange in line with each other **(see illustration)**. This is to make sure the driveshaft is reinstalled in the same position to preserve the balance.

9   Remove the rear driveshaft bolts **(see illustration)**. Turn the driveshaft (or wheels) as necessary to bring the bolts into the most accessible position.

10   Mark the position of the center support bearing, then unbolt the center support bearing from the floor pan. **Caution:** *Be careful to avoid damaging the rubber boot on the center bearing.*

11   Remove the bolts from the front drive yoke at the transfer case.

12   Replace any components that require it. If the center bearing needs work, take it to a dealer or well-equipped automotive shop for service. If the front universal joint must be replaced, refer to Sections 10 and 11.

13   Reconnect the driveshaft to the pinion flange. Be sure to align the marks and tighten the fasteners to the torque listed in this Chapter's Specifications.

14   Reconnect the center support bearing. Be sure to align the marks and tighten the fasteners to the torque listed in this Chap-

ter's Specifications. Finally, connect the front yoke to the transfer case flange, aligning the marks.

10   Universal joint - general information and check

1   Universal joints are mechanical couplings which connect two rotating components that meet each other at different angles.

2   These joints are composed of a yoke on each side connected by a crosspiece called a trunnion. Cups at each end of the trunnion contain needle bearings which provide smooth transfer of the torque load. Snap-rings, either inside or outside of the bearing cups, hold the assembly together.

3   Wear in the needle roller bearings is characterized by vibration in the driveline, noise during acceleration, and in extreme cases of lack of lubrication, metallic squeaking and ultimately grating and shrieking sounds as the bearings disintegrate.

4   It is easy to check if the needle bearings are worn with the driveshaft in position, by trying to turn the shaft with one hand, the other hand holding the rear axle flange when the rear universal joint is being checked, and

9.9 Insert a screwdriver through the driveshaft yoke to prevent the shaft from turning as you loosen the bolts

the front half coupling when the front universal joint is being checked. Any movement between the driveshaft and the front half couplings, and around the rear half couplings, is indicative of considerable wear. Another method of checking for universal joint wear is to use a prybar inserted into the gap between the universal joint and the driveshaft or flange. Leave the vehicle in gear and try to pry the joint both radially and axially. Any looseness should be apparent with this method. A final test for wear is to attempt to lift the shaft and note any movement between the yokes of the joints.

5   If any of the above conditions exist, replace the universal joints with new ones.

11   Universal joint - replacement

Refer to illustrations 11.2, 11.4 and 11.9

Note: *A large vise or a press is required for this procedure. It may be advisable to take the driveshaft to a dealer service department, service station or machine shop where the universal joints can be replaced for you.*

1   Refer to Section 9 and remove the driveshaft.

2   Use pliers to remove the snap-rings from the spider **(see illustration)**.

3   While supporting the driveshaft, place it in position on a workbench equipped with a vise.

4   Place a piece of pipe or a large socket, having an inside diameter slightly larger than the outside diameter of the bearing caps, over one of the bearing caps. Position a socket with an outside diameter slightly smaller than that of the opposite bearing cap over that cap, and use the vise or press to force the bearing cap out (inside the pipe or large socket). Use the vise or large pliers to work the bearing cap the rest of the way out **(see illustration)**.

5   Transfer the sockets to the opposite sides and press the other bearing cap out in the same manner.

6   Pack the new joints with grease. Usually, specific instructions will be included with the

11.2 Needle-nose pliers can be used to remove the universal joint snap-rings

11.4 To press the universal joint out of the driveshaft yoke, set it up in a vise with the small socket pushing the joint and bearing cap into the large socket

universal joint kit. Follow them carefully.
7   Position the spider into the yoke and partially install one bearing cap in the yoke.
8   Start the spider into the bearing cap, then partially install the other bearing cap. Press the bearing caps into place, keeping the spider correctly centered as you do so. Be careful to avoid damaging the dust seals.
9   Use the smaller socket to press the caps fully into place. Install the snap-rings. If you have difficulty in seating them, strike the driveshaft yoke sharply with a hammer. This will spring the yoke ears slightly and allow the snap-rings to seat in their grooves **(see illustration)**.
10   If the universal joint has a grease fitting, install it now and add grease using a grease gun.
11   Install the driveshaft.

12   Driveshaft coupling (4WD models) - description, removal and installation

Note: *The driveshaft coupling is only installed on later models. Early models use a driveshaft that connects directly to the rear axle assembly in a conventional manner. A viscous unit in the transfer case handles the power-splitting function in early models.*

Description

The coupling unit used on later models is installed between the rear of the driveshaft and the front of the rear axle assembly. Its purpose is to adjust the amount of engine power going to the rear wheels. The 4WD computer can electrically adjust its clutch pack to lock, and thus give exactly half of the engine's power to the rear wheels (usually at low speeds and in slippery conditions). Under normal driving conditions, the clutch

pack releases somewhat in order to direct the bulk of the engine's output to the front wheels.
The 4WD computer that operates the coupling is located under the driver's seat. Any trouble in this system will cause the 4WD lamp on the instrument panel to flash while driving. Have the vehicle checked at a dealer or other service facility as soon as possible. Internal service of the coupling is beyond the scope of this manual.

Removal and installation
1   Raise the vehicle and support it securely on jackstands.
2   Remove the bolts that secure the rear of the driveshaft to the coupling assembly.
3   Pry the driveshaft forward to separate it and support it out of the way with wire.
4   Disconnect the wiring harness from the coupling.
5   Remove the mounting bolts and pry the coupling out of the front of the rear axle housing.
6   Installation is the reverse of removal.

13   Pinion oil seal - replacement

Removal

Refer to illustrations 13.3, 13.4 and 13.7
Warning: *If the vehicle is equipped with electronically modulated air suspension, make sure that the height control switch is turned off.*
1   Raise the rear of the vehicle and support it securely on jackstands. Block the front wheels to prevent the vehicle from rolling. Place the transmission in Neutral with the parking brake off.
2   Mark the relationship of the driveshaft to the pinion flange, then unbolt the driveshaft from the flange (see Section 9). Suspend the driveshaft with a piece of wire (don't let it hang by the center support bearing).
3   Using a hammer and a punch, unstake the pinion flange nut. Mark the position of the pinion nut to the flange and the flange to the pinion shaft with dabs of paint. If you have access to a beam-type inch-pound torque wrench, you can use it instead to measure the

11.9 If the snap-ring won't seat in its groove, strike the yoke with a brass hammer - this will relieve the tension that has set up in the yoke and slightly spring the yoke ears (this should be done if the joint feels tight when assembled)

pinion bearing drag. Record your reading so the pinion nut can be tightened later to give the same amount of drag **(see illustration)**.

4   A flange holding tool will be required to keep the companion flange from moving while the self-locking pinion nut is loosened. A chain wrench will also work **(see illustration)**.

5   Remove the pinion nut.

6   Withdraw the flange. It may be necessary to use a two-jaw puller engaged behind the flange to draw it off. Do not attempt to pry or hammer behind the flange or hammer on the end of the pinion shaft.

7   Pry out the old seal and discard it **(see illustration)**.

Installation

Refer to illustration 13.8

8   Lubricate the lips of the new seal and fill the space between the seal lips with wheel bearing grease, then tap it evenly into position with a seal installation tool or a large socket. Make sure it enters the housing squarely and is tapped in to its full depth **(see illustration)**.

13.3 Use an inch-pound torque wrench to check the pinion bearing drag

13.4 A chain wrench can be used to hold the pinion flange while the nut is loosened

9   Install the pinion flange; if necessary, tighten the pinion nut to draw the flange into place. Do not try to hammer the flange into position. Tighten the nut near the torque listed in this Chapter's Specifications until the paint marks made previously are aligned or until the

original amount of bearing preload is reached as measured by the torque wrench.

10   Reconnect the driveshaft to the pinion flange (see Section 9). Check the differential lubricant level and add some, if necessary, to bring it to the appropriate level (see Chapter 1).

14   Driveaxle oil seal (rear) - replacement

1   Raise the rear of the vehicle and support it securely on jackstands. Block the front wheels to prevent the vehicle from rolling. Place the transmission in Neutral with the parking brake off.

2   Remove the driveaxles (see Section 17).

3   Carefully pry out the side gear shaft oil seal with a seal removal tool or a large screwdriver; make sure you don't scratch the seal bore.

4   Using a seal installer or a large deep socket as a drift, install the new oil seal. Drive

13.7 Use a seal removal tool or a large screwdriver to remove the pinion seal (be careful not to disturb the pinion while doing this)

13.8 A large socket with a diameter the same as that of the new seal can be used to drive the pinion seal into the differential housing

16.3 Lift the tabs on the boot clamps with a small screwdriver, then open the clamps

16.4a On tripod-type joints, remove the boot from the inner CV joint and slide the joint housing from the tripod

it into the bore squarely and make sure it's completely seated.

5   Lubricate the lip of the new seal with multi-purpose grease, then install the driveaxles (see Section 17). Be careful not to damage the lip of the new seal.

6   Check the differential lubricant level and add some, if necessary, to bring it to the appropriate level (See Chapter 1).

15   Differential (4WD models) - removal and installation

1   Raise the rear of the vehicle and support it securely on jackstands. Block the front wheels to prevent the vehicle from rolling. Place the transmission in Neutral with the parking brake off. Remove the spare wheel.

2   Disconnect the exhaust pipe hangers and lower the pipe to provide clearance around the right driveaxle.

3   Drain the differential lubricant (see Chapter 1).

4   Mark the relationship of the driveshaft to

the pinion flange, then unbolt the driveshaft from the flange (see Section 9). Suspend the driveshaft with a piece of wire (don't let it hang by the center support bearing).

5   Support the differential with a floor jack. Remove the mounting bracket and differential mounting bolts. Slowly lower the jack.

6   Refer to Section 17 and pry the driveaxles out of the differential. Tie them up with pieces of wire. Avoid letting them hang, as this will damage the joints.

7   Installation is the reverse of the removal procedure. Tighten all fasteners to the torque values listed in this Chapter's Specifications. Fill the differential with the proper lubricant (see Chapter 1).

16   Driveaxle boot - replacement

Disassembly

Refer to illustrations 16.3, 16.4a, 16.4b, 16.6 and 16.7

Note 1: If the CV joint boots must be

replaced, explore all options before beginning the job. Complete rebuilt driveaxles are available on an exchange basis, which eliminates much time and work. Whichever route you choose to take, check on the cost and availability of parts before disassembling the vehicle.

Note 2: Some auto parts stores carry split type replacement boots, which can be installed without removing the driveaxle from the vehicle. This is a convenient alternative; however, the driveaxle should be removed and the CV joint disassembled and cleaned to ensure the joint is free from contaminants such as moisture and dirt which will accelerate CV joint wear. Do NOT disassemble the outboard CV joints. All outer joints are Birfield joints. Inner joints may be tripod, U-type tripod or double offset joints.

Note 3: The procedure shown here is of a tripod-type inner joint. The basic cleaning and checking procedure is the same for all joints.

1   Remove the driveaxle (see Section 17).

2   Mount the driveaxle in a vise with wood lined jaws (to prevent damage to the axleshaft). Check the CV joint for excessive play in the radial direction, which indicates worn parts. Check for smooth operation throughout the full range of motion for each CV joint. If a boot is torn, disassemble the joint, clean the components and inspect for damage due to loss of lubrication and possible contamination by foreign matter.

3   Using a small screwdriver, pry the retaining tabs of the clamps up to loosen them and slide them off (see illustration).

4   Using a screwdriver, carefully pry up on the edge of the outer boot and push it away from the CV joint. Old and worn boots can be cut off. Pull the inner CV joint boot back from the housing and slide the housing off the joint; on double-offset type joints, a wire ring retainer must be removed first (see illustrations).

16.4b On double-offset type joints, remove the wire retainer, then pull the housing off

16.6 Remove the snap-ring with a pair of snap-ring pliers

16.7 Drive the tripod joint from the driveaxle with a brass punch and hammer; be careful not to damage the bearing surfaces or the splines on the shaft

5   Mark the tripod and axleshaft to ensure that they are reassembled properly.

6   Remove the tripod joint snap-ring with a pair of snap-ring pliers **(see illustration)**.

7   Use a hammer and a brass punch to drive the tripod joint from the driveaxle **(see illustration)**.

8   If you haven't already cut them off, remove both boots. **Note:** *Do NOT disassemble the outboard CV joint.*

Check

9   Thoroughly clean all components with solvent - including the outer CV joint assembly - until the old CV joint grease is completely removed. Inspect the bearing surfaces of the inner tripods and housings for cracks, pitting, scoring and other signs of wear. It's not possible to inspect the bearing surfaces of the inner and outer races of the outer CV joint, but you can at least check the surfaces of the ball bearings themselves. If they're in good shape, so are the races; if they're not, neither are the races. If the inner CV joint is worn, you can buy a new inner CV joint and install

16.10a Wrap the splined area of the axleshaft with tape to prevent damage to the boots when installing them

it on the old axleshaft; if the outer CV joint is worn, you'll have to purchase a new outer CV joint and axleshaft (they're sold pre-assembled).

16.10b Install the tripod with the recessed portion of the splines facing the axle shaft

Reassembly

Refer to illustrations 16.10a, 16.10b, 16.10c, 16.10d, 16.12a, 16.12b, 16.12c and 16.12d

10   Wrap the splines on the inner end of the axleshaft with electrical or duct tape to protect the boots from the sharp edges of the splines. Slide the clamps and boot(s) onto the axleshaft, then place the tripod or double-offset on the shaft. Apply grease to the tripod assembly and inside the housing. Insert the tripod into the housing and pack the remainder of the grease around the tripod **(see illustrations)**. If you're working on a double-offset joint, install the wire retainer.

11   Slide the boot into place, making sure both ends seat in their grooves. Adjust the length of the driveaxle, positioning it midway through its travel.

12   Equalize the pressure in the boot, then tighten and secure the boot clamps **(see illustrations)**.

13   Install the driveaxle assembly (see Section 17).

16.10c Place grease at the bottom of the CV joint housing

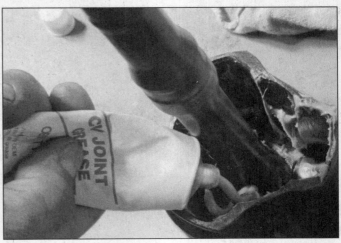

16.10d Install the boot clamps onto the axleshaft, then insert the tripod (or double-offset joint) into the housing, followed by the rest of the grease

16.12a Equalize the pressure inside the boot by inserting a small, dull screwdriver between the boot and the outer race

16.12b To install the new clamps, bend the tang down . . .

16.12c . . . then tap the tabs over to hold it in place

16.12d If your replacement boot came with crimp-type clamps, a special tool such as this one (available at most auto parts stores) will be required to tighten them properly

17.1 Loosen the driveaxle/hub nut with a long breaker bar

17.7 To separate the inner end of the driveaxle from the transaxle, pry on the CV joint housing like this with a large screwdriver or prybar - you may need to give the prybar a sharp rap with a brass hammer

17.8a Pry the old spring clip from the inner end of the driveaxle with a small screwdriver or awl

the driveaxle with a plastic hammer. Support the outer end of the driveaxle with a piece of wire to avoid unnecessary strain on the inner CV joint.

7   Carefully pry the inner end of the drive-axle from the transaxle - or, on models so equipped, the intermediate shaft - using a large screwdriver or prybar positioned between the transaxle or bearing support and the CV joint housing **(see illustration)**. Support the CV joints and carefully remove the driveaxle from the vehicle.

Installation

Refer to illustrations 17.8a and 17.8b

8   Pry the old spring clip from the inner end of the driveaxle and install a new one **(see illustrations)**. Lubricate the differential or intermediate shaft seal with multi-purpose grease and raise the driveaxle into position while supporting the CV joints.

9   Insert the splined end of the inner CV joint or the intermediate shaft into the differential side gear and make sure the spring clip

17   Driveaxles - removal and installation

Front

Removal

Refer to illustrations 17.1 and 17.7

1   Remove the wheel cover or hubcap. Remove the cotter pin and break the drive-axle/hub nut loose **(see illustration)**. Loosen the wheel lug nuts.

2   Raise the vehicle and support it securely on jackstands. Remove the wheel.

3   Drain the transaxle lubricant (see Chapter 1).

4   Disconnect the wheel speed sensor from its bracket. Disconnect the brake hose assembly from the bracket.

5   Remove the two bolts from the lower strut and steering knuckle. Pull the knuckle free of the strut.

6   Swing the knuckle/hub assembly out

(away from the vehicle) until the end of the driveaxle is free of the hub. **Note:** *If the drive-axle splines stick in the hub, tap on the end of*

17.8b To install the new spring clip, start one end in the groove and work the clip over the shaft end, into the groove locks in its groove. **Note:** *When installing the driveaxle, make sure the gap in the spring clip is facing down (this will allow it to compress and engage with its groove more easily).*

10   Apply a light coat of multi-purpose grease to the outer CV joint splines, pull out on the strut/steering knuckle assembly and install the stub axle into the hub.

11   Reconnect the balljoint to the lower control arm and tighten the nuts (see the torque specifications in Chapter 10).

12   Install the driveaxle/hub nut with the convex side of the washer facing out. Tighten the hub nut securely, but don't try to tighten it to the actual torque specification until you've lowered the vehicle to the ground.

13   Grasp the inner CV joint housing (not the driveaxle) and pull out to make sure the driveaxle has seated securely in the transaxle.

14   Install the wheel and lug nuts, then lower the vehicle.

15   Tighten the lug nuts to the torque listed in the Chapter 1 Specifications. Tighten the driveaxle/hub nut to the torque listed in this Chapter's Specifications. Install a new cotter pin.

16   Refill the transaxle with the recommended type and amount of lubricant (see Chapter 1).

Rear (4WD models)

Removal

17   Remove the wheel cover or hubcap.

18   Raise the vehicle and support it securely on jackstands.

19   Remove the cotter pin from the rear driveaxle/hub nut and remove the nut.

20   Refer to Section 15 and disconnect and lower the differential enough so the driveaxles can be pried out of the differential. Support the inner ends of the driveaxles with wire so the outer joint won't be stressed.

21   Tap the driveaxles out of the hubs with a soft-face hammer while supporting their weight.

Installation

22   Pry the old spring clip from the inner end of the driveaxle and install a new one. Lubricate the driveaxle end splines with multi-purpose grease and raise the driveaxle into posi-

tion while supporting the CV joints.

23   Insert the driveaxle into the hub and install the nut finger tight.

24   Put the differential into position and insert the splined end of the inner CV joint or the intermediate shaft into the differential side gear, making sure the spring clip locks in its groove. **Note:** *When installing the driveaxle, make sure the gap in the spring clip is facing down (this will allow it to compress and engage with its groove more easily).*

25   The remainder of installation is the reverse of removal. Tighten the lug nuts to the torque listed in the Chapter 1 Specifications. Tighten the hub nut to the torque listed in this Chapter's Specifications.

26   Refill the differential with the recommended type and amount of lubricant (see Chapter 1).

Notes

Chapter 9 Brakes

Contents

Specifications

General

Brake fluid type	DOT 3 or DOT 4
Brake pedal	
Height with carpet removed	8.19 to 8.21 inches (208 to 213 mm)
Freeplay	1/8 to 5/16 inch (3 to 8 mm)
Brake light switch body-to-pedal clearance	3/64 to 1/8 inch (1 to 3 mm)

Disc brakes

Minimum brake pad thickness	See Chapter 1
Disc minimum thickness	Cast into disc
Disc runout limit	0.0016 inch (0.04 mm)

Parking brake shoe minimum thickness
1/32-inch (0.8 mm)

Torque specifications

Ft-lbs (unless otherwise indicated) **Nm**

Note: *One foot-pound (ft-lb) of torque is equivalent to 12 inch-pounds (in-lbs) of torque. Torque values below approximately 15 ft-lbs are expressed in inch-pounds, since most foot-pound torque wrenches are not accurate at these smaller values.*

	Ft-lbs	Nm
Master cylinder-to-booster nuts	72 to 96 in-lbs	8 to 12
Booster mounting nuts	72 to 84 in-lbs	8 to 10
Brake hose banjo fitting bolt	18 to 22	25 to 30
Brake line flare nuts	120 to 144 in-lbs	13 to 17
Caliper mounting bolts	16 to 24	22 to 32
Caliper mounting bracket bolts		
Front	58 to 74	80 to 100
Rear	37 to 44	50 to 60
Rear hub flange nut, 2WD models	See Chapter 10	
Wheel lug nuts	See Chapter 1	

Note: *Replace all self-locking fasteners with new ones after removing them.*

2.2 The ABS actuator assembly is located on the right side of the engine compartment on some models; on other models it's on the left side

1   General information

The vehicles covered by this manual are equipped with hydraulically operated front and rear disc brake systems. These brakes are self-adjusting and automatically compensate for pad wear.

Hydraulic system

The hydraulic system consists of two separate circuits. The master cylinder has separate reservoirs for the two circuits, and, in the event of a leak or failure in one hydraulic circuit, the other circuit will remain operative.

Power brake booster

The power brake booster utilizes engine manifold vacuum and atmospheric pressure to provide assistance to the hydraulically operated brakes. The booster is mounted on the firewall in the engine compartment.

Parking brake

The parking brake operates the rear brakes only, through cable actuation. It's activated by a lever mounted in the center console.

Service

After completing any operation involving disassembly of any part of the brake system, always test-drive the vehicle to check for proper braking performance before resuming normal driving. When testing the brakes, perform the tests on a clean, dry, flat surface. Conditions other than these can lead to inaccurate test results.

Test the brakes at various speeds with both light and heavy pedal force. The vehicle should stop evenly without pulling to one side or the other. Avoid locking the brakes, because this slides the tires and diminishes braking efficiency and control of the vehicle.

Tires, vehicle load and wheel alignment are factors that also affect braking performance.

Precautions

There are some general cautions and warnings involving the brake system on this vehicle:

a) *Use only brake fluid conforming to DOT 3 or DOT 4 specifications.*
b) *The brake pads and linings contain fibers that are hazardous to your health if inhaled. Whenever you work on brake system components, clean all parts with brake system cleaner. Do not allow the fine dust to become airborne. Also, wear an approved filtering mask.*
c) *Safety should be paramount whenever any servicing of the brake components is performed. Do not use parts or fasteners that are not in perfect condition, and be sure that all clearances and torque specifications are adhered to. If you are at all unsure about a certain procedure, seek professional advice. Upon completion of any brake system work, test the brakes carefully in a controlled area before putting the vehicle into normal service. If a problem is suspected in the brake system, don't drive the vehicle until it's fixed.*
d) *Clean up any spilled brake fluid immediately and wash the area with large amounts of water. This is especially true for any finished, painted or plastic surfaces.*

2   Anti-lock Brake System (ABS) - general information

1   The Anti-lock Brake System (ABS) is designed to maintain vehicle steerability, directional stability and optimum deceleration under severe braking conditions and on most road surfaces. It does so by monitoring the rotational speed of each wheel and controlling the brake line pressure to each wheel during braking. This prevents the wheel from locking up. The ABS system is primarily designed to prevent wheel lockup during heavy braking, but the information provided by the wheel speed sensors of the ABS system is shared with several optional systems that can use the data to control vehicle handling.

Components

Hydraulic electronic control unit

Refer to illustration 2.2

2   The actuator assembly is mounted in the engine compartment. It consists of an electric hydraulic pump and solenoid valves **(see illustration)**.

a) *The electric pump provides hydraulic pressure to charge the reservoirs in the actuator, which supplies pressure to the braking system. The pump and reservoirs are housed in the actuator assembly.*
b) *The solenoid valves modulate brake line pressure during ABS operation.*

3   The ABS computer is mounted in the control unit and is the brain for the ABS system. The function of the computer is to accept and process information received from the wheel speed sensors to control the hydraulic line pressure, avoiding wheel lock up. The computer also constantly monitors the system, even under normal driving conditions, to find faults within the system.

Speed sensors

4   These sensors are located at each wheel and generate small electrical pulsations when the toothed sensor rings are turning, sending a signal to the electronic controller indicating wheel rotational speed.
5   The front speed sensors are mounted to the front steering knuckles in close relationship to the toothed sensor rings, which are integral with the front driveaxle outer CV joints.
6   The rear wheel sensors are bolted to the rear suspension trailing arms. The sensor rings are integrated with the rear hub assemblies.

Diagnosis and repair

7   If a dashboard warning light comes on and stays on while the vehicle is in operation, the ABS system requires attention. Although special electronic ABS diagnostic testing tools are necessary to properly diagnose the system, you can perform a few preliminary checks before taking the vehicle to a dealer service department.

a) *Check the brake fluid level in the reservoir.*
b) *Verify that the computer electrical connectors are securely connected.*
c) *Check the electrical connectors at the hydraulic control unit.*
d) *Check the fuses.*
e) *Follow the wiring harness to each wheel and verify that all connections are secure and that the wiring is undamaged.*

8   If the above preliminary checks do not rectify the problem, the vehicle should be diagnosed by a dealer service department or other qualified repair shop. Due to the complexity of this system, all actual repair work must be done by a qualified automotive tech-

2.12a Front wheel speed sensor mounting bolt

2.12b Rear wheel speed sensor mounting bolt

nician. **Warning:** *Do NOT try to repair an ABS wiring harness. The ABS system is sensitive to even the smallest changes in resistance. Repairing the harness could alter resistance values and cause the system to malfunction. If the ABS wiring harness is damaged in any way, it must be replaced.* **Caution:** *Make sure the ignition is turned off before unplugging or reattaching any electrical connections.*

Wheel speed sensor - removal and installation

Refer to illustrations 2.12a and 2.12b

9   Loosen the wheel lug nuts, raise the vehicle and support it securely on jackstands. Remove the wheel

10   Make sure the ignition key is turned to the Off position.

11   Trace the wiring back from the sensor, detaching all brackets and clips while noting its correct routing, then disconnect the electrical connector.

12   Remove the mounting bolt and carefully pull the sensor out from the knuckle or trailing arm **(see illustrations)**.

13   Installation is the reverse of the removal procedure. Tighten the mounting fastener securely.

14   Install the wheel and lug nuts, tightening them securely. Lower the vehicle and tighten the lug nuts to the torque listed in the Chapter 1 Specifications.

3   Disc brake pads - replacement

Refer to illustrations 3.5, 3.6a through 3.6k and 3.7a through 3.7i

Warning: *Disc brake pads must be replaced on both front or rear wheels at the same time - never replace the pads on only one wheel. Also, the dust created by the brake system is harmful to your health. Never blow it out with compressed air and don't inhale any of it. An approved filtering mask should be worn when working on the brakes. Do not, under any circumstances, use petroleum-based solvents to clean brake parts. Use brake system cleaner only!*

1   Remove the cap from the brake fluid reservoir.

2   Loosen the wheel lug nuts, raise the front or rear of the vehicle and support it securely on jackstands. Block the wheels at the opposite end. **Warning:** *If the vehicle is equipped with an electronically modulated air suspension, make sure that the height control switch is turned off before raising the vehicle.*

3   Remove the wheels. Work on one brake assembly at a time, using the assembled brake for reference if necessary.

4   Inspect the brake disc carefully as outlined in Section 5. If machining is necessary, follow the information in that Section to remove the disc, at which time the pads can be removed as well.

5   Push the piston back into its bore to provide room for the new brake pads. A C-clamp can be used to accomplish this **(see illustration)**. As the piston is depressed to the bottom of the caliper bore, the fluid in the master cylinder will rise. Make sure that it doesn't overflow. If necessary, siphon off some of the fluid.

6   If you're replacing the front brake pads, follow the accompanying photos, beginning with **illustration 3.6a**. Be sure to stay in order

3.5 Before removing the caliper, slowly depress the piston in the caliper bore by using a large C-clamp between the outer brake pad and the back of the caliper

3.6a Always wash the brakes with brake cleaner before disassembling anything

3.6b For brake pad replacement, remove the lower caliper bolt (to detach the caliper completely, remove both caliper bolts, but do not let the caliper hang by the brake hose)

3.6c Pivot the caliper up (be careful not to damage the boot for the upper slide pin)

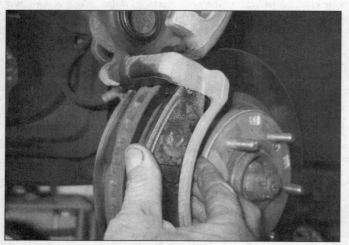

3.6d Remove the outer pad . . .

3.6e . . . and the inner pad

3.6f Remove the upper and lower pad support plates; make sure they are a tight fit and aren't worn. If necessary, replace them

3.6g Install the upper and lower pad support plates

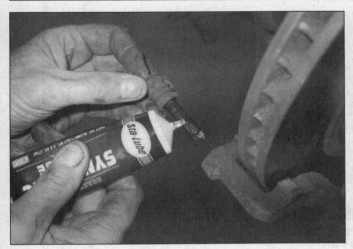

3.6h Pull out the upper and lower sliding pins and clean them. Apply a coat of high-temperature grease to the pins and reinstall them. Be careful not to damage the pin boots, replace any boots that are worn or damaged

3.6i Install the inner pad, making sure that the ends are seated correctly on the pad support plates

3.6j Install the outer pad, making sure that the ends are seated correctly on the pad support plates

3.6k Swing the caliper down and tighten the caliper lower mounting bolt to the torque listed in this Chapter's Specifications

and read the caption under each illustration.

7   If you're replacing the rear brake pads, wash the brake assembly (see illustration 3.6a), then follow the accompanying photos, beginning with illustration 3.7a. Be sure to stay in order and read the caption under each illustration.

8   When reinstalling the caliper, be sure to tighten the mounting bolts to the torque listed in this Chapter's Specifications. After the job has been completed, firmly depress the brake pedal a few times to bring the pads into contact with the disc. Check the level of the brake fluid, adding some if necessary. Check the operation of the brakes carefully before placing the vehicle into normal service.

3.7a Wash the brake with brake system cleaner (see illustration 3.6a), then depress the piston using a C-clamp

3.7b Remove the upper caliper mounting bolt

3.7c Pivot the caliper down for access to the brake pads

3.7d Remove the inner brake pad . . .

3.7e . . . and the outer brake pad

3.7f Remove the upper and lower pad support plates; make sure they are a tight fit and aren't worn. If necessary, replace them

3.7g Install the brake pads in the caliper mounting bracket

3.7h Pull out the sliding pins, clean them, then apply a coat of high-temperature grease to the pins and install them. Replace any boots that are worn or damaged

3.7i Swing the caliper back into place, install the bolt and tighten it to the torque listed in this Chapter's Specifications

4.2a Using a piece of rubber hose of the appropriate size, plug the brake line banjo fitting to prevent brake fluid from leaking out and to prevent dirt and moisture from contaminating the fluid in the hose

4.2b If you're just removing the caliper for access to other components, hang it from the strut bracket with a piece of wire; do not allow the caliper to hang by the flexible brake hose

4 Disc brake caliper - removal and installation

Warning: *Dust created by the brake system is harmful to your health. Never blow it out with compressed air and don't inhale any of it. An approved filtering mask should be worn when working on the brakes. Do not, under any circumstances, use petroleum-based solvents to clean brake parts. Use brake system cleaner only!*
Note: *Always replace the calipers in pairs - never replace just one of them.*

Removal

Refer to illustrations 4.2a, 4.2b, 4.3a and 4.3b
1   Loosen the wheel lug nuts, raise the vehicle and support it securely on jackstands.

Remove the wheels
2   Remove the brake hose banjo bolt and disconnect the hose from the caliper. Plug the hose to keep contaminants out of the brake system and to prevent losing any more brake fluid than is necessary **(see illustration)**. **Note:** *If you're just removing the caliper for access to other components, don't detach the hose, but be sure to support the caliper with a piece of wire - don't let it hang by the hose* **(see illustration)**.
3   Remove the caliper mounting bolts **(see illustrations)**.
4   Remove the caliper. If necessary, remove the caliper bracket from the steering knuckle or rear knuckle.

Installation
5   Install the caliper by reversing the

removal procedure. Tighten the caliper mounting bolts (and bracket bolts, if removed) to the torque listed in this Chapter's Specifications. Install *new* sealing washers on both sides of the brake hose banjo fitting, then tighten the banjo bolt to the torque listed in this Chapter's Specifications.
6   Bleed the brake system (see Section 8).
7   Install the wheels and lug nuts. Lower the vehicle and tighten the lug nuts to the torque listed in the Chapter 1 Specifications. **Warning:** *Depress the brake pedal several times before moving the vehicle to bring the brake pads into contact with the discs. Failure to do so will cause loss of braking at first. Check the operation of the brakes carefully before driving the vehicle.*

4.3a Front brake caliper mounting details

A   Brake hose banjo fitting bolt
B   Caliper mounting bolts

4.3b Rear brake caliper mounting details

A   Brake hose banjo fitting bolt
B   Caliper mounting bolts

5.2 To remove the front caliper bracket from the steering knuckle, remove these two bolts (rear caliper bracket similar)

5.3 The brake pads on this vehicle were obviously neglected, as they wore down completely and cut deep grooves into the disc - wear this severe means the disc must be replaced

5   Brake disc - inspection, removal and installation

Inspection

Refer to illustrations 5.2, 5.3, 5.4a, 5.4b, 5.5a and 5.5b

1   Loosen the wheel lug nuts, raise the vehicle and support it securely on jackstands. Remove the wheel and install the lug nuts to hold the disc in place. If the rear brake disc is being worked on, release the parking brake

2   Remove the brake caliper as outlined in Section 4. It isn't necessary to disconnect the brake hose. After removing the caliper bolts, suspend the caliper out of the way with a piece of wire **(see illustration 3.6d)**. Remove the caliper bracket bolts and remove the bracket **(see illustrations)**.

3   Visually inspect the disc surface for score marks and other damage. Light scratches and shallow grooves are normal after use and may

not always be detrimental to brake operation, but deep scoring - over 0.039-inch (1.0 mm) - requires disc removal and refinishing by an automotive machine shop. Be sure to check both sides of the disc **(see illustration)**. If pulsating has been noticed during application of the brakes, suspect disc runout.

4   To check disc runout, place a dial indicator at a point about 1/2-inch from the outer edge of the disc **(see illustration)**. Set the indicator to zero and turn the disc. The indicator reading should not exceed the specified allowable runout limit. If it does, the disc should be refinished by an automotive machine shop. **Note:** *Professionals recommend resurfacing the discs whenever the pads are replaced regardless of the dial indicator reading, as this will impart a smooth finish and ensure a perfectly flat surface, eliminating any brake pedal pulsation or other undesirable symptoms. At the very least, if you elect not to have the discs resurfaced, remove the glaze from the*

surface with sandpaper or emery cloth using a swirling motion **(see illustration)**.

5   It's absolutely critical that the disc not be machined to a thickness under the specified minimum allowable refinish thickness. The minimum wear (or discard) thickness is cast into the inside of the disc **(see illustration)**. The disc thickness can be checked with a micrometer **(see illustration)**.

Removal

Refer to illustrations 5.7a and 5.7b

6   Remove the lug nuts that were put on to hold the disc in place.

7   Remove the Phillips-head screws from the disc and slide the disc off the hub. If the rear disc won't come off, it may be interfering with the parking brake shoes; remove the plug **(see illustration)** and rotate the adjuster to back the parking brake shoes away from the drum surface within the disc **(see illustration)**.

5.4a Use a dial indicator to check disc runout; if the reading exceeds the maximum allowable runout limit, the disc will have to be machined or replaced

5.4b Using a swirling motion, remove the glaze from the disc surface with sandpaper or emery cloth

5.5a The minimum wear dimension is cast into the rear of the disc (typical)

5.5b Use a micrometer to measure disc thickness

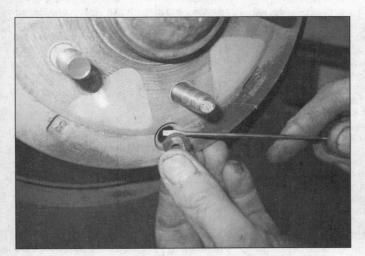

5.7a If the rear disc is difficult to remove, remove this plug . . .

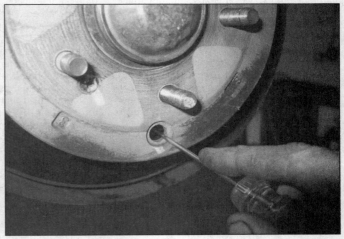

5.7b . . . insert a screwdriver through the hole (the hole must be at the 6 o'clock position) and rotate the adjuster to back the parking brake shoes away from the drum surface in the disc

Installation

8   Place the disc in position over the threaded studs.

9   Install the caliper, tightening the bolts to the torque listed in this Chapter's Specifications. Bleeding won't be necessary unless the brake hose was disconnected from the caliper.

10   If you're installing a rear disc, adjust the parking brake shoes as described in Section 10.

11   Install the wheel and lug nuts. Lower the vehicle and tighten the lug nuts to the torque listed in the Chapter 1 Specifications. **Warning:** *Depress the brake pedal several times before moving the vehicle to bring the brake pads into contact with the discs. Failure to do so will cause loss of braking at first.* Check the operation of the brakes carefully before driving the vehicle.

6   Master cylinder - removal and installation

Removal

Refer to illustration 6.3

Caution: *Brake fluid will damage paint or finished surfaces. Cover all body parts and be careful not to spill fluid during this procedure. Clean up any spilled brake fluid immediately and wash the area with large amounts of water.*

1   Remove the air filter housing and the air intake duct (see Chapter 4).

2   Remove as much fluid as possible from the reservoir with a syringe.

3   Unplug the electrical connector for the brake fluid level warning switch **(see illustration)**.

4   Place rags under the fittings and prepare caps or plastic bags to cover the ends of the lines once they're disconnected.

6.3 Master cylinder mounting details

A   *Electrical connector*
B   *Hydraulic line fittings*
C   *Mounting nut (one of two shown)*

6.9 The best way to bleed air from the master cylinder before installing it on the vehicle is with a pair of bleed tubes

5   Loosen the fittings at the ends of the brake lines where they enter the master cylinder. To prevent rounding off the flats, use a flare-nut wrench, which wraps around the fitting hex.

6   Carefully move the brake lines away from the master cylinder and plug the ends to prevent contamination.

7   Remove the nuts attaching the master cylinder to the power booster. Pull the master cylinder off the studs to remove it. Again, be careful not to spill fluid or bend the brake lines as this is done. **Note:** *If necessary, remove brake lines going to the ABS actuator from the master cylinder if they cannot be moved aside without damaging them.*

Installation

Refer to illustration 6.9

8   Bench bleed the new master cylinder before installing it. Because it will be necessary to depress the master cylinder piston and, at the same time, control flow from the brake line outlets, it is recommended that the master cylinder be mounted in a vise.

9   Attach a pair of master cylinder bleeder tubes to the outlet ports of the master cylinder **(see illustration)**. On models with an auxiliary type reservoir, place the bleeder tubes into the small tank mounted on the master cylinder.

10   Fill the reservoir with brake fluid of the recommended type (see Chapter 1).

11   Slowly push the pistons into the master cylinder (a large Phillips screwdriver can be used for this) - air will be expelled from the pressure chambers and into the reservoir. Because the tubes are submerged in fluid, air can't be drawn back into the master cylinder when you release the pistons.

12   Repeat the procedure until no more air bubbles are present.

13   Remove the bleed tubes, one at a time, and install plugs in the open ports to prevent fluid leakage and air from entering.

14   Install the reservoir cover, then install the master cylinder over the studs on the power brake booster and tighten the attaching nuts only finger tight at this time.

15   Thread the brake line fittings into the master cylinder. Since the master cylinder is still a bit loose, it can be moved slightly in order for the fittings to thread in easily. Do not strip the threads as the fittings are tightened.

16   Tighten the mounting nuts to the torque listed in this Chapter's Specifications, then tighten the brake line fittings securely.

17   Fill the master cylinder reservoir with fluid, then bleed the master cylinder and the brake system as described in Section 8. To bleed the cylinder on the vehicle, have an assistant pump the brake pedal several times slowly, then hold the pedal to the floor. Loosen the fitting nut to allow air and fluid to escape. Repeat this procedure on both fittings until the fluid is clear of air bubbles. **Caution:** *Have plenty of rags on hand to catch the fluid - brake fluid will ruin painted surfaces.*

18   If it was necessary to remove the master cylinder-to-ABS actuator brake lines, also bleed the lines at the ABS control unit.

19   The remainder of installation is the reverse of removal. Test the operation of the brake system carefully before placing the vehicle into normal service. **Warning:** *Do not operate the vehicle if you are in doubt about the effectiveness of the brake system. On*

models equipped with ABS, it is possible for air to become trapped in the anti-lock brake system hydraulic control unit, so, if the pedal continues to feel spongy after repeated bleedings or the BRAKE or ANTI-LOCK light stays on, have the vehicle towed to a dealer service department or other qualified shop to be bled with the aid of a scan tool.

7   Brake hoses and lines - inspection and replacement

Inspection

1   About every six months, with the vehicle raised and supported securely on jackstands, the rubber hoses which connect the steel brake lines with the front and rear brake assemblies should be inspected for cracks, chafing of the outer cover, leaks, blisters and other damage. These are important and vulnerable parts of the brake system and inspection should be complete. A light and mirror will be helpful for a thorough check. If a hose exhibits any of the above conditions, replace it with a new one.

Replacement

Front brake hose

Refer to illustrations 7.3 and 7.4

2   Loosen the wheel lug nuts, raise the vehicle and support it securely on jackstands. Remove the wheel.

3   At the frame bracket, unscrew the brake line fitting from the hose **(see illustration)**. Use a flare-nut wrench to prevent rounding off the corners.

4   Remove the U-clip from the female fitting at the bracket with a pair of pliers **(see illustration)**, then pass the hose through the bracket.

5   At the caliper end of the hose, remove the banjo-fitting bolt, then separate the hose from the caliper. Note that there are two copper sealing washers on each side of the fitting

7.3 Unscrew the brake line threaded fitting with a flare-nut wrench to protect the fitting corners from being rounded off

7.4 Remove the brake hose-to-bracket U-clip with a pair of pliers

- they should be replaced with new ones during installation.
6 Remove the fastener from the strut bracket and then detach the hose from it.
7 To install the hose, pass the caliper fitting end through the strut bracket, then connect the fitting to the caliper with the banjo bolt and new sealing washers. Make sure the locating lug on the fitting is engaged with the hole in the caliper, then tighten the bolt to torque listed in this Chapter's Specifications.
8 Push the metal support into the strut bracket and install the U-clip. Make sure the hose isn't twisted between the caliper and the strut bracket.
9 Route the hose into the frame bracket, again making sure it isn't twisted, then connect the brake line fitting, starting the threads by hand. Install the clip and E-ring, if equipped, then tighten the fitting securely.
10 Bleed the caliper (see Section 8).
11 Install the wheel and lug nuts, lower the vehicle and tighten the lug nuts to the torque listed in the Chapter 1 Specifications.

Rear brake hoses
12 Perform Steps 2, 3 and 4 above, then repeat Steps 3 and 4 at the other end of the hose. Be sure to bleed the caliper (see Section 8).

Metal brake lines
13 When replacing brake lines, be sure to use the correct parts. Don't use copper tubing for any brake system components. Purchase genuine steel brake lines from a dealer or auto parts store.
14 Prefabricated brake line, with the tube ends already flared and fittings installed, is available at auto parts stores and dealer parts departments.
15 When installing the new line, make sure it's securely supported in the brackets and has plenty of clearance between moving or hot components.
16 After installation, check the master cylinder fluid level and add fluid as necessary. Bleed the brake system (see Section 8) and test the brakes carefully before driving the vehicle in traffic.

8 Brake hydraulic system - bleeding

Refer to illustration 8.8
Warning: *Wear eye protection when bleeding the brake system. If the fluid comes in contact with your eyes, immediately rinse them with water and seek medical attention.*
Note: *Bleeding the hydraulic system is necessary to remove any air that manages to find its way into the system when it's opened during removal and installation of a hose, line, caliper or master cylinder.*
1 You'll probably have to bleed the system at all four brakes if air has entered it due to low fluid level, or if the brake lines have been disconnected at the master cylinder.

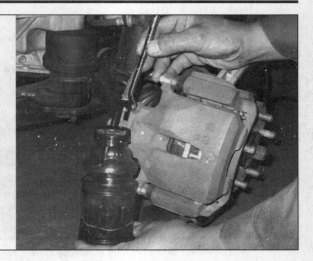

8.8 When bleeding the brakes, a hose is connected to the bleeder valve at the caliper or wheel cylinder, then submerged in brake fluid. Air will be seen as bubbles in the tube and container. All air must be expelled before moving to the next wheel

2 If a brake line was disconnected only at a wheel, then only that caliper must be bled.
3 If a brake line is disconnected at a fitting located between the master cylinder and any of the brakes, that part of the system served by the disconnected line must be bled.
4 Remove any residual vacuum from the brake power booster by applying the brake several times with the engine off.
5 Remove the master cylinder reservoir cover and fill the reservoir with brake fluid. Reinstall the cover. *Note: Check the fluid level often during the bleeding operation and add fluid as necessary to prevent the fluid level from falling low enough to allow air bubbles into the master cylinder.*
6 Have an assistant on hand, as well as a supply of new brake fluid, a clear container partially filled with clean brake fluid, a length of tubing to fit over the bleeder valve and a wrench to open and close the bleeder valve.
7 Beginning at the right rear wheel, loosen the bleeder valve slightly, then tighten it to a point where it's snug but can still be loosened quickly and easily.
8 Place one end of the tubing over the bleeder valve and submerge the other end in brake fluid in the container **(see illustration)**.
9 Have the assistant depress the brake pedal slowly, then hold the pedal down firmly.
10 While the pedal is held down, open the bleeder valve just enough to allow a flow of fluid to leave the valve. Watch for air bubbles to exit the submerged end of the tube. When the fluid flow slows after a couple of seconds, close the valve and have your assistant release the pedal.
11 Repeat Steps 9 and 10 until no more air is seen leaving the tube, then tighten the bleeder valve and proceed to the left front wheel, the left rear wheel and the right front wheel, in that order, and perform the same procedure. Be sure to check the fluid in the master cylinder reservoir frequently.
12 Never use old brake fluid. It contains moisture that will deteriorate the brake system components.
13 Refill the master cylinder with fluid at the end of the operation.

14 Check the operation of the brakes. The pedal should feel solid when depressed, with no sponginess. If necessary, repeat the entire process. **Warning:** *Do not operate the vehicle if you are in doubt about the effectiveness of the brake system. It's possible for air to become trapped in the ABS hydraulic control unit, so, if the pedal continues to feel spongy after repeated bleedings or the BRAKE or ANTI-LOCK light stays on, have the vehicle towed to a dealer service department or other qualified shop to be bled with the aid of a scan tool.*

9 Power brake booster - check, removal and installation

Operating check
1 Depress the brake pedal several times with the engine off and make sure there's no change in the pedal reserve distance.
2 Depress the pedal and start the engine. If the pedal goes down slightly, operation is normal.

Airtightness check
3 Start the engine and turn it off after one or two minutes. Depress the brake pedal slowly several times. If the pedal depresses less each time, the booster is airtight.
4 Depress the brake pedal while the engine is running, then stop the engine with the pedal depressed. If there's no change in the pedal reserve travel after holding the pedal for 30 seconds, the booster is airtight.

Removal
Refer to illustration 9.9
5 Power brake booster units shouldn't be disassembled. They require special tools not normally found in most automotive repair stations or shops. They're fairly complex and, because of their critical relationship to brake performance, should be replaced with new or rebuilt ones.

9.9 Power brake booster mounting nuts

10.4 Before disassembling it, be sure to wash the parking brake assembly with brake cleaner

6   Remove the brake master cylinder (see Section 6). To provide room for booster removal, some models may require that the brake lines that cross in front of the master cylinder be removed entirely (at both ends), and not just disconnected from the master cylinder. Other brake lines that cross in front of the brake booster can be separated from the firewall and carefully moved aside.

7   Carefully disconnect the vacuum hose from the brake booster.

8   Remove the brake pedal return spring near the top of the brake pedal. Remove the clevis pin retaining clip with pliers and pull out the pin.

9   Remove the four fasteners holding the brake booster to the firewall (see illustration). Slide the booster straight out from the firewall until the studs clear the holes.

Installation

10   Installation procedures are basically the reverse of removal. Tighten the booster mounting nuts to the torque listed in this Chapter's Specifications.

11   After the final installation of the master cylinder and brake hoses and lines, the brake pedal height and freeplay must be adjusted and the system must be bled. See the appropriate Sections of this Chapter for those procedures.

---

10   Parking brake shoes - inspection and replacement

Refer to illustrations 10.4, 10.5a through 10.5u, 10.7a and 10.7b

Warning 1: *Dust created by the brake system is hazardous to your health. Never blow it out with compressed air and don't inhale any of it. An approved filtering mask should be worn when working on the brakes. Do not, under any circumstances, use petroleum-based sol-* vents to clean brake parts. Use brake system cleaner only!

Warning 2: *Parking brake shoes must be replaced on both wheels at the same time - never replace the shoes on only one wheel.*

1   Remove the rear brake discs (see Section 5).

2   Inspect the thickness of the lining material on the shoes. If the lining has worn down to 1/32-inch or less, the shoes must be replaced.

3   Remove the hub and bearing assembly (see Chapter 10). **Note:** *It is possible to perform the shoe replacement procedure without removing the hub and bearing assembly, although working room is very limited.*

4   Wash off the brake parts with brake system cleaner (see illustration).

5   Follow the accompanying illustrations for the brake shoe replacement procedure (see illustrations 10.5a through 10.5u). Be sure to stay in order and read the caption under each illustration.

10.5a Referring to Chapter 10, unstake the hub nut and remove the hub for easier access to the parking brake components, then remove the return springs

10.5b Lift off the retainer plate

10.5c Spread the shoes and remove the strut

10.5d Remove the star-wheel mechanism, noting which end is facing forward

10.5e Remove the shoe hold-down springs and retainers

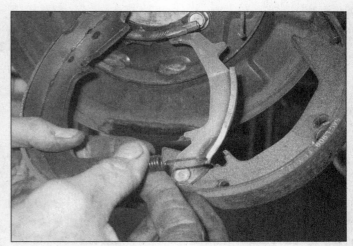

10.5f Remove the lower spring

10.5g Disconnect the shoe from the parking brake cable and set all the components aside for cleaning

10.5h Apply brake lubricant to the backing plates at the raised areas that support the shoes

10.5i Lightly lubricate the star-wheel threads and friction surfaces

10.5j Install the front shoe . . .

10.5k . . . followed by its hold-down spring and retainer

10.5l Install the rear shoe, hold-down spring and retainer

10.5m Install the star-wheel with the correct (threaded) end facing forward

10.5n Install the lower spring

10.5o Install the strut with its spring on the forward end

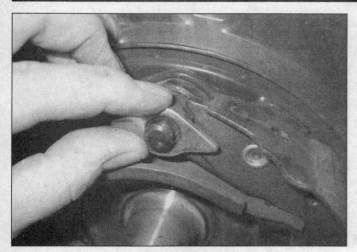

10.5p Install the upper retainer

10.5q Install the front spring . . .

10.5r . . . and the rear spring

10.5s The upper section should now look like this

10.5t This is how the complete parking brake assembly should look when you're done!

10.5u Tighten the hub nut to the torque listed in this Chapter's Specifications, then stake the nut to the spindle. It may be necessary to shorten the adjuster to get the brake disc on

10.7a   To adjust the parking brake shoes, first remove this rubber plug

10.7b   Use a screwdriver to rotate the star-wheel until the shoes lock, then back them off five clicks

6   Install the brake disc. Temporarily thread three of the wheel lug nuts onto the studs to hold the disc in place.

7   Remove the hole plugs from the brake discs. Adjust the parking brake shoe clearance by turning the adjuster star wheel with a brake adjusting tool or screwdriver until the shoes contact the discs and the discs can't be turned **(see illustrations)**. Back off the adjusters five notches, then install the hole plugs.

8   Install the brake caliper (see Section 4). Be sure to tighten the bolts to the torque listed in this Chapter's Specifications.

9   Install the wheel and tighten the lug nuts to the torque specified in Chapter 1.

10   Set the parking brake with about 45 pounds of force and count the number of clicks that it travels. It should be about seven clicks - if it's not, adjust the parking brake as described in Section 11.

11   Parking brake - adjustment

Refer to illustration 11.5

1   Pull the parking brake lever with about 45 pounds of force and count the number of clicks from the handle. It should take about seven clicks to apply the parking brake. If it travels less than five clicks, there's a chance the parking brake might not be releasing completely. If it travels more than seven clicks, the parking brake may not hold adequately on an incline, allowing the car to roll. Release the lever.

2   Raise the rear of the vehicle and support it securely on jackstands. Be sure to block the front wheels. The parking brake should be released.

3   Refer to Step 7 in Section 10 to adjust the parking brake shoes.

4   Remove the console cover (see Chapter 11).

5   Adjust the nut on the end of the cable rod to get the correct number of clicks when operating the parking brake lever **(see illustration)**.

6   With the lever released, move the rear wheels by hand to make sure that the parking brake isn't dragging.

7   Reinstall the console cover and lower the vehicle.

12   Brake light switch - removal, installation and adjustment

Removal and installation

Refer to illustration 12.1

1   The brake light switch is located on a bracket at the top of the brake pedal **(see illustration)**.

11.5   The parking brake adjusting nut is located at the base of the handle. Loosen the locknut (A) and turn the adjusting nut (B) to obtain adjustment

12.1   The brake light switch is located on a bracket near the top of the brake pedal. Loosen the locknut and unscrew the switch from its bracket

92008-9-15.6 HAYNES

12.6 To adjust the brake light switch, loosen the locknut and rotate the switch until the plunger distance (A) is within the range listed in this Chapter's Specifications, then tighten the locknut

13.1 Brake pedal height and freeplay measuring and adjustment points

A   *Clevis locknut*
B   *Brake light switch adjusting nut/ locknut*
C   *Pedal height measurement point (to steel floor)*
D   *Freeplay measurement point*

92095-9-13.1 HAYNES

2   Disconnect the wiring harness at the brake light switch.
3   Loosen the locknut and unscrew the switch from the pedal bracket.
4   Installation is the reverse of removal.

Adjustment

Refer to illustration 12.6

5   Check and, if necessary, adjust brake pedal height (see Chapter 1).
6   Loosen the switch locknut, adjust the switch so that the pedal has freeplay as listed in this Chapter's Specifications (see Section 13) **(see illustration)**.
7   Plug the electrical connector into the switch. Make sure the brake lights come on when the brake pedal is depressed and go off when the pedal is released. If not, repeat the adjustment procedure until the brake lights function properly.

8   Check and, if necessary, adjust brake pedal freeplay (see Section 13).

13   Brake pedal - adjustment

Pedal height

Refer to illustration 13.1

1   The height of the brake pedal is the distance the pedal sits off the floor. If the pedal height is not within Specifications, it must be adjusted **(see illustration)**.
2   To adjust the brake pedal, loosen the locknut and back the pushrod out for clearance. Turn the pushrod to adjust the pedal height in the middle of the specified range, then retighten the locknut.
3   At the brake pedal, loosen the locknut on the brake switch and retract the switch. Before measuring the brake pedal height, make sure the pedal is in the fully-returned position. Measure the pedal height and adjust it if necessary (see Step 2). To get an accurate mea-

surement, the carpet must be pulled back.
4   Adjust the brake pedal switch by turning it clockwise until the switch body just contacts the pedal arm, then rotate it counterclockwise to gain the clearance in this Chapter's Specifications, and tighten the switch locknut.

Pedal freeplay

5   The freeplay is the pedal slack, or the distance the pedal can be depressed before it begins to have any effect on the brake system. If the pedal freeplay is not within the specified range, it must be adjusted.
6   To adjust the pedal freeplay, loosen the brake pedal switch. Adjust it to get the freeplay to the specified range, then retighten the locknut.
7   Before adjusting brake pedal freeplay, depress the brake pedal several times (with the engine off). Measure the freeplay and adjust it if necessary. Loosen the locknut on the pushrod, then back off the pushrod to adjust the pedal freeplay to the specified range and retighten the locknut.

Notes

Chapter 10
Suspension and steering systems

Contents

Specifications

Torque specifications

Note: *One foot-pound (ft-lb) of torque is equivalent to 12 inch-pounds (in-lbs) of torque. Torque values below approximately 15 ft-lbs are expressed in inch-pounds, since most foot-pound torque wrenches are not accurate at these smaller values.*

	Ft-lbs (unless otherwise indicated)	Nm
Front suspension		
Balljoint self-locking nuts	74 to 88	100 to 120
Control arm-to-subframe bolts	74 to 88	100 to 120
Stabilizer bar		
Stabilizer bar link nuts	74 to 88	100 to 120
Stabilizer bushing/retainer bolts	33 to 41	45 to 55
Strut		
Strut upper mounting nuts	33 to 44	45 to 60
Lower mounting nuts	74 to 88	100 to 120
Self-locking nuts	44 to 52	60 to 70
Subframe mounting bolts	33 to 41	45 to 55
Rear suspension		
Driveaxle/hub nut (4WD models)	148 to 192	200 to 260
Rear hub spindle nut (2WD models)	148 to 192	200 to 260
Rear hub-to-trailing arm nuts (4WD models)	59 to 66	80 to 90
Shock absorber		
Upper mounting nut	15 to 22	20 to 30
Lower mounting nut	88 to 103	120 to 140
Stabilizer bar		
Stabilizer bar link-to-strut assembly	74 to 88	100 to 120
Stabilizer bushing/retainer bolts	33 to 41	45 to 55
Subframe mounting bolts	104 to 118	140 to 160
Suspension arm mounting bolts	118 to 133	160 to 180
Upper and lower arms-to-knuckle bolts	74 to 81	100 to 120
Upper arm cam bolts	104 to 118	140 to 160
Steering system		
Airbag module screws	36 to 48 in-lbs	4 to 6
Steering wheel nut	26 to 33	35 to 45
Steering gear mounting bolts/nuts	59 to 73	80 to 100
Steering shaft universal joint pinch bolt	11 to 14	15 to 20
Tie-rod end-to-steering knuckle nut	18 to 25	24 to 34
Tie-rod end lock nut	37 to 40	50 to 55
Power steering pump mounting bolts		
Short	13 to 19	17 to 26
Long	17 to 24	22 to 28
Wheel lug nuts	See Chapter 1	

1.1 Front suspension and steering components

1 Subframe	3 Tie-rod end	5 Balljoint
2 Steering gear	4 Steering knuckle	6 Control arm

1.2 Rear suspension components

1   Rear suspension crossmember
2   Trailing arm
3   Upper arm

4   Lower arm
5   Stabilizer bar and link

6   Coil spring
7   Shock absorber

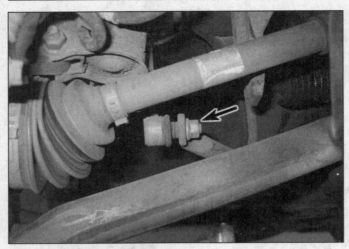

2.3 To detach the stabilizer bar link from the bar, remove the lower nut; if you're removing the strut (or replacing the link), remove the upper nut

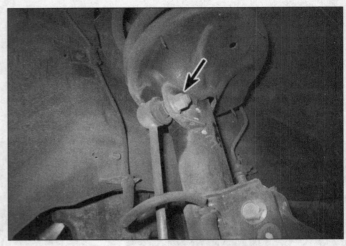

3.2 Disconnect the top of the stabilizer bar link from the strut

1   General information

Refer to illustrations 1.1 and 1.2

The front suspension is a MacPherson strut design. The upper end of each strut is attached to the vehicle's body strut support. The lower end of the strut is connected to the upper end of the steering knuckle. The steering knuckle is attached to a balljoint mounted on the outer end of the suspension control arm **(see illustration)**.

The rear suspension uses a trailing arm and an upper and lower control arm on each side **(see illustration)**. They connect to a hub assembly. Each hub assembly uses a coil spring and a shock absorber to control its movement.

The power-assisted rack-and-pinion steering gear, which is located behind the engine/transaxle assembly, is mounted on the engine cradle. The steering gear actuates the tie-rods, which are attached to the steering knuckles. The steering column is designed to collapse in the event of an accident.

Frequently, when working on the suspension or steering system components, you may come across fasteners that seem impossible to loosen. These fasteners on the underside of the vehicle are continually subjected to water, road grime, mud, etc., and can become rusted or frozen, making them extremely difficult to remove. In order to unscrew these stubborn fasteners without damaging them (or other components), be sure to use lots of penetrating oil and allow it to soak in for a while. Using a wire brush to clean exposed threads will also ease removal of the nut or bolt and prevent damage to the threads. Sometimes a sharp blow with a hammer and punch will break the bond between nut and bolt threads, but care must be taken to prevent the punch from slipping off the fastener and ruining the threads. Heating the stuck fastener and surrounding area with a torch sometimes helps

too, but isn't recommended because of the obvious dangers associated with fire. Long breaker bars and extension, or cheater, pipes will increase leverage, but never use an extension pipe on a ratchet - the ratcheting mechanism could be damaged. Sometimes tightening the nut or bolt first will help to break it loose. Fasteners that require drastic measures to remove should always be replaced with new ones.

Since most of the procedures dealt with in this Chapter involve jacking up the vehicle and working underneath it, a good pair of jackstands will be needed. A hydraulic floor jack is the preferred type of jack to lift the vehicle, and it can also be used to support certain components during various operations. **Warning:** *Never, under any circumstances, rely on a jack to support the vehicle while working on it. Whenever any of the suspension or steering fasteners are loosened or removed they must be inspected and, if necessary, replaced with new ones of the same part number or of original equipment quality and design. Torque specifications must be followed for proper reassembly and component retention. Never attempt to heat or straighten any suspension or steering components. Instead, replace any bent or damaged part with a new one.*

2   Stabilizer bar bushings and links (front) - removal and installation

Refer to illustration 2.3

Note: *If a stabilizer bar becomes damaged, it is most likely the result of an accident that was severe enough to damage other major components (such as the subframe itself). Damage this severe will require the services of an auto body shop.*

1   Loosen the front wheel lug nuts, then raise the front of the vehicle and support it securely on jackstands.

2   Remove the front wheels.

3   Disconnect the stabilizer bar links from the bar **(see illustration)**.

4   Detach both stabilizer bar bushing retainers from the subframe.

5   While the stabilizer bar is detached, slide off the retainer bushings and inspect them. If they're cracked, worn or deteriorated, replace them. Also inspect the stabilizer bar links for loose ballstuds.

6   Clean the bushing area of the stabilizer bar with a stiff wire brush to remove any rust or dirt.

7   Lubricate the inside and outside of the new bushings with vegetable oil (used in cooking) to simplify reassembly. **Caution:** *Don't use petroleum or mineral-based lubricants or brake fluid - they will lead to deterioration of the bushings.*

8   Install the retainers and bolts, tightening the bolts to the torque listed in this Chapter's Specifications.

9   Install the links, tightening the link nuts to the torque listed in this Chapter's Specifications.

3   Strut assembly (front) - removal, inspection and installation

Removal

Refer to illustrations 3.2, 3.4 and 3.7

1   Loosen the wheel lug nuts, raise the vehicle and support it securely on jackstands. Remove the wheel. Support the control arm with a floor jack.

2   Disconnect the stabilizer bar link from the strut **(see illustration)**.

3   Remove the brake hose bracket and the wheel speed sensor wiring harness from the strut.

4   Mark the position of the steering knuckle to the strut to help preserve the camber

3.4 Mark the position of the knuckle to the strut before removing the bolts

3.7 Remove the upper strut mounting nuts. Warning: *Don't try to remove the large nut in the center at this time. If you wish, you may loosen it*

adjustment **(see illustration)**. Remove the strut-to-knuckle nuts and knock the bolts out with a hammer and punch.

5   Separate the strut from the steering knuckle. Be careful not to overextend the inner CV joint. Also, don't let the steering knuckle fall outward, as the brake hose could be damaged.

6   If the strut is to be disassembled, loosen, but do not remove, the damper shaft nut (in the center of the upper mount).

7   Support the strut and spring assembly with one hand (or have an assistant hold it) and remove the three strut-to-shock tower nuts in the engine compartment **(see illustration)**. Remove the assembly out from the fenderwell.

Inspection

8   Check the strut body for leaking fluid, dents, cracks and other obvious damage that would warrant repair or replacement.

9   Check the coil spring for chips or cracks in the spring coating (this can cause premature spring failure due to corrosion). Inspect the spring seat for cuts, hardness and general deterioration.

10   If any undesirable conditions exist, proceed to the strut disassembly procedure (see Section 4).

Installation

11   Guide the strut assembly up into the fenderwell and insert the upper mounting studs through the holes in the shock tower. Once the studs protrude from the shock tower, install the nuts so the strut won't fall back through. This is most easily accomplished with the help of an assistant, as the strut is quite heavy and awkward.

12   Slide the steering knuckle into the strut flange and insert the two bolts. Install the nuts, match the position of the strut to the steering knuckle that was previously marked and tighten them to the torque listed in this Chapter's Specifications.

13   Reattach the brake hose bracket and the wheel speed sensor wiring harness bracket to the strut.

14   Install the wheel and lug nuts, then lower the vehicle and tighten the lug nuts to the torque listed in the Chapter 1 Specifications.

15   Tighten the three upper mounting nuts to the torque listed in this Chapter's Specifications.

4   Strut/coil spring assembly - replacement

1   If the struts or coil springs exhibit the telltale signs of wear (leaking fluid, loss of damping capability, chipped, sagging or cracked coil springs), explore all options before beginning any work. The strut/shock absorber assemblies are not serviceable and must be replaced if a problem develops. However, strut assemblies complete with springs may be available on an exchange basis, which eliminates much time and work. Whichever route you choose to take, check on the cost and availability of parts before disassem-

bling your vehicle. **Warning:** *Disassembling a strut is potentially dangerous and utmost attention must be directed to the job, or serious injury may result. Use only a high-quality spring compressor and carefully follow the manufacturer's instructions furnished with the tool. After removing the coil spring from the strut assembly, set it aside in a safe, isolated area.*

Disassembly

Refer to illustrations 4.3, 4.4, 4.5, 4.6 and 4.7

2   Remove the strut and spring assembly (see Section 3). Mount the strut assembly in a vise. Line the vise jaws with wood or rags to prevent damage to the unit and don't tighten the vise excessively.

3   Following the tool manufacturer's instructions, install the spring compressor (which can be obtained at most auto parts stores or equipment yards on a daily rental basis) on the spring and compress it sufficiently to relieve all pressure from the upper spring seat **(see illustration)**. This can be verified by wiggling the spring.

4.3 **Install the spring compressor in accordance with the tool manufacturer's instructions and compress the spring until all pressure is relieved from the upper spring seat**

4.4 Remove the damper shaft nut

4.5 Lift the suspension support off the damper shaft

4   Unscrew the damper shaft nut **(see illustration)**.

5   Remove the nut and suspension support **(see illustration)**. Inspect the bearing in the suspension support for smooth operation. If it doesn't turn smoothly, replace the suspension support. Check the rubber portion of the suspension support for cracking and general deterioration. If there is any separation of the rubber, replace it.

6   Remove the upper spring seat from the damper shaft **(see illustration)**. Check the spring seat for cracking and hardness; replace it if necessary. Remove the upper insulator.

7   Carefully lift the compressed spring from the assembly **(see illustration)** and set it in a safe place. **Warning:** *Never place your head near the end of the spring!*

8   Slide the rubber bumper off the damper shaft.

9   Check the lower insulator for wear, cracking and hardness and replace it if necessary.

Reassembly

Refer to illustrations 4.11 and 4.12

10   If the lower insulator is being replaced, set it into position with the dropped portion seated in the lowest part of the seat. Extend the damper rod to its full length and install the rubber bumper.

11   Carefully place the coil spring onto the lower insulator, with the end of the spring resting in the lowest part of the insulator **(see illustration)**.

4.6 Remove the spring seat from the damper shaft

4.7 Remove the compressed spring assembly - keep the ends of the spring pointed away from your body

4.11 When installing the spring, make sure the end fits into the recessed portion of the lower seat

4.12 The flats on the damper shaft must match up with the flats in the spring seat

5.2 Remove the pinch bolt that secures the balljoint and use a prybar to separate the control arm/balljoint assembly from the knuckle

12 Install the upper insulator on the spring. Install the spring seat, making sure that the flats in the hole in the seat match up with the flats on the damper shaft (see illustration).
13 Align the holes in the upper spring seat with those in the lower.
14 Install the damper nut and tighten it to the torque listed in this Chapter's Specifications. Don't allow the holes in the spring seats to become misaligned. Remove the spring compressor tool.
15 Install the strut/spring assembly.

5   Control arm - removal, inspection and installation

Removal

Refer to illustrations 5.2 and 5.3

1 Loosen the wheel lug nuts on the side to be dismantled, raise the front of the vehicle, support it securely on jackstands and remove the wheel.
2 Remove the nut and balljoint pinch bolt (see illustration). Use a prybar to disconnect the balljoint from the control arm, being careful not to damage the balljoint boot.
3 Remove the pair of bolts that attach the short leg of the control arm to the subframe (see illustration).
4 Remove the single bolt that attaches the longer leg of the control arm to the subframe.
5 Remove the control arm.

Inspection

6 Make sure the control arm is straight. If it's bent, replace it. Do not attempt to straighten a bent control arm.
7 Inspect the bushings. The rear bushing can be removed, and the new one installed, with a hydraulic press. At the time of writing, the pivot shaft bushing was not available separately, necessitating replacement of the control arm.

Installation

8 Installation is the reverse of removal. Be sure to tighten all fasteners to the torque listed in this Chapter's Specifications.
9 Install the wheel and lug nuts, lower the vehicle and tighten the lug nuts to the torque listed in the Chapter 1 Specifications.
10 It's a good idea to have the front wheel alignment checked, and if necessary, adjusted after this job has been performed.

6   Balljoints - replacement

1 Loosen the wheel lug nuts, raise the vehicle and support it securely on jackstands. Remove the wheel.
2 Refer to Section 5 and remove the lower control arm from the vehicle.
3 Remove the rubber boot from the balljoint.
4 Use snap-ring pliers to remove the snap-ring from the balljoint
5 Support the bottom the control arm and separate the balljoint from the control arm

by striking the stud with a plastic-face hammer.
6 The new balljoint can be installed by using a large socket that fits around the outer rim of the balljoint and a hammer. A hydraulic press can also be used by a repair shop to press the new balljoint into place.
7 Installation is the reverse of removal.

7   Steering knuckle and hub - removal and installation

Warning: *Dust created by the brake system is harmful to your health. Never blow it out with compressed air and don't inhale any of it. Do not, under any circumstances, use petroleum-based solvents to clean brake parts. Use brake system cleaner only.*

Removal

1 Loosen the driveaxle/hub nut (see Chapter 8). Loosen the wheel lug nuts, raise the vehicle and support it securely on jackstands.

5.3 Remove the bolts from both legs of the control arm

9.3 Disconnect the rear stabilizer bar link from the bar

9.4 Remove the stabilizer bar bushing retainers

Remove the wheel.
2   Remove the wheel speed sensor from the knuckle and remove the brake disc from the hub (see Chapter 9).
3   Loosen, but do not remove, the strut-to-steering knuckle bolts **(see illustration 3.4)**.
4   Separate the tie-rod end from the steering knuckle arm (see Section 17).
5   Separate the balljoint from the steering knuckle and pull the control arm down (see Section 5). The strut-to-knuckle bolts can now be removed.
6   Push the driveaxle from the hub as described in Chapter 8. Support the end of the driveaxle with a piece of wire.
7   Separate the steering knuckle from the strut.

Installation
8   Guide the knuckle and hub assembly into position, inserting the driveaxle into the hub.
9   Push the knuckle into the strut flange and install the bolts and nuts, but don't tighten them yet.
10   Connect the balljoint to the control arm and install the pinch bolt and nut (don't tighten it yet).
11   Attach the tie-rod to the steering knuckle arm (see Section 17). Tighten the strut bolt nuts and the tie-rod nut to the torque values listed in this Chapter's Specifications. Replace all cotter pins with new ones.
12   Place the brake disc on the hub and install the caliper and wheel speed sensor as outlined in Chapter 9.
13   Install the driveaxle/hub nut and tighten it securely (final tightening will be carried out when the vehicle is lowered).
14   Install the wheel and lug nuts, lower the vehicle and tighten the lug nuts to the torque listed in the Chapter 1 Specifications.
15   Tighten the driveaxle/hub nut to the torque listed in the Chapter 8 Specifications (see Chapter 8).

8   Hub and bearing assembly (front) - removal and installation

Due to the special tools and expertise required to press the hub and bearing from the steering knuckle, this job should be left to a professional shop. However, the steering knuckle and hub may be removed and the assembly taken to a dealer service department or other qualified repair shop. See Section 7 for the steering knuckle and hub removal procedure.

9   Stabilizer bar and bushings (rear) - removal and installation

Refer to illustrations 9.3 and 9.4

1   Loosen the rear wheel lug nuts for one wheel. Raise the rear of the vehicle and support it securely on jackstands. Remove one rear wheel.
2   Disconnect the exhaust system hangers if needed to provide clearance.
3   Disconnect the stabilizer bar links from

the bar **(see illustration)**.
4   Unbolt the stabilizer bar bushing retainers **(see illustration)**.
5   The stabilizer bar can now be removed from the vehicle. Remove the bushings from the stabilizer bar, noting their positions.
6   Check the bushings for wear, hardness, distortion, cracking and other signs of deterioration, replacing them if necessary. Check the stabilizer bar links for loose ballstuds.
7   Using a wire brush, clean the areas of the bar where the bushings ride. Lubricate the inside and outside of the new bushings with vegetable oil (used in cooking). **Caution:** *Don't use petroleum or mineral-based lubricants or brake fluid - they will lead to deterioration of the bushings.*
8   Installation is the reverse of removal.

10 Shock absorbers (rear) - replacement

Refer to illustrations 10.3a, 10.3b, 10.3c and 10.4

1   Raise the rear of the vehicle and support

10.3a Pry off the plastic shock mount covers from inside the rear compartment

10.3b Remove the rubber cap

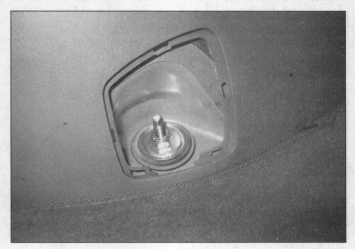

10.3c Hold the end of the stud with a small wrench or pliers while
removing the nut

10.4 Rear shock
absorber lower
mounting nut

it securely on jackstands placed under the
body jacking points.
2   Support the trailing arm with a floor jack
placed under the area of the coil spring.
3   Remove the nut from the top of the shock
absorber **(see illustrations)**.
4   Remove the nut from the bottom of the
shock absorber **(see illustration)**. If the nut
won't loosen due to rust, apply some penetrating oil and allow it to soak in.
5   Extend the new shock absorber as far as
possible.
6   Installation is the reverse of removal.
Tighten the fasteners to the torque values
listed in this Chapter's Specifications.

11 Coil spring (rear) - removal and installation

1   Support the trailing arm with a floor jack
placed under the area of the coil spring.
2   Unbolt and disconnect the bottom of the

shock absorber from the trailing arm assembly.
3   Use the floor jack to slowly and carefully
lower the trailing arm until the spring can be

removed by hand from the protrusion on the
trailing arm.
4   Installation is the reverse of removal.

12 Suspension arms (rear) - removal and installation

Note: *When installing any rear suspension
arms, loosely tighten all the bolts, move the
suspension to its normal ride-height angle
and position (a floor jack can be used to do
this), then fully tighten the bolts.*

Upper and lower arms

Refer to illustrations 12.2, 12.4a and 12.4b

1   Loosen the rear wheel lug nuts, raise the
rear of the vehicle and support it securely on
jackstands. Remove the rear wheel.
2   Make marks on the cam adjuster so the
wheel alignment can be preserved during
reassembly **(see illustration)**.
3   Remove the inner pivot bolt.

12.2 Mark the cam
adjusters on the inner
ends of the upper and
lower arms

12.4a Rear upper arm-to-trailing arm bolt

12.4b Rear lower arm-to-trailing arm bolt

12.11 Disconnect the brake hose, the parking brake cable and the wiring from the trailing arm

12   Refer to Section 10 and disconnect the shock absorber from the trailing arm.

13   Refer to Section 11 and remove the coil spring.

14   Disconnect the upper and lower arms from the trailing arm (see Steps 1 through 5).

15   Remove the trailing arm pivot bolt **(see illustration)**.

16   **Note:** *An assistant would be helpful for this Step.* Remove the trailing arm from the vehicle. If you're working on a 4WD model, remove the outer end of the driveaxle from the hub as this is done, then support the driveaxle with a piece of wire - don't let it hang by the inner CV joint.

17   Installation is the reverse of removal. Be sure to tighten all fasteners to the torque listed in this Chapter's Specifications.

18   Install the wheel and lug nuts, then lower the vehicle to the ground. Tighten the wheel lug nuts to the torque listed in the Chapter 1 Specifications. If you're working on a 4WD model, tighten the driveaxle/hub nut to the torque listed in the Chapter 8 Specifications.

19   Have the rear wheel alignment checked and, if necessary, adjusted.

4   Remove the cotter pin from the outer rod end, then remove the nut **(see illustrations)**.

5   Remove the outer rod end from the trailing arm. If it's stuck, use a tie-rod removal tool to pop it free.

6   Installation is the reverse of removal. Align the marks you made previously when installing the bar, and be sure to use new cotter pins at the outer ends.

7   It's a good idea to have the rear wheel alignment checked and, if necessary, adjusted.

Trailing arm

Refer to illustrations 12.11 and 12.15

8   Loosen the rear wheel lug nuts. If you're working on a 4WD model, loosen the drive-axle/hub nut.

9   Raise the rear of the vehicle and support it securely on jackstands. Block the front wheels to prevent the vehicle from rolling. Remove the wheel.

10   Disconnect the lower end of the stabilizer bar link from the trailing arm (see Section 9).

11   Refer to Chapter 9 and disconnect the parking brake cables from the shoes (this requires complete disassembly of the brakes). Disconnect the cables from the trailing arms **(see illustration)**. Disconnect the wheel speed sensor wiring harness.

12.15 Trailing arm pivot bolt

13.4 On 2WD models, the rear hub assembly is secured with a staked nut - be sure to stake it back into the notch in the spindle after tightening it to the torque listed in this Chapter's Specifications

15.2 The screws retaining the airbag module have Torx heads - be sure to use the correct socket when removing them

13 Hub and bearing assembly (rear) - removal and installation

1 Loosen the rear wheel lug nuts. If you're working on a 4WD model, loosen the drive-axle/hub nut. Raise the vehicle and support it securely on jackstands.

2WD models

Refer to illustration 13.4

2 Remove the cap, nut and washer from the rear hub. Use a hammer and punch to unstake the nut.
3 Refer to Chapter 9 and remove the brake disc.
4 Remove the spindle nut and lift off the hub assembly. The hub, bearing and wheel flange are a unit that must be replaced as an assembly. Be sure to restake the hub nut during installation **(see illustration)**.

4WD models

5 Refer to Chapter 9 and remove the brake disc and the entire parking brake assembly.
6 Disconnect the rear wheel speed sensor wiring harness.
7 Working through the holes in the flange, remove the four nuts from the end of the rear bearing housing.
8 Attach a large two-jaw puller to the rear hub. These pullers are available at rental centers and auto supply stores. Pull the hub assembly from the bearing housing. Remove the brake backing plate.
9 The bearing housing can be unbolted from the trailing arm. Use snap-ring or needle-nose pliers to remove the snap-ring from the wheel bearing.
10 The wheel bearing race can be removed by a shop equipped with a press.
11 Installation is the reverse of removal.

Tighten all fasteners to the torque values listed in this Chapter's Specifications.

14 Steering system - general information

All models are equipped with rack-and-pinion steering. The steering gear is bolted to the subframe and operates the steering knuckles via tie-rods. The inner ends of the tie-rods are protected by rubber boots that should be inspected periodically for secure attachment, tears and leaking lubricant.

The power assist system consists of a belt-driven pump and the associated lines and hoses. The fluid level in the power steering pump reservoir should be checked periodically (see Chapter 1).

The steering wheel operates the steering shaft, which actuates the steering gear through universal joints. Looseness in the steering can be caused by wear in the steering shaft universal joints, the steering gear, the tie-rod ends and loose retaining bolts.

15 Steering wheel - removal and installation

Warning: *The models covered by this manual are equipped with Supplemental Restraint Systems (SRS), more commonly known as airbags. Always disable the airbag system before working in the vicinity of any airbag system component to avoid the possibility of accidental deployment of the airbag(s), which could cause personal injury (see Chapter 12).*

Removal

Refer to illustrations 15.2, 15.3, 15.4, 15.5 and 15.6

1 Turn the steering wheel so that the wheels are pointing straight ahead. Turn the ignition key to Off, then disconnect the cable from the negative terminal of the battery (see Chapter 5, Section 1).
2 Use a Torx socket to remove the captive screws on each side of the steering wheel **(see illustration)**.
3 Carefully pull off the airbag module **(see illustration)**.

15.3 Lift the airbag module from the steering wheel, but be careful to avoid pulling on the wiring

15.4 The airbag wiring has a safety latch that must be released prior to pulling it out

15.5 The steering shaft and the steering wheel must have matchmarks made so they can be assembled in the same orientation

4   Disconnect the wiring **(see illustration)** and place the airbag in a safe location with the pad facing up.

5   Make match marks on the steering shaft and the hub so the steering wheel can be replaced in exactly the same position **(see illustration)**. Remove the nut.

6   Remove the two screws securing the horseshoe collar and remove it **(see illustration)**. Disconnect the horn wiring.

7   Try to remove the steering wheel by shaking the rim back and forth manually. If this fails, attach a steering wheel puller. **Caution:** *Don't use a hammer in any way on the steering wheel or column.*

8   Lift the wheel from the column while carefully threading the wires through it.

Installation

9   Make sure that the front wheels are facing straight ahead. If the clockspring has turned and is not centered, turn the hub in

either direction until it stops (don't apply too much force). Now, rotate the hub in the other direction, counting the number of turns it takes to reach the opposite stop. Divide that number by two, then turn the hub back that many turns, approximately, until the neutral position indicator is aligned with its corresponding mark.

10   To install the wheel, align the mark on the steering wheel hub with the mark on the shaft and slip the wheel onto the shaft. Install the nut and tighten it to the torque listed in this Chapter's Specifications.

11   Plug in the electrical connectors for the airbag module and any other connectors. Make sure the module connector locks are pushed back into position.

12   Install the airbag module and tighten the retaining screws to the torque listed in this Chapter's Specifications.

13   Connect the negative battery cable (see Chapter 5, Section 1).

16   Steering column - removal and installation

Removal

Refer to illustrations 16.7, 16.9 and 16.10

1   Park the vehicle with the wheels pointing straight ahead. Disconnect the cable from the negative terminal of the battery.

2   Remove the steering wheel (see Section 15), then turn the ignition key to the LOCK position to prevent the steering shaft from turning. **Caution:** *If this is not done, the airbag clockspring could be damaged.*

3   Remove the steering column upper and lower covers (see Chapter 11).

4   Disconnect the wiring and remove the multi-function switch.

5   Remove the switch from the left end of the knee bolster.

6   Remove the knee bolster.

7   Disconnect all interfering wiring and

15.6 Remove the horseshoe-shaped collar from the steering wheel

16.7 Remove the knee bolster reinforcement for access to the steering shaft universal joint

16.9 Be sure to make alignment marks for the orientation of the steering shaft before you disassemble it

16.10 Steering column upper mounting bolts

unbolt the knee bolster reinforcement (**see illustration**).

8   Mark the position of the universal joint at the steering gear pinion shaft.

9   Unscrew the steering shaft-to-universal joint pinch bolt (**see illustration**).

10 Unscrew the mounting bolts, then remove the steering column and shaft.

Installation

11   Guide the steering column into position, connect the intermediate shaft, then install the connecting fasteners, but don't tighten them yet.

12   Tighten the column mounting fasteners to the torque listed in this Chapter's Specifications.

13   Install the pinch bolt, tightening it to the torque listed in this Chapter's Specifications.

14   The remainder of installation is the reverse of removal.

17   Tie-rod ends - removal and installation

Removal

Refer to illustrations 17.2a, 17.2b and 17.4

1   Loosen the wheel lug nuts. Raise the front of the vehicle, support it securely on jackstands, block the rear wheels and set the parking brake. Remove the front wheel.

2   Hold the tie-rod with a pair of locking pliers or wrench and loosen the jam nut enough to mark the position of the tie-rod end in relation to the threads (**see illustrations**).

3   Remove the cotter pin and loosen the nut on the tie-rod end stud.

4   Disconnect the tie-rod from the steering knuckle arm with a puller (**see illustration**). Remove the nut and separate the tie-rod.

5   Unscrew the tie-rod end from the tie-rod.

17.2a Hold the tie-rod end with a wrench and break the jam nut loose with another wrench

17.2b Back off the jam nut and mark the exposed threads to ensure that the new tie-rod end is threaded on the same number of turns

17.4 Install a small puller to separate the tie-rod end from the steering knuckle

Installation

6   Thread the tie-rod end on to the marked position and insert the tie-rod stud into the steering knuckle arm. Tighten the jam nut securely.
7   Install the castle nut on the stud and tighten it to the torque listed in this Chapter's Specifications. Install a new cotter pin.
8   Install the wheel and lug nuts. Lower the vehicle and tighten the lug nuts to the torque listed in the Chapter 1 Specifications.
9   Have the alignment checked by a dealer service department or an alignment shop.

18   Steering gear boots - replacement

Refer to illustration 18.3

1   Loosen the lug nuts, raise the vehicle and support it securely on jackstands. Remove the wheel.
2   Remove the tie-rod end and jam nut (see Section 17).
3   Remove the steering gear boot clamps and slide off the boot **(see illustration)**.
4   Before installing the new boot, wrap the threads and serrations on the end of the steering rod with a layer of tape so the small end of the new boot isn't damaged.
5   Slide the new boot into position on the steering gear until it seats in the groove in the steering rod, and install new clamps.
6   Remove the tape and install the tie-rod end (see Section 17).
7   Install the wheel and lug nuts. Lower the vehicle and tighten the lug nuts to the torque listed in the Chapter 1 Specifications.
8   Have the alignment checked by a dealer service department or an alignment shop.

19   Steering gear - removal and installation

Warning: *Make sure the steering shaft is not turned while the steering gear is removed or you could damage the spiral cable for the air-*

18.3 Remove the outer clamp from the steering gear boot with a pair of pliers; the inner clamp must be cut or pried off

bag system. To prevent the shaft from turning, place the ignition key in the lock position or thread the seat belt through the steering wheel and clip it into place.

Removal

Refer to illustration 19.5

1   Park the vehicle with the front wheels pointing straight ahead. Loosen the front wheel lug nuts, raise the front of the vehicle and support it securely on jackstands. Apply the parking brake and remove the wheels. Remove the engine under-covers on models so equipped.
2   Place a drain pan under the steering gear. Detach the power steering pressure and return lines and cap the ends to prevent excessive fluid loss and contamination. **Caution:** *Use a flare-nut wrench for detaching the lines from the steering gear or the fittings could be severely damaged.*
3   Mark the relationship of the intermediate shaft to the steering shaft U-joint and remove the pinch bolt.
4   Separate the tie-rod ends from the steering knuckle arms (see Section 17).
5   Remove the steering gear mounting bolts **(see illustration)**.

6   Separate the intermediate shaft U-joint from the steering gear input shaft, then maneuver the steering gear down and out from the subframe.
7   Check the steering gear mounting grommets for excessive wear or deterioration, replacing them if necessary.

Installation

8   Raise the steering gear into position and connect the intermediate shaft U-joint to the steering input shaft, aligning the marks. If you're installing a new steering gear, center the pinion in the center of its travel by counting the number of turns lock to lock and setting the pinion midway.
9   Install the mounting bolts and nuts and tighten them to the torque listed in this Chapter's Specifications.
10   Connect the tie-rod ends to the steering knuckle arms and tighten them to the torque listed in this Chapter's Specification (see Section 17).
11   Install the steering shaft U-joint pinch bolt (in the passenger cab) and tighten it to the torque listed in this Chapter's Specifications. Make certain that the alignment marks match if the intermediate shaft was separated from the steering shaft U-joint.
12   Connect the power steering pressure and return hoses to the steering gear and fill the power steering pump reservoir with the recommended fluid (see Chapter 1). Reattach the bracket to the top of the steering gear assembly.
13   Lower the vehicle and bleed the steering system (see Section 21).
14   Have the alignment checked by a dealer service department or an alignment shop.

20   Power steering pump - removal and installation

Note: *Access to the steering pump is extremely tight on most models. Remove or disconnect the components that interfere on your particular model.*

19.5 Steering gear mounting bolts

Removal

Refer to illustration 20.5

1   Disconnect the cable from the negative battery terminal (see Chapter 5, Section 1).
2   Using a large syringe or suction gun, suck as much fluid out of the power steering fluid reservoir as possible. Place a drain pan under the vehicle to catch any fluid that spills out when the hoses are disconnected.
3   Loosen the drivebelt (see Chapter 1) and lift it from the power steering pump pulley.
4   Detach the fluid suction hose from the pump. Disconnect the electrical connector from the power steering pressure switch.
5   Disconnect the pressure line from the pump **(see illustration)**. Take care to avoid losing the seals.
6   Remove the mounting bolts and remove the pump.

Installation

7   Installation is the reverse of removal. Be sure to tighten the mounting bolts to the torque listed in this Chapter's Specifications. Adjust the drivebelt tension (see Chapter 1).
8   Top up the fluid level in the reservoir (see Chapter 1) and bleed the system (see Section 21).

21   Power steering system - bleeding

1   Following any operation in which the power steering fluid lines have been disconnected, the power steering system must be bled to remove all air and obtain proper steering performance.
2   With the front wheels in the straight-ahead position, check the power steering fluid level and, if low, add fluid.
3   Start the engine and allow it to idle. Recheck the fluid level and add more if necessary.
4   Bleed the system by turning the wheels fully from side to side, without hitting the stops. It may take several dozen turns to bleed the

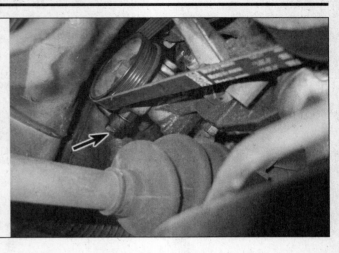

20.5 Power steering pressure line fitting

system. This will work the air out of the system. Keep the reservoir full of fluid as this is done. **Note:** *This procedure can be done with the front of the vehicle raised with a jack and supported on jackstands. This makes it easier to turn the wheels back and forth during the bleeding process.*
5   When the air is worked out of the system, return the wheels to the straight-ahead position and leave the vehicle running for several more minutes before shutting it off.
6   Road test the vehicle to be sure the steering system is functioning normally and noise free.
7   Recheck the fluid level to be sure it is up to the Hot mark on the dipstick while the engine is at normal operating temperature. Add fluid if necessary (see Chapter 1).

22   Subframe - removal and installation

Refer to illustration 22.11

1   Disconnect the cable from the negative battery terminal (see Chapter 5, Section 1).
2   Loosen the front wheel lug nuts, raise the front of the vehicle and support it securely on jackstands. Remove both front wheels. **Note:**

The jackstands must be behind the front suspension subframe, not supporting the vehicle by the subframe.
3   Remove any interfering front bumper trim components.
4   Disconnect the stabilizer bar bushing retainers from the subframe.
5   Disconnect the control arms from the steering knuckles (see Section 5).
6   Remove the steering gear mounting bolts from the subframe (see Section 19). **Note:** *Support the steering gear from above with a rope.*
7   Inspect the subframe for any hose, line or harness brackets that may be attached, and detach them.
8   Support the engine from above using an engine hoist or support fixture (see Chapter 2C). **Warning:** *DO NOT place any part of your body under the engine when it's supported only by a hoist or other lifting device.*
9   Detach all engine and transaxle mounts from the subframe (see Chapter 2)
10   Using two floor jacks, support the subframe. Position one jack on each side of the subframe, midway between the front and rear mounting points.
11   With the jacks sufficiently supporting the subframe, remove the subframe mounting bolts **(see illustration)**.
12   With the use of an assistant to steady the subframe, carefully lower the jacks until the subframe is sufficiently resting on the ground.

Installation

13   Installation is the reverse of removal. Tighten all suspension and subframe fasteners to the torque listed in this Chapter's Specifications. Tighten the engine mount fasteners to the torque listed in the Chapter 2 Specifications.

23   Wheels and tires - general information

Refer to illustration 23.1

1   All vehicles covered by this manual are

22.11 Subframe mounting bolts

METRIC TIRE SIZES
P 185 / 80 R 13

TIRE TYPE
P-PASSENGER
T-TEMPORARY
C-COMMERCIAL

ASPECT RATIO
(SECTION HEIGHT)
(SECTION WIDTH)
70
75
80

RIM DIAMETER
(INCHES)
13
14
15

SECTION WIDTH
(MILLIMETERS)
185
195
205
ETC

CONSTRUCTION TYPE
R-RADIAL
B-BIAS - BELTED
D-DIAGONAL (BIAS)

SECTION WIDTH

SECTION HEIGHT

23.1 Metric tire size code

equipped with metric-sized fiberglass or steel belted radial tires (**see illustration**). Use of other size or type of tires may affect the ride and handling of the vehicle. Don't mix different types of tires, such as radials and bias belted, on the same vehicle as handling may be seriously affected. It's recommended that tires be replaced in pairs on the same axle, but if only one tire is being replaced, be sure it's the same size, structure and tread design as the other.

2   Because tire pressure has a substantial effect on handling and wear, the pressure on all tires should be checked at least once a month or before any extended trips (see Chapter 1).

3   Wheels must be replaced if they are bent, dented, leak air, have elongated bolt holes, are heavily rusted, out of vertical symmetry or if the lug nuts won't stay tight. Wheel repairs that use welding or peening are not recommended.

4   Tire and wheel balance is important in the overall handling, braking and performance of the vehicle. Unbalanced wheels can adversely affect handling and ride characteristics as well as tire life. Whenever a tire is installed on a wheel, the tire and wheel should be balanced by a shop with the proper equipment.

CAMBER ANGLE (FRONT VIEW)

Vertical

C

A

B

Centerline of Vehicle

CASTER ANGLE (SIDE VIEW)

Vertical

D

Centerline of Ball Joint Axis

FRONT

TOE-IN (TOP VIEW)

F

G

FRONT

E

24.1 Camber, caster and toe-in angles

A minus B = C (degrees camber)
D = caster (expressed in degrees)
E minus F = toe-in (measured in inches)
G = toe-in (expressed in degrees)

24 Wheel alignment - general information

Refer to illustration 24.1

A wheel alignment refers to the adjustments made to the wheels so they are in proper angular relationship to the suspension and the ground. Wheels that are out of proper alignment not only affect vehicle control, but also increase tire wear. The alignment angles normally measured are camber, caster and toe-in **(see illustration)**.

Getting the proper wheel alignment is a very exacting process, one in which complicated and expensive machines are necessary to perform the job properly. Because of this, you should have a technician with the proper equipment perform these tasks. We will, however, use this space to give you a basic idea of what is involved with a wheel alignment so you can better understand the process and deal intelligently with the shop that does the work.

Toe-in is the turning in of the wheels. The purpose of a toe specification is to ensure parallel rolling of the wheels. In a vehicle with zero toe-in, the distance between the front edges of the wheels will be the same as the distance between the rear edges of the wheels. The actual amount of toe-in is normally only a fraction of an inch. On the front end, toe-in is controlled by the tie-rod end position on the tie-rod. On the rear end, it's controlled by cam bolts at the inner ends of the upper and lower arms. Incorrect toe-in will cause the tires to wear improperly by making them scrub against the road surface.

Camber is the tilting of the wheels from vertical when viewed from one end of the vehicle. When the wheels tilt out at the top, the camber is said to be positive (+). When the wheels tilt in at the top the camber is negative (-). The amount of tilt is measured in degrees from vertical and this measurement is called the camber angle. This angle affects the amount of tire tread, which contacts the road and compensates for changes in the suspension geometry when the vehicle is cornering or traveling over an undulating surface.

Caster is the tilting of the front steering axis from the vertical. A tilt toward the rear is positive caster and a tilt toward the front is negative caster. Too little caster will make the front end wander, while too much caster can make the steering effort higher.

Notes

Chapter 11 Body

Contents

1 General information

These models feature a "unibody" layout, using a floor pan with integral side frame rails that support the body components, front and rear suspension systems and other mechanical components.

Certain components are particularly vulnerable to accident damage and can be unbolted and repaired or replaced. Among these parts are the body moldings, bumpers, front fenders, the hood and trunk lid, doors and all glass.

Only general body maintenance practices and body panel repair procedures within the scope of the do-it-yourselfer are included in this Chapter. **Warning:** *The front seat belts on some models are equipped with pre-tensioners, which are pyrotechnic (explosive) devices designed to retract the seat belts in the event of a collision. On models equipped with pre-tensioners, do not remove the front seat belt retractor assemblies, and do not disconnect the electrical connectors leading to the assemblies. Problems with the pre-tensioners will turn on the SRS (airbag) warning light on the dash. If any pre-tensioner problems are suspected, take the vehicle to a dealer service department.*

2 Body - maintenance

1 The condition of your vehicle's body is very important, because the resale value depends a great deal on it. It's much more difficult to repair a neglected or damaged body than it is to repair mechanical components. The hidden areas of the body, such as the wheel wells, the frame and the engine compartment, are equally important, although they don't require as frequent attention as the rest of the body.
2 Once a year, or every 12,000 miles, it's a good idea to have the underside of the body steam-cleaned. All traces of dirt and oil will be removed and the area can then be inspected carefully for rust, damaged brake lines, frayed electrical wires, damaged cables and other problems.
3 At the same time, clean the engine and the engine compartment with a steam cleaner or water-soluble degreaser.
4 The wheel wells should be given close attention, since undercoating can peel away and stones and dirt thrown up by the tires can cause the paint to chip and flake, allowing rust to set in. If rust is found, clean down to the bare metal and apply an anti-rust paint.
5 The body should be washed about once a week. Wet the vehicle thoroughly to soften

the dirt, then wash it down with a soft sponge and plenty of clean soapy water. If the surplus dirt is not washed off very carefully, it can wear down the paint.

6   Spots of tar or asphalt thrown up from the road should be removed with a cloth soaked in kerosene. Scented lamp oil is available in most hardware stores and the smell is easier to work with than straight kerosene.

7   Once every six months, wax the body and chrome trim. If chrome cleaner is used to remove rust from any of the vehicle's plated parts, remember that the cleaner also removes part of the chrome, so use it sparingly. On any plated parts where chrome cleaner is used, use a good paste wax over the plating for extra protection.

3   Vinyl trim - maintenance

Don't clean vinyl trim with detergents, caustic soap or petroleum-based cleaners. Plain soap and water works just fine, with a soft brush to clean dirt that may be ingrained. Wash the vinyl as frequently as the rest of the vehicle.

After cleaning, application of a high quality rubber and vinyl protectant will help prevent oxidation and cracks. The protectant can also be applied to weather stripping, vacuum lines and rubber hoses, which often fail as a result of chemical degradation, and to the tires.

4   Upholstery and carpets - maintenance

1   Every three months remove the floormats and clean the interior of the vehicle (more frequently if necessary). Use a stiff whisk broom to brush the carpeting and loosen dirt and dust, then vacuum the upholstery and carpets thoroughly, especially along seams and crevices.

2   Dirt and stains can be removed from carpeting with basic household or automotive carpet shampoos available in spray cans. Follow the directions and vacuum again, then use a stiff brush to bring back the nap of the carpet.

3   Most interiors have cloth or vinyl upholstery, either of which can be cleaned and maintained with a number of material-specific cleaners or shampoos available in auto supply stores. Follow the directions on the product for usage, and always spot-test any upholstery cleaner on an inconspicuous area (bottom edge of a backseat cushion) to ensure that it doesn't cause a color shift in the material.

4   After cleaning, vinyl upholstery should be treated with a protectant. **Note:** *Make sure the protectant container indicates the product can be used on seats - some products may make a seat too slippery.* **Caution:** *Do not use protectant on steering wheels.*

5   Leather upholstery requires special care. It should be cleaned regularly with saddle-soap or leather cleaner. Never use alcohol,

gasoline, nail polish remover or thinner to clean leather upholstery.

6   After cleaning, regularly treat leather upholstery with a leather conditioner, rubbed in with a soft cotton cloth. Never use car wax on leather upholstery.

7   In areas where the interior of the vehicle is subject to bright sunlight, cover leather seating areas of the seats with a sheet if the vehicle is to be left out for any length of time.

5   Body repair - minor damage

Flexible plastic body panels (front and rear bumper fascia)

The following repair procedures are for minor scratches and gouges. Repair of more serious damage should be left to a dealer service department or qualified auto body shop. Below is a list of the equipment and materials necessary to perform the following repair procedures on plastic body panels. Although a specific brand of material may be mentioned, it should be noted that equivalent products from other manufacturers may be used instead.

Wax, grease and silicone removing solvent
Cloth-backed body tape
Sanding discs
Drill motor with three-inch disc holder
Hand sanding block
Rubber squeegees
Sandpaper
Non-porous mixing palette
Wood paddle or putty knife
Curved-tooth body file
Flexible parts repair material

1   Remove the damaged panel, if necessary or desirable. In most cases, repairs can be carried out with the panel installed.

2   Clean the area(s) to be repaired with a wax, grease and silicone removing solvent applied with a water-dampened cloth.

3   If the damage is structural, that is, if it extends through the panel, clean the backside of the panel area to be repaired as well. Wipe dry.

4   Sand the rear surface about 1-1/2 inches beyond the break.

5   Cut two pieces of fiberglass cloth large enough to overlap the break by about 1-1/2 inches. Cut only to the required length.

6   Mix the adhesive from the repair kit according to the instructions included with the kit, and apply a layer of the mixture approximately 1/8-inch thick on the backside of the panel. Overlap the break by at least 1-1/2 inches.

7   Apply one piece of fiberglass cloth to the adhesive and cover the cloth with additional adhesive. Apply a second piece of fiberglass cloth to the adhesive and immediately cover the cloth with additional adhesive in sufficient quantity to fill the weave.

8   Allow the repair to cure for 20 to 30 minutes at 60-degrees to 80-degrees F.

9   If necessary, trim the excess repair material at the edge.

10   Remove all of the paint film over and around the area(s) to be repaired. The repair material should not overlap the painted surface.

11   With a drill motor and a sanding disc (or a rotary file), cut a "V" along the break line approximately 1/2-inch wide. Remove all dust and loose particles from the repair area.

12   Mix and apply the repair material. Apply a light coat first over the damaged area; then continue applying material until it reaches a level slightly higher than the surrounding finish.

13   Cure the mixture for 20 to 30 minutes at 60-degrees to 80-degrees F.

14   Roughly establish the contour of the area being repaired with a body file. If low areas or pits remain, mix and apply additional adhesive.

15   Block sand the damaged area with sandpaper to establish the actual contour of the surrounding surface.

16   If desired, the repaired area can be temporarily protected with several light coats of primer. Because of the special paints and techniques required for flexible body panels, it is recommended that the vehicle be taken to a paint shop for completion of the body repair.

Steel body panels
See photo sequence

Repair of minor scratches

17   If the scratch is superficial and does not penetrate to the metal of the body, repair is very simple. Lightly rub the scratched area with a fine rubbing compound to remove loose paint and built up wax. Rinse the area with clean water.

18   Apply touch-up paint to the scratch, using a small brush. Continue to apply thin layers of paint until the surface of the paint in the scratch is level with the surrounding paint. Allow the new paint at least two weeks to harden, then blend it into the surrounding paint by rubbing with a very fine rubbing compound. Finally, apply a coat of wax to the scratch area.

19   If the scratch has penetrated the paint and exposed the metal of the body, causing the metal to rust, a different repair technique is required. Remove all loose rust from the bottom of the scratch with a pocket knife, then apply rust inhibiting paint to prevent the formation of rust in the future. Using a rubber or nylon applicator, coat the scratched area with glaze-type filler. If required, the filler can be mixed with thinner to provide a very thin paste, which is ideal for filling narrow scratches. Before the glaze filler in the scratch hardens, wrap a piece of smooth cotton cloth around the tip of a finger. Dip the cloth in thinner and then quickly wipe it along the surface of the scratch. This will ensure that the surface of the filler is slightly hollow. The scratch can now be painted over as described earlier in this Section.

Repair of dents

20   When repairing dents, the first job is to pull the dent out until the affected area is as close as possible to its original shape. There is no point in trying to restore the original shape completely as the metal in the damaged area will have stretched on impact and cannot be restored to its original contours. It is better to bring the level of the dent up to a point that is about 1/8-inch below the level of the surrounding metal. In cases where the dent is very shallow, it is not worth trying to pull it out at all.

21   If the back side of the dent is accessible, it can be hammered out gently from behind using a soft-face hammer. While doing this, hold a block of wood firmly against the opposite side of the metal to absorb the hammer blows and prevent the metal from being stretched.

22   If the dent is in a section of the body which has double layers, or some other factor makes it inaccessible from behind, a different technique is required. Drill several small holes through the metal inside the damaged area, particularly in the deeper sections. Screw long, self-tapping screws into the holes just enough for them to get a good grip in the metal. Now the dent can be pulled out by pulling on the protruding heads of the screws with locking pliers.

23   The next stage of repair is the removal of paint from the damaged area and from an inch or so of the surrounding metal. This is easily done with a wire brush or sanding disk in a drill motor, although it can be done just as effectively by hand with sandpaper. To complete the preparation for filling, score the surface of the bare metal with a screwdriver or the tang of a file or drill small holes in the affected area. This will provide a good grip for the filler material. To complete the repair, see the Section on filling and painting.

Repair of rust holes or gashes

24   Remove all paint from the affected area and from an inch or so of the surrounding metal using a sanding disk or wire brush mounted in a drill motor. If these are not available, a few sheets of sandpaper will do the job just as effectively.

25   With the paint removed, you will be able to determine the severity of the corrosion and decide whether to replace the whole panel, if possible, or repair the affected area. New body panels are not as expensive as most people think and it is often quicker to install a new panel than to repair large areas of rust.

26   Remove all trim pieces from the affected area except those which will act as a guide to the original shape of the damaged body, such as headlight shells, etc. Using metal snips or a hacksaw blade, remove all loose metal and any other metal that is badly affected by rust. Hammer the edges of the hole in to create a slight depression for the filler material.

27   Wire brush the affected area to remove the powdery rust from the surface of the metal. If the back of the rusted area is accessible, treat it with rust inhibiting paint.

28   Before filling is done, block the hole in some way. This can be done with sheet metal riveted or screwed into place, or by stuffing the hole with wire mesh.

29   Once the hole is blocked off, the affected area can be filled and painted. See the following subsection on filling and painting.

Filling and painting

30   Many types of body fillers are available, but generally speaking, body repair kits which contain filler paste and a tube of resin hardener are best for this type of repair work. A wide, flexible plastic or nylon applicator will be necessary for imparting a smooth and contoured finish to the surface of the filler material. Mix up a small amount of filler on a clean piece of wood or cardboard (use the hardener sparingly). Follow the manufacturer's instructions on the package, otherwise the filler will set incorrectly.

31   Using the applicator, apply the filler paste to the prepared area. Draw the applicator across the surface of the filler to achieve the desired contour and to level the filler surface. As soon as a contour that approximates the original one is achieved, stop working the paste. If you continue, the paste will begin to stick to the applicator. Continue to add thin layers of paste at 20-minute intervals until the level of the filler is just above the surrounding metal.

32   Once the filler has hardened, the excess can be removed with a body file. From then on, progressively finer grades of sandpaper should be used, starting with a 180-grit paper and finishing with 600-grit wet-or-dry paper. Always wrap the sandpaper around a flat rubber or wooden block, otherwise the surface of the filler will not be completely flat. During the sanding of the filler surface, the wet-or-dry paper should be periodically rinsed in water. This will ensure that a very smooth finish is produced in the final stage.

33   At this point, the repair area should be surrounded by a ring of bare metal, which in turn should be encircled by the finely feathered edge of good paint. Rinse the repair area with clean water until all of the dust produced by the sanding operation is gone.

34   Spray the entire area with a light coat of primer. This will reveal any imperfections in the surface of the filler. Repair the imperfections with fresh filler paste or glaze filler and once more smooth the surface with sandpaper. Repeat this spray-and-repair procedure until you are satisfied that the surface of the filler and the feathered edge of the paint are perfect. Rinse the area with clean water and allow it to dry completely.

35   The repair area is now ready for painting. Spray painting must be carried out in a warm, dry, windless and dust free atmosphere. These conditions can be created if you have access to a large indoor work area, but if you are forced to work in the open, you will have to pick the day very carefully. If you are working indoors, dousing the floor in the work area with water will help settle the dust which would otherwise be in the air. If the repair area is confined to one body panel, mask off the surrounding panels. This will help minimize the effects of a slight mismatch in paint color. Trim pieces such as chrome strips, door handles, etc., will also need to be masked off or removed. Use masking tape and several thickness of newspaper for the masking operations.

36   Before spraying, shake the paint can thoroughly, then spray a test area until the spray painting technique is mastered. Cover the repair area with a thick coat of primer. The thickness should be built up using several thin layers of primer rather than one thick one. Using 600-grit wet-or-dry sandpaper, rub down the surface of the primer until it is very smooth. While doing this, the work area should be thoroughly rinsed with water and the wet-or-dry sandpaper periodically rinsed as well. Allow the primer to dry before spraying additional coats.

37   Spray on the top coat, again building up the thickness by using several thin layers of paint. Begin spraying in the center of the repair area and then, using a circular motion, work out until the whole repair area and about two inches of the surrounding original paint is covered. Remove all masking material 10 to 15 minutes after spraying on the final coat of paint. Allow the new paint at least two weeks to harden, then use a very fine rubbing compound to blend the edges of the new paint into the existing paint. Finally, apply a coat of wax.

6   Body repair - major damage

1   Major damage must be repaired by an auto body shop specifically equipped to perform unibody repairs. These shops have the specialized equipment required to do the job properly.

2   If the damage is extensive, the body must be checked for proper alignment or the vehicle's handling characteristics may be adversely affected and other components may wear at an accelerated rate.

3   Due to the fact that some of the major body components (hood, fenders, doors, etc.) are separate and replaceable units, any seriously damaged components should be replaced rather than repaired. Sometimes the components can be found in a wrecking yard that specializes in used vehicle components, often at considerable savings over the cost of new parts.

7   Hinges and locks - maintenance

Once every 3000 miles, or every three months, the hinges and latch assemblies on the doors, hood and trunk (or liftgate) should be given a few drops of light oil or lock lubricant. The door latch strikers should also be lubricated with a thin coat of grease to reduce wear and ensure free movement. Lubricate the door and trunk (or liftgate) locks with spray-on graphite lubricant.

These photos illustrate a method of repairing simple dents. They are intended to supplement *Body repair - minor damage* in this Chapter and should not be used as the sole instructions for body repair on these vehicles.

1 If you can't access the backside of the body panel to hammer out the dent, pull it out with a slide-hammer-type dent puller. In the deepest portion of the dent or along the crease line, drill or punch hole(s) at least one inch apart . . .

2 . . . then screw the slide-hammer into the hole and operate it. Tap with a hammer near the edge of the dent to help 'pop' the metal back to its original shape. When you're finished, the dent area should be close to its original contour and about 1/8-inch below the surface of the surrounding metal

3 Using coarse-grit sandpaper, remove the paint down to the bare metal. Hand sanding works fine, but the disc sander shown here makes the job faster. Use finer (about 320-grit) sandpaper to feather-edge the paint at least one inch around the dent area

4 When the paint is removed, touch will probably be more helpful than sight for telling if the metal is straight. Hammer down the high spots or raise the low spots as necessary. Clean the repair area with wax/silicone remover

5 Following label instructions, mix up a batch of plastic filler and hardener. The ratio of filler to hardener is critical, and, if you mix it incorrectly, it will either not cure properly or cure too quickly (you won't have time to file and sand it into shape)

6 Working quickly so the filler doesn't harden, use a plastic applicator to press the body filler firmly into the metal, assuring it bonds completely. Work the filler until it matches the original contour and is slightly above the surrounding metal

7 Let the filler harden until you can just dent it with your fingernail. Use a body file or Surform tool (shown here) to rough-shape the filler

8 Use coarse-grit sandpaper and a sanding board or block to work the filler down until it's smooth and even. Work down to finer grits of sandpaper - always using a board or block - ending up with 360 or 400 grit

9 You shouldn't be able to feel any ridge at the transition from the filler to the bare metal or from the bare metal to the old paint. As soon as the repair is flat and uniform, remove the dust and mask off the adjacent panels or trim pieces

10 Apply several layers of primer to the area. Don't spray the primer on too heavy, so it sags or runs, and make sure each coat is dry before you spray on the next one. A professional-type spray gun is being used here, but aerosol spray primer is available inexpensively from auto parts stores

11 The primer will help reveal imperfections or scratches. Fill these with glazing compound. Follow the label instructions and sand it with 360 or 400-grit sandpaper until it's smooth. Repeat the glazing, sanding and respraying until the primer reveals a perfectly smooth surface

12 Finish sand the primer with very fine sandpaper (400 or 600-grit) to remove the primer overspray. Clean the area with water and allow it to dry. Use a tack rag to remove any dust, then apply the finish coat. Don't attempt to rub out or wax the repair area until the paint has dried completely (at least two weeks)

9.3 Draw alignment marks around the hood hinges to ensure proper alignment of the hood when it's reinstalled

9.4 Support the hood with your shoulder while removing the hood bolts

8 Windshield and fixed glass - replacement

Replacement of the windshield and fixed glass requires the use of special fast-setting adhesive/caulk materials and some specialized tools and techniques. These operations should be left to a dealer service department or a shop specializing in glass work.

9 Hood - removal, installation and adjustment

Note: *The hood is awkward to remove and install; at least two people should perform this procedure.*

9.9a Remove the plastic clips and remove the latch cover

Removal and installation

Refer to illustrations 9.3 and 9.4

1   Open the hood, then place blankets or pads over the fenders and cowl area of the body. This will protect the body and paint as the hood is lifted off.
2   Disconnect any cables or wires that will interfere with removal. Disconnect the windshield washer tubing.

3   Make marks around the hood hinges to ensure proper alignment during installation **(see illustration)**.
4   Have an assistant support one side of the hood. Take turns removing the hinge-to-hood bolts and lift off the hood **(see illustration)**.
5   Installation is the reverse of removal.

9.9b To adjust the hood latch horizontally or vertically, loosen the mounting bolts and reposition it

Align the hinge bolts with the marks made in Step 3.

Adjustment

Refer to illustrations 9.9a, 9.9b and 9.10

6   Fore-and-aft and side-to-side adjustment of the hood is done by moving the hood in the hinge plate slots after loosening the bolts.
7   If you haven't done so already, mark around the entire hinge plate so you can determine the amount of movement.
8   Loosen the bolts and move the hood into correct alignment. Move it only a little at a time. Tighten the hinge bolts and carefully lower the hood to check the position.
9   If necessary after installation, the entire hood latch assembly can be adjusted up-and-down as well as from side-to-side on the radiator support, so the hood closes securely and flush with the fenders. Scribe a line or mark around the hood latch mounting bolts to provide a reference point, then loosen them and reposition the latch assembly, as necessary **(see illustrations)**. Following adjustment, retighten the mounting bolts.
10   Finally, adjust the hood bumpers on the radiator support so the hood, when closed, is flush with the fenders **(see illustration)**.

9.10 To adjust the vertical height of the leading edge of the hood so that it's flush with the fenders, rotate each edge cushion

10.2 Pry the cable retainer from the latch and disengage the cable end

11   The hood latch assembly, as well as the hinges, should be periodically lubricated with white lithium-base grease to prevent binding and wear.

10   Hood latch and release cable - removal and installation

Latch

Refer to illustration 10.2

1   Scribe a line around the latch to aid alignment when installing, then remove the retaining bolts securing the hood latch to the radiator support **(see illustration 9.9b)**. Remove the latch.

2   Disconnect the hood release cable by disengaging the cable from the latch **(see illustration)**.

3   Installation is the reverse of removal. **Note:** *Adjust the latch so the hood engages securely when closed and the hood bumpers are slightly compressed.*

Cable

Refer to illustration 10.8

4   Working in the passenger compartment, lift the hood release handle lever upward, then pull down on the cable housing end and disengage the cable from the hood release lever handle **(see illustration)**.

5   Attach a piece of thin wire or string to the end of the cable.

6   Disconnect the hood release cable from the latch as described in Steps 1 and 2.

7   Remove the left inner plastic fender well.

8   Unclip all the cable retaining clips on the radiator support and the outer fenderwell **(see illustration)**.

9   Pull the cable forward into the wheel well until you can see the wire or string, then remove the wire or string from the old cable and fasten it to the new cable.

10   With the new cable attached to the wire or string, pull the wire or string back through the body until the new cable reaches the inside handle.

11   Working in the passenger compartment, install the new cable into the hood release

lever, making sure the cable housing fits snugly into the notch in the handle bracket. **Note:** *Pull on the cable with your fingers from the passenger compartment until the cable stop seats in the grommet on the body.*

12   The remainder of the installation is the reverse of removal.

11   Bumpers - removal and installation

Front bumper

Refer to illustrations 11.3, 11.4 and 11.5

1   Apply the parking brake, raise the vehicle and support it securely on jackstands.

2   Disconnect the wiring from the fog lights by reaching behind the bumper.

3   Remove the six screws securing the top front of the bumper cover **(see illustration)**.

4   Raise the vehicle and support it securely on jackstands. Remove the screws secur-

10.8 Remove the left plastic inner fender liner to get access to the hood release cable

11.3 The top bumper cover clips are visible after lifting the hood

11.4 Lower front bumper cover retainer locations

11.5 End bumper cover retainer locations

ing the lower edge of the bumper cover (**see illustration**).

5   Remove the screws on each side that attach the bumper cover to the wheel well liner (**see illustration**). Lift off the bumper cover.

6   Installation is the reverse of removal.

Rear bumper

Refer to illustrations 11.7, 11.8 and 11.9

7   Open the liftgate, lift up the weatherstrip and remove the six screws at the top of the bumper cover (**see illustration**).

8   Raise the vehicle and support it securely on jackstands. Remove the eight lower screws attaching the bumper cover to the frame and the wheel well liners (**see illustration**).

9   Remove the screws on each side attaching the bumper cover to the wheel wells (**see illustration**). Lift the bumper cover off.

10   Installation is the reverse of removal.

12 Front fender - removal and installation

Refer to illustrations 12.2, 12.5, 12.6, 12.7 and 12.8

1   Loosen the front wheel lug nuts. Raise the vehicle, support it securely on jackstands and remove the front wheel.

2   Open the hood. Remove the upper edge fender bolts (**see illustration**).

3   Remove the headlight housing (see Chapter 12).

4   Detach the inner fenderwell fasteners, then remove the inner fender splash shield. Detach the front bumper cover from the fender to be removed (see Section 11).

11.7 The upper bumper cover screws are under the weatherstrip

11.8 Lower bumper cover screw locations

11.9 The screws for the bumper ends are in the wheel wells

12.2 Top fender bolt locations

12.5 Remove the retainer and slide this cladding forward to release it (only if you need to transfer it to a new fender)

12.6 Lower rear fender bolt locations - the upper rear bolt is accessible after opening the door

12.7 Upper rear fender bolt

12.8 The inner fender bolts can only be reached after removing the plastic fender liner

5   To remove the lower rear plastic cladding, remove the clip and slide the lower body cladding forward to disengage it from its retainer (see illustration).
6   Remove the fender-to-body bolts at the lower rear edge (see illustration).
7   Open the door and remove the upper rear fender bolt (see illustration).
8   Reach behind the front bumper and remove the fender bolts (see illustration).
9   Lift off the fender. It's a good idea to have an assistant support the fender while it's being moved away from the vehicle to prevent damage to the surrounding body panels.

10   Installation is the reverse of removal. Check the alignment of the fender to the hood and front edge of the door before final tightening of the fender fasteners.

13   Radiator grille - removal and installation

Refer to illustration 13.1
1   Open the hood. Remove the fasteners along the top of the grille (see illustration).
2   Detach the grille from the hood.
3   Installation is the reverse of removal.

14   Cowl cover and vent tray - removal and installation

Refer to illustrations 14.2 and 14.3
1   Remove the wiper arms (see Chapter 12). They are retained by nuts.

13.1 Radiator grille fasteners

14.2 Lift off the cowl weatherstrip - it's held in place by plastic pins

14.3 Cowl fastener locations

15.2 The screw at the door handle is under a plastic cover

15.3 There is a screw at the bottom of the pull handle

2   Remove the cowl weatherstrip, being careful to avoid losing the plastic retainers **(see illustration)**.

3   Remove the pushpin fasteners securing the cowl cover **(see illustration)**. Note: *Use a small screwdriver to pop the center button up on the plastic fasteners, but do not try to remove the center buttons; they stay in the fastener.* Disengage the remaining clips and remove the cowl cover.

4   Installation is the reverse of removal.

15   Door trim panels - removal and installation

Warning: *The models covered by this manual are equipped with Supplemental Restraint systems (SRS), more commonly known as airbags. Always disarm the airbag system before working in the vicinity of any airbag system component to avoid the possibility of accidental deployment of the airbag, which could cause personal injury (see Chapter 12).*
Caution: *Wear gloves when working inside the door openings to protect against cuts from sharp metal edges.*

Doors

Refer to illustrations 15.2, 15.3, 15.4a, 15.4b, 15.5, 15.6, 15.7 and 15.8

1   Disconnect the cable from the negative battery terminal (see Chapter 5, Section 1).

2   Remove the screw at the door latch handle **(see illustration)**.

3   Remove the screw in the door pull handle/armrest on front doors **(see illustration)**.

4   Remove the screws at the front and rear of the panel **(see illustrations)**.

5   Pry the cover from the outside mirror and speaker enclosure **(see illustration)**.

6   Carefully pry the panel out until the clips

15.4a Fasteners at the door front edge (the upper one is under a small cover)

15.4b Door panel rear edge fasteners (under small covers)

15.5 The outside mirror cover can be pried off using a trim tool or a screwdriver wrapped with electrical tape

15.6 Use a trim tool to release the door panel - start at a corner and work slowly around the door panel

15.7 Disconnect the light and also the switches as you remove the panel

15.8 The water shield is sealed with butyl - keep it flat as you gently pull it free

disengage **(see illustration).** Work slowly and carefully around the outer edge of the trim panel until it's free. Unplug any wiring harness connectors and remove the panel.

7   Disconnect the light at the lower rear edge and the switches in the armrest **(see illustration).**

8   For access to the door outside handle or the door window regulator inside the door, raise the window fully, then carefully peel back the plastic watershield **(see illustration).**

9   Installation is the reverse of removal.

Liftgate

Refer to illustrations 15.10a, 15.10b, 15.11a, 15.11b, 15.12 and 15.13

10   Remove screw covers and the two fasteners, then lift off the center high-mounted stoplight **(see illustration).** Disconnect the wiring from the light **(see illustration).**

15.10a Pry the covers from the screws at the stoplight and remove the two screws

15.10b Disconnect the wiring to remove the unit completely

15.11a Pry the top trim off . . .

15.11b . . . and the side pieces

15.12 Remove the screws from the bottom tailgate trim panel (left side shown)

11   Remove the upper and side trim panels from the liftgate window **(see illustrations)**.
12   Remove the screws from the trim panel **(see illustration)**.
13   Using a screwdriver or trim removal tool, pry out the clips and remove the trim panel from the liftgate **(see illustration)**. Work slowly and carefully around the outer edge of the trim panel until it's free. Unplug any wiring harness connectors and remove the panel.
14   For access to other components inside the door, carefully peel back the plastic watershield.
15   Installation is the reverse of removal.

16   Door - removal, installation and adjustment

Note: *The door is heavy and somewhat awkward to remove and install - at least two people should perform this procedure.*

Removal and installation
Refer to illustration 16.5
1   Raise the window completely in the door and disconnect the cable from the negative battery terminal (see Chapter 5, Section 1).
2   Open the door all the way and support it from the ground on jacks or blocks covered with rags to prevent damaging the paint.
3   Remove the door trim panel and watershield as described in Section 15.
4   Disconnect all electrical connections, ground wires and harness retaining clips from the door. **Note:** *It is a good idea to label all connections to aid the reassembly process.*
5   From the door side, detach the rubber conduit between the body and the door **(see illustration)**. Pull the wiring harness through

15.13 Use a trim tool to pry the panel off

16.5 Door conduit (A), door stop strut (B) and the upper door hinge bolts (C)

16.13 Adjust the door lock striker by loosening the mounting fasteners and gently tapping the striker in the desired direction

17.2 The control rods are attached with plastic clips

the conduit hole and remove it from the door.

6   Remove the door stop strut bolt (see illustration 16.5).

7   Mark around the door hinges with a pen or a scribe to facilitate realignment during reassembly.

8   With an assistant holding the door, remove the hinge-to-door bolts and lift the door off.

9   Installation is the reverse of removal.

Adjustment

Refer to illustration 16.13

10   Having proper door-to-body alignment is a critical part of a well-functioning door assembly. First check the door hinge pins for excessive play. Fully open the door and lift up and down on the door without lifting the body. If a door has 1/16-inch or more excessive play, the hinges should be replaced.

11   Door-to-body alignment adjustments are made by loosening the hinge-to-body bolts or hinge-to-door bolts and moving the door. Proper body alignment is achieved when the top of the doors are parallel with the roof section, the front door is flush with the fender, the rear door is flush with the rear quarter panel and the bottom of the doors are aligned with the lower rocker panel. If these goals can't be reached by adjusting the hinge-to-body or hinge-to-door bolts, body alignment shims may have to be purchased and inserted behind the hinges to achieve correct alignment.

12   To adjust the door-closed position, scribe a line or mark around the striker plate to provide a reference point, then check that the door latch is contacting the center of the latch striker. If not, adjust the up and down position first.

13   Finally adjust the latch striker sideways position, so that the door panel is flush with the center pillar or rear quarter panel and provides positive engagement with the latch mechanism (see illustration).

17   Door latch, lock cylinder and handles - removal and installation

Caution: *Wear gloves when working inside the door openings to protect against cuts from sharp metal edges.*

Door latch

Refer to illustrations 17.2 and 17.4

1   Raise the window, then remove the door trim panel and watershield (see Section 15).

2   Working through the large access hole, disengage the rods from the handle and lock cylinder (see illustration). All door lock rods are attached by plastic clips. The plastic clips can be removed by unsnapping the portion engaging the connecting rod, then pulling the rod out of its locating hole.

3   Disconnect the electrical connectors at the latch. Disengage the handle-to-latch cables (see Steps 11 and 12).

4   Remove the screws securing the latch to the door (see illustration). Remove the latch assembly through the door opening.

5   Installation is the reverse of removal.

Outside handle and door lock cylinder

Refer to illustration 17.8

6   To remove the outside handle and lock cylinder assembly, raise the window and remove the door trim panel and watershield (see Section 15). **Caution:** *Take care not to scratch the paint on the outside of the door.* Wide masking tape applied around the handle opening before beginning the procedure can help avoid scratches.

7   Working through the access hole, disengage the plastic clips that secure the outside door lock-to-latch rod and the outside door handle-to-latch rod (see illustration 17.2).

8   Remove the handle and lock cylinder retaining screws from the inside of the door and remove the handle and lock cylinder (see illustration).

9   Installation is the reverse of removal.

Inside door handle

Refer to illustration 17.11

10   Remove the door trim panel (see Section 15).

17.4 Door latch mounting screws

17.8 Outer door handle screw locations

17.11 Inner door handle mounting fasteners

18.4 Raise the window to access the glass retaining bolts through the holes in the door frame

11   Remove the handle retaining screws and nut and disengage the handle from the door **(see illustration)**.
12   Disengage the handle-to-latch cables and remove the handle from the door.
13   Installation is the reverse of removal.

18   Door window glass - removal and installation

Caution: *Wear gloves when working inside the door openings to protect against cuts from sharp metal edges.*

Door glass

Refer to illustration 18.4
1   Remove the door trim panel and the plastic watershield (see Section 15).
2   Lower the window glass all the way down into the door.
3   Remove the door speaker (see Chapter 12).
4   Raise the window just enough to access the window retaining bolts through the holes in the door frame **(see illustration)**. Remove

the two glass mounting bolts.
5   Remove the glass by pulling it up and out.
6   Installation is the reverse of removal.

Liftgate glass

7   Replacement of the liftgate glass requires the use of special fast-setting adhesive/caulk materials and some specialized tools and techniques. These operations should be left to a shop specializing in glass work.

19   Door window glass regulator - removal and installation

Refer to illustration 19.4
Caution: *Wear gloves when working inside the door openings to protect against cuts from sharp metal edges.*
1   Remove the door trim panel and the plastic watershield (see Section 15).
2   Remove the window glass (see Section 18).
3   Disconnect the electrical connector from the window regulator motor. Detach the cables from the inside handle.

4   Remove the regulator/motor module mounting bolts **(see illustration)**.
5   Remove the regulator/motor module assembly.
6   Installation is the reverse of removal. Lubricate the rollers and wear points on the regulator with white grease before installation.

20   Mirrors - removal and installation

Outside mirrors

Refer to illustrations 20.1 and 20.2
1   Remove the mirror trim panel using a panel removing tool or a screwdriver with the blade wrapped with tape **(see illustration)**.
2   Disconnect the electrical connector from the mirror, then remove the three mirror retaining bolts and detach the mirror from the vehicle **(see illustration)**.
3   Installation is the reverse of removal.

Inside mirror

4   Disconnect the electrical connector from the mirror, if equipped.
5   On some models the mirror can be removed by carefully prying between the mirror mount and the notch in the base of the mirror stalk with a screwdriver tip covered with tape. There is a hairpin-type spring holding the mirror stalk in the base. Push the screwdriver in about 3/4-inch to release the spring. On some other models, the mirror can be removed by removing the set screw located at the base of the mirror stalk.
6   On models without a set screw, to install the mirror, reinsert the spring if it was removed earlier. Insert the mirror stalk's lug into the mount, pushing downward until the mirror is secured.
7   If the mount plate itself has come off the windshield, adhesive kits are available at auto parts stores to resecure it. Follow the instructions included with the kit.

19.4 Window regulator/motor module bolts

20.1 The outside mirror trim panel is simply pried off

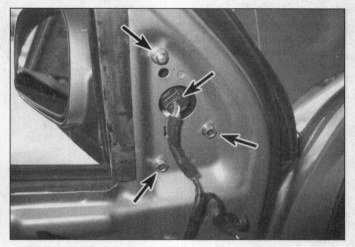

20.2 Disconnect the wiring and remove the three fasteners while supporting the mirror through the open window

21 Liftgate - removal, installation and adjustment

Note: *The liftgate is heavy and somewhat awkward to remove and install - at least two people should perform this procedure.*

Removal and installation

Refer to illustration 21.7

1 Disconnect the cable from the negative battery terminal (see Chapter 5, Section 1).
2 Open the liftgate all the way.
3 Remove the liftgate trim panel as described in Section 15.
4 Disconnect all electrical connections, ground wires and harness retaining clips from the liftgate. **Note:** *It is a good idea to label all connections to aid the reassembly process.*
5 From the liftgate side, detach the rubber conduit between the body and the liftgate. Pull the wiring harness through the conduit hole and remove it from the liftgate.

6 Detach the liftgate support struts by either unbolting them at the top or using a small screwdriver to separate the ball socket connection. Have an assistant hold the weight of the liftgate.
7 Mark around the liftgate hinges with a pen or a scribe to facilitate realignment during reassembly **(see illustration)**.
8 With the assistant still holding the liftgate, remove the hinge-to-liftgate bolts and lift the liftgate off.
9 Installation is the reverse of removal.

Adjustment

10 Having proper liftgate-to-body alignment is a critical part of a well-functioning liftgate assembly. First check the liftgate hinge pins for excessive play. Fully open the liftgate and lift up and down on the liftgate without lifting the body. If a liftgate has 1/16-inch or more excessive play, the hinges should be replaced.
11 Liftgate-to-body alignment adjustments are made by loosening the hinge-to-body bolts or hinge-to-liftgate bolts and moving the

liftgate. Proper body alignment is achieved when the top of the liftgate is parallel with the roof section and the sides of the liftgate are flush with the rear quarter panels and the bottom of the liftgate is aligned with the lower liftgate sill. If these goals can't be reached by adjusting the hinge-to-body or hinge-to-liftgate bolts, body alignment shims may have to be purchased and inserted behind the hinges to achieve correct alignment.
12 To adjust the liftgate-closed position, scribe a line or mark around the striker plate to provide a reference point, then check that the liftgate latch is contacting the center of the latch striker. If not, adjust the up and down position first.
13 Finally adjust the latch striker sideways position, so that the liftgate panel is flush with the rear quarter panel and provides positive engagement with the latch mechanism.

22 Liftgate latch, lock cylinder and handle - removal and installation

Liftgate latch

Refer to illustration 22.5

1 Disconnect the cable from the negative battery terminal (see Chapter 5, Section 1).
2 Open the liftgate and remove the door trim panel and watershield as described in Section 15.
3 Working through the large access hole, disengage the outside liftgate handle-to-latch cable and the outside liftgate lock-to-latch rod. Disconnect the electrical connector for the power lock.
4 All liftgate lock rods are attached by plastic clips. The plastic clips can be removed by unsnapping the portion engaging the connecting rod, then pulling the rod out of its locating hole.

21.7 Mark around the liftgate hinges so it can be installed in the same position

22.5 Liftgate latch assembly

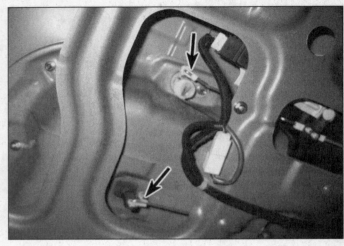

22.8 The rods that connect the handle and lock to the latch are secured with plastic clips

5   Remove the fasteners securing the latch to the liftgate **(see illustration)**. Remove the latch assembly.
6   Installation is the reverse of removal.

Liftgate lock cylinder

Refer to illustration 22.8
7   Open the liftgate and remove the door trim panel as described in Section 15.
8   Working through the large access hole, disengage the outside liftgate lock-to-latch rod **(see illustration)**.
9   All liftgate lock rods are attached by plastic clips. The plastic clips can be removed by unsnapping the portion engaging the connecting rod, then pulling the rod out of its locating hole.
10   Remove the lock cylinder retaining fasteners. Remove the lock cylinder.
11   Installation is the reverse of removal.

Liftgate outside handle

Refer to illustration 22.13
12   Open the liftgate and remove the door trim panel and watershield as described in Section 15.

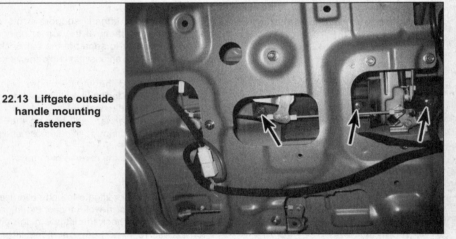

22.13 Liftgate outside handle mounting fasteners

13   Working through the large access hole, disengage the outside liftgate handle-to-latch rod **(see illustration)**.
14   Remove the handle retaining fasteners through the holes in the door frame and detach the handle from the liftgate.
15   Installation is the reverse of removal.

23   Center console - removal and installation

Refer to illustrations 23.1, 23.2 and 23.3
Warning: *The models covered by this manual are equipped with Supplemental Restraint systems (SRS), more commonly known as airbags. Always disable the airbag system before working in the vicinity of any airbag system component to avoid the possibility of accidental deployment of the airbag, which could cause personal injury* (see Chapter 12).
1   Remove the side trim covers at the front of the console **(see illustration)**.
2   Remove the retaining screws from inside the console **(see illustration)**.
3   Loosen the two screws at the front of the shifter handle and pull it off **(see illustration)**. If the button is removed, be sure to reinstall it in the same orientation.
4   Lift off the console.
5   Installation is the reverse of removal. Push the button in part way to align it with the cable end when installing the handle.

23.1 There are exposed side cover screws on each side of the console

23.2 Lift the carpet in the bottom of the console storage area to access the screws beneath

23.3 These screws secure the shift handle; make sure that the button engages the shift mechanism when installing it

24.4 Instrument cluster bezel screws

instrument panel mounting screws. Some of the covers use fasteners, and others are easily pried off with a screwdriver or trim stick. If you're going to remove the instrument panel, remove all of the covers.

2   Disconnect the cable from the negative terminal of the battery (see Chapter 5, Section 1).

Instrument cluster bezel

Refer to illustrations 24.4 and 24.5

3   Refer to Section 25 and remove the steering column covers.

4   Remove the bezel retaining screws **(see illustration)**.

5   Remove the bezel by pulling it rearward **(see illustration)**.

Driver's knee bolster

Refer to illustrations 24.6 and 24.7

6   Remove the three retaining screws **(see illustration)**.

24 Dashboard trim panels - removal and installation

Warning: *Models covered by this manual are equipped with a Supplemental Restraint System (SRS), more commonly known as*
airbags. Always disable the airbag system before working in the vicinity of any airbag system component to avoid the possibility of accidental deployment of the airbag, which could cause personal injury (see Chapter 12).

1   These panels provide access to various

24.5 Pry the bezel rearward to remove it

24.6 The knee bolster is retained by three screws and several concealed clips

24.7 The switch panel can be pried out - disconnect the wiring harnesses after it's loose

24.11 The center trim panel screws are behind the ashtray

24.13 There's no need to remove the heater control knobs prior to removing the trim panel

7   Pry the switch assembly out with a trim stick or a screwdriver wrapped with tape (see illustration). Disconnect the wiring from it.
8   Pull the panel rearward to disengage it from its clips.
9   Installation is the reverse of removal.

Center trim panel

Refer to illustrations 24.11 and 24.13

10   Remove the ashtray.
11   Remove the two screws behind the ashtray (see illustration).
12   Use a trim stick or a screwdriver with the tip wrapped with electrical tape to pry the panel off.
13   Disconnect the wiring from the rear of the assembly (see illustration).
14   Installation is the reverse of the removal procedure. Make sure the clips are engaged properly before pushing the panel firmly into place.

24.15 The glove box door can be lowered after the glove box support cord is disconnected - push inward on its sides to lower it fully

24.17 The glove box door hinge screws can be removed when the door is allowed to fall downward

25.2a Remove the screws from the lower half . . .

25.2b . . . then unsnap the upper and lower covers

Glove box door

Refer to illustrations 24.15 and 24.17

15   Open the glove box and disconnect the support cord **(see illustration)**.
16   Push firmly inward on both sides of the glove box to release it.
17   Remove the screws from the hinge **(see illustration)**.
18   Installation is the reverse of removal.

Glove box side trim panel

19   Remove the trim panel at the right of the glove box by removing the screw at its lower edge.
20   Use a trim stick or a screwdriver with the tip wrapped with electrical tape to pry the panel off.
21   Installation is the reverse of removal.

25   Steering column covers - removal and installation

Refer to illustrations 25.2a, 25.2b and 25.2c

Warning: *Models covered by this manual are equipped with a Supplemental Restraint System (SRS), more commonly known as airbags. Always disable the airbag system before working in the vicinity of any airbag system component to avoid the possibility of accidental deployment of the airbag, which could cause personal injury (see Chapter 12).*

1   Disconnect the cable from the negative terminal of the battery (see Chapter 5, Section 1). Move the column to the lowest position
2   Remove the four lower screws, then separate the halves and remove the upper and lower steering column covers **(see illustrations)**.
3   Installation is the reverse of the removal procedure.

26   Instrument panel - removal and installation

Refer to illustrations 26.8a, 26.8b, 26.8c, 26.9, 26.11, 26.12, 26.14a, 26.14b and 26.14c

Warning: *Models covered by this manual are equipped with a Supplemental Restraint System (SRS), more commonly known as airbags. Always disable the airbag system before working in the vicinity of any airbag system component to avoid the possibility of accidental deployment of the airbag, which could cause personal injury (see Chapter 12).*

Note 1: *This is a difficult procedure for the home mechanic. There are many hidden fasteners, difficult angles to work in and many electrical connectors to tag and disconnect/connect. We recommend that this procedure be done only by an experienced do-it-yourselfer.*

Note 2: *During removal of the instrument panel, make careful notes of how each piece comes off, where it fits in relation to other pieces and what holds it in place. If you note how each part is installed before removing it, getting the instrument panel back together again will be much easier.*

Note 3: *It is not necessary, but it is suggested to remove both front seats to allow additional working space and lessen the chance of damage to the seats during this procedure.*

1   Disconnect the cable from the negative battery terminal (see Chapter 5, Section 1).
2   Refer to Section 27 and remove the front seats for easier access.
3   Remove the multi-function switch (see Chapter 12).
4   Remove the dashboard trim panels (see Section 24) and the center floor console (see Section 23).
5   Remove the glove box (see Section 24).
6   Remove the instrument cluster (see Chapter 12).
7   Disconnect the electrical connector from the passenger's side airbag.
8   Remove the audio unit and air conditioning control panel at the center of the dash-

25.2c Snap this small cover back into place after replacing the lower column cover over the tilt lever

26.8a The audio trim panel is secured by these screws

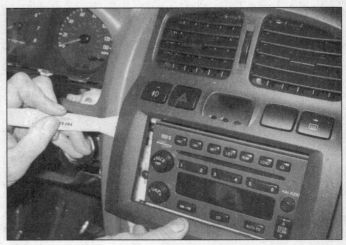

26.8b After removing the screws, pry the trim panel to the rear

26.8c Disconnect the hazard, defogger and fog light switches when you have enough clearance

board **(see illustrations)**.

9   Refer to Section 24 and remove the driver's knee bolster and reinforcement panel.

10   Unscrew the bolts securing the steering column to the instrument panel and lower it (see Chapter 10).

11   Remove the front pillar trim **(see illustration)**.

12   Remove the kick panels **(see illustration)**.

13   A number of electrical connectors must be disconnected in order to remove the instrument panel. Most are designed so that they will only fit on the matching connector (male or female), but if there is any doubt, mark the connectors with masking tape and a marking pen before disconnecting them.

14   Remove all of the fasteners holding the instrument panel to the body **(see illustrations)**. Once all are removed, lift the panel then pull it away from the windshield and take it out through the door opening. **Note:** *This is a two-person job.*

15   Installation is the reverse of removal.

27   Seats - removal and installation

Front seat

Refer to illustrations 27.2a and 27.2b

Warning 1: *The front seat belts on some models are equipped with pre-tensioners, which are pyrotechnic (explosive) devices designed to retract the seat belts in the event of a collision. On models equipped with pre-tension-*

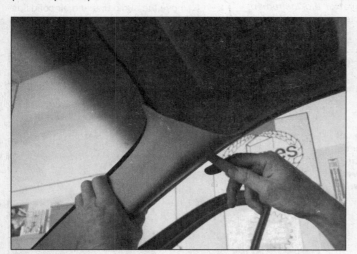

26.11 Pry off the covers from the A pillars using a trim stick or a screwdriver wrapped with electrical tape

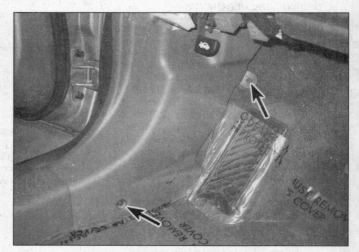

26.12 Pry the kick panels off after removing their retaining screws

26.14a The instrument panel is secured with bolts at the left end . . .

26.14b . . . the right end . . .

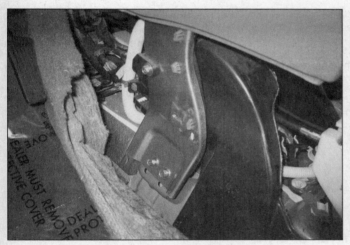

26.14c . . . and at the center

27.2a Remove the front . . .

ers, do not remove the front seat belt retractor assemblies, and do not disconnect the electrical connectors leading to the assemblies. Problems with the pre-tensioners will turn on the SRS (airbag) warning light on the dash. If any pre-tensioner problems are suspected, take the vehicle to a dealer service department. Also on these models, be sure to disable the airbag system (see Chapter 12).

Warning 2: On models with side-impact airbags, be sure to disarm the airbag system before beginning this procedure (see Chapter 12).

1   Pry off any plastic covers to access the seat tracks and their mounting bolts. Keep them in order, as they are not identical.

2   Remove the retaining bolts (**see illustrations**).

27.2b . . . and the rear bolts

27.5 After lifting the seat cushion, remove the plastic cover

27.6 The seat cushion assembly can now be unbolted
and removed

3   Tilt the seat upward to access the under-side, then disconnect any electrical connectors and lift the seat from the vehicle.
4   Installation is the reverse of removal.

Rear seat

Refer to illustrations 27.5 and 27.6

5   Flip the seat cushion up and forward, then remove the plastic seat bottom tray **(see illustration)**.

6   Remove the bolts from the lower seat **(see illustration).** Lift out the seat cushion assembly.
7   Remove the bolts from the seat back and lift it out.
8   Installation is the reverse of removal.

Chapter 12
Chassis electrical system

Contents

1 General information

The electrical system is a 12-volt, negative ground type. Power for the lights and all electrical accessories is supplied by a lead/acid-type battery, which is charged by the alternator.

This Chapter covers repair and service procedures for the various electrical components not associated with the engine. Information on the battery, alternator and starter motor can be found in Chapter 5.

It should be noted that when portions of the electrical system are serviced, the cable should be disconnected from the negative battery terminal to prevent electrical shorts and/or fires.

2 Electrical troubleshooting - general information

Refer to illustrations 2.5a and 2.5b

A typical electrical circuit consists of an electrical component, any switches, relays, motors, fuses, fusible links or circuit breakers related to that component and the wiring and connectors that link the component to both the battery and the chassis. To help you pinpoint an electrical circuit problem, wiring diagrams are included at the end of this Chapter.

Before tackling any troublesome electrical circuit, first study the appropriate wiring diagrams to get a complete understanding of what makes up that individual circuit. For instance, noting whether other components related to the circuit are operating correctly can often narrow down potential causes of trouble. If several components or circuits fail at one time, chances are the problem is in a fuse or ground connection, because several circuits are often routed through the same fuse and ground connections.

Electrical problems usually stem from simple causes, such as loose or corroded connections, a blown fuse, a melted fusible link or a failed relay. Visually inspect the condition of all fuses, wires and connections in a problem circuit before troubleshooting the circuit.

If test equipment and instruments are going to be utilized, use the diagrams to plan ahead of time where you will make the necessary connections in order to accurately pinpoint the trouble spot.

2.5a   The most useful tool for electrical troubleshooting is a digital multimeter that can check volts, amps, and test continuity

2.5b   A simple test light is a very handy tool for testing voltage

The basic tools needed for electrical troubleshooting include a circuit tester or voltmeter (a 12-volt bulb with a set of test leads can also be used), a continuity tester, which includes a bulb, battery and set of test leads, and a jumper wire, preferably with a circuit breaker incorporated, which can be used to bypass electrical components **(see illustrations)**. Before attempting to locate a problem with test instruments, use the wiring diagram(s) to decide where to make the connections.

Voltage checks

Refer to illustration 2.6

Voltage checks should be performed if a circuit is not functioning properly. Connect one lead of a circuit tester to either the negative battery terminal or a known good ground. Connect the other lead to a connector in the circuit being tested, preferably nearest to the

battery or fuse **(see illustration)**. If the bulb of the tester lights, voltage is present, which means that the part of the circuit between the connector and the battery is problem free. Continue checking the rest of the circuit in the same fashion. When you reach a point at which no voltage is present, the problem lies between that point and the last test point with voltage. Most of the time the problem can be traced to a loose connection. **Note:** *Keep in mind that some circuits receive voltage only when the ignition key is in the Accessory or Run position.*

Finding a short

One method of finding shorts in a live circuit is to remove the fuse and connect a test light in place of the fuse terminals (fabricate two jumper wires with small spade terminals, plug the jumper wires into the fuse box and connect the test light). There should be voltage present in the circuit. Move the suspected

wiring harness from side-to-side while watching the test light. If the bulb goes off, there is a short to ground somewhere in that area, probably where the insulation has rubbed through.

Ground check

Perform a ground test to check whether a component is properly grounded. Disconnect the battery and connect one lead of a continuity tester or multimeter (set to the ohm scale), to a known good ground. Connect the other lead to the wire or ground connection being tested. If the resistance is low (less than 5 ohms), the ground is good. If the bulb on a self-powered test light does not go on, the ground is not good.

Continuity check

Refer to illustration 2.9

A continuity check is done to determine if there are any breaks in a circuit - if it is pass-

2.6   In use, a basic test light's lead is clipped to a known good ground, then the pointed probe can test connectors, wires or electrical sockets - if the bulb lights, the circuit being tested has battery voltage

2.9   With a multimeter set to the ohm scale, resistance can be checked across two terminals - when checking for continuity, a low reading indicates continuity, a high reading or infinity indicates lack of continuity

3.1a The engine compartment fuse and relay box is located at the left side of the engine compartment. There's a guide on the cover

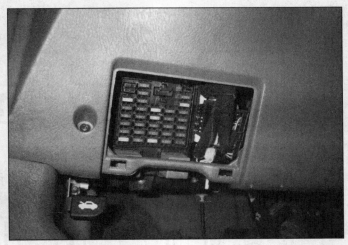

3.1b There's also a fuse box inside the vehicle, at the left end of the dash, behind a small access door marked OBD

ing electricity properly. With the circuit off (no power in the circuit), a self-powered continuity tester or multimeter can be used to check the circuit. Connect the test leads to both ends of the circuit (or to the "power" end and a good ground), and if the test light comes on the circuit is passing current properly **(see illustration)**. If the resistance is low (less than 5 ohms), there is continuity; if the reading is 10,000 ohms or higher, there is a break somewhere in the circuit. The same procedure can be used to test a switch, by connecting the continuity tester to the switch terminals. With the switch turned On, the test light should come on (or low resistance should be indicated on a meter).

Finding an open circuit

When diagnosing for possible open circuits, it is often difficult to locate them by sight because the connectors hide oxidation or terminal misalignment. Merely wiggling a connector on a sensor or in the wiring harness may correct the open circuit condition. Remember this when an open circuit is indicated when troubleshooting a circuit. Intermit-

tent problems may also be caused by oxidized or loose connections.

Electrical troubleshooting is simple if you keep in mind that all electrical circuits are basically electricity running from the battery, through the wires, switches, relays, fuses and fusible links to each electrical component (light bulb, motor, etc.) and to ground, from which it is passed back to the battery. Any electrical problem is an interruption in the flow of electricity to and from the battery.

Connectors

Most electrical connections on these vehicles are made with multi-wire plastic connectors. The mating halves of many connectors are secured with locking clips molded into the plastic connector shells. The mating halves of large connectors, such as some of those under the instrument panel, are held together by a bolt through the center of the connector.

To separate a connector with locking clips, use a small screwdriver to pry the clips apart carefully, then separate the connector halves. Pull only on the shell, never pull

on the wiring harness as you may damage the individual wires and terminals inside the connectors. Look at the connector closely before trying to separate the halves. Often the locking clips are engaged in a way that is not immediately clear. Additionally, many connectors have more than one set of clips.

Each pair of connector terminals has a male half and a female half. When you look at the end view of a connector in a diagram, be sure to understand whether the view shows the harness side or the component side of the connector. Connector halves are mirror images of each other, and a terminal shown on the right side end-view of one half will be on the left side end view of the other half.

3 Fuses and fusible links - general information

Fuses

Refer to illustrations 3.1a, 3.1b and 3.3

The electrical circuits of the vehicle are protected by a combination of fuses, circuit breakers and fusible links. Fuse blocks are located under the left side of the instrument panel and in the engine compartment **(see illustrations)**.

Each of the fuses is designed to protect a specific circuit, and the various circuits are identified on the fuse panel cover.

Miniaturized fuses are employed in the fuse blocks. These compact fuses, with blade terminal design, allow fingertip removal and replacement. If an electrical component fails, always check the fuse first. The best way to check a fuse is with a test light. Check for power at the exposed terminal tips of each fuse. If power is present on one side of the fuse but not the other, the fuse is blown. A blown fuse can also be confirmed by visually inspecting it **(see illustration)**.

3.3 When a fuse blows, the element between the terminals melts

BAD

GOOD

5.3a These two relays are typical normally open types; the one above completes a single circuit (terminal 5 to terminal 3) when energized - the lower relay type completes two circuits (6 and 7, and 3 and 5) when energized

5.3b These relays are normally closed types, where current flows though one circuit until the relay is energized, which interrupts that circuit and completes the second circuit

Be sure to replace blown fuses with the correct type. Fuses of different ratings are physically interchangeable, but only fuses of the proper rating should be used. Replacing a fuse with one of a higher or lower value than specified is not recommended. Each electrical circuit needs a specific amount of protection. The amperage value of each fuse is molded into the fuse body.

If the replacement fuse immediately fails, don't replace it again until the cause of the problem is isolated and corrected. In most cases, this will be a short circuit in the wiring caused by a broken or deteriorated wire.

Fusible links

Some circuits are protected by fusible links. The links are used in circuits that are not ordinarily fused, such as the high-current side of the charging or starting circuits. Conventional inline fusible links, such as those used in the starter cable, are characterized by a bulge in the cable. Newer cartridge-type fusible links, which are similar in appearance to a large cartridge-type fuse, are located in their own fusible link block in the engine compartment fuse and relay box **(see illustration 3.1a)**. After disconnecting the cable from the negative battery terminal, simply remove the fusible link and replace it with a unit of the same amperage.

4   Circuit breakers - general information

Circuit breakers protect certain circuits, such as the power windows or heated seats. Depending on the vehicle's accessories, there might be circuit breakers in or near either of the fuse and relay boxes.

Because the circuit breakers reset automatically, an electrical overload in a circuit-breaker-protected system will cause the circuit to fail momentarily, then come back on. If the circuit does not come back on, check it immediately.

For a basic check, pull the circuit breaker up out of its socket on the fuse panel, but just far enough to probe with a voltmeter. The breaker should still contact the sockets.

With the voltmeter negative lead on a good chassis ground, touch each end prong of the circuit breaker with the positive meter probe. There should be battery voltage at each end. If there is battery voltage only at one end, the circuit breaker must be replaced.

Some circuit breakers must be reset manually.

5   Relays - general information and testing

General information

1   Several electrical accessories in the vehicle, such as the fuel injection system, horns, starter, and fog lamps use relays to transmit

5.6 To test a typical four-terminal normally open relay, connect an ohmmeter to the two terminals of the power circuit - the meter should indicate continuity with the relay energized and no continuity with the relay not energized

6.5 On most models the turn signal and hazard flasher relay is located near the instrument panel fuse/relay block

the electrical signal to the component. Relays use a low-current circuit (the control circuit) to open and close a high-current circuit (the power circuit). If the relay is defective, that component will not operate properly. Most relays are mounted in the engine compartment fuse/relay box, with some specialized relays located in the underhood box at the fender. If a faulty relay is suspected, it can be removed and tested using the procedure below or by a dealer service department or a repair shop. Defective relays must be replaced as a unit. Identification of the circuit the relay controls is often marked on the top of the relay, but the decal or imprint inside the cover of the relay box should also indicate which circuits they control.

Testing

Refer to illustrations 5.3a, 5.3b and 5.6

2   Refer to the wiring diagrams for the circuit to determine the proper connections for the relay you're testing. If you can't determine the correct connection from the wiring diagrams, however, you may be able to determine the test connections from the information that follows.

3   There are four basic types of relays used on these models **(see illustrations)**. Some are normally open type and some normally closed, while others include a circuit of each type.

4   On most relays, two of the terminals are the relay control circuit (they connect to the relay coil which, when energized, closes the large contacts to complete the circuit). The other terminals are the power circuit (they are connected together within the relay when the control-circuit coil is energized).

5   Some relays may be marked as an aid to help you determine which terminals make up the control circuit and which make up the power circuit. If the relay is not marked, refer to the wiring diagrams at the end of this Chap-

ter to determine the proper hook-ups for the relay you're testing.

6   To test a relay, connect an ohmmeter across the two terminals of the power circuit, continuity should not be indicated **(see illustration)**. Now connect a fused jumper wire between one of the two control circuit terminals and the positive battery terminal. Connect another jumper wire between the other control circuit terminal and ground. When the connections are made, the relay should click and continuity should be indicated on the meter. On some relays, polarity may be critical, so, if the relay doesn't click, try swapping the jumper wires on the control circuit terminals.

7   If the relay fails the above test, replace it.

---

6   Turn signal and hazard flasher relay - check and replacement

Warning: *The models covered by this manual are equipped with Supplemental Restraint Systems (SRS), more commonly known as airbags. Always disable the airbag system before working in the vicinity of any airbag system component to avoid the possibility of accidental deployment of the airbags, which could cause personal injury (see Section 24).*

Check

1   When the turn signal and hazard flasher relay is functioning properly, you can hear a click when it's operating.

2   If the turn signals fail on one side or the other and the flasher unit does not make its characteristic clicking sound, or if a bulb on one side of the vehicle flashes much faster than normal but the bulb at the other end of the vehicle (on the same side) doesn't light at all, a turn signal bulb is probably faulty.

3   If both turn signals fail to blink, the problem might be a blown fuse, a faulty flasher

unit, a defective switch or a loose or open connection. If a quick check of the fuse box indicates that the turn signal fuse has blown, check the wiring for a short before installing a new fuse.

Replacement

Refer to illustration 6.5

Note: *The turn signal and hazard flasher relay is located behind the knee bolster, next to the instrument panel junction block on most models.*

4   Open the fuse and relay center access door (near the driver's left knee) or remove the knee bolster completely (see Chapter 11).

5   Locate the turn signal and hazard flasher relay near the instrument panel fuse/relay block **(see illustration)**.

6   Disconnect the electrical connector from the flasher unit.

7   Remove the flasher unit from the instrument panel junction block.

8   Make sure that the replacement unit is identical to the original. Compare the old one to the new one before installing it.

9   Installation is the reverse of removal.

---

7   Ignition switch and key lock cylinder - replacement

Refer to illustrations 7.4, 7.5, 7.6a and 7.6b

Warning: *The models covered by this manual are equipped with Supplemental Restraint Systems (SRS), more commonly known as airbags. Always disable the airbag system before working in the vicinity of any airbag system component to avoid the possibility of accidental deployment of the airbag(s), which could cause personal injury (see Section 24).*

1   Disconnect the cable from the negative terminal of the battery (see Chapter 5, Section 1).

7.4 Disconnect all the electrical wiring harnesses from the switch unit

7.5 Remove the screws and detach the shift interlock cable

2   Remove the upper and lower steering column covers (see Chapter 11).
3   Remove the driver's knee bolster trim panel (see Chapter 11).
4   Disconnect the electrical connectors from the ignition switch **(see illustration)**.
5   Disconnect the shift interlock cable from the bottom of the ignition lock assembly **(see illustration)**.
6   The ignition key assembly is mounted to the steering column using a pinch-bolt with a break-off head **(see illustration)**. Attach locking pliers to clamp the bolt head so the nut on the rear can be removed **(see illustration)**.
7   Pull the switch out and remove it from the key lock cylinder housing.
8   The lock cylinder can now be removed from the assembly.
9   Installation is the reverse of the removal. Tighten the new bolt until the head breaks off.

8   Multi-function switches - replacement

Refer to illustrations 8.3 and 8.4
Warning: *The models covered by this manual are equipped with Supplemental Restraint Systems (SRS), more commonly known as airbags. Always disable the airbag system before working in the vicinity of any airbag system components to avoid the possibility of accidental deployment of the airbag(s), which could cause personal injury (see Section 24).*
Note: *The multi-function switches (also referred to as combination switches or steering column switches) are two separate switch units connected to a central plastic housing known as the switch body, which encircles the steering column. The left multi-function switch controls the headlights and the turn signals; the right switch controls the wind-shield washer/wiper system. Either switch can be replaced separately.*
1   Disconnect the cable from the negative terminal of the battery (see Chapter 5, Section 1).
2   Remove the steering wheel and the upper and lower steering column covers (see Chapters 10 and 11).
3   Disconnect the electrical connectors from the switch **(see illustration)**.
4   Remove the switch **(see illustration)**.
5   Installation is the reverse of removal. If the clockspring has turned and is not centered, turn the hub in either direction until it stops (don't apply too much force). Now, rotate the hub in the other direction, counting the number of turns it takes to reach the opposite stop. Divide that number by two, then turn the hub back that many turns, approximately, until the neutral position indicator is aligned with its corresponding mark.

7.6a The pinch-bolt that the factory uses to clamp the ignition switch has a head that is broken off during assembly - the smooth head must be held from turning while the nut is removed

7.6b Locking pliers will secure the shear-head bolt in order for the nut on the other side of the clamp to be removed

8.3 Unplug the wiring from the multi-function switch

8.4 Multi-function switch screw locations

9.2 The instrument dimmer control and TCS switch are in a panel that can simply be pried out of the driver's knee bolster with a trim tool or a screwdriver wrapped with electrical tape

Instrument brightness control and traction control switch

Refer to illustration 9.2

2   Carefully pry the switch panel out of the instrument panel with a suitable trim panel tool **(see illustration)**.
3   To replace the switches, disconnect the electrical connector and remove the switch from the switch panel.
4   Installation is the reverse of the removal procedure.

Hazard warning light, fog light and rear window defogger switches

Refer to illustrations 9.6, 9.7 and 9.8

5   Remove the lower center trim panel (see Chapter 11).
6   Remove the two screws from the bottom of the upper trim panel **(see illustration)**.
7   Use a trim tool to pry the upper panel off **(see illustration)**.
8   Disconnect the wiring from the switches

9   Instrument panel switches - replacement

Warning: *The models covered by this manual are equipped with Supplemental Restraint Systems (SRS), more commonly known as airbags. Always disable the airbag system* *before working in the vicinity of any airbag system component to avoid the possibility of accidental deployment of the airbag(s), which could cause personal injury (see Section 24).*

1   Disconnect the cable from the negative battery terminal (see Chapter 5, Section 1).

9.6 These screws secure the bottom of the center trim panel - the rest of the panel is held by clips

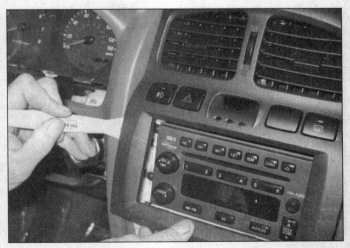

9.7 Use a plastic tool to pry the panel rearward and release the clips

and remove the assembly **(see illustration)**. **Note:** *The fog light and defogger switches have identical electrical connectors. Make clear marks on them to avoid mixing them up later.*

9   Remove the individual switches as necessary.

10   Installation is the reverse of removal.

10   Instrument cluster - removal and installation

Refer to illustration 10.3

Warning: *The models covered by this manual are equipped with Supplemental Restraint Systems (SRS), more commonly known as airbags. Always disable the airbag system before working in the vicinity of any airbag system component to avoid the possibility of accidental deployment of the airbag(s), which could cause personal injury (see Section 24).*

1   Disconnect the cable from the negative battery terminal (see Chapter 5, Section 1).

2   Remove the instrument cluster bezel (see Chapter 11).

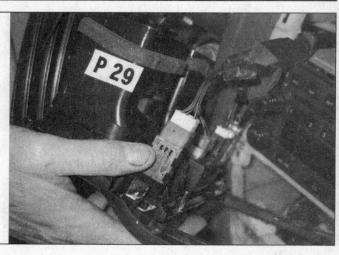

9.8 When the panel is loose, you will be able to disconnect the wiring and replace the switch individually

3   Remove the cluster mounting screws **(see illustration)** and pull the instrument cluster towards the steering wheel.

4   Disconnect the electrical connectors from the rear of the cluster.

5   Installation is the reverse of removal.

11   Radio and speakers - removal and installation

Warning: *The models covered by this manual are equipped with Supplemental Restraint Systems (SRS), more commonly known as airbags. Always disable the airbag system before working in the vicinity of any airbag system component to avoid the possibility of accidental deployment of the airbag(s), which could cause personal injury (see Section 24).*

Radio

Refer to illustrations 11.2 and 11.3

1   Disconnect the cable from the negative battery terminal (see Chapter 5, Section 1).

2   Remove the center trim panel (see Section 9). Remove the radio mounting screws **(see illustration)**.

3   Pull out the radio and disconnect the electrical connectors from the radio assembly **(see illustration)**.

4   Installation is the reverse of removal.

10.3 To detach the instrument cluster, remove these mounting screws

11.2 Remove the center trim panel to remove the audio unit mounting screws

11.3 Pull out the antenna lead and disconnect the wiring harnesses

Speakers

Refer to illustration 11.8

5   To access the upper speakers, pry off the speaker panel from the inside of the mirror.

6   Disconnect the wiring and remove the speaker from the panel.

7   To access the main door speaker, first remove the door trim panel (see Chapter 11).

8   Disconnect the electrical connector from the speaker, remove the speaker mounting screws **(see illustration)** and remove the speaker.

9   Installation is the reverse of removal.

12   Antenna - replacement

The vehicles covered by this manual are equipped with a wire grid-type antenna attached to the rear window glass. If there's a problem with it, you can repair the antenna grid the same way that you'd repair the rear window defogger grid (see Section 14).

13   Wiper motor - check and replacement

Wiper motor circuit check

Note: *Refer to the wiring diagrams for the following checks. When checking for voltage, probe a grounded 12-volt test light to each terminal at a connector until it lights; this verifies voltage (power) at the terminal. If the following checks fail to locate the problem, have the system diagnosed by a dealer service department or other properly equipped repair facility.*

1   If the wipers work slowly, make sure that the battery is in good condition and has a strong charge (see Chapter 5). If the battery is in good condition, remove the wiper motor

11.8 Main door speaker mounting screws

(see below) and operate the wiper arms by hand. Check for binding linkage and pivots. Lubricate or repair the linkage or pivots as necessary. Reinstall the wiper motor. If the wipers still operate slowly, check for loose or corroded connections, especially the ground connection. If all connections look OK, replace the motor.

2   If the wipers fail to operate when activated, check the fuse in the driver's side interior fuse panel. If the fuse is OK, connect a jumper wire between the wiper motor's ground terminal and ground, then retest. If the motor works now, repair the ground connection. If the motor still doesn't work, turn the wiper switch to the HI position and check for voltage at the motor. **Note:** *The cowl cover will have to be removed (see Chapter 11) to access the wiper motor electrical connector.*

3   If there's voltage at the connector, remove the motor and check it off the vehicle with fused jumper wires from the battery. If the motor now works, check for binding linkage (see Step 1). If the motor still doesn't work, replace it. If there's no voltage to the motor, check for voltage at the wiper control relays. If

there's voltage at the wiper control relays and no voltage at the wiper motor, have the switch tested. If the switch is OK, the wiper control relay is probably bad. See Section 5 for relay testing.

4   If the interval (delay) function is inoperative, check the continuity of all the wiring between the switch and wiper control module.

5   If the wipers stop at the position they're in when the switch is turned off (fail to park), check for voltage at the park feed wire of the wiper motor connector when the wiper switch is OFF but the ignition is ON. If no voltage is present, check for an open circuit between the wiper motor and the fuse panel.

Replacement

Windshield wiper motor

Refer to illustrations 13.6, 13.7, 13.10 and 13.11

6   Remove the wiper arm mounting nuts **(see illustration)**.

7   Mark the position of each wiper arm to its shaft, then remove the arms **(see illustration)**.

13.6 The wiper arms are secured to their shafts by decorative nuts

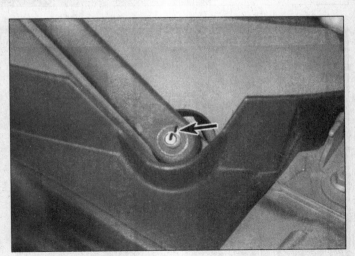

13.7 Mark the positions of the arms so they can be correctly installed

8   Remove the plastic cowl cover (see Chapter 11).
9   Disconnect the electrical connector from the wiper motor.
10   Remove the wiper motor and link assembly mounting bolts **(see illustration)** and remove the wiper motor and link assembly from the cowl area.
11   Use a screwdriver to pry the linkage rod from the crank arm pivot of the wiper motor **(see illustration)**.
12   Remove the crank arm nut, mark the relationship of the crank arm to the motor shaft and remove the crank arm from the shaft.
13   Remove the wiper motor mounting bolts and separate the motor from the link rod assembly.
14   Installation is the reverse of removal.

Rear wiper motor

Refer to illustration 13.19

15   Remove the rear wiper arm retaining nut (see Step 6).
16   Mark the relationship of the rear wiper arm to the motor shaft, then remove the arm (see Step 7).
17   Remove the trim panel from the rear

13.10 The wiper assembly is retained by three bolts - remove them after disconnecting the wiring, then lift the entire unit out of the cowl

hatch (see Chapter 11).
18   Disconnect the electrical connector from the rear wiper motor.
19   Remove the rear wiper motor mounting bolts **(see illustration)** and remove the motor.
20   Installation is the reverse of removal.

14   Rear window defogger - check and repair

1   The rear window defogger consists of a number of horizontal elements baked onto the glass surface.
2   Small breaks in the element can be repaired without removing the rear window.

Check

Refer to illustrations 14.4, 14.5 and 14.7

3   Turn the ignition switch and defogger system switches to the ON position. Using a voltmeter, place the positive probe against the defogger grid positive terminal and the negative probe against the ground terminal. If battery voltage is not indicated, check the fuse, defogger switch and related wiring. If voltage is indicated, but all or part of the defogger doesn't heat, proceed with the following tests.
4   When measuring voltage during the next two tests, wrap a piece of aluminum foil around the tip of the voltmeter positive probe and press the foil against the heating element with your finger **(see illustration)**. Place the negative probe on the defogger grid ground terminal.

13.11 Pry the link from the crank arm; the crank arm can then be removed from the motor shaft if required

13.19 Liftgate wiper motor mounting bolts

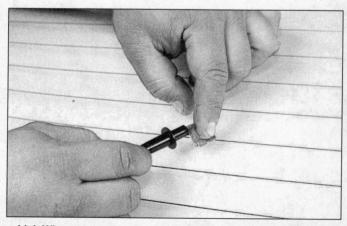

14.4 When measuring the voltage at the rear window defogger grid, wrap a piece of aluminum foil around the positive probe of the voltmeter and press the foil against the wire with your finger

14.5 To determine if a heating element has broken, check the voltage at the center of each element - if the voltage is 5 or 6-volts, the element is unbroken - if the voltage is 10 or 12-volts, the element is broken between the center and the ground side - if there is no voltage, the element is broken between the center and the positive side

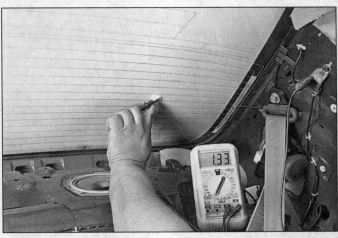

14.7 To find the break, place the voltmeter negative lead against the defogger ground terminal, place the voltmeter positive lead with the foil strip against the heating element at the positive terminal end and slide it toward the negative terminal end - the point at which the voltmeter reading changes abruptly is the point at which the element is broken

5   Check the voltage at the center of each heating element (see illustration). If the voltage is 5 or 6-volts, the element is okay (there is no break). If the voltage is zero, the element is broken between the center of the element and the positive end. If the voltage is 10 to 12-volts the element is broken between the center of the element and ground. Check each heating element.

6   Connect the negative lead to a good body ground. The reading should stay the same. If it doesn't, the ground connection is bad.

7   To find the break, place the voltmeter negative probe against the defogger ground terminal. Place the voltmeter positive probe with the foil strip against the heating element at the positive terminal end and slide it toward the negative terminal end. The point at which the voltmeter deflects from several volts to zero is the point at which the heating element is broken (see illustration).

Repair

Refer to illustration 14.13

8   Repair the break in the element using a repair kit specifically recommended for this purpose, available at most auto parts stores. Included in this kit is plastic conductive epoxy.

9   Prior to repairing a break, turn off the system and allow it to cool off for a few minutes.

10   Lightly buff the element area with fine steel wool, then clean it thoroughly with rubbing alcohol.

11   Use masking tape to mask off the area being repaired.

12   Thoroughly mix the epoxy, following the instructions provided with the repair kit.

13   Apply the epoxy material to the slit in the masking tape, overlapping the undamaged area about 3/4-inch on either end (see illustration).

14   Allow the repair to cure for 24 hours before removing the tape and using the system.

15 Headlight bulbs - replacement

Refer to illustrations 15.2 and 15.4

Warning: *Gas-filled bulbs are under pressure and may shatter if the surface is scratched or the bulb is dropped. Wear eye protection and handle the bulbs carefully, grasping only the base whenever possible. Do not touch the surface of the bulb with your fingers because the oil from your skin could cause it to overheat and fail prematurely. If you do touch the bulb surface, clean it with rubbing alcohol.*

1   Refer to Section 16 and remove the headlight housing, disconnecting the wiring harnesses as you do so. **Note:** *The bulbs are accessible without removing the entire assembly, but it's easier with the assembly on a workbench.*

2   Remove the cover from the rear of the housing (see illustration).

3   Disconnect the wiring.

4   Release the retaining spring and pull out

14.13 To use a defogger repair kit, apply masking tape to the inside of the window at the damaged area, then brush on the special conductive coating

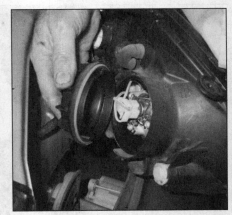

15.2 Unscrew the cover from the rear of the headlight housing

15.4 The spring-loaded wire retains the bulb

16.1 Remove these three bolts . . .

the old bulb **(see illustration)**.

5   Without touching the bulb glass with your bare fingers, insert the new bulb assembly into the headlight housing.

6   Attach the bulb retaining spring and connect the wiring.

7   Install the cover, connect the wiring harness and replace the headlight assembly.

---

16   Headlight housing - replacement

Refer to illustrations 16.1 and 16.2
Warning: *These vehicles are equipped with gas-filled headlight bulbs that are under pressure and may shatter if the surface is damaged or the bulb is dropped. Wear eye protection and handle the bulbs carefully, grasping only the base whenever possible. Do not touch the surface of the bulb with your fingers because the oil from your skin could cause it to overheat and fail prematurely. If you do touch the bulb surface, clean it with rubbing alcohol.*

16.2 . . . then remove the headlight assembly

1   Open the hood for access to the mounting bolts **(see illustration)**.

2   Remove the three headlight mounting bolts and maneuver the assembly from the bumper cover **(see illustration)**.

3   Disconnect the wiring from the headlight assembly.

4   Installation is the reverse of removal.

5   Be sure to check headlight adjustment when you're done (see Section 17).

---

17   Headlights - adjustment

Refer to illustrations 17.2, 17.5a and 17.5b
Note: *The headlights must be aimed correctly. If adjusted incorrectly they could blind the driver of an oncoming vehicle and cause a serious accident or seriously reduce your ability to see the road. The headlights should be checked for proper aim every 12 months and any time a new headlight is installed or front-end bodywork is performed. It should be*

emphasized that the following procedure is only an interim step, which will provide temporary adjustment until a properly equipped shop can adjust the headlights.

1   There are several methods of adjusting the headlights. The simplest method requires masking tape, a blank wall and a level floor.

2   Position masking tape vertically on the wall in reference to the vehicle centerline and the centerlines of both headlights **(see illustration)**.

3   Position a horizontal tape line in reference to the centerline of all the headlights. **Note:** *It may be easier to position the tape on the wall with the vehicle parked only a few inches away.*

4   Adjustment should be made with the vehicle parked 25 feet from the wall, sitting level, the gas tank half-full and no unusually heavy load in the vehicle.

5   With the low beams on, position the high intensity zone so it is two inches below the horizontal line. Make the adjustment by turning the adjusting screw to raise or lower the beam **(see illustrations)**.

6   With the high beams on, the high intensity zone should be vertically centered with the exact center just below the horizontal line. **Note:** *It may not be possible to position the headlight aim exactly for both high and low beams. If a compromise must be made, keep in mind that the low beams are the most used and have the greatest effect on driver safety.*

7   Have the headlights adjusted by a dealer service department or service station at the earliest opportunity.

---

18   Horn - check and replacement

Warning: *The models covered by this manual are equipped with Supplemental Restraint Systems (SRS), more commonly known as* *airbags. Always disable the airbag system before working in the vicinity of any airbag system components to avoid the possibility of accidental deployment of the airbag(s), which could cause personal injury (see Section 24).*

Check

Note: *Check the fuses before beginning electrical diagnosis.*

1   Disconnect the electrical connector from the horn.

2   To test the horn, connect battery voltage to the horn terminal with a jumper wire. If the horn doesn't sound, replace it.

3   If the horn does sound, check for voltage at the terminal when the horn button is depressed. If there's voltage at the terminal, check for a bad ground at the horn.

4   If there's no voltage at the horn, check the relay (see Section 5).

5   If the relay is OK, check for voltage to the relay power and control circuits. If either of the circuits is not receiving voltage, inspect the wiring between the relay and the fuse panel.

6   If both relay circuits are receiving voltage, depress the horn button and check the circuit from the relay to the horn button for continuity to ground. If there's no continuity, check the circuit for an open. If there's no open circuit, replace the horn button.

7   If there's continuity to ground through the horn button, check for an open or short in the circuit from the relay to the horn.

Replacement

Refer to illustration 18.9

Note: *There are two horns. One is located behind the left headlight assembly and the other is located in the center of the vehicle in front of the condenser (on most models).*

17.2 Headlight adjustment details

17.5a Some of the headlight adjusters have caps that must be flipped open

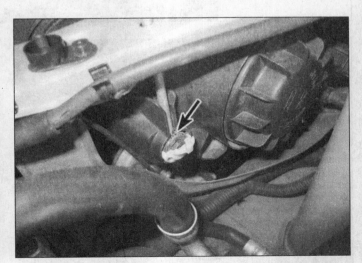

17.5b To turn the adjuster wheels, insert a Phillips screwdriver into the hole in the radiator support, engage the head of the screwdriver with the teeth on the adjuster wheel and turn the wheel

8   For access to the center-mounted horn (on models so equipped), refer to Chapter 11 and remove the bumper cover.
9   Disconnect the electrical connector **(see illustration)**.
10   Remove the bracket bolt.
11   Installation is the reverse of removal.

---

19   Bulb replacement

Exterior light bulbs

Front turn signal bulbs

Refer to illustration 19.2

Note: *The front turn signal/parking and side-marker light bulbs are located in the headlight housing.*

1   Reach behind the headlight housing. The bulbs are all accessible without removing the headlight assembly.
2   Remove the bulb holder from the headlight housing **(see illustration)**.
3   Remove the bulb from the holder.
4   Installation is the reverse of removal.

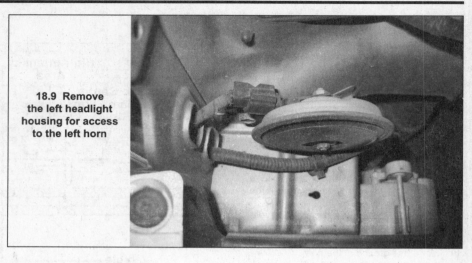

18.9 Remove the left headlight housing for access to the left horn

Front side marker lights

Refer to illustration 19.6

5   Remove the mounting screw from the lens. Maneuver the assembly out through the hole in the fender.

6   Disconnect the wiring harness from the bulb holder **(see illustration)**.
7   Turn the bulb holder counterclockwise to remove it.
8   Pull the bulb from its socket.
9   Installation is the reverse of removal.

Fog lamp bulbs

Refer to illustration 19.11

10   Refer to Chapter 11 and remove the front bumper cover. Alternatively, you can remove the plastic inner fender liners, although reaching through the opening is more difficult.
11   Disconnect the electrical connector from the fog lamp bulb holder **(see illustration)**.
12   Turn the fog lamp bulb holder counterclockwise and pull it out of the fog lamp housing.
13   Installation is the reverse of removal.

Center high-mounted brake light

Refer to illustrations 19.14 and 19.15

Note: *The center high-mounted brake light bulb is located in the upper edge of the rear hatch.*

19.2 To remove the bulb holder for the front turn signal/parking light bulb, rotate it counterclockwise and pull it out of the headlight housing

19.6 To remove the front turn signal/parking and sidemarker light unit, remove the screw and slide the unit rearward

19.11 The fog lights are mounted in the front bumper cover - either remove the bumper cover or the inner fender liner for access

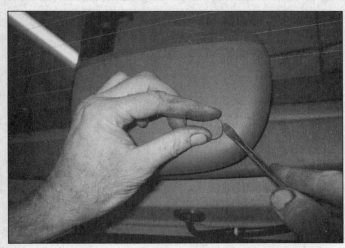

19.14 The center high-mounted brake light screws have covers that can be removed with a screwdriver

19.15 Disconnect the wiring harness and disassemble the housing to access the bulbs

16   Remove the center high-mounted brake light bulb holder from the housing.

17   Remove the center high-mounted brake light bulb from the holder.

18   Installation is the reverse of removal.

Rear brake/tail, turn signal, brake and back-up light bulbs

Refer to illustrations 19.19, 19.20, 19.21 and 19.22

19   Open the rear hatch. Use a Phillips screwdriver to remove the two mounting screws **(see illustration)**.

20   Pull the forward section of the light assembly straight out from the side of the vehicle to release the front pin **(see illustration)**.

21   Remove the bulb holder from the taillight housing by turning it counter-clockwise **(see illustration)**.

22   Remove the bulb from its holder **(see illustration)**.

23   Installation is the reverse of removal.

19.19 The taillight housing is retained by two screws at the rear . . .

19.20 . . . and a stud at the front; be sure to pull it out to the side of the vehicle - not towards the rear

14   Open the rear hatch and remove the screw covers **(see illustration)**, then remove the mounting screws.

15   Disconnect the electrical connector from the center high-mounted brake light bulb holder **(see illustration)**.

19.21 Rotate the taillight bulb holders to pull them out . . .

19.22 . . . then remove the bulbs

19.25a Pry down in this area of the dome light lens to avoid breaking the tabs

19.25b The cargo area light also has a specific area to insert a screwdriver to avoid breakage

License plate light bulbs

24   Remove the two screws securing the license plate light housing(s) and pull the housing from the liftgate. Detach the bulb holder from the housing. Pull the bulb straight out of the holder to replace it.

Interior light bulbs

Luggage compartment light and dome light bulbs

Refer to illustrations 19.25a, 19.25b and 19.26

25   Remove the lens from the map reading light housing by prying it off with a screwdriver inserted into the small slot **(see illustrations)**.
26   Lift the lens off and remove the bulb from the terminals **(see illustration)**.
27   Installation is the reverse of removal.

Glove box light

Note: *Some models have glove box light bulbs that are replaceable by prying the lens down from inside the glove compartment.*
28   Referring to Chapter 11, lower the glove

box door fully and remove the inner glove box shell.
29   Disconnect the wiring from the light.
30   Remove the bulb holder, remove the bulb and replace it.
31   Installation is the reverse of removal.

20   Electric side view mirrors - description

1   Most electric side view mirrors use two motors to move the glass; one for up and down adjustments and one for left-right adjustments.
2   The control switch has a selector portion that sends voltage to the left or right side mirror. With the ignition ON but the engine OFF, roll down the windows and operate the mirror control switch through all functions (left-right and up-down) for both the left and right side mirrors.
3   Listen carefully for the sound of the electric motors running in the mirrors.
4   If the motors can be heard but the mirror glass doesn't move, there's a problem

with the drive mechanism inside the mirror. Remove and disassemble the mirror to locate the problem.
5   If the mirrors do not operate and no sound comes from the mirrors, check the fuse (see Chapter 1).
6   If the fuse is OK, remove the mirror control switch from the dashboard. Have the switch continuity checked by a dealership service department or other qualified automobile repair facility.
7   Test the ground connections. Refer to the wiring diagrams at the end of this Chapter.
8   If the mirror still doesn't work, remove the mirror and check the wires at the mirror for voltage.
9   If there's not voltage in each switch position, check the circuit between the mirror and control switch for opens and shorts.
10   If there's voltage, remove the mirror and test it off the vehicle with jumper wires. Replace the mirror if it fails this test.

21   Cruise control system - description

1   The cruise control system maintains vehicle speed with a vacuum actuated servo located in the engine compartment, which is connected to the throttle body by a cable. The system consists of the cruise control unit, brake switch, control switches, vacuum hose and vehicle speed sensor. Some features of the system require special testers and diagnostic procedures that are beyond the scope of this manual. Listed below are some general procedures that may be used to locate common problems.
2   Locate and check the fuse (see Section 3).
3   Check the brake light switch (see Chapter 9).
4   Visually inspect the control cable between the actuator assembly and the accel-

19.26 To remove a light bulb from the reading light housing, grasp it firmly and pull it straight down from the terminal clips. If necessary, pry only on the metal ends of the bulb, not the glass

erator pedal for free movement, replace if necessary.

5   Test drive the vehicle to determine if the cruise control is now working. If it isn't, take it to a dealer for further diagnosis.

22   Power window system - description

1   The power window system operates electric motors, mounted in the doors, which lower and raise the windows. The system consists of the control switches, relays, the motors, regulators, glass mechanisms and associated wiring.

2   The power windows can be lowered and raised from the master control switch by the driver or by remote switches located at the individual windows. Each window has a separate motor that is reversible. The position of the control switch determines the polarity and therefore the direction of operation.

3   The circuit is protected by a fuse and a circuit breaker. Each motor is also equipped with an internal circuit breaker; this prevents one stuck window from disabling the whole system.

4   The power window system will only operate when the ignition switch is ON. In addition, many models have a window lockout switch at the master control switch that, when activated, disables the switches at the rear windows and, sometimes, the switch at the passenger's window also. Always check these items before troubleshooting a window problem.

5   These procedures are general in nature, so if you can't find the problem using them, take the vehicle to a dealer service department or other properly equipped repair facility.

6   If the power windows won't operate, always check the fuse and circuit breaker first.

7   If only the rear windows are inoperative, or if the windows only operate from the master control switch, check the rear window lockout switch for continuity in the unlocked position. Replace it if it doesn't have continuity.

8   Check the wiring between the switches and fuse panel for continuity. Repair the wiring, if necessary.

9   If only one window is inoperative from the master control switch, try the other control switch at the window. **Note:** *This doesn't apply to the driver's door window.*

10   If the same window works from one switch, but not the other, check the switch for continuity. Have the switch checked at a dealer service department or other qualified automobile repair facility.

11   If the switch tests OK, check for a short or open in the circuit between the affected switch and the window motor.

12   If one window is inoperative from both switches, remove the trim panel from the affected door and check for voltage at the switch and at the motor while the switch is operated.

13   If voltage is reaching the motor, disconnect the glass from the regulator (see Chapter 11). Move the window up and down by hand while checking for binding and damage. Also check for binding and damage to the regulator. If the regulator is not damaged and the window moves up and down smoothly, replace the motor. If there's binding or damage, lubricate, repair or replace parts, as necessary.

14   If voltage isn't reaching the motor, check the wiring in the circuit for continuity between the switches and motors. You'll need to consult the wiring diagram for the vehicle. If the circuit is equipped with a relay, check that the relay is grounded properly and receiving voltage.

15   Test the windows after you are done to confirm proper repairs.

23   Power door lock system - description

1   A power door lock system operates the door lock actuators mounted in each door. The system consists of the switches, actuators, a control unit and associated wiring. Diagnosis can usually be limited to simple checks of the wiring connections and actuators for minor faults that can be easily repaired.

2   Power door lock systems are operated by bi-directional solenoids located in the doors. The lock switches have two operating positions: Lock and Unlock. When activated, the switch sends a ground signal to the door lock control unit to lock or unlock the doors. Depending on which way the switch is activated, the control unit reverses polarity to the solenoids, allowing the two sides of the circuit to be used alternately as the feed (positive) and ground side.

3   Some vehicles may have an anti-theft system incorporated into the power locks. If you are unable to locate the trouble using the following general Steps, consult a dealer service department or other qualified repair shop.

4   Always check the circuit protection first. Some vehicles use a combination of circuit breakers and fuses.

5   Operate the door lock switches in both directions (Lock and Unlock) with the engine off. Listen for the click of the solenoids operating.

6   Test the switches for continuity. Remove the switches and have them checked by a dealer service department or other qualified automobile repair facility.

7   Check the wiring between the switches, control unit and solenoids for continuity. Repair the wiring if there's no continuity.

8   Check for a bad ground at the switches or the control unit.

9   If all but one lock solenoid operate, remove the trim panel from the affected door (see Chapter 11) and check for voltage at the solenoid while the lock switch is operated. One of the wires should have voltage in the Lock position; the other should have voltage in the Unlock position.

10   If the inoperative solenoid is receiving voltage, replace the solenoid.

11   If the inoperative solenoid isn't receiving voltage, check the relay for an open or short in the wire between the lock solenoid and the control unit. **Note:** *It's common for wires to break in the section of harness that goes between the body and door because opening and closing the door fatigues and eventually breaks the wires.*

24   Airbag system - general information

All models are equipped with a Supplemental Restraint System (SRS), more commonly known as the airbag system. The airbag system is designed to protect the driver and the front seat passenger from serious injury in the event of a head-on or frontal collision. It consists of the impact sensors, a driver's airbag module in the center of the steering wheel, a passenger's airbag module in the glove box area of the instrument panel and a sensing/diagnostic module mounted in the center of the floorpan, in the center console. Some models are also equipped with side-impact airbags.

Airbag modules
Driver's airbag

The airbag inflator module contains a housing incorporating the cushion (airbag) and inflator unit, mounted in the center of the steering wheel. The inflator assembly is mounted on the back of the housing over a hole through which gas is expelled, inflating the bag almost instantaneously when an electrical signal is sent from the system. A clockspring assembly on the steering column under the steering wheel carries this signal to the module. This clockspring assembly can transmit an electrical signal regardless of steering wheel position. The igniter in the airbag converts the electrical signal to heat and ignites the powder, which inflates the bag.

Passenger's airbag

The airbag is mounted inside the right end of the instrument panel, in the vicinity of the glove box compartment. It's similar in design to the driver's airbag, except that it's larger than the steering wheel unit. The passenger airbag is mounted between the instrument panel reinforcement bar and the underside of the instrument panel. The trim cover (on the side of the instrument panel that faces toward the passenger) is textured and colored to match the instrument panel and has a molded seam that splits open when the bag inflates.

Side impact airbags

Extra protection is provided by side-impact airbags on some models. These are smaller devices, which are located on the outer sides of the seat backs, and deploy in the event of a severe side-impact collision.

Sensing and diagnostic module

The sensing and diagnostic module supplies the current to the airbag system in the event of the collision, even if battery power is cut off. It checks this system every time the vehicle is started, causing the "AIR BAG" light to go on then off, if the system is operating properly. If there is a fault in the system, the light will go on and stay on, flash, or the dash will make a beeping sound. If this happens, the vehicle should be taken to your dealer immediately for service.

Disarming the system and other precautions

Warning: *Failure to follow these precautions could result in accidental deployment of the airbag and personal injury.*

Whenever working in the vicinity of the steering wheel, steering column or any of the other SRS system components, the system must be disarmed.

To disarm the airbag system:

a) *Point the wheels straight ahead and turn the key to the Lock position.*
b) *Disconnect the cable from the negative battery terminal.*
c) *Wait at least two minutes for the back-up power supply to be depleted.*

Whenever handling an airbag module:

Always keep the airbag opening (the trim side) pointed away from your body. Never place the airbag module on a bench or other surface with the airbag opening facing the surface. Always place the airbag module in a safe location with the airbag opening facing up.

Never measure the resistance of any SRS component. An ohmmeter has a built-in battery supply that could accidentally deploy the airbag.

Never use electrical welding equipment on a vehicle equipped with an airbag without first disconnecting the electrical connector for each airbag.

Never dispose of a live airbag module. Return it to a dealer service department or other qualified repair shop for safe deployment and disposal.

Component removal and installation

Driver's side airbag module and spiral cable

Refer to Chapter 10, *Steering wheel - removal and installation*, for the driver's side airbag module and clockspring removal and installation procedures.

Other airbag modules

We don't recommend removing any of the other airbag modules. These jobs are best left to a professional.

---

25 Remote keyless entry system - battery replacement and matching the transmitter to the vehicle

---

1   Here's how the transmitter inside the remote keyless entry fob should work:
•   *When you press the UNLOCK button, the driver's door unlocks. If you press the UNLOCK button a second time within four seconds, all the doors unlock.*
•   *Pressing the lock button sets the alarm and locks all of the doors and the lift-gate.*

Battery replacement

2   When the transmitter becomes weak, operation will become intermittent and require you to be closer to the vehicle for it to work. Eventually it won't work at all.
3   To replace the transmitter battery, carefully pry open the keyless entry fob by inserting a coin or screwdriver into the notch in the body of the transmitter and separate the halves of the fob.
4   Carefully pry out the old battery with a small screwdriver.
5   Installation is the reverse of removal. Make sure the two halves of the cover snap together tightly to keep out dirt, dust, humidity and rain.

Matching the transmitter to the vehicle

6   Remove the driver's side knee bolster (see Chapter 11, Section 24).
7   Locate the keyless entry receiver under

the instrument panel, near the steering column. Slide the switch on the receiver from the Off position to the Set position.
8   Push the Lock or Unlock button on the transmitter. If a second transmitter is to be programmed, do the same thing with it at this time. **Note:** *Only two transmitters can be programmed.*
9   Slide the switch on the receiver from Set back to Off.

---

26 Ignition key - programming

Note: *This procedure is used for adding an additional master key if a master key (or both of them) has been lost. It will be necessary to have the ID key (identified by the Hyundai logo) in order to perform this procedure. If the ID key has been lost, this procedure must be performed at a dealer service department or other repair shop equipped with a Hi-Scan diagnostic tool.*
1   Place the ID key into the ignition lock cylinder and turn it to the On position, then the Off position.
2   With ten seconds, insert the key to be added into the ignition lock cylinder and turn it to the On position, then the Off position. The new key is now registered to work with the immobilizer system.
3   If another key is to be added, repeat Step 2. **Note:** *Only two master keys can be registered.*

---

27 Wiring diagrams - general information

Since it isn't possible to include all wiring diagrams for every year covered by this manual, the following diagrams are those that are typical and most commonly needed.

Prior to troubleshooting any circuits, check the fuse and circuit breakers (if equipped) to make sure they're in good condition. Make sure the battery is properly charged and check the cable connections (see Chapter 1).

When checking a circuit, make sure that all connectors are clean, with no broken or loose terminals. When unplugging a connector, do not pull on the wires - pull only on the connector housings.

Starting and charging systems - manual transaxle models

Starting and charging systems - automatic transaxle models

Exterior lighting system (1 of 2)

Exterior lighting system (2 of 2)

Interior lighting system

Instrument cluster warning system

Heating and air conditioning system - 2001 models

Manual heating and air conditioning system - 2002-2006 models

Automatic heating and air conditioning system - 2002-2006 models

Power windows system

Power door locks system

Cruise control system - typical

Base audio system

Wiper and washer system

Index

Haynes Automotive Manuals

NOTE: If you do not see a listing for your vehicle, consult your local Haynes dealer for the latest product information.

(Continued on other side)

Haynes North America, Inc., 861 Lawrence Drive, Newbury Park, CA 91320-1514 • (805) 498-6703 • http://www.haynes.com

Haynes Automotive Manuals (continued)

NOTE: If you do not see a listing for your vehicle, consult your local Haynes dealer for the latest product information.

GMC
Vans & Pick-ups - see CHEVROLET

HONDA
42010 **Accord CVCC** all models '76 thru '83
42011 **Accord** all models '84 thru '89
42012 **Accord** all models '90 thru '93
42013 **Accord** all models '94 thru '97
42014 **Accord** all models '98 thru '02
42015 **Honda Accord** models '03 thru '07
42020 **Civic 1200** all models '73 thru '79
42021 **Civic 1300 & 1500 CVCC** '80 thru '83
42022 **Civic 1500 CVCC** all models '75 thru '79
42023 **Civic** all models '84 thru '91
42024 **Civic & del Sol** '92 thru '95
42025 **Civic** '96 thru '00, **CR-V** '97 thru '01, **Acura Integra** '94 thru '00
42026 **Civic** '01 thru '05, **CR-V** '02 thru '06
42035 **Honda Odyssey** all models '99 thru '04
42037 **Honda Pilot** '03 thru '07, **Acura MDX** '01 thru '07
42040 **Prelude CVCC** all models '79 thru '89

HYUNDAI
43010 **Elantra** all models '96 thru '06
43015 **Excel & Accent** all models '86 thru '98
43050 **Santa Fe** all models '01 thru '06
43055 **Sonata** all models '99 thru '08

ISUZU
Hombre - see CHEVROLET S-10 (24071)
47017 **Rodeo, Amigo & Honda Passport** '89 thru '02
47020 **Trooper & Pick-up** '81 thru '93

JAGUAR
49010 **XJ6** all 6 cyl models '68 thru '86
49011 **XJ6** all models '88 thru '94
49015 **XJ12 & XJS** all 12 cyl models '72 thru '85

JEEP
50010 **Cherokee, Comanche & Wagoneer Limited** all models '84 thru '01
50020 **CJ** all models '49 thru '86
50025 **Grand Cherokee** all models '93 thru '04
50029 **Grand Wagoneer & Pick-up** '72 thru '91 Grand Wagoneer '84 thru '91, Cherokee & Wagoneer '72 thru '83, Pick-up '72 thru '88
50030 **Wrangler** all models '87 thru '03
50035 **Liberty** '02 thru '04

KIA
54070 **Sephia** '94 thru '01, **Spectra** '00 thru '04

LEXUS
ES 300 - see TOYOTA Camry (92007)

LINCOLN
Navigator - see FORD Pick-up (36059)
59010 **Rear-Wheel Drive** all models '70 thru '05

MAZDA
61010 **GLC Hatchback (rear-wheel drive)** '77 thru '83
61011 **GLC (front-wheel drive)** '81 thru '85
61015 **323 & Protegé** '90 thru '00
61016 **MX-5 Miata** '90 thru '97
61020 **MPV** all models '89 thru '98
Navajo - see Ford Explorer (36024)
61030 **Pick-ups** '72 thru '93
Pick-ups '94 thru '00 - see Ford Ranger (36071)
61035 **RX-7** all models '79 thru '85
61036 **RX-7** all models '86 thru '91
61040 **626 (rear-wheel drive)** all models '79 thru '82
61041 **626/MX-6 (front-wheel drive)** '83 thru '92
61042 **626, MX-6/Ford Probe** '93 thru '01

MERCEDES-BENZ
63012 **123 Series Diesel** '76 thru '85
63015 **190 Series four-cyl models** '84 thru '88
63020 **230/250/280 6 cyl sohc models** '68 thru '72
63025 **280 123 Series gasoline models** '77 thru '81
63030 **350 & 450** all models '71 thru '80
63040 **C-Class: C230/C240/C280/C320/C350** '01 thru '07

MERCURY
64200 **Villager & Nissan Quest** '93 thru '01
All other titles, see FORD Listing.

MG
66010 **MGB** Roadster & GT Coupe '62 thru '80
66015 **MG Midget, Austin Healey Sprite** '58 thru '80

MITSUBISHI
68020 **Cordia, Tredia, Galant, Precis & Mirage** '83 thru '93
68030 **Eclipse, Eagle Talon & Ply. Laser** '90 thru '94

68031 **Eclipse** '95 thru '05, **Eagle Talon** '95 thru '98
68035 **Mitsubishi Galant** '94 thru '03
68040 **Pick-up** '83 thru '96 & **Montero** '83 thru '93

NISSAN
72010 **300ZX** all models including Turbo '84 thru '89
72011 **350Z & Infiniti G35** all models '03 thru '08
72015 **Altima** all models '93 thru '06
72020 **Maxima** all models '85 thru '92
72021 **Maxima** all models '93 thru '04
72030 **Pick-ups** '80 thru '97 **Pathfinder** '87 thru '95
72031 **Frontier Pick-up, Xterra, Pathfinder** '96 thru '04
72032 **Nissan Frontier & Xterra** '05 thru '08
72040 **Pulsar** all models '83 thru '86
Quest - see MERCURY Villager (64200)
72050 **Sentra** all models '82 thru '94
72051 **Sentra & 200SX** all models '95 thru '04
72060 **Stanza** all models '82 thru '90

OLDSMOBILE
73015 **Cutlass V6 & V8 gas models** '74 thru '88
For other OLDSMOBILE titles, see BUICK, CHEVROLET or GENERAL MOTORS listing.

PLYMOUTH
For PLYMOUTH titles, see DODGE listing.

PONTIAC
79008 **Fiero** all models '84 thru '88
79018 **Firebird** V8 models except Turbo '70 thru '81
79019 **Firebird** all models '82 thru '92
79040 **Mid-size Rear-wheel Drive** '70 thru '87
For other PONTIAC titles, see BUICK, CHEVROLET or GENERAL MOTORS listing.

PORSCHE
80020 **911** except Turbo & Carrera 4 '65 thru '89
80025 **914** all 4 cyl models '69 thru '76
80030 **924** all models including Turbo '76 thru '82
80035 **944** all models including Turbo '83 thru '89

RENAULT
Alliance & Encore - see AMC (14020)

SAAB
84010 **900** all models including Turbo '79 thru '88

SATURN
87010 **Saturn** all models '91 thru '02
87011 **Saturn Ion** '03 thru '07
87020 **Saturn** all L-series models '00 thru '04
87040 **Saturn VUE** '02 thru '07

SUBARU
89002 **1100, 1300, 1400 & 1600** '71 thru '79
89003 **1600 & 1800** 2WD & 4WD '80 thru '94
89100 **Legacy** all models '90 thru '99
89101 **Legacy & Forester** '00 thru '06

SUZUKI
90010 **Samurai/Sidekick & Geo Tracker** '86 thru '01

TOYOTA
92005 **Camry** all models '83 thru '91
92006 **Camry** all models '92 thru '96
92007 **Camry, Avalon, Solara, Lexus ES 300** '97 thru '01
92008 **Toyota Camry, Avalon and Solara and Lexus ES 300/330** all models '02 thru '06
92015 **Celica Rear Wheel Drive** '71 thru '85
92020 **Celica Front Wheel Drive** '86 thru '99
92025 **Celica Supra** all models '79 thru '92
92030 **Corolla** all models '75 thru '79
92032 **Corolla** all rear wheel drive models '80 thru '87
92035 **Corolla** all front wheel drive models '84 thru '92
92036 **Corolla & Geo Prizm** '93 thru '02
92037 **Corolla** models '03 thru '05
92040 **Corolla Tercel** all models '80 thru '82
92045 **Corona** all models '74 thru '82
92050 **Cressida** all models '78 thru '82
92055 **Land Cruiser FJ40, 43, 45, 55** '68 thru '82
92056 **Land Cruiser FJ60, 62, 80, FZJ80** '80 thru '96
92060 **Matrix & Pontiac Vibe** '03 thru '08
92065 **MR2** all models '85 thru '87
92070 **Pick-up** all models '69 thru '78
92075 **Pick-up** all models '79 thru '95
92076 **Tacoma, 4Runner, & T100** '93 thru '04
92077 **Tacoma** all models '05 thru '09
92078 **Tundra** '00 thru '06 & **Sequoia** '01 thru '06
92079 **4Runner** all models '03 thru '09
92080 **Previa** all models '91 thru '95
92081 **Prius** all models '01 thru '08
92082 **RAV4** all models '96 thru '05

92085 **Tercel** all models '87 thru '94
92090 **Toyota Sienna** all models '98 thru '06
92095 **Highlander & Lexus RX-330** '99 thru '06

TRIUMPH
94007 **Spitfire** all models '62 thru '81
94010 **TR7** all models '75 thru '81

VW
96008 **Beetle & Karmann Ghia** '54 thru '79
96009 **New Beetle** '98 thru '05
96016 **Rabbit, Jetta, Scirocco & Pick-up** gas models '75 thru '92 & Convertible '80 thru '92
96017 **Golf, GTI & Jetta** '93 thru '98 & **Cabrio** '95 thru '02
96018 **Golf, GTI, Jetta** '99 thru '05
96020 **Rabbit, Jetta & Pick-up** diesel '77 thru '84
96023 **Passat** '98 thru '05, **Audi A4** '96 thru '01
96030 **Transporter 1600** all models '68 thru '79
96035 **Transporter 1700, 1800 & 2000** '72 thru '79
96040 **Type 3 1500 & 1600** all models '63 thru '73
96045 **Vanagon** all air-cooled models '80 thru '83

VOLVO
97010 **120, 130 Series & 1800 Sports** '61 thru '73
97015 **140 Series** all models '66 thru '74
97020 **240 Series** all models '76 thru '93
97040 **740 & 760 Series** all models '82 thru '88
97050 **850 Series** all models '93 thru '97

TECHBOOK MANUALS
10205 **Automotive Computer Codes**
10206 **OBD-II & Electronic Engine Management**
10210 **Automotive Emissions Control Manual**
10215 **Fuel Injection Manual, 1978 thru 1985**
10220 **Fuel Injection Manual, 1986 thru 1999**
10225 **Holley Carburetor Manual**
10230 **Rochester Carburetor Manual**
10240 **Weber/Zenith/Stromberg/SU Carburetors**
10305 **Chevrolet Engine Overhaul Manual**
10310 **Chrysler Engine Overhaul Manual**
10320 **Ford Engine Overhaul Manual**
10330 **GM and Ford Diesel Engine Repair Manual**
10333 **Engine Performance Manual**
10340 **Small Engine Repair Manual, 5 HP & Less**
10341 **Small Engine Repair Manual, 5.5 - 20 HP**
10345 **Suspension, Steering & Driveline Manual**
10355 **Ford Automatic Transmission Overhaul**
10360 **GM Automatic Transmission Overhaul**
10405 **Automotive Body Repair & Painting**
10410 **Automotive Brake Manual**
10411 **Automotive Anti-lock Brake (ABS) Systems**
10415 **Automotive Detailing Manual**
10420 **Automotive Electrical Manual**
10425 **Automotive Heating & Air Conditioning**
10430 **Automotive Reference Manual & Dictionary**
10435 **Automotive Tools Manual**
10440 **Used Car Buying Guide**
10445 **Welding Manual**
10450 **ATV Basics**
10452 **Scooters, Automatic Transmission 50cc to 250cc**

SPANISH MANUALS
98903 **Reparación de Carrocería & Pintura**
98904 **Carburadores para los modelos Holley & Rochester**
98905 **Códigos Automotrices de la Computadora**
98910 **Frenos Automotriz**
98913 **Electricidad Automotriz**
98915 **Inyección de Combustible 1986 al 1999**
99040 **Chevrolet & GMC Camionetas** '67 al '87
99041 **Chevrolet & GMC Camionetas** '88 al '98
99042 **Chevrolet & GMC Camionetas Cerradas** '68 al '95
99055 **Dodge Caravan & Plymouth Voyager** '84 al '95
99075 **Ford Camionetas y Bronco** '80 al '94
99077 **Ford Camionetas Cerradas** '69 al '91
99088 **Ford Modelos de Tamaño Mediano** '75 al '86
99091 **Ford Taurus & Mercury Sable** '86 al '95
99095 **GM Modelos de Tamaño Grande** '70 al '90
99100 **GM Modelos de Tamaño Mediano** '70 al '88
99106 **Jeep Cherokee, Wagoneer & Comanche** '84 al '00
99110 **Nissan Camioneta** '80 al '96, **Pathfinder** '87 al '95
99118 **Nissan Sentra** '82 al '94
99125 **Toyota Camionetas y 4Runner** '79 al '95

Over 100 Haynes motorcycle manuals also available

6-09